Routledge Revivals

Devaluation and Pricing Decisions

First published in 1974, *Devaluation and Pricing Decisions* is based on case studies of the export pricing decisions made by nineteen major British companies after the 1967 devaluation. The aim was to look in detail at the decisions that major British firms took after devaluation and to see how they had responded to this major change in government policy. This book shows how far the firms had anticipated the devaluation; what company objectives were at that time and what changes in these objectives, or in pricing and marketing policies, were made to take advantage of new opportunities for exporting and for import substitution. The researchers also examined the actual process of decision making to find what information was available to the decision makers and how they used it.

The book is directed to businessmen taking decisions on export prices and marketing in the world of today where foreign exchange rates change frequently. It is also directed towards those responsible for shaping national economic policy. For students of economics, it represents a study showing, in considerable detail, how a number of businesses responded to the 1967 devaluation.

T0341160

Devaluation and Pricing Decisions

A Case Study Approach

D. C. Hague, E. Oakeshott and A. Strain

Routledge
Taylor & Francis Group

First published in 1974
by George Allen & Unwin

This edition first published in 2022 by Routledge
2 Park Square, Milton Park, Abingdon, Oxon, OX14 4RN

and by Routledge
605 Third Avenue, New York, NY 10017

Routledge is an imprint of the Taylor & Francis Group, an informa business

© Crown Copyright 1974

Publisher's Note
The publisher has gone to great lengths to ensure the quality of this reprint but points out that some imperfections in the original copies may be apparent.

Disclaimer
The publisher has made every effort to trace copyright holders and welcomes correspondence from those they have been unable to contact.

A Library of Congress record exists under ISBN: 0046582118

ISBN: 978-1-032-19778-4 (hbk)
ISBN: 978-1-003-26103-2 (ebk)
ISBN: 978-1-032-19824-8 (pbk)

Book DOI 10.4324/9781003261032

Devaluation and Pricing Decisions

A Case Study Approach

D. C. HAGUE
W. E. F. OAKESHOTT
A. A. STRAIN

London
GEORGE ALLEN & UNWIN LTD
RUSKIN HOUSE   MUSEUM STREET

First published in 1974

ISBN 0 04 658211 8

Printed in Great Britain
in 10 point Times Roman type
by The Lavenham Press Limited
Lavenham, Suffolk

Preface

This book is based on nineteen case studies of the way that British firms responded to devaluation. The field work was carried out by Evelyn Oakeshott and Adrian Strain, under the supervision of Douglas Hague, over a period of about two years, beginning in January 1969.

Adrian Strain, who worked on the project until January 1972, wrote a draft of much of the book, which was put into its final form by Douglas Hague. Evelyn Oakeshott, who left the project in October 1970, made extensive and valuable comments on the manuscript.

The research was financed by the Government, first, through the Department of Economic Affairs, then the Ministry of Technology and, finally, the Department of Trade & Industry. We should like to express our thanks for this support, without which the work would not have been carried out.

We also wish to thank those in the firms studied. In most cases the decision-takers themselves were interviewed. They were given the opportunity to criticise the drafts of the case studies which we wrote. We are grateful for their help, criticism and the illumination they provided. We should also like to thank the members of a small advisory panel, set up by the Centre for Business Research, and consisting of businessmen and civil servants, as well as those carrying out the research. The panel met periodically to discuss the cases as they were written, to make suggestions for their improvement and to supervise the project generally. In particular we owe a great debt to Mr Plymen, of Messrs W. Greenwell, who was chairman of the advisory panel and whose enthusiasm and support were a great encouragement to us. We also thank those in the Centre for Business Research and in Government departments, especially the Department of Economic Affairs and the Department of Trade & Industry, for the information and advice that helped us to complete this study. Nevertheless, while this work was commissioned by the Secretary of State for Economic Affairs, neither the Department for Trade and Industry, which assumed the responsibility of the Department of Economic Affairs for this work, nor Her Majesty's Stationery Office are in any way responsible for any view expressed in this book.

Finally, we are extremely grateful to Miss Rosemary Weston for compiling the index, and Brenda Hague who read the proofs.

D. C. Hague
W. E. F. Oakeshott
A. A. Strain

Contents

PART II   THE CASE STUDIES

CASE STUDY

Part I

CHAPTER 1

Introduction

At 9.30 p.m. on Saturday 18 November 1967, the Chancellor of
the Exchequer, Mr James Callaghan, announced the devaluation
of sterling by 14·3% from $2·80 to £1. While the precise timing
of this move may have come as a surprise, it was certainly not
unexpected. Devaluation rumours had been growing stronger for
some months, and economists and economic journalists had been
forecasting, and indeed advocating, devaluation with steadily
increasing enthusiasm since the major payments crisis in 1964. To
remind readers of the situation at the time of devaluation, we
shall first outline briefly the development of the balance of
payments of the UK from 1964 to 1970.

1.1 The Background: 1964–67

1.1.1 THE PAYMENTS IMBALANCE: 1964–66

Even before 1960, Britain's balance of payments had often been
unhealthy, but the slowdown in the economy in 1961 and 1962
temporarily improved the position. As Table 1.1 shows, there was
a current surplus of £122M in 1962. With relatively rapid growth
of the GNP resuming in early 1963, the position on current account

TABLE 1.1 *UK balance of payments 1962–70*

Year	Visible exports	Visible imports	Visible balance	Invisible balance	Current balance
1962	+3993	−4095	−102	+224	+122
1963	+4282	−4362	− 80	+204	+124
1964	+4486	−5005	−519	+143	−376
1965	+4817	−5054	−237	+185	− 52
1966	+5182	−5255	− 73	+156	+ 83
1967	+5122	−5674	−552	+254	−298
1968	+6273	−6916	−643	+355	−288
1969	+7061	−7202	−141	+581	+440
1970	+7885	−7882	+ 3	+576	+579

Source: National Institute Economic Review, No. 58 (November 1971)

and on long-term capital account worsened sharply. While there was still a current account surplus of £124M in 1963, in 1964 the current deficit was £376M. During 1964, the combined deficit on the current and long-term capital accounts was running at an annual rate of nearly £800M. In addition, in the latter half of 1964 there was a dramatic outflow of short-term funds, due both to fears of devaluation and to the attractions of relatively high interest rates abroad. The Labour government which came into power in October 1964 decided not to devalue, but instead brought in a series of restrictive measures, the most controversial of which were the introduction of a tax rebate on export earnings equivalent to about 2% of their value, and the imposition of a temporary surcharge of 15% on all imports except of food and some raw materials. (This was reduced to 10% in April 1965 and removed in November 1966.) Despite these measures, which were reinforced by a moderately restrictive budget in November 1965, and a sharp rise in bank rate, heavy selling of sterling continued until the government announced, around the middle of November, that it had secured substantial foreign credits.

The balance of payments situation eased somewhat during the next two years. The import surcharge and the slowing-down of economic growth within the UK between them meant that the volume of visible imports did not rise in 1965 and rose by only 4% in 1966. Since the volume of exports rose by 6% in 1965 and 4% in 1966, the visible trade deficit fell in both years. As usual, the UK had a surplus on invisible trade, and the current balance improved to show a deficit of about £50M in 1965 and a surplus of about £80M in 1966. Nevertheless, there was continued nervousness among those who were in a position to take funds out of Britain. Their anxiety was not eased by the continuing increase in the domestic price level in the UK, or by the fact that the budgets of 1965 and 1966 were only mildly deflationary. By June 1966 it became clear that more drastic action was necessary if there was not to be a further run on sterling.

Confidence in Britain's ability to maintain the sterling parity was low, and heavy selling of sterling took place through the early summer. At the same time, interest rates abroad were rising relative to those in the UK. In July 1966, therefore, the government introduced a series of measures designed to restrain demand in the UK and so to restore foreign confidence. Bank rate was increased, taxes were raised and a six-month standstill was decreed for wages and prices, to be followed by a period of 'severe restraint'. Once again, large credits were obtained from abroad.

1.1.2 DEVELOPMENTS IN 1967

These measures were unsuccessful, though it is difficult to judge precisely why. It is true that the balance of payments actually went into surplus in the fourth quarter of 1966, but this was probably due to special factors, including the delayed effects of the seamen's strike and a fall in imports as traders waited for the import surcharge to be ended towards the end of 1966. Nonetheless, this improvement was taken by the authorities to be the first sign of a more favourable trend, and the feeling spread that there would be a substantial surplus on the balance of payments in 1967. A modest degree of reflation was allowed, to counter uncomfortably high unemployment. Bank rate was reduced in three steps, each of $\frac{1}{2}\%$, in January, March and May 1967. The budget in April was neutral, with increases in expenditure roughly matched by increases in revenue. The situation did not seem to warrant more restriction.

However, the current balance deteriorated sharply in the first two quarters of 1967. For the year as a whole, the volume of visible imports was to fall by 7%, and the volume of exports to fall by 2%, but these two figures are misleading. They were affected by a dock strike. But there was a current deficit of about £300M in 1967.

It is not surprising that confidence in sterling remained weak. In March 1967 the authorities had to negotiate a large credit from the Bank for International Settlement in order to counter pressure on the reserves. The situation worsened considerably after the outbreak of the 'Six-day' Arab-Israeli war at the beginning of June and the closure of the Suez Canal. This delayed exports and increased the cost of some imports, especially fuel and raw materials. The unfavourable balance of payments deficit on current account was accompanied by a heavy outflow of short-term funds, attracted in part by higher interest rates abroad. Yet the authorities remained confident of achieving a surplus on the balance of payments, and the leading 'unofficial' forecaster, the National Institute of Economic and Social Research, in the August issue of its *Economic Review*, was still predicting a small current surplus for 1967 as a whole. The government felt able to continue the gentle domestic expansion which it saw as desirable, given the continued high level of unemployment. At the end of August, it made some small reductions in hire purchase restrictions.

The devaluation monetary crisis really got under way at the beginning of October 1967. Despite official optimism, rumours of devaluation had been growing stronger month by month and its possibility was being discussed, if not quite openly, at least in private. Confidence in the pound was badly damaged by an unfavourable report on the economic position of the UK, made by the International Monetary Fund at the beginning of September. A month later, the EEC Commission reported on the application for membership which the UK had made in May 1967. It severely criticised the British economic and financial situation, and implied that the current sterling exchange rate could not be sustained. Indeed, the British press reported that the Commission's unofficial view was that a large devaluation of sterling would be a pre-requisite for British entry to the EEC. With these comments, with a continuing trade deficit, and with relaxation of the hire purchase restrictions, the outflow of short-term funds reached crisis proportions at the end of September 1967.

Over the next week or two, several factors reinforced the devaluation rumours. On 12 October the Finnish mark was devalued by 32% in order to counteract the effect of Finland's domestic inflation on its balance of payments. Combined with the weakness of sterling, this development unsettled the foreign exchange markets. On the next day, the influential London and Cambridge Economic Bulletin appeared in *The Times*. It forecast a continuing, and indeed increasing, deficit on the current balance of payments unless drastic action was taken. Then came the announcement that the reserves were at the lowest level since April 1965 and that the deficit on visible trade in September was the highest since the crisis month of July 1966. A few days later, the effects of a strike in the London docks were estimated to be equivalent to a reduction in exports of over £100M. On 19 October the Bank Rate was raised by $\frac{1}{2}$% to 6%; 'to defend the pound against rising interest rates abroad'. But this was much less than had been anticipated and there was further selling of sterling. By the end of the month, the Chancellor of the Exchequer felt obliged to state formally that sterling would not be devalued.

Heavy selling of sterling continued into November and by the first week of the month sterling was at its lowest price for a decade. It was obvious that the rise in Bank Rate had not stemmed the wave of speculation, and the financial press began to suggest that devaluation was almost certain within the next two or three weeks. Bank Rate was raised again on 9 November, but only by $\frac{1}{2}$% because of the high level of unemployment. Once more, this increase was less than had been expected and heavy selling of sterling continued. On 13 November the *Financial Times* carried a report that the government was trying to negotiate yet another massive credit from the Bank for International Settlement, but it was soon rumoured that the loan would be made conditional on sterling being devalued. On 15 November a statement by the Treasury ruled out the use of import controls to reduce the pressure on sterling, which was seen as implying that devaluation was the only alternative. On the same day the Chancellor, speaking in the House of Commons, refused to confirm or deny the press rumours about the BIS negotiations, or indeed to say anything specific about the crisis. This was taken by the City as an admission that immediate devaluation was being seriously contemplated, and a further wave of selling of sterling ensued. Finally, on 18 November devaluation was announced.

1.2   The Results of Devaluation

1.2.1   THE DEVALUATION PACKAGE

When devaluation came, there was little surprise. It is now known that for the previous fortnight Britain had been conducting secret negotiations with other major industrial countries in order to forestall a wave of retaliatory devaluations. As a result of these discussions, substantial credits were secured, but the Chancellor had to give an undertaking that strongly deflationary measures would be introduced within the UK. Indeed, domestic economic policy was to be kept under scrutiny for a time by the IMF.

In addition to devaluation, Bank Rate was raised to 8%, the export rebate was cancelled and the SET premium was withdrawn from all manufacturing activity outside the development areas. Increased restrictions on hire purchase and bank lending were announced, and it was explained that in the next budget Corporation tax would be increased from 40 to $42\frac{1}{2}$% together with other unspecified deflationary measures. Initial cuts of £200M were to be made in government expenditure. A month later, on 19 December, a further review of government expenditure was begun. This resulted in further cuts, amounting to about £300M, being announced in the middle of January 1968. The Prices and Incomes Board was instructed to monitor price increases in the home market resulting from devaluation, in order to prevent profits rising. When the 1968 budget was introduced in March, the net increase in taxation amounted to £923M for a full year.

1.2.2   THE INITIAL REACTION

The initial reaction of most businessmen to devaluation was cautious. Much press comment argued that the deflationary measures accompanying devaluation would reduce the buoyancy of the home market, while any increase in exports would take a considerable time to materialise. This was certainly the view of the Confederation of British Industry, which sent out a newsletter couched in these terms to its members a few days after devaluation. There were also complaints from business that the removal of the export rebate would rob devaluation of much of its effectiveness. All the businessmen who gave press interviews confirmed that they would increase their export effort, though not necessarily through price reductions. A significant number of businessmen we interviewed in this study claimed that the general tenor of ministerial speeches was in favour of price cutting, though a study of the speeches themselves does not confirm this view. In his broadcast after devaluation, the Prime Minister claimed that it had been forced on Britain by foreign speculators, and that it was up to the British exporter now to show his mettle. However, while again some of those we interviewed claimed that Mr Wilson implied that cuts in export prices would be the most desirable response to devaluation, he certainly did not say so explicitly.

1.2.3 THE RESULTS OF DEVALUATION

In his Letter of Intent to the International Monetary Fund a few days after devaluation, the Chancellor of the Exchequer explained that the measures accompanying it were designed to secure an improvement in the balance of payments of about £500M per annum; that is, a surplus running at an annual rate of £200M by the second half of 1968. These hopes were finally fulfilled, but not during 1968. The improvement in the balance of payments took longer to effect than many people had expected. However, the slow response is not surprising. It takes a longish time to reap the advantages of a devaluation. In firms making capital goods, as many British firms do, the time needed to take extra export business, and then to produce the goods concerned, must be measured in years rather than months. Yet import prices immediately rise by the amount of devaluation, unless foreign suppliers reduce their prices. In fact, the index of British import prices increased by nearly 12% between 1967 and 1968, and by roughly another 5% between 1968 and 1969.

Between 1967 and 1968, the sterling value of both imports and exports of goods and services rose by about 20%. The volume of all physical goods exported rose by 14%, after a slight fall in 1967 (it will be remembered that a dock strike affected these figures), while the volume of such physical goods imported rose by 27 % compared with a fall of 7 % in 1967. Because of devaluation, British export prices, in foreign currency, fell. The index of sterling prices for British exports of visible items rose by 8 % in 1968, implying a fall in foreign-currency prices of about 6 %. The terms of trade (that is, export prices of British goods divided by import prices) fell from 104 to 101, between 1967 and 1968. In 1963, the terms of trade had been 100.

The result was a rise in the visible trade deficit by £91 million, between 1967 and 1968, to £643M. The rise in exports took time to achieve, while the level of imports rose sharply, partly to provide the raw materials necessary for increased exports, partly no doubt to provide for the consumer spending boom before the 1968 budget and to replenish stocks afterwards. Most of the increase in the volume of imports was accounted for by an increase in imports of manufactured goods. Yet the hope had been that the fall in the value of sterling would raise the price of such of these goods as Britain could produce reasonably efficiently herself, and would lead to import substitution away from imported and towards British goods.

As a result of these developments, around the middle of 1968 many people were wondering whether devaluation would ever 'work'. By the end of 1968, it was clear that the balance of payments was improving rapidly. In 1969, the volume of visible imports rose by only 1 %, while the volume of exports increased by 10 %. The terms of trade remained constant between 1968 and 1969 at 101. So far as the balance of payments alone was concerned, the beneficial effect of devaluation was being experienced; the Government's economic policy was manifestly 'working'. However, the effects of this policy on British exports were being steadily eroded by the continuing rise in sterling export prices, under the pressure of rising costs at home. Not only had devaluation increased the sterling costs of many raw materials. The increase in the sterling cost of imports was raising the cost of living and helping to encourage wage claims, so raising export costs further.

The experience of 1967 and 1968 has had a considerable impact on the thinking of British economists, who now emphasise that Britain's response to devaluation is bound to be 'J-shaped', as in Figure 1.1. The vertical axis in this figure shows the size of the balance of payments surplus or deficit; time is measured along the horizontal axis. Here we have assumed that there is a zero surplus when devaluation takes place, at the point of time represented by the origin. Its immediate effect is to worsen the balance of payments, increasing (or causing) the deficit. Sterling import prices begin to rise at once while import volume, if it ever falls in a country which produces few raw materials itself, does not do so at once. Firms cannot immediately find new suppliers. Similarly, sterling export prices tend to fall. The balance of payments worsens temporarily, as the 'J-shaped' curve in Figure 1.1 shows. However, after a time, export volume begins to increase, with lower foreign-currency prices, and this increase in export volume leads to an improvement in the balance of payments position and, in Figure 1.1 at least, to a substantial surplus. This was the course of events after devaluation in 1967. It is the rough pattern of events that British economists now expect from any devaluation by the UK.

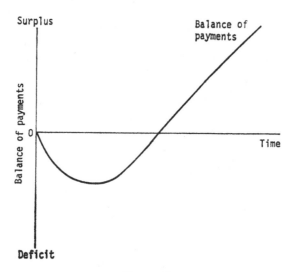

Figure 1.1

While there seems little doubt that devaluation played a significant part in improving the balance of payments position in 1969, and perhaps in 1970, it is impossible to show conclusively how big an effect devaluation had. While the increase in British exports in 1968 and 1969 was much bigger than in any year during the previous decade, it was obviously helped by the fact that there was a boom in world trade at the time. The value of world exports of manufactured goods increased by about 15% between 1967 and 1968 and by a further 17% in 1969. While there seems to have been little change in world export prices in 1968, they rose by about 3% in 1969. Similarly, the value of world trade in manufactures rose by about 15% between 1969 and 1970, though there was a rise in export prices of about 6% during this period. Britain's share of world trade in manufactured goods continued to decline. However, having fallen from 13·2% to 12·2% between 1966 and 1967 and from 12·2% to 11·3% in 1968, the rate of decrease in Britain's share does then seem to have slackened for a time. Between 1968 and 1969 it remained roughly constant, though the fall in share was resumed in 1970, with a decline to 10·5%. There seems to be a *prima facie* case for arguing that devaluation temporarily slowed the decline.

Whatever the reasons, Britain did improve her current balance of payments markedly in 1968 and afterwards. A minor factor in 1968 was almost certainly that the dock strike towards the end of 1967 meant that exports for 1967 were understated and that the true rise in export volume in 1968 was smaller than Table 1.2 suggests. More important, the slow rate of growth in British real GNP after 1967 held down the demand for imports, and so sustained the balance of payments surplus. With a real growth rate in GNP of 4 or 5% per annum, the balance of payments would have been much less satisfactory, and probably in deficit. At the same time, one has to remember that much of the effect of devaluation was being eroded by rapidly increasing incomes, and therefore costs, within the UK. Nevertheless, the unusually large increases in British exports in 1968 and 1969 must have owed a good deal to devaluation.

We end this brief summary of the background to our study, in 1970. The reason is that, as one would expect from a once-for-all stimulus like devaluation, its effects seem to have largely disap-

TABLE 1.2 *Annual changes in UK visible trade 1964–70*

Year	Change in volume of exports compared with previous year, %	Change in volume of imports compared with previous year, %
1964	+ 3	+11
1965	+ 6	+ 0
1966	+ 4	+ 4
1967	− 2	− 7
1968	+14	+27
1969	+10	+ 1
1970	+ 4	+ 6

Source: calculated from *National Institute Economic Review*, No. 58 (November 1971).

peared by that year. So far as the balance of payments was concerned, there was a further improvement in the visible trade balance in 1970, although this seems to have owed more to an improvement in the terms of trade than to a change in export volume. In 1970, the volume of British visible goods exported rose by only 4%, while the volume of imports of these goods rose by 6%, but the terms of trade rose from 101 in 1969 to 104 in 1970. As a result, Britain actually had a surplus on her visible trade balance for the first time for more than a decade, and a surplus on the current balance of payments of about £600M. Once again, however, world trade in manufactured goods seems to have increased rapidly. It rose, in real terms, by about 8% in 1970, and in value by 15%.

It is perhaps worth spending a little time, at this stage, looking at longer-term trends in imports and exports. One problem implicit in a good deal of what has been said so far is that it is not easy to discover what effect a devaluation *would have had* on export and import volumes at a given level of GNP (or GDP), because GNP is usually changing, if only because of the direct and multiplier effects of the devaluation itself. The most appropriate procedure for looking at long-run export and import performance therefore seems to be the one used in Table 1.3, where we show exports and imports as percentages of gross domestic product (GDP). Changes in exports and imports are then seen in relation to a changing GDP.

Table 1.3 shows a significant increase in the proportion of GDP both imported *and* exported. From 1960 to 1963 there was little change in the percentage of either exports or imports to GDP, with both steady, at about 21% of GDP. In 1964, with rapid economic growth in the UK, there was a substantial increase in imports, to 23% of GDP, and, while growth slowed markedly, this percentage was maintained until 1966, though exports represented a lower percentage. There was a further increase in imports to 24% of GDP in 1967, while exports, as a percentage of GDP, continued to lag two percentage points behind imports.

The figures in Table 1.3 suggest that devaluation, in 1967, had little short- or long-run effect on the percentage of GDP imported. By 1971, it had risen to 27%, perhaps in part because of moves towards trade liberalisation, like the Kennedy Round of tariff reductions. On this evidence, devaluation does not seem to have led to significant import substitution. The most one could claim is that it may have held down the percentage of imports to GDP at 25%, in 1968 and 1969. Every other year since 1966 saw an increase of one percentage point. The import substitution hoped

TABLE 1.3   *Exports and imports of goods and services as percentages of gross domestic product* 1960–71 (at 1963 prices)

Year	Exports	Imports
1960	21	21
1961	21	21
1962	21	22
1963	21	21
1964	21	23
1965	22	23
1966	21	23
1967	22	24
1968	24	25
1969	26	25
1970	27	26
1971	28	27

for after devaluation simply did not take place on an observable scale. However, presumably because of devaluation, there was a substantial increase in the percentage of Britain's GDP that was exported, from 21 % in 1966 to 28 % in 1971.

We shall not pursue the interesting question of how far one can expect the proportions of GDP imported and exported to rise in the future, except to note one point. Since the increase in both percentages, during the 1960's, seems to have been linked with trade liberalisation, the reduction in tariffs which will take place now that Britain is a member of the EEC is likely to give a fresh impetus to the process. All that we have tried to do here is to give the essential background information against which the devaluation decisions studied in this book can be better understood.

1.3   The Research Process

1.3.1   AIMS AND METHODS

The purpose of the book is to look in detail at the decisions that nineteen individual British firms took after devaluation. We wanted to see how they responded to such a major change in government policy and therefore in their economic environment. One problem about much empirical research in economics is that one can rarely study the way in which two or more firms respond to exactly the same change in the economic influences affecting them. We were therefore enthusiastic to take this opportunity of studying the effects of devaluation, because devaluation represented a major change in the economic environment affecting the whole of British industry. We wanted, for example, to see how far our firms anticipated devaluation. We wished to discover what their objectives were at that time and whether they thought that changes in these objectives, or in their pricing and marketing policies, were necessary if they were to take advantage of new opportunities for exporting and for import-substitution. We wanted to examine the actual process of decision-taking. We wanted to find out what information was available to decision-takers and how they used it. We hope that our study will help firms which have to decide how to act when the pound sterling or other currencies are devalued, or revalued, in the future.

We also hope that, in a small way, this study will help those responsible for making British economic policy. While it looks in detail only at the way in which nineteen firms responded to devaluation, it may tell us something about the way firms respond to other changes in economic policy. It may be possible to learn something from it about the way that firms would respond, say, to major changes in taxation policy, in investment incentives or to other similar measures. Whether they are deciding to devalue or to change some other element in economic policy, those responsible for government policy measures have to rely on the response of individual firms being what was expected.

The reason for choosing to study nineteen firms is that we wanted to look at enough firms to learn something from detailed case studies, and to generalise a little. However, we also wanted to complete the work before devaluation was so far in the past that those we talked to in firms had abandoned memory for rationalisation. We therefore examined nineteen firms. We wrote seventeen detailed case studies, and one rather less detailed one (Hertford Stoves). Nottingham Confectionery gave us only very limited information and we were not able to write a case study for it, though we have used the information we were able to collect from it in the remainder of the book. Our case research began early in 1969 and all case material had been collected by the end of 1970. The participating firms generously provided a good deal of confidential information about their devaluation decisions, including papers which were circulated at the time of devaluation and then filed away. In all firms except Hertford Stoves and Nottingham Confectionery, such written material was supplemented by long and detailed interviews with both senior and middle management. However, in all firms we believe that we obtained an accurate picture of the way the decisions after devaluation were taken.

1.4   The Firms

It will be helpful at this stage to introduce the firms we shall be dealing with throughout the book (see Table 1.4). They have been given false names, to disguise their identities. It must be emphasised that should there be any real-world firms with these names, we did not study them. The case studies themselves are also disguised. The products that our firms appear to be making are not the true ones, though the type of product and the markets they are sold in are sufficiently similar for the case studies to be realistic. The reason for the use of disguise is the need to conceal information which the firms regard as capable of damaging their competitive position, even if published so long after the event. Nevertheless, we emphasise that all essential elements in each case are undisguised and unaltered. We regret the need for camouflage, but the firms gave us no alternative.

All the firms we studied were manufacturing businesses. About half of them (or their parent companies) were members of the Centre for Business Research, while the other half were selected in the hope that the total sample would cover a reasonably representative selection of firms. We do not know how representative the sample is, though we probably biased it by trying to find firms which we thought were major exporters. The representativeness of the sample must also have been reduced by the fact that the particular division, company or plant we studied was chosen for us by the top management of the firm or group. The local management then selected a product, or product group, for us to study. All we can say is that our studies show considerable diversity. Our firms came from different industries, exported different percentages of their output and experienced different degrees of export success.

The firms seem to give a reasonable spread of different types of producer. Six of them manufactured consumer-goods on a large scale; three produced consumer durables and three non-durables. The remaining thirteen firms produced industrial goods. Five manufactured components, four concentrated on processing raw or intermediate materials and four made large and expensive capital goods to customers' specifications. Some firms produced several types of products. For example, Tottenham Piping manufactured both a raw material and three types of component. Similarly, we were able to study decisions taken for two different product groups in both Durham Plates and Peterborough Tubes.

It is difficult to classify our firms by size. On the one hand, most of them belonged to large groups; on the other, the product groups we studied seldom accounted for a major part of the whole

TABLE 1.4 *The firms studied*

Consumer durables	Consumer non-durables	Components	Basic materials	Capital goods
Ealing Electrical Appliances	Birmingham Cakes	Durham Plates	Acton Chemicals	Cardiff Instruments
Hertford Stoves	Gatley Hosiery	Kendal Accessories	Fulham Castings	Inverness Plant Builders
Jarrow Furniture	Nottingham Confectionery	London Switches	Rugby Processing	Oxford Furnaces
		Peterborough Tubes	Tottenham Piping	Quantox Construction
		Stratford Equipment		

business. However, judged by the scale and/or capital intensiveness of their activities, Acton Chemicals, Ealing Electrical Appliances, Fulham Castings, Nottingham Confectionery, Oxford Furnaces, Peterborough Tubing, Quantox Construction, Rugby Processing and Tottenham Piping were nine large firms. Birmingham Cakes, London Switches and Stratford Equipment were three small ones. Cardiff Instruments, Durham Plates, Gatley Hosiery, Hertford Stoves, Inverness Plant Builders, Jarrow Furniture, and Kendal Accessories were seven medium-sized firms.

Most of our firms met many more significant competitors in their export markets than in their home markets. Three firms faced no competition in their home markets for the product we studied; four more had only one effective competitor. Nine firms faced few other producers at home, while three operated in home markets where there were large numbers of firms. However, the numbers of competitors our firms met in the UK market, and the extent to which their capacity was usually engaged on producing for the UK, often influenced their attitudes towards exporting. At the time of devaluation, the home markets for most of our firms were depressed and the long-run rate of growth of their sales was usually rather slow.

In export markets, the number of competitors our firms had naturally varied from country to country; not all competitors were active in each overseas market. The capital-goods manufacturers usually faced a small number of competitors for each tender they submitted, although they were not always sure who these were. The component and basic-material manufacturers also usually met a small number of competitors in each overseas country. The consumer-goods manufacturers tended to meet more.

1.5 The Firms Described

A brief description of each firm is given below:

Acton Chemicals was part of a very large group. There was only one other British manufacturer of the product with a significant market share, although imports into the UK represented 20% of total UK sales. Abroad, Acton's sales were confined to Europe for logistic reasons; in Europe, there were few firms producing (or selling) in any country. The proportion of Acton's sales which was exported was small and the volume of these had not increased much for several years. There was a considerable amount of spare capacity among the European producers. Margins on all exports were therefore narrow.

Until just before devaluation, Acton had treated its export sales as being less important to it than its sales in the UK and was prepared, if necessary, to abandon exports altogether. However, a series of difficulties in converting Acton's plant to use a new process had led to fears that Acton would be short of capacity. In working out the distribution arrangements for its product, Acton had decided to give exports higher priority than in the past. Acton felt that devaluation confirmed this as the correct policy.

Birmingham Cakes was a much smaller company and most of its activities were concentrated on one range of products. The number of firms in its industry had fallen steadily, so that Birmingham Cakes had become the only producer of its main product. It also faced little direct competition for this product in its export markets. However, there was a great deal of indirect competition from similar products made by a large number of other producers, both at home and abroad. Consequently, the total market in which Birmingham's products were sold was shared between a large number of firms, each selling similar, but not identical, products and each with a small market share. There was what economists call monopolistic competition (for a definition of monopolistic competition, see section 2.3). Birmingham Cakes was an enthusiastic exporter, with about one-third of its output going abroad at the time of devaluation. A very high proportion of its exports went to a few European countries, about which it was very well informed.

Cardiff Instruments had only recently been established. It was one company in a large group making capital equipment. Its products were both advanced technically and made to the specifications of individual customers. They were built by assembling a set of standard parts. Historically, technical excellence had always been a major objective of the parent firm. The growth of Cardiff Instrument's sales had been explosive. At the time of devaluation, Cardiff Instruments was exporting a significant proportion of its output but, when taking business, made no distinction between home and export sales. Competition both in the home market and in overseas markets came from much the same small number of producers. There was what economists call oligopoly (for a definition of oligopoly, see section 2.4).

Durham Plates was the largest of four British producers in its industry. It concentrated on the manufacture of two types of component. For one of these it was a monopolist. Export prices of the other product, where Durham Plates faced a few other UK producers, were greatly influenced by the industry's export cartel. Competition abroad came mainly from two European producers. The number of export markets in which Durham Plates sold was large and Durham had agents in more than forty countries. However, because demand for the product of the whole industry was cyclical, Durham Plates' export effort tended to fluctuate inversely with the current level of demand in the home market. At the time of devaluation, Durham Plates was exporting only a small proportion of its output, while its profits had been falling for some time because of rising costs.

Ealing Electrical Appliances was a comparatively small producer, by world standards, in a capital intensive industry, where there was a small number of very large firms. It concentrated on the more expensive end of the total market, and its most serious competition in the UK came from imports. Abroad, Ealing's markets were spread over the whole world, with no one country taking a large proportion of its output. The number and identity of Ealing's competitors varied from market to market, but Ealing usually met a large number of competing producers in each European country. There was therefore oligopoly in the UK market and something closer to monopolistic competition overseas. Ealing's competitive position abroad had been weakening in recent years, so that the volume of its exports was falling, although Ealing was still exporting well over a third of its output.

Fulham Castings was part of a multi-national firm, selling a wide range of semi-manufactures. The prices for its products were set in an international market. Production from its UK plants was integrated with that of its plants abroad, so that exports from the UK were intended to 'top-up' the outputs of its European plants. Exports therefore fluctuated sharply from year to year. At the time of devaluation, they accounted for nearly a quarter of Fulham's UK output. The world price was expressed in dollars and most of the competition abroad came from a few producers based in the USA. Fulham feared that any price cutting on its part would provoke swift retaliatory cuts by its competitors. Fulham Castings is notable in being one of the few firms in our sample which drew up plans, in advance, for dealing with devaluation.

Gatley Hosiery was an old-established manufacturer, operating in a home market where there was a large number of producers. The company was keen to develop abroad, and had established manufacturing and marketing facilities overseas. Sales overseas accounted for more than a third of its turnover. However, direct exports represented only a small proportion of its UK output. Its main markets were in Europe—East and West—and in North

America. Gatley Hosiery changed its product range and price list every few months, with fashion changes. At the time of devaluation, almost all its indirect export business for the current season had already been arranged.

Hertford Stoves dominated the UK market for its products and exported about 90% of its output to about a hundred markets. By far the most important market was the USA, and exports to that country had been rising rapidly. Hertford Stoves concentrated on the more expensive products in its industry, and most of the competition it met in export markets came from a small number of foreign producers, competing with Hertford Stoves throughout the world. Hertford had correctly anticipated, in the summer of 1967, the percentage by which sterling would be devalued, so that by the autumn it had a contingency plan which showed how it would respond to devaluation in each of the hundred or so countries. It put these decisions into effect immediately after devaluation.

Inverness Plant Builders was an important division of a large group, producing capital equipment. It specialised in making large custom-built products. Several years elapsed between the order being received and the completion of the contract. Only a few competitors, all foreign, were likely to be tendering for any one contract, either in the UK or abroad. However, the competitors for a contract of a given type would not necessarily be the same on each occasion. Until shortly before devaluation, Inverness had treated exports as secondary to its home sales. Inverness Plant Builders had expanded its capacity substantially during the few years before devaluation, at a time when the home market was shrinking and, in 1967, was therefore very keen to obtain export business. Some months before devaluation, it had been able to obtain a very large contract from the USA which was highly profitable. The returns on its other export business were low.

Jarrow Furniture dominated the UK furniture industry, and accounted for practically all its exports. Because it had met increasing competition in export markets from a large and growing number of foreign producers, the proportion of Jarrow's output exported had been declining in the years before devaluation. However, at the end of 1967, three-quarters of its ouptut was still exported—to a large number of countries. Jarrow's most important markets were in the USA and Europe, but its performance in Europe had been unsatisfactory before devaluation. The fall in export sales, together with a fall in profit margins, meant that Jarrow was in a serious financial position. Devaluation was welcomed as a way of improving profitability.

Kendal Accessories was a division of a large firm manufacturing capital equipment, which produced a number of products. It specialised in a component not much used by its parent group. Kendal Accessories was the largest and oldest firm in its industry in the UK, which was oligopolistic. Exports accounted for about a third of Kendal's output. They were regulated by the industry's export cartel, which fixed minimum prices for major markets.

London Switches was a small, independent company operating in a rapidly growing industry whose exports accounted for about a quarter of its production. There was only one competitor in the UK, and that firm was also London's keenest competitor in export markets. These were world-wide and several of them were of equal importance to London Switches. Because London's total sales were growing so rapidly, it had little spare capacity.

Nottingham Confectionery was a large firm producing a range of consumer goods, in a number of other fields as well as confectionery. Sales turnover had been increasing rapidly before devaluation and it made considerable expenditures on research and development. Exports had always been important to Nottingham Confectionery and, in the year ended March 1967, overseas earnings had exceeded earnings within the UK for the first time. This trend towards an increased emphasis on exports continued. Nottingham Confectionery sold its products throughout the world, and there was monopolistic competition, both at home and in most of its markets overseas.

Oxford Furnaces was part of a large, diversified engineering firm which exported a high percentage of its output. However, only a small proportion of Oxford Furnace's own output was exported. Oxford met few competitors in any of its markets—home or abroad—but competition was keen in all markets and margins were low. The industry had experienced sharp swings of demand in the years before 1967 and at the time of devaluation Oxford Furnaces had a good deal of spare capacity.

Peterborough Tubes was part of a large group with an impressive export record. We studied two separate devaluation decisions, each by a product group under relatively independent management. For one group (X-ply) Peterborough Tubes was the only licensee in the UK and Europe; with Product D, it was the dominant supplier in the UK. Export markets for both products were expanding rapidly.

Quantox Construction was one of the few firms in the world capable of producing the expensive capital goods in which it specialised. It exported about three-quarters of its output. Even so, it gave priority to the more-profitable home market. When devaluation occurred, both home and export markets were depressed and foreign competition for the few contracts available was very strong. The industry was strongly oligopolistic.

Rugby Processing was part of a large group, using very capital-intensive production methods. It manufactured a basic material for consumer-goods producers. Rugby Processing was the main supplier of the material in the UK, but the product faced competition from a limited number of indirect substitutes. Rugby exported a quarter of its output and its main markets were in Europe. Direct competition from the small number of European producers was significant, but Rugby's prices were highly competitive, because it had a strategy for expanding its sales in Europe ready at the time of devaluation, to consolidate its position in Europe. It had, however, been making marginal price increases for some months in order to raise its profits on sales to Europe to a rate similar to that on profits on its home market.

Stratford Equipment was part of a large group. It exported a great deal of its output in 1967; a third went to some 100 countries. Both home and export markets were growing rapidly and profit margins were good. There was only one UK competitor of any importance. Abroad, there were few competitors and the UK producer was the most important of them.

Tottenham Piping was a group with its headquarters in the UK, but with substantial overseas interests. It put great emphasis on exports. Tottenham Piping sold raw materials and components, and our study dealt with its basic material and with three components. The basic material was produced mainly for consumption within the group itself and exports were small, but growing steadily. Tottenham Piping dominated the British market for the basic material and had became price leader for exports when its industry's export cartel ceased to operate, because there was so much excess capacity that prices fell sharply. Abroad, there were also few producers or customers.

For each component we studied, Tottenham Piping was the dominant producer both in the UK and throughout the world, although there was a considerable amount of indirect competition from other products. However, all markets for the component were growing rapidly. Value-added represented only a small proportion of the price of all the products we studied. The biggest cost was that of the main raw material going into them, and its price was determined by supply and demand in the world market.

CHAPTER 2

The Firm and Devaluation

In this chapter we look at the considerations that a firm has to take into account when responding to devaluation. We do this using the tools that economic theory has traditionally used, assuming that both before and after devaluation the firm maximises profits. However, our objective is simply to clarify the issues. There is no implication that firms always *do* maximise profit. We wish simply to show how cost, price and output are related in devaluation decisions.

We confine our attention to the simple case where a firm exports its total output to one export market, and look at what happens in the four types of market situation most usually discussed by economists. These are: perfect competition, monopoly, monopolistic competition and oligopoly. We do not consider how firms should set marketing expenditure, only how price should be determined after devaluation. This is not because we believe that other marketing factors are unimportant, but simply because most of the firms we studied concentrated on whether to change export prices. To keep the analysis simple, we shall ignore the inter-relationships between the home and export markets. We concentrate on how a firm sets its export prices after a devaluation if it is maximising profit. We assume that costs are a continuous function of the output of each product, and that demand for it is a continuous function of price. This means that the theory cannot be directly applied to situations where firms are producing a few very big products, especially if each product is made to the specification of an individual customer. There will then be discontinuities in the demand and cost functions. However, even there, a similar analysis can be used, provided 'the margin' is defined broadly enough.

Since we assume that all firms maximise profit both before and after devaluation, we follow economic theory in assuming that they equate marginal cost (MC) and marginal revenue (MR). Readers not acquainted with economic theory should note that all we are doing is to apply the general mathematical rule that to maximise the difference between two functions (here the cost and revenue functions) one equates the derivatives of the two functions.

We are using diagrams where marginal cost is the derivative of the total cost function and marginal revenue is the derivative of the total revenue function. To maximise profit we have to find the output where the derivatives are equal.

2.1   Perfect Competition

Perfect competition is the limiting case where price and output adjust easily to changes in demand and supply conditions. In perfect competition, each firm in the industry is too small relative to the whole industry for anything it does to affect market price. Firms are price takers, not price makers. Consequently, if the firm cut its price it would merely reduce its profits. Being so small, it can always sell at the market price everything that it is able to produce. If the firm raises its price it loses all its customers, who buy instead from other firms at the market price. Since we are assuming that the firm seeks to maximise profit, it sells all that it can at the going price. There can be perfect competition only if all firms sell identical (homogeneous) products. It follows that price is then the only marketing variable.

We concentrate on a situation where a large number of firms are selling in a world market, but where the number of British firms is too small for even all of them together to influence the world price of the product. We did not meet any firms in this situation in our study. However, Fulham Castings and Tottenham Piping produced homogeneous products, though the number of firms in their markets was not big enough for there to be perfect competition. This analysis of perfect competition is consequently a useful starting point.

In theory, one could have the reverse situation, where a large percentage of the world output of a homogeneous product was made in the UK, so that all British firms together did influence world price. We ignore this possibility. Perfect competition usually occurs in markets for primary products and raw materials and it would be very unusual for the UK to produce a large proportion of the world output of such a product.

What happens after devaluation in perfect competition is shown in Figure 2.1. Price per unit is measured up the y axis, in sterling. (While we shall work entirely in domestic currency, readers should note that we should reach exactly the same conclusions if the analysis were carried out in foreign currency.) Exports are measured along the x axis. In Figure 2.1 the line PP represents the firm's average revenue curve, which economists use to relate the volume of sales to price per unit. In perfect competition the

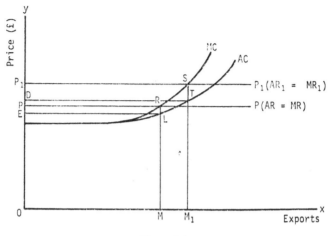

Figure 2.1

average revenue curve (AR) is identical with the marginal revenue curve (MR); both are given by the same horizontal straight line. The firm can sell all that it produces at £OP per unit. Price per unit (average revenue) and the addition to total receipts from selling one additional unit of output (marginal revenue) are both equal to £OP at all levels of exports.

The demand curve facing all producers in the world market is likely to slope downwards to the right. Its position and slope will be determined by consumers' incomes and by the strength of their tastes for the products of this and other industries. However, each individual firm in the industry has to take as given whatever price is set in the world market. It can sell all it wishes to produce at this price, but the price itself will be determined by the balance between supply and demand in the world market.

Before devaluation, the firm in Figure 2.1 is maximising its profits by exporting OM units of output in each period of time. It sells these at the market price of £OP per unit. Marginal cost at each level of exports is shown by the curve MC. Average (unit) cost is given by the average cost curve. Marginal cost is equal to marginal revenue if exports are OM; the two curves MR and MC intersect vertically above M, at R. Since we are looking only at exports, export profit is equal to total receipts minus total costs. It is therefore given by the area $ELRP$. In Figure 2.1, the average cost curve shows cost per unit, and the average revenue curve price per unit. Consequently, the area $ELRP$ represents the difference between total receipts ($OMRP$) and total costs ($OMLE$) at the output OM.

If sterling is now devalued, higher profits can be obtained from exports. In Figure 2.1 a British firm is selling in a world market, where the price of the product is expressed in foreign-currency. We now assume that sterling is devalued by a percentage which, in Figure 2.1, increases the sterling equivalent of the world price of the product, from OP to OP_1. If the average and marginal cost curves remain unchanged the profit-maximising export volume is now OM_1, at the new world price of OP_1. Because the sterling equivalent of the world price has risen, the firm simply increases its exports until marginal cost again equals marginal revenue, now with exports of OM_1. Profit increases from $ELRP$ to $DTSP_1$.

In perfect competition, the firm has no real decision to make after devaluation. There is a world market price for the product, set in foreign currency, which is unaltered by devaluation. The firm therefore increases its exports in order to profit from the increase in the sterling equivalent of the (unaltered) world price. We have here assumed that the average and marginal cost curves remain the same after devaluation. If the firm uses imported materials, their costs are likely to increase immediately after devaluation and there may be consequential increases in the costs of other inputs later. However, even if costs are raised by devaluation, this makes no difference of principle to our argument. Of course, if costs *do* increase, this will mean that M_1 is closer to M than in Figure 2.1, so that exports increase by less than MM_1.

The conclusion is therefore that, in perfect competition, devaluation leads the firm simply to increase its exports in order to take advantage of the higher sterling price for its product. This world (foreign currency) price can be assumed unchanged if very few of the firms selling the product are British. The increase in their exports will not affect the balance between world supply and demand. However, it should be intuitively obvious that if a large percentage of the firms selling the product were British the sterling equivalent of the world price would fall somewhat, the size of the fall being bigger the bigger the increase in British exports. To increase their profits, British firms will increase their exports. With a given demand curve for the product, the increase in supply relative to demand would then reduce the price somewhat.

2.2 Monopoly

We now deal with the other limiting case: monopoly. The

monopolist is the only producer of a product which has no close substitutes. The firm is now the industry. We assume that all its output is exported. Like the demand curve for the industry implicit in the discussion in section 2.1, the monopolist's average revenue curve (AR) slopes downwards to the right. The firm retains some customers if it increases its price. However, if it lowers its price, it gains only a limited number of customers. The firm's average revenue curve slopes downwards; it is not horizontal. Because there are no effective substitutes for the monopolist's product, the amount bought is not very responsive to changes in its price.

2.2.1 ELASTICITY OF DEMAND

Economists then say that demand for the product is relatively 'inelastic'. Elasticity of demand is a technical economic concept which measures the responsiveness of the demand for a product to a change in its price. Elasticity of demand at any point on an average revenue curve is given by the formula:

$$\text{Elasticity of demand} = \frac{\text{Percentage change in quantity demanded}}{\text{Percentage change in price}}$$

If a given percentage reduction in price increases demand by a bigger percentage, it is said that the demand for the product is 'inelastic'. Numerical elasticity of demand is greater than one. For example, if price is cut by 1% and the quantity demanded increases by 2%, it is said that elasticity of demand is 2. Whenever demand is elastic—whenever elasticity of demand is greater than one—total receipts from selling the product *increase* as its price is reduced.

Similarly, if a given percentage change in price leads to a less than proportional change in quantity demanded, it is said that demand is 'inelastic'. Numerical elasticity of demand is less than one. For example, if price is reduced by 2% and quantity demanded increases by only 1%, numerical elasticity of demand equals one-half. Where elasticity of demand is less than one, a reduction in price leads to a *fall* in total receipts from sales of the product. We shall find that elasticity of demand is an extremely useful concept in this book. However, we shall find it unnecessary to go farther than to distinguish between 'elastic' and 'inelastic' demands, as defined above.

[Strictly, the above formula gives elasticity of demand at a point on an average revenue curve and one should therefore discuss only infinitesimal changes in price. However, provided changes in price are small, we can use this formula for 'point' elasticity of demand. Where changes are large, a formula for calculating 'arc' elasticity over a range of an average revenue curve may be used. See, for example, D. C. Hague, *Managerial Economics*, p 55, London (1969)].

2.2.2   MONOPOLY AND DEVALUATION

We now look at the effect of devaluation on the price and quantity of a monopolist's exports. Of course, price is not now the only marketing variable available to the firm. A monopolist can increase exports by spending money to persuade people to buy more of his product as well as by reducing its price. However, the firms in our study paid little attention to the possibility of increasing exports by spending more on sales promotion or on changing the product physically. We therefore concentrate here on decisions to change export prices rather than decisions to change sales promotion expenditure, or to alter the product.

We consider the position of the monopolist shown in Figure 2.2. Again, sterling price is measured up the y axis and the volume of exports along the x axis. Before devaluation, price is £OP and

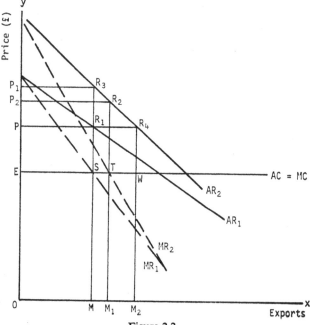

Figure 2.2

sales are OM. Marginal cost and marginal revenue are equal at S. For simplicity, we assume that costs are constant so that the average and marginal cost curves coincide. In this original situation, profits are ESR_1P.

We now assume that there is a devaluation of a given percentage. Since the monopolist is the only producer of his product, the reactions of his competitors are unimportant. The average and marginal revenue curves automatically rise from AR_1 and MR_1 to AR_2 and MR_2. Since there are no effective competitors, the quantity of product which would be bought at each foreign-currency price remains the same; and at each foreign-currency price the sterling equivalent is now bigger. Because devaluation is by a given percentage, the absolute distance between the old and the new revenue curves is bigger the higher the foreign-currency price. Marginal cost and marginal revenue are now equal at T, the new profit-maximising price is OP_2 and exports at that price are OM_1. As can be seen, devaluation has increased both price and output. Similarly, profits have increased from ESR_1P to ETR_2P_2. If the monopolist wishes to maximise profits, he moves from R_1 to R_2 after devaluation. However, because the firm is a monopolist, it has a choice. Unlike the firm in perfect competition, it is not restricted simply to adjusting output in response to a change in the world price for its product. Because it has no competitors, the firm can choose one of the two extreme courses of action open to it, or one between them. First, it can continue to export the original amount, OM. If it does this, price will rise to OP_1 and profit to ESR_3P_1. Second, at the other extreme, the firm can leave price at OP. The quantity sold is then OM_2 and profit EWR_4P. Alternatively, the firm could choose some position between these two extremes.

What can we conclude? In Figure 2.2, we assume constant costs. Moving to R_4, keeping the sterling price unchanged and allowing output to increase to OM_2 is the worst reaction to devaluation in terms of profit. However, there is little difference between profit at R_2 and R_3. Profit is not significantly less if the sterling price is reduced to OP_2, when exports rise to OM_1, or if exports are held at OM. Although OM_1 is the profit maximising export volume after devaluation, with a price of £OP_2, profit is not much bigger than if exports are held at OM rather than increased to OM_1. Indeed, the sacrifice in profit that a monopolist makes, by choosing to move to R_3 rather than R_2, is always likely to be relatively small because a monopolist's average revenue curve is likely to be rather inelastic. The difference in profit between R_2 and R_3 will be smaller the steeper the slope of the firm's average revenue curve, the steeper the (upward) slope of its cost curve and the smaller percentage devaluation.

We may therefore conclude that where a monopolist is uncertain about demand conditions in his export markets, but is convinced that demand for his product is inelastic and his average revenue curve therefore steep, there is a strong case for doing nothing. The monopolist can take the whole benefit of devaluation in extra sterling profit at the current level of exports, rather than reducing sterling prices in the hope of reaching R_2. The difference in profit is likely to be small, and the more sharply unit costs increase as output increases the more true this will be. However, if cost per unit (average cost) falls as exports exceed OM, the conclusions are less clear-cut. All will depend on how steep the slope of the average cost curve is. Even so, unless it slopes downward very steeply, holding price at OP and moving to R_4 would still be the worst alternative, though the difference in profit between the other two positions would still be small. We shall later suggest other reasons why a monopolist, like Peterborough Tubes for X-ply, may leave export prices unchanged after devaluation. However, this is one possible explanation. Moreover, doing this still leaves the monopolist with the possibility of reducing prices later, if he feels that it will pay him to do so, whereas if he cuts prices at once he may find it harder to raise them later.

2.3 Monopolist Competition

A firm selling under monopolistic competition faces a large number of competitors, as does one seller in perfect competition. However, each firm now differentiates its product a little in the eyes of customers, from those offered by its rivals. It may do so by differentiating the product physically, by advertising or by spending money on some other form of sales promotion which emphasises that the product is a little different from the others in the industry. As a result, the firm can increase its price without suffering quite as large a fall in exports as it would in perfect competition, even if its competitors do not increase their prices. If it cuts its price it will gain a good deal of business if other firms do not cut theirs; but it will gain much less business if they do. Birmingham Cakes and Nottingham Confectionery were selling in monopolistically competitive markets both in the UK and abroad.

With monopolistic competition, the nationality of competitors in export markets is again important, as under perfect competition and, again, the effect of devaluation on sterling prices in export markets will depend on whether most of the competition met

abroad comes from British or from foreign firms. We begin with
Figure 2.3a. Here, we assume that a British firm faces competition
in its export markets mainly from other British firms. In Figure
2.3a, the vertical axis again shows amounts of sterling. The average
revenue curve DD for our firm is drawn on the assumption that
all firms charge the same price, shown on the y axis. The average
revenue curve dd is drawn on the assumption that our firm alone
charges the price shown on the y axis, while all other firms charge
OP. The dd curve is consequently more elastic than the DD curve.

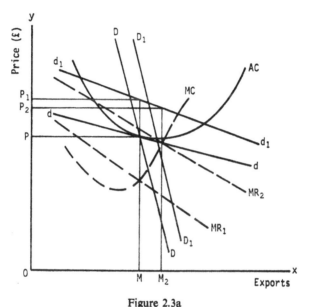

Figure 2.3a

Because there are so many producers in the industry, each firm
realises that if it cuts its price it can increase its export sales
significantly at the expense of all its competitors together, taking
only a negligible amount of export business from any one of them.
All firms in the industry will therefore be tempted to treat dd as
the average revenue curve and cut their export prices. This will
lead to general price cutting, as a large number of firms see the
attractiveness of price cuts. So, the exports of each individual
firm will depend not on the slope of dd but on that of DD. The
dd curve facing the individual firm slides down the DD curve. As
prices fall, profits fall and the least efficient firms in the industry

will be driven out, or so economic theory says. Indeed, the theory holds that the *dd* curve will continue to slide downwards until the industry as a whole is earning only the amount of profit required to keep in the industry the number of firms that can just make a profit. In practice, profit may well not be reduced so far, but there will be a tendency for profit to fall in some degree.

In the firm shown in Figure 2.3a, the profit-maximising export volume before devaluation is OM and export price is OP. Marginal cost equals marginal revenue with exports of OM. How will devaluation affect this situation?

2.3.1 NO FOREIGN COMPETITION

If all firms come from the devaluing country, here assumed to be the UK, the DD curve in Figure 2.3a will move to $D_1 D_1$ and the *dd* curve to $d_1 d_1$. With no foreign firms in the industry, the curves are shifted upwards by the full percentage of devaluation. We make the usual assumption for monopolistic competition, namely, that the demand curve for exports, where all British producers charge the same price, (DD), will be fairly steep, so that the horizontal shift to $D_1 D_1$ after devaluation will be small. However, each individual firm will appear to be faced with a more-elastic demand curve like $d_1 d_1$. The firm has the same three possibilities as the monopolist in Figure 2.2. It can maintain exports at OM and raise price by the full amount of devaluation to OP_1. Alternatively, it can charge the profit-maximising price, OP_2, and expand exports to OM_2. Or it can charge a price between OP_1 and OP_2, with exports increasing to the extent given by the new average revenue curve $d_1 d_1$.

In theory, what happens will depend on what profits on exports our firms require. If they were not satisfied with export profits before devaluation, they may well raise the sterling export price to OP_1. However, that assumes unanimity among the firms. The theory assumes that some firms will cut prices and cause the others to follow. But practice may be different. If they were happy with profits before devaluation, some firms at least may try to expand exports by cutting prices below OP_1. If they are initially successful in expanding sales along $d_1 d_1$, this may induce more and more firms to do the same, to maintain market share, until the demand curve facing each firm slides down $D_1 D_1$. Economic theory would argue that the export price would then be reduced to something like OP_1, with the exports of each individual firm increased only marginally. Sterling profit would be roughly the same as before devaluation.

2.3.2 FOREIGN COMPETITION

We were assuming above that there were no foreign competitors in overseas markets and that profits were satisfactory before devaluation. We now assume that there is considerable foreign competition overseas.

When most competition comes from foreign firms it is easier to work in terms of foreign currency, and to show devaluation as lowering the marginal cost curve by the percentage of devaluation, less the increase in costs which it causes by raising the prices of imported inputs, as in Figure 2.3b. If we now suppose that most competitors in export markets are foreign, the supply curve for the whole industry (British and foreign) in export markets is unlikely to fall very far, because now only a few of the firms are British. Similarly, even if devaluation increases the export output of all British firms, it will not increase it by a significant proportion of the output of the whole industry. Moreover, devaluation will alter world supply only to the extent that firms in the industry *are* operating from Britain.

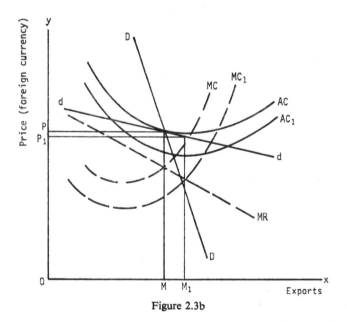

Figure 2.3b

Devaluation will allow British firms, like the one in Figure 2.3b to extend sales along the demand curve *dd*, because their foreign currency costs will have been reduced by devaluation. Again, there are three options, but this time a move to the profit-maximising price (OP_1), with an output of OM_1, is the most likely one. Where a firm exporting in monopolistic competition already faces competition overseas mainly from foreign businesses, the most profitable course will be to take advantage of this situation. The firm will maximise profits by making only small reductions in foreign-currency prices. Because the British firms represent only a few of those operating in the overseas market, it will be most profitable for them to assume that demand curves in the overseas market are unchanged and merely to adjust supply. Even if British firms *do* cut prices, the fact that there are so few of them in the overseas market may well mean that prices will not fall far. Again the theory assumes that some firms are bound to a set of general price cutting. But, again, the theory may be different.

2.3.3 CONCLUSIONS

Economic theory therefore argues that where there is monopolistic competition in an overseas market the extent to which a British firm can increase its sterling prices after devaluation will depend on the relative numbers of British and foreign firms operating in export markets. Sterling prices are most likely to be increased where: (a) most competition in export markets comes from foreign firms; or (b) most competitors in export markets are British, but they all regard the export profits they were earning before devaluation as unsatisfactory and see no profit advantage in cutting export prices. Sterling prices are less likely to be increased where: (a) most competitors in export markets are British; and (b) these firms were satisfied with profits before devaluation and are prepared to cut prices to increase export volume and profit. It is clearly difficult to generalise, but we shall see during our study of Birmingham Cakes and Nottingham Confectionery what happened to those of our firms that were selling in monopolistic competition.

2.4 Oligopoly

The final type of situation we shall study is oligopoly, where only a small number of producers sell in any overseas market. Most of the firms studied in this book were selling in oligopolistic markets. Again, we shall have to analyse the situation differently according to whether the competitors met in export markets are mainly British or foreign.

We deal first with the situation where the firm faces mainly its own nationals in export markets (Figure 2.4a) and shall measure sterling prices up the y axis. Where the firm faces mainly foreign competitors, we work in foreign currency (Figure 2.4b).

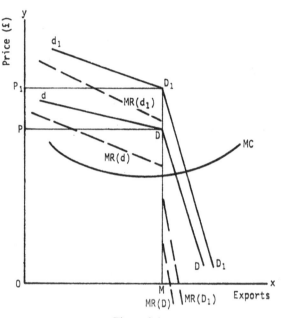

Figure 2.4a

In oligopoly, firms are interdependent because, with few sellers in each market, if one firm cuts its price then its competitors are likely to find their own sales significantly reduced and will therefore feel bound to respond with retaliatory price cuts of their own. It follows that, in oligopoly, an average revenue curve for the product of any individual firm can be drawn only if its competitors' reactions are known or assumed. In a sense, there is no such thing as an average revenue curve under oligopoly at all. At each price, there are a number of quantities of product that an oligopolist might sell, according to the way his competitors react.

We can make all the points we need to make if we use a device known as a kinked demand curve, shown in Figure 2.4a. The firm's average revenue curve is now in two parts. The lower part (*DD*) assumes that the prices of all firms in the market, including its own, move up and down together. The prices the firms charge need not be identical, though they may be. The upper part of the average revenue curve (*dD*) assumes that the firm can change its own prices independently, without any retaliation by its competitors. The demand curve facing the firm before devaluation is therefore *dDD* in Figure 2.4a. There is a 'kink' at the ruling price of *OP*.

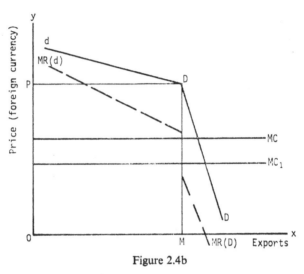

Figure 2.4b

2.4.1 NO FOREIGN COMPETITION

Figure 2.4a assumes that the export market is depressed. A number of our firms were in this position, for example, Acton Chemicals, Inverness Plant Builders and Quantox Construction. The reason why the average revenue curve takes the shape shown in Figure 2.4a is that our firm fears that if it reduces its price below *OP* its competitors will immediately match its price reductions in order to maintain their market shares. Again, because the market is depressed, the firm fears that if it raises its price above *OP* its competitors will be reluctant to follow. It thinks they will hope that, by raising its price independently, it will simply lose market share. *OP* is a price which is neither low enough to threaten competitors' market shares and so invite retaliation, nor high enough to put the firm's own market share at risk. There is therefore a tendency for prices to remain at *OP* unless demand or supply conditions change very greatly. There is too much risk in making any change.

In Figure 2.4a, therefore, competitors are likely to match any price cut the firm makes, but not any increase. One could draw a similar diagram for buoyant market conditions. Here, the kink in the average revenue curve would be in the opposite direction. However, since we can point by analogy, where necessary, to what is likely to happen if there is oligopoly in a buoyant market we shall not draw this diagram here. [Readers who wish to see an analysis of what happens under oligopoly in such conditions, using a kinked demand curve, are referred, for example, to D. C. Hague, *Managerial Economics*, pp 96 and 97, London (1969).] We shall concentrate on the situation in a depressed oligopolistic market.

Where the oligopolist's average revenue curve is kinked, the associated marginal revenue curve will not be continuous. For example, with the depressed market shown in Figure 2.4a, the left-hand part of the marginal revenue curve ends and the right-hand part begins immediately below the kink. There is a 'gap' in the marginal revenue curve. This is because the marginal revenue curves associated with the two portions of the average revenue curve have very different slopes and positions. At the level of output where there is the kink, the firm suddenly switches from the marginal revenue curve $MR(d)$ which is marginal to the gently sloping half (dD) of the kinked average revenue curve to the marginal revenue curve $MR(d)$ which is marginal to the much steeper part, DD. Hence there is the gap. In Figure 2.4a, where the marginal cost curve passes through the 'gap' in the marginal revenue curve, it pays the firm to charge the price OP. This analysis suggests that if price is originally OP, only a considerable rise or fall in the marginal cost curve will make it profitable to alter price. Only a big rise or fall in marginal cost will make it worth risking the reactions of competitors, which are expected to be unhelpful whether price is increased or decreased. This is why many economists believe that, in depressed conditions, oligopoly prices are often 'sticky'. They believe that prices change only infrequently and then only in response to big changes in the situation facing the firm.

How will the oligopolist in Figure 2.4a react to devaluation? In oligopoly where all firms selling in an export market are British, devaluation will increase the sterling profit to be earned from a given level of exports. The two halves of the demand curve (in domestic currency) shift upwards, with the kink remaining at the same level of output. Since all firms are British and the market is depressed, they decide (gratefully) to take the benefit of devaluation in extra sterling profits. Diagrammatically, what happens is that the average revenue curve now takes the shape of the dotted line $d_1 D_1 D_1$ in Figure 2.4a. If the oligopolists wish to maximise profit, there is no incentive to reduce the foreign-currency price below its new sterling equivalent (OP_1) unless devaluation is big enough for the lower part of the new marginal revenue curve $MR(D_1)$ to intercept the marginal cost curve to the right of M. However, even if this happened, the extra profit to be obtained from reducing price below OP_1 to the profit-maximising level, would probably leave profit very little above what it would be if the firm left price at OP_1. This is because (as we have seen) the D_1D_1 section of the average revenue curve is likely to be very steep. The firm's competitors will match any price cut, so that cutting price will bring in little extra profit, even if the devaluation is substantial.

2.4.2 FOREIGN COMPETITION

We now assume that all other firms in the overseas market, except the one we are studying, are foreign. This situation is shown in Figure 2.4b, where we still assume depressed market conditions, but the y axis now shows prices in foreign currency. The demand curve facing the firm therefore does not change after devaluation. What does change, now that Britain has devalued, is the position of the marginal cost curve, measured in foreign currency. It falls from MC to MC_1. For simplicity, we use a horizontal marginal cost curve, both before and after devaluation. It falls after devaluation by the percentage of devaluation minus the increase in costs caused by devaluation, because devaluation raises the cost of imports.

Again, in the depressed market shown in Figure 2.4b, the downward shift in the cost curve (in foreign currency) will not lead the firm to cut its foreign-currency prices unless the marginal cost curve moves downwards far enough to intersect the lower part of the marginal revenue curve $MR(D)$ associated with the right-hand (DD) part of the average revenue curve. In Figure 2.4b, it does not. Unless this happens, the profit-maximising price remains at OP and the profit-maximising output at OQ. However, since the DD part of the average revenue curve is likely to be rather inelastic, and the dD part rather elastic, the 'gap' between the two parts of the marginal revenue curve is also likely to be big. So, unless the firm's cost curve before devaluation was very close to the bottom of the 'gap', the amount of devaluation required to increase the profit-maximising level of output much beyond OQ may well have to be large. Similarly, the steeper is the slope of the DD curve the smaller is the extra profit obtained after devaluation if the firm charges a lower price than OP.

2.4.3 CONCLUSION

To summarise, in an oligopolistic market where the firm seeks maximum profit, devaluation is at least likely to lead to a reduction in the foreign-currency price that an oligopolist charges for his exports if the export market is very depressed and/or if most competitors are from the devaluing country and/or if the percentage of devaluation is small. If many exporters are from the devaluing country, all will fear retaliation if they are the first to cut prices. Similarly, the theory assumes that only if the percentage of devaluation is very large can the firm take the risk that cutting its prices will lead to retaliation by its competitors. The argument is that a large percentage of devaluation will allow the firm to reduce its prices by more than its competitors can afford to do, especially if these are from overseas countries whose currency has not been devalued. This was the kind of situation that Inverness Plant Builders met in New Zealand, when competing with Italian firms.

However, such an analysis over-simplifies a complex situation. It assumes that any price cut by our firm would lead to an immediate price cut by all competitors. However, if ours were the only British firm in an overseas market, even a depressed one, competitors might *not* follow a price cut that it made, even if the cut were relatively small. They might feel unable to do so because profits were already low, and their own costs, measured in local currency, were not changed by devaluation. The British firm would then be able to reduce foreign-currency prices without causing retaliation and so be able to gain market share.

By analogy, economic theory would argue that where demand in an oligopolistic overseas market was buoyant, there would be little need for a British firm to cut prices. Price cuts would be likely only where a large proportion of the competitors were British and/or one or more of them was seeking an opportunity to raise its share of the overseas market.

This discussion simply emphasises the difficulty of making general statements about what may happen in oligopoly. There are too many possibilities. All we can safely do is to await the results of our analysis of the case material, and then see whether we can generalise about what *our* oligopolistic firms did.

2.5 Summary

The conclusions we have reached so far are as follows, though it must be emphasised that they are all based on the assumption that firms maximise profits.

In perfect competition, the firm adjusts its exports to the price set in the world market. Where most firms in the industry are foreign, and where the world price is set in foreign currency, that world price is unaffected by devaluation. The sterling price increases by the amount of devaluation and the firm expands exports to adjust to the new sterling price.

In monopoly, since the firm's average revenue curve slopes downwards, it will respond to devaluation by reducing its foreign-currency price and expanding its exports. The fall in the foreign-currency price will be smaller the steeper the (downward-sloping) marginal revenue curve and the (upward-sloping) marginal cost curve. But even if the firm's marginal cost curve is sloping downwards very steeply, and demand for the product is very elastic, it will always pay the firm to charge a higher sterling price than before devaluation. A monopolist is likely to find that the extra profit it obtains by moving to the profit-maximising position after devaluation, as compared with holding its exports and its foreign currency export price at the pre-devaluation level, is rather small. There will be a big benefit from moving to the profit-maximising position rather than keeping exports at the same level only where: (a) the size of devaluation is considerable; (b) demand is elastic (which is unlikely in monopoly); (c) economies of scale are very substantial, so that the marginal cost curve slopes steeply downwards.

In monopolistic competition, where most of the firm's competitors in export markets are from its own country, it is likely to have to reduce its foreign currency-prices without obtaining much increase in sales. However, where most competition in export markets comes from foreign firms, it is unlikely to need to reduce its foreign-currency price much, if at all.

In oligopoly, generalisations are more difficult. However, it seems probable that, where the market is depressed, the foreign-currency price will not be reduced, for fear of retaliation. This is especially the case where most of the competition comes from firms in the country which has devalued. Similarly, if the overseas market is buoyant, there will be no need to cut prices unless the firm regards its market share as too small, or one of its competitors cuts its price and the firm feels bound to match this price cut for some reason.

To reach our conclusions we have made a number of simplifying assumptions, all of which may be unrealistic. The most important is the assumption of profit maximisation. While profit is obviously necessary for survival, we shall see later that the majority of our firms aimed in 1967 at increasing sales rather than profit, in their general export policies. However, they followed rather different objectives at the time of devaluation and this makes generalisation difficult.

2.6 Some Jargon

This is a convenient point at which to introduce some jargon that we shall find useful later. This chapter has shown that one reaction to devaluation is to reduce foreign-currency prices by as much as possible. However, this will rarely mean reducing them by the full amount of devaluation. Devaluation also increases costs, especially because it directly increases the cost of imports. So, if a firm's national currency is devalued by 15% but its costs are also expected to increase by 5%, the firm can afford to cut its prices by only 10% if it is not to suffer a fall in profits. For the remainder of this book, we shall therefore describe the total amount of devaluation (15% in the example we have just used) as the 'full amount of devaluation'. However, we shall use the term 'net amount of devaluation' to describe this amount of devaluation less the increase in costs to which devaluation is expected to give rise. In the above example, this is 10%. Not surprisingly, where our firms cut foreign-currency prices, they usually cut them by the *net*, rather than the full, amount of devaluation. To have done otherwise would have been to reduce profit.

Another concept that we shall frequently use is 'contribution'. If a firm is to make a profit, it obviously has to cover its total costs. Especially for pricing decisions, it is useful to divide the firm's costs into fixed and variable costs. In order to make a profit, the firm must cover both its fixed and variable costs and have something left over. One difficulty in business is that while it is usually possible to identify the variable costs incurred in producing different amounts of a given product, it is often not possible to do the same with fixed costs. It follows that, strictly, all that one can legitimately say about the profitability of any individual product is that it has covered the variable costs incurred in its production and sale and contributed a certain amount towards covering fixed costs and making profit. This is why 'contribution' is a key concept in the remainder of this book. One needs to know what 'contribution' each product is making, over and above its variable costs, towards meeting the firm's total fixed cost and enabling it to earn a profit. How easy it is to define 'contribution' will depend on the precise shape of the cost and revenue functions facing the firm. It may be worth adding, although this should be obvious, that if the firm does *not* cover its fixed costs, then it will make a loss.

The meaning of 'contribution' can be seen most easily if we take a situation where the firm is able to sell as much as it can at the 'going' price. We saw earlier in this chapter that this will be the case where the firm is selling in conditions of perfect competition. Price per unit is constant, however much or little the firm is selling. If, at the same time, variable cost per unit of output is also constant, we have the situation shown in Figure 2.5. Here, price per unit of output is *OP* and variable cost per unit is *OC*. Average variable cost (or variable cost per unit) is simply total variable cost divided by output. (Where average variable cost is constant, it is equal to marginal cost.) The convenient thing about this simple situation is that, since price and average variable cost are both constant at every level of output, 'contribution' can easily be defined.

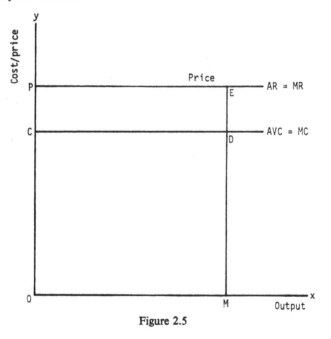

Figure 2.5

It is worth distinguishing two meanings of the word 'contribution'. Contribution per unit of output is the difference between the price per unit of product and the average variable cost incurred in producing and selling that unit. This is often known as the 'contribution margin' or 'unit contribution'. In Figure 2.5, it is

CP (=ED) per unit. So, for example, if the variable cost of producing each unit of output were 8p and each unit could be sold for 10p, unit contribution would be 2p. Because we are making the simple assumption that both price and variable cost per unit of output are constant then, in Figure 2.5, we can define price (OP), average variable cost (OC) and contribution margin (CP) unambiguously. They are the same at every output between zero and OM.

Difficulties arise in the more usual situation where price changes as output rises and where variable cost also changes with output. Unit contribution can then be calculated accurately only if the cost and revenue functions are known. Unit contribution will be different at different levels of output. It is then usually much more useful to think in terms of the 'total contribution' from the whole output of a given product, rather than of contribution per unit. We can see what is meant by total contribution from our simple diagram, Figure 2.5. In this figure, total contribution is $CDEP$, with sales of OM.

While it can be a somewhat difficult concept to use, we shall find that 'contribution' was one which several of our firms used when taking their devaluation decisions.

We have now completed the preliminaries. We proceed to look in detail at our firms' devaluation decisions, beginning with the objectives they pursued at the time of devaluation.

CHAPTER 3

Export Objectives

Like all other business decisions, decisions about devaluation
have to be taken with some objective in view. In the first section
of this chapter we look at the general attitude of our firms towards
exports at the time of devaluation. We then turn to the narrower
objectives that our firms pursued as they took their devaluation
decisions. We see how far the general objectives they had been
pursuing up to the time of devaluation limited the range of
alternatives which their managements seriously considered when
it occurred. Indeed, one issue we must study is whether devaluation stimulated the managements of our firms into changing their
export objectives.

The way exports fit into a firm's overall marketing strategy
obviously owes a good deal to historical accident, to the psychology of individual managers and collective managements, and
so on. Such influences are usually least important in large, long-
established firms whose export policies have been shaped less by
individual attitudes or accidental factors and more by deliberate
decisions of the entire management team over a long period. In
smaller firms, because they have fewer managers, the roles and
attitudes of individuals are often more important. Indeed, in some
of the smaller firms we studied, individuals exerted a major
influence even on general export policies.

In at least five firms, both large and small, individuals played a
major role in reaching the decisions about devaluation. Even
where more than one person was involved, the group was rarely
very large and rarely a top management one. For example, the
devaluation decisions were often taken by the marketing department. This would usually *not* be true with a decision to make a
fundamental change in the firm's whole marketing strategy, or
in its total export strategy. While neither we nor the firms would
argue that devaluation is not an important economic event, the
significant part that individuals were allowed to play in taking
the devaluation decisions confirms the general impression that
our firms regarded the reaction to devaluation as a rather technical
matter.

3.1 Attitudes to Exporting

Our firms approached exporting in one of two ways. Five of them saw it as something of an expedient to be resorted to when the home market was depressed. They were: Durham Plates, Ealing Electrical Appliances, Inverness Plant Builders, Kendal Accessories and Quantox Construction. To save space, we shall describe these firms as 'anti-cyclical' exporters. They were firms that took exports seriously only when the home market was cyclically depressed and which largely ignored them when it was buoyant. The remaining fourteen firms believed that exporting could and should form a permanent and important part of their activities. We shall describe these firms as 'regular' exporters.

3.2 Anti-cyclical Exporters

Demand in the UK for the products of the five anti-cyclical exporters was cyclical. At times when home demand was good, profits from sales in the UK were higher than from exports. As a result, when sales in the UK were buoyant, the incentive to export was reduced. Indeed, at such times the receipt of export orders could be embarrassing because capacity was too small to meet both home and export demand. Order books became unacceptably long, delivery dates lengthened and exports were reduced. When the domestic market was weak, however, exporting became more attractive. To maintain the amount of employment they were offering and to prevent losses becoming unbearably large, these firms then increased exports, if necessary at prices close to marginal cost.

Our anti-cyclical exporters said that because export prices were so low they were hesitant about investing in extra capacity to produce exports. They argued that they did not earn enough profit on exports for it to be worth installing sufficient extra capacity to be able quickly to meet all the orders they would receive if they were to make substantial exports at a time when demand in the home market was high.

An element in the anti-cyclical approach to exporting was that the firm committed only relatively small amounts of money to overseas marketing. For example, Quantox Construction had invested very little in marketing activities outside the UK. It was in an industry where it was relatively easy to discover where overseas business was available and was so well-known internationally that it was almost always invited to tender for potential business. Inverness Plant Builders and Kendal Accessories used overseas commission agents mainly to obtain initial enquiries. They relied on their own technical and marketing experts, sent from the UK, to do the actual selling. This not only kept down the expense of overseas marketing; with few resources permanently devoted to stimulating them, there was little need to maintain a steady level of export sales. The most important reason was that, in both firms, the value of a typical export order was very large (though smaller than for Quantox Construction) so that overseas agents could earn substantial commissions from providing business, even if they brought in rather infrequent orders. The converse is obviously true as well. Thus, although we have classified it as an anti-cyclical exporter, Ealing Electrical Appliances found that it could not allow its exports of caravans to fall too far at any time because it had made a substantial investment in setting up an overseas marketing organisation. Finding this very valuable at times when the home market was depressed, Ealing continued to spend money on it when the home market recovered.

We now look in detail at the anti-cyclical exporters, though emphasising that they were not completely opportunistic. They did not treat exports simply as a source of short-run employment and profit, but exported some output at all times. We are simply grouping together those firms where exports were substantially reduced when their business in the UK was good, and vice versa.

Three of these firms did not have separate export departments at the time of devaluation. Durham Plates' export sales were handled by the same department as dealt with home sales. Inverness Plant Builders and Kendal Accessories did obtain large export orders from their commission agents abroad, but so infrequently that they did not think it worth having separate home and export marketing departments. While Ealing Electrical Appliances also altered its export effort inversely to fluctuations in home market demand, it did so to a smaller extent than the other three firms, because of its big investment in its export marketing organisation. When trade in the UK was depressed, home sales alone were too small to give Ealing the economies of scale it needed to be able to keep its costs and prices low enough to compete effectively abroad. The technology of caravan production meant that to break even Ealing had to sell larger and larger numbers of each succeeding model of caravan.

At the time of devaluation, the home sales of all the anti-cyclical exporters were low. All five had therefore been trying to increase their exports for some time. Durham Plates' total sales had been falling for about two years; Inverness Plant Builders and Kendal Accessories had also suffered sharp falls in their total orders since 1965, as their customers cut back on investment after a period of excessive optimism about economic growth in the UK which had led to them to over-order. Ealing Electrical Appliances was in a slightly better position because home sales of caravans had remained roughly constant since 1964, but we have seen that to keep its costs down Ealing had continually to increase the total sales of each succeeding model of caravan. Moreover, Ealing's exports were falling. All these firms knew that when home sales fell unit costs rose considerably, unless exports could be increased.

All five firms were therefore actively seeking export business at the time of devaluation, but as a matter of necessity rather than choice and with no intention at this stage that doing so would leave them with a major and permanent commitment to export when home demand recovered. An increase in exports was seen as the only way of keeping activity, and hopefully profit as well, at acceptable levels in the short run. While it had its more-permanent commitment to its overseas sales organisation, even Ealing Electrical still felt a greater commitment to the home market than to exports.

However, up to the time of devaluation, the success of three of the anti-cyclical exporters (Durham Plates, Ealing Electrical Appliances and Kendal Accessories) in increasing exports had been limited. Despite a bigger marketing effort overseas, Ealing Electrical Appliances' exports were falling steadily. So were exports of Durham Plates' main product, although this fall had been offset by rising exports of its other products. Kendal Accessories' exports had also fallen. On the other hand, Inverness Plant Builders had been fortunate in obtaining a series of very large orders from one customer in the USA, which had provided enough extra business to cancel out the decline in home sales turnover, though not enough to prevent a fall in profits.

Quantox Construction was unique among our firms. The price of every one of its products was many times greater than for any other firm. Its policy had been to keep sufficient capacity available to be able to give priority to the home market whenever demand there was at a peak, but the last occasion when home demand had been high was around 1957. Quantox Construction had therefore been forced to build up a substantial export business. At the time of devaluation, it was exporting three-quarters of its output and had established an elaborate overseas marketing organisation, including a strong team at Quantox's head office. However, competition in the industry was so keen that the contribution to profit that Quantox was earning on its export business just before devaluation was small. On some contracts, it was not even receiving any 'contribution'. Quantox's hopes for long-term survival depended on an upturn in business in the more-profitable UK market and, in 1967, there were hopes that this would soon occur. Because, at the time of devaluation, Quantox Construction had not yet fully broken with its tradition of maintaining at least some capacity to meet a possible increase of demand in the home market, we classify it as an anti-cyclical exporter.

3.3 Regular Exporters

What we call 'regular' exporting was carried out in the belief that it was in the firm's best interests to develop a continuing export business in at least some overseas markets. This keenness to export a substantial percentage of output permanently, often reflected the belief that only then would total production be big enough to keep costs down to a competitive level. All our regular exporters had discovered that they could rely on demand from their export markets being reasonably stable. They had therefore been happy to treat extra exports as part of the 'base load' on which they relied when planning to increase their capacity. Indeed, Jarrow Furniture and Hertford Stoves had made some very big investments in extra capacity, which depended for their profitability wholly on increased exports. In the other firms, of course, investment in increased capacity was carried out to cater for increased sales in both home and export markets.

Our fourteen regular exporters included all the firms not listed above as anti-cyclical exporters. All of them, except London Switches, Stratford Equipment and Rugby Processing, had large and established marketing and selling organisations. Indeed, all the other regular exporters (except Acton Chemicals) had set up wholly-owned marketing companies to deal with their export business in important markets. For less-important markets all fourteen firms, except Fulham Castings, used commission agents. Five of the regular exporters (Fulham Castings, Gatley Hosiery, Jarrow Furniture, Oxford Furnaces and Peterborough Tubes) had manufacturing plants overseas.

Although they exported a large percentage of their outputs, both London Switches and Stratford Equipment had virtually one-man export organisations, their export departments consisting of little more than their managing directors. The export marketing team of Birmingham Cakes was also very small, even though Birmingham was a very active exporter.

All the overseas representatives of Birmingham Cakes, London Switches and Stratford Equipment were commission agents.

Stratford Equipment, and more especially London Switches, had no close relationships with their agents. However, though Birmingham Cakes had few overseas agents, all were of long standing and all had an intimate association with the firm.

For all the regular exporters except Fulham Castings, a major reason why they put so much emphasis on exports in 1967 was that they saw only limited opportunities for increasing sales within the UK at that time. Birmingham Cakes was the most extreme example of this. It was the only producer of its particular product, in a market where many similar products competed, so that there was monopolistic competition. Like demand for the whole set of products taken together, the market for Birmingham Cakes' own particular products had been saturated for some years. A continuing growth in total turnover could be obtained only by selling new products in the UK or by exporting. However, Birmingham Cakes could find no market in the UK with good sales prospects that was not outside the bakery industry altogether. It had therefore chosen to increase its exports instead.

Hertford Stoves and Jarrow Furniture were virtual monopolists in the UK. They accounted for almost all home sales of their products. Even so, this gave them home markets that were too small to allow them to achieve the economies of scale they needed if they were to be able to compete effectively in international markets. As a result, they had made strenuous efforts to increase exports during 1967. By the time of devaluation, Hertford Stoves was exporting about 90% of its output and Jarrow Furniture over 70%. Peterborough Tubes and Rugby Processing also almost completely monopolised the markets for their particular products in the UK. Peterborough Tubes had traditionally been the biggest exporter in its industry and the emphasis it had always put on exporting considerably influenced the way it marketed the products we studied, though it is true that sales prospects for these products were better abroad than in the UK. Because of its limited home market, Rugby Processing was keen to expand into any profitable export market it could find. In particular, it was seeking to become an established supplier in Europe. So, at the time of devaluation, Rugby Processing was treating its exports to Europe in exactly the same way as its sales within the UK, so far as delivery, credit terms and customer service arrangements were concerned. For Tottenham Piping, there had been no growth at all in total UK sales for some years and, with Tottenham already the largest firm in its industry in the UK, it had sought to increase exports.

The home markets of both London Switches and Stratford Equipment had been expanding rapidly for several years, but export demand had grown even faster, as a result of technological changes both in their products and in the production methods of the industries they supplied. Nevertheless, London Switches had no coherent exporting strategy and it was just before devaluation that Stratford Equipment had set down its broad export objectives for the first time, and then only under pressure from its parent firm.

Cardiff Instruments had been exporting for only five years before devaluation, but its overseas sales had been increasing rapidly. It was already the largest exporter in its own industry in the UK, though exports had never accounted for more than a quarter of its turnover. Despite this leading position, Cardiff Instruments had no special export strategy.

Oxford Furnaces saw itself as a major exporter, though it exported only 14% of the output of the product we studied. Indeed, Oxford claimed that as a firm it had more experience of exporting than of any of its UK competitors, having been doing so for several decades. Oxford's markets, in the UK and elsewhere, were subject to sharp, cyclical swings. Partly because of depressed conditions overseas, Oxford's export sales had been disappointing for some years before 1967.

Fulham Castings is the odd one out among the regular exporters. Its attitude towards exporting was determined by the fact that its technology made it cheaper to produce locally in Europe, so long as capacity was available there, rather than export to Europe from the UK. Fulham Castings' exports were therefore limited to the difference between the capacity of its European plants and European demand for its products. Since the world price for its product was beyond Fulham Casting's control, its main objective was to co-ordinate the allocation of orders to its various plants so as to minimise costs.

In contrast to the anti-cyclical exporters, most of our 'regular' exporters had earned roughly the same rate of profit from their exports as from home sales during most of the post-war period. However, at the time of devaluation, profits on exports in most of these firms were lower than at home. We feel that we can assert this confidently despite the difficulty of calculating 'profit per unit' for any product. The basic problem, of course, is that calculating 'profit' on an individual unit of any product means attempting to allocate fixed costs to it. Here, we have an extra difficulty. To talk of 'profit' on each unit of output exported means trying to allocate costs correctly to an individual unit of *export* output. Most of our firms claimed that, at the time of devaluation, 'profit' on exports was lower than on home sales.

Many of our firms did not allocate costs at all, but worked in terms of contribution. Some actually earned more 'contribution' on a unit of output exported than on a unit sold at home. Thus, Hertford Stoves sent most of its exports (and indeed most of its output) to the USA, where contribution per unit of product sold was considerably higher than in the small UK market. Jarrow Furniture's exports to the USA also appeared to be earning a slightly higher 'unit contribution' than its home sales. Again, Stratford Equipment was able to charge a higher price in the USA than in the UK for a new product launched after devaluation. Cardiff Instruments and London Switches charged roughly the same prices, both within the UK and abroad, for most of their products.

While the remaining firms claimed that the export 'profit margin', at the time of devaluation, was often lower than the margin on home sales, none of them saw contribution per unit exported as unacceptably low. Even so, Jarrow Furniture (outside the USA), Oxford Furnaces and Tottenham Piping were selling in depressed export markets at the time of devaluation, and were not very happy about 'contribution' from exports.

The management of Acton Chemicals had changed its export philosophy shortly before devaluation, and devaluation confirmed it in this decision. Until 1967, Acton Chemicals had regarded its export business as less worthwhile than its home business because it was usually less profitable. It had therefore operated on a strictly anti-cyclical basis, reducing its exports dramatically whenever its home market revived. However, since devaluation, Acton Chemicals had decided to become a permanent, if rather small, exporter. We classify it here as a regular exporter.

3.4   General Objectives

3.4.1   OVERALL OBJECTIVES

Sixteen of our nineteen firms had overall objectives that required them to achieve a particular sales volume or market share, subject to earning some rate of profit. However, we can divide the sixteen firms into three groups.

First, twelve of the firms aimed at a particular sales volume or market share, subject to earning a specified rate of profit on either capital or turnover. For example, Cardiff Instruments aimed at increasing its overall share of the UK market from 30 to 33%, while earning 15% on capital employed. Similarly, Ealing Electrical Appliances aimed to keep its 8% share of the UK market and if possible increase it. In London Switches and Stratford Equipment, demand was running so far ahead of their abilities to supply, that for each the overall objective was to meet as much demand as it could, at profitable levels of price. Both were therefore expanding rapidly, although one of London's objectives was to finance all expansion from retained earnings, and this appeared to have held back the growth of its capacity.

The second group contained two firms, each of which aimed at maximum sales, subject to earning a given rate of return on capital. They were Gatley Hosiery and Rugby Processing. Gatley Hosiery aimed to increase its total sales as rapidly as possible, subject to earning the rate of profit required by its budget. Rugby Processing aimed at the maximum level of sales compatible with increasing its return on capital employed from 10 to 13%.

In the third group, also containing two firms, the situation was more complicated. Jarrow Furniture sought to achieve specified market shares in different countries, but to earn the maximum profit compatible with doing so. Quantox Construction sought to maximise contribution from what it saw as the maximum attainable level of sales. But we think that, in a conflict, sales would have come first.

Only three firms, namely, Hertford Stoves, Birmingham Cakes and Fulham Castings, had unqualified profit objectives—to maximise 'contribution'. Hertford Stoves and Birmingham Cakes both aimed explicitly at maximising contribution. Fulham Castings sought to minimise costs, which came to much the same thing.

It follows from this that in their general objectives only three firms were unambiguously concerned with profit though, in addition, Jarrow Furniture and Quantox Construction sought maximum profit from given sales, or production, capacities. The remaining fourteen were seeking market-share or sales-volume objectives, subject to a particular rate of profit (in the case of Jarrow Furniture and Rugby Processing the maximum profit) being earned.

We may compare these conclusions with those reached in an earlier CBR book, *Pricing in Business*, by D. C. Hague [London (1971)]. That study, which considered thirteen pricing decisions in detail, found that eight of the thirteen firms studied were 'satisficers' in the sense that in their pricing decisions for the products studied they aimed to ensure that at least two objectives, for example, for market share, level of sales or rate of return on capital, were simultaneously met. A 'satisficing' firm will be content if it is at least meeting all its objectives—its 'aspiration levels'; it will not take remedial action unless it fails to achieve one of them. If that happens all attention will be given, for the time, to making the changes which seem necessary in order to meet that particular objective again. How far does the fact that in the devaluation study sixteen of our nineteen firms were aiming at particular levels of sales—in several cases maximum sales— subject to earning a given rate of profit, mean that these firms were significantly different from those in the earlier study?

First, neither sample of firms was in any way a random one. Second, the UK economy was much more depressed in 1967 than it had been in 1964 and 1965, when most of the pricing studies of 'satisficers' were made. This may mean that the firms we studied after devaluation were looking more keenly for opportunities to increase both home and export sales than those studied in *Pricing in Business*. The fact that they were insisting on some minimum rate of profit on sales was therefore presumably intended to prevent sales from increasing too far at the expense of profit. However, this does not necessarily mean that these firms were in the other category often distinguished by economists—maximising sales, subject to earning a minimum rate of profit. It is quite likely that many of the fourteen firms which were neither unambiguously concerned with profit nor interested in increasing profit or contribution from given sales or capacity, were 'satisficers'. Because *Pricing in Business* was based on studies which, for the satisficers at least, were written at a time when business was good because the UK economy was prosperous, it was not difficult for them to meet all their objectives. The 'satisficing' process was easy for us to observe. By 1967, it was often extremely difficult for a firm to meet all its objectives. The way our firms were behaving was, in many cases, the way a 'satisficer' would behave if trade was depressed.

If a 'satisficing' firm finds it sales objectives hard to meet, it will concentrate on achieving the desired level of sales. While our firms claimed that they were attempting to do this subject to their profit objectives being met, in most cases, sales, and therefore the amount of employment the firm could offer to its labour force, appeared to come first. Indeed, in several firms the required rate of profit was *not* being earned. We continue to believe that most firms are run by satisficing procedures. The evidence we collected certainly does not clearly show that our firms were sales maximisers rather than satisficers.

The complexity of most business organisations is such that only a computer model, as used in some firms in the oil industry, could have any hope of keeping the firm continuously in an optimal position. Even this would be possible only if the model covered all aspects of the firm including, for example, both finance and manpower which, so far as we know, no model actually being used yet does. Even it had such a model, it is far from certain that a firm would be prepared to make changes in its prices, sales promotion activities, etc. with the rapidity that continuous optimisation would require. It remains our conviction that most British firms 'satisfice' in controlling their total activities though, within this, they may take some decisions (for example, on pricing or investment) which aim at maximum profits. It may well be that economists who wish simply to predict the results of changes in the external environment of the firm, for example, in the tax system or in market demand, can safely do so on the assumption that firms maximise sales subject to earning a minimum rate of profits on turnover or capital, or indeed that they unambiguously maximise profit. But we believe that the best way to *describe* how most (perhaps all) firms run their total operations is to regard them as satisficers. Cyert and March, who propounded the idea of 'satisficing', would expect the 'pure' satisficer whose sales are below the required level, because of the kind of depression experienced in British firms in 1966–67, to concentrate on increasing sales to the desired level, even though this might lead to a failure to meet other objectives. Since at the time of devaluation many of our firms faced depressed home markets, they were anxious to increase sales but also having difficulty in earning the desired rate of profit, they may have felt unwilling to take the risk of behaving like 'pure' satisficers. While putting the emphasis on increasing sales, their insistence on earning a minimum rate of profit may have been intended to ensure that they did not, as a result, fall too far short of their profit objectives.

3.4.2 EXPORT OBJECTIVES

We turn now to export objectives. Our firms had both operational and non-operational export objectives, using the standard definition of operational objectives, namely, that they can be stated precisely and therefore pursued without difficulty. Non-operational objectives are nebulous, so that no one could know exactly what action would be required in any given circumstances to reach them. For example, a firm may say that its aim is 'to sell innovation'. It will be very difficult to decide whether to take a particular contract at a particular price without more specific, operational objectives being set. The objective: 'our aim is to sell innovation' is non-operational.

Not surprisingly, the export objectives which our firms were pursuing before devaluation were similar to their overall objectives. Hertford Stoves and Birmingham Cakes were seeking to expand exports at whatever rate would give maximum contribution to profit. The other firms were more concerned with increasing export volume. In theory, they were simultaneously pursuing the objective of earning an 'acceptable' rate of profit on exports, but that rate was usually lower than for home sales and, at the time of devaluation, often not being earned. Despite this, all our firms saw a need at least to maintain the level of exports and usually to increase them. For most firms, restrictive economic policies within the UK meant that they had a good deal of excess capacity. It was worth exporting at 'marginal' prices that gave *some* 'contribution' in order to keep up employment and output and to prevent too big a fall in profit.

Turning to operational export objectives, we find that the firms we studied can be divided into three groups. These objectives had been set as the basis for general export decisions and not simply to allow the firm to react to devaluation. The first group of firms had specific, quantitative objectives for each major market before devaluation—for sales turnover, market share, sales promotion expenditure, and so on. The nine firms in this category were: Acton Chemicals, Birmingham Cakes, Ealing Electrical Appliances, Gatley Hosiery, Hertford Stoves, Jarrow Furniture, Kendal Accessories, London Switches and Rugby Processing. Six of these firms produced consumer goods.

The second group contained those firms whose export objective was to sell goods with a given total sterling sales value. There were three firms in this category, two of them producing intermediate goods and one consumer goods. They were: Durham Plates, Fulham Castings and Nottingham Confectionery. However, as we have seen, Fulham Castings was an international business, which did not treat exports from the UK at all differently from exports from any other country.

The third group contained seven firms, four of them producing capital equipment. They were: Cardiff Instruments, Inverness Plant Builders, Oxford Furnaces, Peterborough Tubes, Quantox Construction, Stratford Equipment and Tottenham Piping. All felt unable to draw up detailed export targets for each overseas market, mainly because their business fluctuated too much, though they did regard themselves as actively seeking export business in some countries, while neglecting others. For all these firms, the export objective was to increase the sales effort in particular countries, rather than to achieve a particular volume of export turnover in any of them.

The non-operational objectives of the firms we studied varied widely with the nature of their business. Three firms stressed the need to keep prices as stable as possible, so that small cost increases (but *not* those resulting from devaluation) would be absorbed wherever possible and for as long as possible. These firms also stressed that the price changes which devaluation itself caused for existing products would be treated as of a once-and-for-all nature, at least for the life of the product. In this sense, the firms seemed to be thinking of periods of up to three years. Other firms thought that to be 'patriotic' they ought to cut prices.

3.5 Devaluation Objectives

In taking their devaluation decisions, all but four of our firms pursued one of two objectives. However, Peterborough Tubes pursued one objective for X-ply and another for Product D, while Tottenham Piping pursued one devaluation objective for Products M, A and B and another for Product C. For our present purpose, we can therefore think of both Peterborough Tubes and Tottenham Piping as represented by two different 'firms'. This means that, if we leave out the four exceptions, we have seventeen (not fifteen) 'firms' to consider. These seventeen 'firms' may be divided into two groups of ten and seven, respectively.

The first ten 'firms', namely, Acton Chemicals, Fulham Castings, Gatley Hosiery, Jarrow Furniture, Kendal Accessories, London Switches, Nottingham Confectionery, Peterborough Tubes (for X-ply), Rugby Processing and Tottenham Piping (for Products M, A and B) sought to increase sterling prices (and therefore profit) per unit of sales by the full amount of devaluation. All of them assumed that, since this meant leaving foreign-currency prices unchanged, there would be no change in their sales volume. As we shall see later, things did not always work out like this. The other seven 'firms', namely, Cardiff Instruments, Oxford Furnaces, Peterborough Tubes (for Product D), Quantox Construction, Tottenham Piping (for Product C), Ealing Electrical Appliances and Inverness Plant Builders aimed at the maximum possible increase in sales, subject to not reducing profit per unit.

This leaves the four firms we see as exceptions. Hertford Stoves sought to obtain the maximum possible increase in contribution to profit from its devaluation decisions. The other two firms sought only a 'moderate' increase in profit. They believed that it would, in some way, be 'wrong' to take advantage of the difficulties that had led the UK to devalue by making much extra profit from devaluation. These two firms were Stratford Equipment and

Durham Plates. In the case of Stratford Equipment, the managing director took the view that it would be 'wrong' to seek more than a moderate increase in profit. In Durham Plates, the feeling was that the firm should attempt to increase profits to 'acceptable' levels, but not to make the maximum possible increase. Birmingham Cakes sought to increase sales and to obtain an 'acceptable' increase in profit.

Although we have included London Switches and Kendal Accessories among firms which sought the maximum possible increase in profit per unit, we shall see later that what they were actually able to do depended on what action their competitors decided to take after devaluation. London Switches faced the same major competitor both in the UK and in export markets, and this competitor was not prepared to increase its prices by as much as London suggested. As a result, much against its will, London was forced to accept a relatively small increase in sterling prices. Similarly, while Kendal Accessories wished to increase profit as much as possible after devaluation, the members of its export pricing association decided to make rather smaller increases. However, unlike London Switches' competitor, they based their decisions on the strength of competition in overseas markets and not on more nebulous objectives of their own.

To summarise: our 'firms' may be divided into three groups. The first ten wanted to maintain foreign-currency prices, and take the benefit from devaluation in the form of increased sterling profits on the same volume of exports. The second group of seven 'firms' aimed at using devaluation to increase exports, by the maximum amount compatible with not reducing sterling profit margins on exports. Of the remaining four 'firms', Hertford Stoves wanted to maximise contribution after devaluation, while Birmingham Cakes, Durham Plates and Stratford Equipment sought 'moderate' increases in profit.

It is perhaps worth emphasising that we are not at this point attempting to go behind our firms' explicit devaluation objectives to try to discover whether or not they were aiming to maximise profit or export sales in taking their devaluation decisions. As practical men, faced with the need to decide what to do after devaluation, the decision takers in our firms put their devaluation objectives in operational terms. For the moment, we shall accept them in that form, but in section 8.15 we shall try to go behind them and see whether or not the firms seem to have been seeking maximum profit or maximum exports (subject to a profit constraint) after devaluation.

Table 3.1 classifies our firms in terms of two characteristics.

TABLE 3.1 *The objectives of our firms in responding to devaluation*

	Maximise the increases in 'contribution'	Maximise the increase in profit per unit of output, assuming no change in sales volume	Maximise the increases in sales volume, subject to no fall in profit per unit	Achieve a moderate increase in profit
Regular exporters	Hertford Stoves	Acton Chemicals Fulham Castings Gatley Hosiery Jarrow Furniture London Switches Nottingham Confectionery Peterborough Tubes (X-ply) Rugby Processing Tottenham Piping (Products M, A and B)	Cardiff Instruments Oxford Furnaces Peterborough Tubes (Product D) Tottenham Piping (Product C)	Birmingham Cakes Stratford Equipment
Anti-cyclical exporters		Kendal Accessories	Ealing Electrical Appliances Inverness Plant Builders Quantox Construction	Durham Plates

The columns show the objectives the twenty-one 'firms' (including Tottenham Piping and Peterborough Tubes twice) pursued at the time of devaluation. The rows divide them into regular and anti-cyclical exporters. This table shows that, of the five anti-cyclical exporters, Ealing Electrical Appliances, Inverness Plant Builders and Quantox Construction were seeking the maximum increase in sales compatible with not reducing profit per unit. Durham Plates was seeking merely to restore profit to an 'acceptable' level. Only one of the five anti-cyclical exporters (Kendal Accessories), was seeking the maximum possible increase in profit on its existing volume of exports. Of the regular exporters, nine 'firms' were seeking the maximum increase in sterling profit per unit of export sales, assuming no increase in exports. The other six 'firms' sought increases in sales, four of them maximum increases. So, rather more of the regular exporters were anxious to increase export profitability, with exports unchanged, than were anxious to increase export sales, while four of the five anti-cyclical exporters were anxious to increase export volume provided (at the worst) that the rate of profit did not decline.

3.6   How Objectives Changed after Devaluation

None of our firms saw devaluation as justifying it in embarking on a complete re-thinking of its objectives. The reaction of all of the firms was to see devaluation as helping them to achieve export targets already set, or enabling them to make rather small increases in these. Many of our firms expressed disappointment at the smallness of devaluation, and argued that the additional price advantage that it gave them would be largely offset in the short run by increased import costs and by the ending of the export and SET rebates. In the longer run, they thought that the remainder of the benefit of devaluation would be eliminated by increasing labour costs. Many of our firms therefore argued that the net effect of devaluation was 'too small' to warrant them making a major switch towards exports.

3.7   Summary

Five of our firms were 'anti-cyclical' exporters, which saw exports as something of an expedient, to be given priority only when the home market was depressed. The other fourteen firms were 'regular' exporters, seeing exports as an important and permanent part of their activities.

At the time of devaluation, the home markets of all five anti-cyclical exporters were depressed and they had all therefore been increasing their export effort, but from necessity rather than choice. Their success had been limited. The regular exporters all had export marketing organisations in their important markets and five had production plants overseas. A major reason for the emphasis they put on exports was that they had only limited opportunities for increasing output at home not only in the short run, as with the anti-cyclical exporters, but in the medium and long run too. Several firms already dominated the home market for their products and so saw the best hope for growth in exporting.

The firms whose home markets were growing rapidly had less coherent export policies but still exported a good deal because overseas markets were also growing rapidly. The anti-cyclical exporters were not satisfied with the profits they were earning on overseas sales, but the regular exporters were in a better position, though at the time of devaluation few were earning as much on overseas sales as at home. The difficulty of identifying 'profit' on exports as opposed to home sales makes such comparison difficult, though some firms did work in terms of 'contribution'.

Of our nineteen firms, sixteen had general objectives which required them to increase market share or sales volume, but subject to earning some rate of profit. Only three firms (Hertford Stoves, Birmingham Cakes and Fulham Castings) aimed at maximising contribution.

Export objectives were similar. All firms except Hertford Stoves and Birmingham Cakes were keen to increase export volume provided that a minimum rate of profit was earned. Nine of our nineteen firms had specific, quantitative objectives for each major market in terms of sales volume, market share and/or profit, and altered these only marginally at the time of devaluation. Three firms sought to achieve a budgeted total sterling export turnover. Finally, seven firms found it too difficult to draw up detailed export targets for each individual market, but regarded themselves as actively seeking export business in some countries, while neglecting others. Their export objectives were to increase sales effort in particular countries, rather than to achieve any particular increase in total export turnover.

To study the objectives our firms followed at the time of devaluation, we must look at twenty-one (not nineteen) 'firms' because Peterborough Tubes and Tottenham Piping each pursued two different objectives for the products we studied. After devaluation, nine of our twenty-one 'firms' sought to increase sterling prices by the full amount of devaluation, assuming that export volume would be unchanged. Seven sought the maximum increase in exports, subject to there being no fall in the rate of profit. Durham Plates and Stratford Equipment sought 'modest' increases in profit and Birmingham Cakes an 'acceptable' increase. Hertford Stoves sought to maximise contribution. No firm saw devaluation as requiring it to re-think its overall export objectives.

CHAPTER 4

Market Factors

At the time of devaluation, the problem facing our firms was not how to set initial levels for price and the other marketing variables, except in the limited sense that some of them quoted a separate price for each contract. The question was how big a change to make from the existing levels of price and other marketing variables, set as a result of a whole series of earlier decisions. These earlier decisions had been influenced by internal and external pressures on the firm and had sometimes been taken over a considerable period of time. Before taking its decisions, each firm needed to answer a number of questions. Would it gain profit and/or other advantages from a reduction in its foreign-currency prices? If so, how big a reduction should be made? Was the advantage likely to be long-run or short-run? And which kind was more important? How far would a reduction in foreign-currency prices increase competitiveness? Would sales and profits increase more if the firm held foreign-currency prices constant, and used the extra sterling this provided to increase expenditure on advertising, to change product design or to spend more on other forms of sales promotion? Or should there be a compromise between the two, with limited price reductions and limited increases in sales promotion expenditure?

To answer these questions, a considerable amount of marketing information was required. In this chapter we first outline briefly the market information that any firm needs for its day-to-day export marketing decisions and then consider whether the information our firms had was adequate.

4.1 Background Information Required

A good system for collecting market information would provide basic information about the following factors.

4.1.1 MARKET SEGMENTS

Those taking marketing decisions must have a clear idea of the products being considered. This is not always as simple as it sounds, since the product has to be seen from the customer's viewpoint, which is the only one that matters. Where firms manufacture products to individual customers' specifications, they must have some idea of the importance which the consumer attaches to each characteristic of the product, in order to present him with one which suits his needs. The customer's requirements are not always clear, even to himself.

Similar factors are important in selling apparently standardised products at list prices. Products that are exported may have to meet different physical conditions in different countries, as well as having to serve different kinds of market, in terms of age structure, income distribution, type of industrial user, etc. Once again, the customer's needs have to be identified and catered for, even if this means considering whether to re-design products for sale to some countries.

4.1.2 PRICES

While the relevant price is obviously the one the customer actually pays, this need not be the list price, because of discounts. The prices actually charged in any market may vary considerably between customers. Similarly, actual prices may differ between countries. The firm will obtain a misleading impression of its competitive position in any overseas country if it looks only at average prices there, and not at the distribution around this average. It therefore needs fairly detailed information about the discounts it offers to particular customers and about the proportions of customers in each country obtaining different rates or types of discount. While the degree of detail needed in this information may vary, the firm will need to distinguish price reductions given, for example, to customers who put in bigger orders, and thereby reduce its costs, from price reductions resulting from competitive pressures.

4.1.3 COMPETITION

Some of the most important information the firm needs is about its competitive position in overseas markets. The firm needs to know what type of competition there is, in terms of the analysis in Chapter 2. Especially where there is oligopoly, the firm needs to know, at least for each major market, its own market share and those of its main competitors, and how these have changed over time. The firm should identify the competitors with the biggest shares in important markets, and discover whether they are price leaders. Similarly, it should look at trends in market shares. Have the sales of competitors which have small market shares been growing so rapidly that they may become more serious competitors in future? The firm should know whether a competitor's stake in a particular overseas market makes that market important to him. For example, it is possible that export sales to a country where a competitor has a large market share nevertheless represent only a small proportion of his total turnover and/or profit. Is the rival firm therefore unlikely to try to maintain its position in that market because that would be costly? To answer this question, it is helpful to know not only the competitors likely to be met in each major overseas market, but how seriously they will be interested in that market. This will help the firm to judge which competitive methods are likely to be most effective in any overseas market, and how hard competitors will fight to remain in that market.

The nationality of competitors in overseas markets may also be important. We saw in Chapter 2 that it makes a difference to a firm whether actual or potential competition in any market comes from firms exporting from its own country, or from overseas firms which are therefore subject to different influences within their domestic economies. [For the results of a study, at the level of the total economy, readers are referred to 'The relationship between UK export performance in manufacture and the internal pressure demand', R. J. Ball, J. R. Eaton and M. D. Steuer, *Economic Journal*, p 501 (1966).] Thus, it has been somewhat facetiously suggested that the best way to improve activity in the British machine tool industry would be to create a boom in Western Germany.

So, for example, if all the competitors met in an overseas market are based in a single overseas country, then the higher is activity in that overseas country, the less serious their competition is likely to be. While the fact that foreign competitors come from a number of countries makes it more difficult to do so, it will still be possible to predict the likelihood that all of them will be simultaneously short of capacity or of orders.

4.1.4 COMPETITIVE METHODS

For good export decisions, firms obviously need to know the marketing methods open to them, and their competitors, in each export market, and so the alternative methods they can use themselves. Should they offer a better quality of product at a given price? Should they increase the amount of sales promotion expenditure? And so on. Consumer-good firms may have a wider choice of competitive methods than those selling intermediate and capital goods, whose customers are fewer in number and more knowledgeable technically. However, even the latter will often have alternatives to price cutting, like improving technical service, credit terms or delivery dates.

4.1.5 MARKET TRENDS

The most obvious information about export markets, and indeed the most commonly collected, is about the size and growth (past, present and, if possible, future) of the total market and of the firm's share of it. Firms seem more willing to collect such time-series information than the 'analytical' information required to enable them to understand the relationship between the important variables lying behind marketing decisions. For instance, they are likely to have information about how sales in particular markets have altered from year to year. They are less likely to have information about how sales in each of those markets would alter if price, or some other marketing variable, were altered.

This is not to say that collecting information about market trends is easy. Firms selling annually only small numbers of expensive capital goods may find it very difficult to measure the size and growth rate of the market in one country, because sales to such a country can fluctuate sharply from year to year, depending on the timing of individual deliveries. However, an attempt should be made. The provision of 'analytical' information would be even harder, but it is correspondingly more useful.

Another important trend is in technology. Technical factors can affect a firm's sales in two ways. A technological break-through by a competitor may reduce his costs and so his prices. Similarly, a technical development may significantly increase the amount of output available from a single production unit, and so lead competitors into aggressive sales activities in order to keep their plants fully employed.

4.1.6 MARKET GROUPING

While, in principle, one could argue that the firm should know exactly what is happening in each overseas market, this may be neither practical nor sensible. For example, a firm like Hertford Stoves, which sold in about a hundred different countries, would find the task formidable. It may often be best to group markets together. The most useful grouping may differ from case to case.

Sometimes, a geographical grouping will be sensible, where neighbouring countries have important characteristics in common as, for example, with the common external tariff of the EEC. Sometimes even neighbouring countries differ significantly in market structure or marketing methods. The collection of market information must be flexible enough to allow for such differences. Overseas countries must be grouped in terms of market factors, not administrative convenience.

4.1.7 THE INFLUENCE OF THE HOME MARKET

Given the links between home and export sales, it is obviously important for information about the home market to be used in formulating an overall sales strategy. Beside the fact that an increase in home sales may reduce exports, there are other links between home and export markets. For example, the main competition at home may be from firms which are also important in export markets. Or firms may depend on overseas competitors for raw materials and patents. Information for home and export markets will then need to be considered together.

4.2 Our Firms' Market Information

While we do not claim that section 4.1 is exhaustive, it does give us a basis for judging our firms on the quality of their information about export markets. Since this information differs considerably between types of product, we group our firms into four categories, distinguishing producers of: consumer goods, components, raw materials and capital goods [Tottenham Piping sold an industrial raw material (Product M) and three components (Products A, B and C). We therefore have twenty 'firms'.]

4.2.1 THE CONSUMER GOOD PRODUCERS

The six consumer-goods manufacturers in our sample were:

> Birmingham Cakes
> Ealing Electrical Appliances
> Gatley Hosiery
> Hertford Stoves
> Jarrow Furniture
> Nottingham Confectionery

They all 'differentiated' their products, by changing their physical characteristics and/or by advertising and/or by other forms of sales promotion expenditure. All saw product differentiation as a major marketing variable and all, except Ealing Electrical Appliances, saw price as a relatively unimportant marketing factor over quite big price ranges. While it still emphasised the importance of product differentiation, competition had forced Ealing Electrical Appliances to pay more attention to price.

None of the six firms faced much direct competition from British competitors in their main export markets. For example, Birmingham Cakes was almost a monopolist in the UK. It had its own limited part of the very fragmented British market, though there was indirect competition with many of the other products. The position was similar for Gatley Hosiery. Hertford Stoves was a monopolist in Britain, while Jarrow Furniture was very much the biggest firm in an oligopolistic market in the UK and accounted for almost all British exports. Ealing Electrical Appliances did face some competition in export markets from its British competitors, and to that extent its freedom in pricing after devaluation was restricted. However by far its most important competition came from abroad.

The amount and type of competition in export markets naturally varied from country to country, though in most there was either monopolistic competition or oligopoly with relatively large numbers of firms. While Birmingham Cakes faced direct competition overseas from only one foreign (German) firm, we have seen that there was rather keen indirect competition. This came from a large number of foreign producers and each overseas 'market' had to be defined to include them. Similarly, foreign competition in each of Gatley Hosiery's export markets came from a large number of firms. Although fewer foreign competitors faced Ealing Electrical Appliances and Jarrow Furniture in their main export markets, there was still a sizeable number. On the other hand, the chief competitors for Hertford Stoves in its main export markets, especially in the USA, were a small number of Japanese producers.

With so many competitors and so much emphasis on product differentiation, there was only limited scope for individual foreign competitors, or indeed groups of them, to retaliate to a price cut by any one of our six consumer-good firms. At the same time, all six had a clear idea what the 'going' price was. In November 1967, all of them, apart from Ealing Electrical Appliances, could safely reduce their prices in overseas markets, knowing that there would be little direct retaliation by foreign competitors to any price cut they made.

No firm made a formal calculation of elasticity of demand, but all had a good idea of how demand was likely to respond to price cuts. However, Ealing Electrical Appliances had been forced to reduce its prices to levels where contribution was inadequate, in a rather unsuccessful effort to maintain its market share. Hertford Stoves and Jarrow Furniture felt that, because they were selling 'high-quality' products, especially in the USA and some other countries, price cuts would damage their reputations as high-quality producers.

Gatley Hosiery, on the other hand, was in a market where each firm sold a range of goods of differing quality. There was a price range for each grade. Unless a price cut was big enough to take the product out of its particular price range altogether, demand was thought to be almost completely inelastic. However, if a product moved into a different price range, there were then difficulties if it was not of the appropriate quality.

Birmingham Cakes perhaps found least difficulty in obtaining information, since it exported to only nine major markets. With only a small number of wholesalers in each of them, it was well informed about its position. It had little difficulty in understanding, for each market, when it was best to use price and when other sales promotion methods.

4.2.2 THE COMPONENT MANUFACTURERS

The component manufacturers we studied were:

> Durham Plates
> Kendal Accessories
> London Switches
> Peterborough Tubes
> Stratford Equipment
> Tottenham Piping (Products A, B and C)

Component manufacturers are in a rather different position, at the time of a devaluation, from consumer-goods manufacturers. The former can stimulate sales of their products to some extent by extra marketing expenditure. Again, because they face large numbers of customers who are relatively ignorant of the technical characteristics of products, competition through product differentiation and sales promotion represent good alternative marketing methods to price competition. Component manufacturers have less choice. They face professional buyers who are well able to judge the technical performance of products, and who also have a good understanding of the attractiveness of competing products. Indeed, buyers often tell component manufacturers what specification of product they require. While this usually means that price is effectively the only competitive weapon, for that component it also means that if price is cut too far competitors may retaliate with price cuts of their own. Our component manufacturers therefore had to worry much more than did our consumer goods manufacturers about the likely reactions of their competitors to price changes.

All six 'firms' in this category were operating in monopolistic or oligopolistic markets, both at home and abroad. Only London Switches and Stratford Equipment faced serious competition from British firms in export markets. Each of these faced its main British competitor overseas. On the other hand, Kendal Accessories sold all its exports at minimum prices laid down by its export cartel. Durham Plates sold about half its exports this way. These two firms therefore faced little price competition from British firms in their export markets. The other half of Durham Plates' business was in speciality products, where it again met no serious British competition. Peterborough Tubes and Tottenham Piping were near-monopolists in the UK. All met some foreign competitors in overseas markets, so that the main information these last four 'firms' needed was about the likely reactions of foreign competitors to any price changes they made.

The six component 'firms' had very few competitors in overseas markets. Durham Plates and its cartel faced only two Austrian competitors in its main European markets, and a small number of other competitors elsewhere. Normally, the marketing policies of the Austrian firms were well known. However, the market was so depressed in November 1967 that the cartel feared that the Austrians would break with past behaviour and retaliate quickly to any price cuts that it made. Kendal Accessories and its cartel faced competition abroad from about six foreign firms, mainly from Japan and Eastern Europe. The Japanese, in particular, were new to the field and had been setting the pace in reducing world prices. Kendal Accessories and its cartel had little doubt that these competitors would match any price reductions they made, at least in the main overseas markets.

Peterborough Tubes had a European monopoly for X-ply and competed, in the rest of the world, with the American company which licenced it to produce X-ply in Europe. Foreign competition for Product D came from a larger number of firms, with different ones competing in different markets. However, most could be identified. There was most scope for price changes in Europe, because there Peterborough had a priviledged market position. Tottenham Piping also operated in a highly oligopolistic world market for its components (Products A, B and C) and met some competition in all markets. However, because each firm tended to remain within its own spheres of influence, some price cuts could be made without provoking immediate retaliation. As we have seen, London Switches and Stratford Equipment competed abroad mainly with their British rivals, and both firms' prices were much the same in all overseas markets.

4.2.3   THE RAW MATERIAL MANUFACTURERS

The four 'firms' here were:

> Acton Chemicals
> Fulham Castings
> Rugby Processing
> Tottenham Piping (Product M)

These 'firms' operated in oligopolistic markets both at home and overseas. Since all firms had to make large capital investments in production plant, there were relatively few of them. There was little product differentiation, because the goods were raw materials. Each company sold at an international price, expressed in a foreign currency. World capacity was greatly in excess of world demand for most of their products, so that world prices were drifting downwards. They therefore feared that a significant price cut overseas by any British firm would provoke retaliation by its competitors. As with the component manufacturers, these firms sold to professional buyers. Although total consumption of all products was increasing in the long term, demand in the short run was inelastic for all firms taken together. Only if a firm could cut its prices below the level being charged by the others, and escape retaliation, could it increase sales. With depressed markets at the time of devaluation, it was seen as dangerous to try to increase sales in this way.

Prices were arrived at mainly by tendering. However, since products were standardised, the number of customers large, and the average size of order small, the process of tendering had become a routine one. Standard discounts were offered, and were usually based on size of order.

Because of this, as with the component manufacturers, the main information the raw material firms needed at the time of devaluation was about the likely reactions of competitors to price cuts. Competition from British firms within the UK was important only for Acton Chemicals, which had to try to predict the reactions of a major British competitor. Rugby Processing was virtually a monopolist in the UK, while competition in the UK for Fulham Castings came mainly from foreign firms. Tottenham Piping was the main UK producer of Product M.

Abroad, all firms faced a small number of competitors. Acton Chemicals, Fulham Castings and Rugby Processing faced about eight competitors in most markets, while Tottenham Piping met about six. Fulham Castings' exports went directly to its own subsidiaries, but the other firms gave discounts to export customers. according to size of order and delivery date. However, they found it difficult to be sure about the size of discount being offered by competitors, because customers often bluffed about discounts in order to obtain better terms.

4.2.4   CAPITAL-GOODS MANUFACTURERS

The four firms here were:

> Cardiff Instruments
> Inverness Plant Builders
> Oxford Furnaces
> Quantox Construction

All four firms made the products they sold mainly to the specifications of customers, and prices were therefore determined by tendering. The nature of their businesses meant that Inverness Plant Builders and Quantox Construction could usually allow devaluation to alter tender prices only as new tenders were put in. In many cases, they could not change the quoted prices on existing contracts or even on outstanding tenders. While both Oxford Furnaces and Cardiff Instruments also sold products made to the specifications of individual customers, there was less variety in the range of products they sold in any year.

The difficulty for these firms was that while demand for their products fluctuated considerably over time, taking or losing any one contract could make a big difference to profit in any one year. Similarly, while total number of contracts available in any year was rather small, the value of each contract was very large and the production cycle long. While the total amount of business available to each group of firms was almost completely inelastic to changes in price, any firm tendering for an individual contract had to take great care when deciding on a price. One problem was that, even where a tender was unsuccessful, the firm was never quite certain whether this was because the price was too high, or because its salesmen had failed to understand the precise requirements of the customer. Yet what needed to be done to improve the situation was obviously different according to which was the correct explanation. All four firms faced this problem, but Oxford Furnaces seemed to have more difficulty than the others.

Of the four firms, only Cardiff Instruments was operating anywhere near capacity, and it was in a new, rapidly growing industry. The other three firms had a great deal of spare capacity because, for all of them, demand both at home and overseas had been contracting sharply since the mid-1960s. For Inverness Plant Builders and Quantox Construction especially, the number of orders was falling, though their average value was increasing. Price competition was therefore becoming increasingly strong.

These four firms faced only a few competitors for any individual home or export order, though the particular competitors differed from tender to tender. The strength of the competition they offered varied inversely with the length of their order books. Only Quantox Construction was confident that it could guess accurately at the state of its competitors' order books. Inverness Plant Builders was introducing an improved system for collecting information about potential competitors, but this was in a very early stage of development. Neither Cardiff Instruments nor Oxford Furnaces had much information about competitors' order books.

Only Quantox Construction had made a detailed study of developments in each major overseas market, to help it to predict when extra business would be available. Cardiff Instruments saw no need to make detailed predictions of what might happen in any overseas market. Instead, it relied on making quarterly revisions of the probabilities it assigned to obtaining particular business, and did not analyse long-term trends systematically. Oxford Furnaces did make annual forecasts, but they were not taken very seriously by its management, which continued to operate in rather a hand-to-mouth way. Like Cardiff Instruments, Inverness Plant Builders made quarterly assessments of the probability that it would obtain outstanding contracts. Once a year, it made general forecasts of what business would be available in each major market during the next year.

Cardiff Instruments saw little need to group its markets, since it exported to only a few countries. While Oxford Furnaces exported to far more countries, it grouped its markets only for administrative convenience. However, Inverness Plant Builders and Quantox Construction had been able to classify their overseas markets in a useful way. They based their classification on the likelihood of doing profitable business in each country. This depended on political attitudes there and on how many local manufacturers there were, as well as on economic trends.

4.3   The Adequacy of Information

We now look at the value of the market information our firms had. We have classified them according to whether their information seemed to be adequate, but our judgements are obviously subjective, reflecting only our impressions. Moreover, for any given firm, the quality of information varied between markets. In each case, we evaluated the firm according to the quality of its information for its most important export markets.

4.3.1   MARKET SEGMENTS

Apart from London Switches, all our firms claimed to have enough information to be able to divide up their customers in each overseas market, or at least each important one, in terms of relevant characteristics. These included the effectiveness of using price changes or other marketing methods to increase sales. Most of our firms had adequate information about the structure of prices and discounts in overseas markets, though London Switches and Acton Chemicals were exceptions. While all our firms would have liked more information about how their competitors were faring in overseas markets, there were only four who perhaps had too little for taking good marketing decisions. They were Gatley Hosiery, Kendal Accessories, Cardiff Instruments and Oxford Furnaces.

4.3.2   MARKET TRENDS

One consumer-goods firm (Gatley Hosiery), two capital-goods firms (Cardiff Instruments and Oxford Furnaces), and four component manufacturers (Durham Plates, Kendal Accessories, London Switches and Stratford Equipment) found it difficult to analyse trends in their overseas markets in any detail. London Switches and Stratford Equipment were not particularly worried by this. Their export markets were growing so rapidly that they did not need such information urgently. Three firms producing components and capital goods had very good information about market trends. They were Peterborough Tubes, Tottenham Piping (for Products A, B and C) and Quantox Construction. Apart from Gatley Hosiery, all the consumer-good and basic-material firms (including Tottenham Piping for Product M) had sufficient information about market trends, not least because they obtained good statistical information from business and governments overseas.

4.3.3 MARKET GROUPINGS

Six firms felt no need to group overseas markets according to their economic characteristics, in order to be able to take good marketing decisions abroad. They included all four raw material firms, one consumer-goods firm (Birmingham Cakes) and one capital-goods firm (Quantox Construction). All sold only to a small number of countries, mainly in Europe, and so felt little need to group overseas markets, to help them to pursue different marketing policies in different groups of countries. This is not to say that these six firms charged the same price in every country. Of the six, only Tottenham Piping (for Products A, B and C) had a standard price list for all markets, and even then competition made it difficult to charge list prices.

4.4 The Minimum Information Required After a Devaluation

We have so far considered what general information about overseas markets our firms had. We now need to decide what is the minimum amount of marketing information that a firm requires in order to take good decisions after devaluation. We can then determine what other information, if any, our firms needed to acquire at the time of devaluation.

For our firms, the main problem was whether or not to cut their foreign-currency prices, and if so by how much. If it decided not to cut foreign-currency prices at all, or only by enough to leave over something for spending on sales promotion, the firm then had to decide how much, if anything, to spend on sales promotion. Many of our firms sold in export markets where price changes were infrequent. A few sold products whose prices fluctuated from day to day. It was more important for the first group of firms to make good pricing decisions after devaluation, since it would inevitably be some time before they could make good any mistakes.

To make good devaluation decisions, a firm needs to know three things about demand conditions. First, how much more of its products would customers buy, both now and as time elapsed, if their prices were reduced, all other prices remaining the same? Second, how far would changes in other marketing variables, like product design or advertising, increase sales, all other things again remaining equal? Third, how far would these other things remain the same? Would competitors make, say, a cut in price, or an increase in expenditure on sales promotion? What other retaliation would there be?

Because it turned out that most of our firms concentrated on whether to change their prices after devaluation, we shall concentrate on prices here. However, non-price factors must not be forgotten. They can be important, even though they were not important to our firms in November 1967.

4.4.1 ELASTICITY OF DEMAND

We have seen that where devaluation decisions are about prices, the firm needs some estimate of elasticity of demand for its products. However, while information about elasticity of demand is the most important information the firm needs, it may not tell the firm all it needs to know. The firm may also need to know how demand for its products is changing over time. Elasticity of demand shows how demand responds to a change in price at a given time—along a given demand curve. The firm may also need to know how demand is changing over time—how the demand curve itself is shifting as time passes. For a product with a given elasticity of demand, a cut in foreign-currency prices may seem less necessary at the time of a devaluation, if demand is increasing rapidly, than if it is constant or falling.

How much attention a firm will pay to the rate at which demand for its products is changing, at the time of a devaluation, will depend on the time period for which it is setting prices. If prices can be changed frequently, information about elasticity of demand will be the essential information. Only if the price changes being decided on at the time of a devaluation are seen as part of a long-run marketing strategy will the firm need to look seriously at the way demand is changing over time.

It follows from this, as was shown in detail in Chapter 2, that the minimum information required about any overseas market after devaluation will be how elastic demand for each of the firm's products is to cuts in foreign-currency prices. If the pricing decisions taken at the time of devaluation are medium or long run, it may also be necessary to consider how fast demand in that marketing is growing. Those markets where demand is growing only slowly are the really serious candidates for price reductions.

If changes in other elements in the marketing mix are being considered as well, or instead, at the time of a devaluation, a similar analysis will be needed of the effect on the firm's objectives of increasing expenditure on sales promotion, changing product quality, and so on. We have seen that, for our firms, changes in these other marketing variables were unimportant. So, we can ignore them here. Nevertheless, the extent to which such changes would meet the firm's objectives needs to be explicitly, and correctly, considered if good devaluation decisions are to be made.

4.4.2   COMPETITORS' REACTIONS

If it is an oligopolist, as most of our firms were, the firm must also decide how its competitors are likely to react, if it reduces its foreign-currency prices. It is quite possible, after devaluation, for a firm to be forced to cut its prices when it would prefer not to, simply because its competitors have cut theirs. This may happen even if the competitors are in countries that have not devalued. For example, the European competitors of Quantox Construction felt that a cut in Quantox's prices was so likely, once Britain devalued, that they had to make immediate reductions of their own. Such price cuts are made less to increase market share than to keep existing market share. Where most competition in overseas markets came from British firms, there might well have been retaliation to price cuts, because devaluation gave these British firms more room for manoeuvre. However, even where most competitors were foreign, we have seen that where trade overseas was sufficiently depressed, foreign competitors sometimes took the initiative in reducing prices.

Obviously, a number of factors determine the likelihood of retaliation by the firm's competitors. They include: the number of competitors in the relevant market, the rate of growth of demand in that market and the financial position and market shares of competitors.

Whether there is retaliation to price cuts after devaluation will depend on the particular circumstances. No general rule can be laid down. However, wherever the number of competitors selling in any one overseas market is less than about ten, and/or trade there is depressed, retaliation is likely enough to need considering seriously.

4.5   The Information Used for the Devaluation Decisions

We have already seen what information our 'firms' collected regularly about overseas markets (again we have twenty 'firms'). We must now see what market information they used in their devaluation decisions. We divide the 'firms' into two groups. The first contains the 'firms' which tried to collect extra market information after devaluation, and the second those which did not.

Firms collecting extra information	Firms collecting no extra information
Birmingham Cakes	Acton Chemicals
Durham Plates	Cardiff Instruments
Hertford Stoves	Ealing Electrical Appliances
Inverness Plant Builders	Fulham Castings
Jarrow Furniture	Gatley Hosiery
Kendal Accessories	Nottingham Confectionery
London Switches	Peterborough Tubes (X-ply)
Oxford Furnaces	Rugby Processing
Peterborough Tubes (Product D)	Tottenham Piping
Quantox Construction	
Stratford Equipment	

As will be seen, the firms are fairly evenly divided between these two groups, with slightly more than half collecting extra information.

However, this conclusion is rather misleading. Durham Plates and Kendal Accessories have been included with the firms which obtained extra marketing information, because they discussed the devaluation decisions in meetings with other cartel members, which meant that they obtained some more information from them. Yet, when they went to the devaluation meetings, neither the two firms nor the other cartel members had much information about elasticity of demand, about the rate of growth of overall demand in overseas markets, or about the likely reactions of competitors in these markets. Nor did either firm attempt to obtain more market information for itself. Similarly, much of the extra information collected by London Switches, Stratford Equipment and Oxford Furnaces before they took their decisions came from telephone conversations with their British competitors.

Of the remaining firms, Inverness Builders, Peterborough Tubes (for Product D) and Quantox Construction were producing products to individual specifications, so that a separate market assessment always had to be made for each order. Even so, after devaluation, these three firms also made a special effort to re-examine each export order separately. They looked both at whether changing its price would make the order easier to obtain and at the danger of competitive retaliation if its price were cut.

The firms which made the biggest effort to get more information for the devaluation decisions were Birmingham Cakes, Hertford Stoves and Jarrow Furniture. In making a contingency plan for devaluation, Hertford Stoves had tried to reassess its competitive position in each export market by looking at all relevant factors.

Though it did not use the concept of elasticity of demand explicitly, it considered the way the volume of its exports would respond to price cuts in a general way. Since it also looked at the possibility of changing market variables other than price after devaluation, Hertford Stoves had no need to seek more information. Although Birmingham Cakes knew its few overseas markets very well, it made its decisions only after considering all the alternatives open to it in each market and after consulting its agents. Jarrow Furniture sold in far more overseas markets, but considered it necessary to re-examine separately the market position in each. Its agents were not consulted.

The fact that the second group of firms did not collect more information after devaluation does not necessarily imply that the information they had was inadequate before taking the devaluation decisions. It may have meant exactly the opposite. Only where the existing information was inadequate for taking these decisions, but the firms nevertheless decided not to collect more, was there a case for criticism. In fact, most of the firms that did not collect more information were well informed about elasticity of demand, at least in a general sense, and about competitors' policies. They had little to gain from searching for more information. Moreover, because most of these firms left foreign-currency prices unchanged they had less need for market information than the firms which were seriously considering cutting their prices. The only firms whose marketing information may not have been adequate for taking good devaluation decisions were Cardiff Instruments and Gatley Hosiery.

CHAPTER 5

Internal Information

We now look at the information about internal factors that the firm needs when making devaluation decisions. As the analysis in Chapter 2 showed, much of this information is about costs.

Devaluation has two effects on costs, which need to be distinguished. First, it increases the cost of producing the existing volume of output. This cost is important to all firms, whether or not they take devaluation decisions that increase output. Second, devaluation increases the incremental, or marginal, cost of producing a slightly bigger output. This cost is relevant to any firm which considers, after devaluation, whether to take decisions that will increase exports and therefore output.

There was a good deal of variation in the quality and quantity of the cost information which our firms used for their devaluation decisions, but most of them seem to have made much the same calculations. In particular, as we have suggested they would need to do, all calculated the effect that devaluation was likely to have on total costs and therefore profit. In some cases, this information was supplemented by separate calculations designed to help those taking decisions for home and export markets. Some firms also made calculations of changes in incremental costs that were intended to help them with decisions aimed at increasing export sales, for example, by reducing prices.

It seems simplest to organise our discussion around this pattern of analysis. We therefore begin by looking at home market costs in section 5.1. In section 5.2, we go on to consider export market costs and in section 5.3 total costs. Incremental costs are discussed in section 5.5.

5.1 Home Market Costs

Although our firms exported more of their output than the average British firm, and Hertford Stoves and Jarrow Furniture the great bulk of output, home market sales usually provided the bulk of revenue, if not profit. The firms therefore looked carefully at the effect that devaluation would have on home market costs. They were anxious that, whatever else might happen, devaluation should not reduce profit from UK sales, as it would do if they did not increase prices in the UK sufficiently to cancel out increased costs caused by devaluation.

In addition, partly because of the 'early warning system', many firms were exercised by the whole question of how to keep home market prices at least in line with increasing costs. Devaluation provided a welcome opportunity to press for price increases to take account not only of the cost increases caused by devaluation itself but earlier increases too. The firms had seen the latter as too small to be worth trying to recoup under the early-warning system.

5.1.1 IMPORTED MATERIALS AND COMPONENTS

The most immediate effect on costs of the 1967 devaluation was the increase that it caused in the costs of imported raw materials and components. The costs of many of these increased almost at once, though not by the same amounts. Where there was a world price, usually in dollars, for materials sold in an international market, the sterling price increased at once by the full amount of devaluation. Where the price of a raw material was set by an individual firm, or a group of firms, the size and timing of the price increase was more difficult to predict. It depended on the number of overseas firms supplying the product and how keenly they competed on price. It also depended on the bargaining strengths of the firms concerned.

Some of our firms, for example, Gatley Hosiery and Birmingham Cakes, did their best to find out at once what would happen to import prices by telephoning their suppliers. However, most of our firms took the simplest way out and assumed the biggest increase they thought likely, arguing that an over-estimate could always be reduced. This approach seemed reasonable, because all British producers were in roughly the same position.

While our firms wanted to be as clear as they could about both the size and timing of price increases, some could influence the increases themselves. For example, Stratford Equipment bought large quantities of raw materials, and so was able to bargain with its suppliers, particularly since all were located in the UK. It knew that they had bought large stocks of the raw material at the prices ruling before devaluation, and therefore resisted an immediate price increase.

5.1.2 ROYALTIES

Royalty payments which our firms had to make to countries which had not devalued, automatically increased by the full amount of devaluation. Acton Chemicals and Peterborough Tubes were the firms most affected. Acton had to pay a royalty on the part of its output that was produced by a particular process. Because of problems in getting the plant to work satisfactorily, Acton found it hard to work out its production plans and so to estimate what its royalty payments would be. In Peterborough Tubes, where royalty payments increased immediately by the full amount of devaluation, production, sales and therefore royalties were much easier to predict.

5.1.3 OTHER COSTS

It follows that devaluation soon increased the size of payments for most of the goods and services used by our firms that had to be made in foreign currency. Given the dependence of the UK on imported materials, the price of virtually all inputs was increased. Credit and warranty charges were particularly important to the firms which produced expensive capital goods paid for over considerable time periods, namely, Cardiff Instruments, Inverness Plant Builders, Oxford Furnaces and Quantox Construction. After a time lag, devaluation affected the major component of our firms' variable costs, namely wages. In the end, devaluation therefore affected almost all the costs of our firms.

Since devaluation increased the prices of many consumer goods in the UK, it was inevitable that workers would attempt to protect themselves from the consequent rise in the cost of living, by making wage claims, and that they would succeed, if only in part. The difficulty, at the time of devaluation, was that it was not at all clear how long it would be before wages increased, or how much they would rise. Indeed, even when such a wage increase had been granted, it was almost impossible to discover how much of it was the result of devaluation and how far wages would have increased in any case. Of course, this was not important for our firms. What they needed to be able to do was to predict how far their wage bills would increase after devaluation, for whatever reason. We feel that firms with strong trade unions, like Ealing Electrical Equipment and Rugby Processing, could perhaps have made a more realistic allowance for wage increases than they did. On the whole, our firms seem to have been too optimistic about the effect that devaluation would have in increasing wages, though perhaps Gatley Hosiery and Jarrow Furniture are exceptions. Moreover, one should not be too critical of the firms that made bad predictions. It was far from easy to make good ones.

Jarrow Furniture's top management specifically instructed its decision takers to remember that wages would increase substantially in the period after devaluation. One reason for this was perhaps that Jarrow's top management was anxious to find ways of restraining its marketing staff from cutting foreign-currency prices too far, especially with most of Jarrow's output being exported. The remaining firms seem to have decided that increased wage costs could best be offset when it became clearer how much they would rise. This was an entirely reasonable attitude, given the uncertainties of what would happen to wages and the downward pressure that the early-warning system and government policy generally were exerting on prices.

5.2 Export Market Costs

The goods which our firms exported were often physically distinct from those sold on the home market, if only because of differences in design, specification or packaging. Extra cost information was therefore needed when decisions were being taken about products for export. The way our firms collected this information did not follow any one pattern, but depended on the firm's particular organisation and circumstances. In most cases, the firm used information for the home market. In other firms, somewhat separate calculations were made.

5.3 The Effect of Devaluation on Total Costs

What our firms most wanted to know was what effect devaluation was likely to have on their cash flows and profit, so that they could work out the minimum increase in prices needed to prevent devaluation making them worse off. This calculation required estimates of both cost and revenue, on the assumption that sales would remain at a particular level, or within some range. Where devaluation decisions implied no increase in exports, the firm needed only information about the way total costs would be affected. Most firms chose to base their calculations either on sales actually achieved in 1966–67, or on those budgeted for 1967–68. In some firms, like Jarrow Furniture, senior management used this information as the basis for giving instructions to those taking devaluation decisions. However, the top management of most firms seemed to decide that it was unnecessary to intervene in this way.

5.4 The Effect of Devaluation on Marginal Costs

As we have explained, the effect of devaluation on marginal costs was important only for those firms taking marketing decisions intended to increase exports beyond the existing level, for example, decisions to reduce foreign-currency prices. As we saw in Chapter 2, marginal cost in this context is the addition to total cost resulting from an increase in exports. While, strictly, marginal cost is the cost of producing one extra unit of output for export, in some contexts it was more sensible to look at the extra cost of producing *all* the additional export output the firm expected to sell after devaluation.

Our firms did not all calculate marginal cost when deciding whether to respond to devaluation in a way that would increase exports. Several firms looked at only average costs. Such a firm first calculated the total cost of producing the level, or levels, of exports they hoped for after devaluation, including the overhead and other indirect costs which they felt could be specifically allocated to exports. These total costs were then divided by anticipated exports, to give a unit (average) cost. In some cases, this gave the firm a number of average cost figures, one for each possible level of exports.

The danger in using average-cost figures is that they conceal information ideally needed for good decision taking. As a growing number of firms recognise, it is usually impossible to allocate overhead costs accurately to individual products, especially when the firm produces several products, as all of ours did. It is even more difficult to allocate them to individual products for export. The best that the firm can do is to allocate its overhead costs to products on the most realistic assumptions that its accountants can make. The problem is that decision takers need information about relevant costs and relevant costs are very often marginal costs. They may not be easy to disentangle from average cost information.

In all our firms, raw material and labour costs made up a significant proportion of marginal cost and we have seen that devaluation led to an immediate increase in the cost of most raw materials. While labour costs rose sooner or later, it was usually some time before this happened. Similarly, especially in the firms making consumer goods, where the marginal cost of producing more goods for export included some advertising and other sales promotion expenditure, devaluation did not usually increase such costs, at least in the short run. Where marginal cost included the cost of employing extra salesmen, or headquarters staff, to deal with exports, their salaries remain unchanged for some time after devaluation.

Very few of our firms made special calculations of the marginal cost of producing and selling exports. The reason was simply that most firms could reasonably assume that marginal cost would be roughly the same, for any likely increase in output, as at the existing output. However, Birmingham Cakes believed that in some markets it could increase exports by slightly changing its export product, and so its cost, for example by improving the quality of packaging. Similarly, Hertford Stoves looked at a 'typical' product for each export market. In both firms, the marginal cost of producing the relevant product was specially calculated for the devaluation decisions.

Strictly, the marginal cost of increased output for export should be calculated separately for each likely level of output. For example, marginal cost might be higher the bigger the expected increase in output; the marginal cost curve might be rising, as in Figure 2.1. Indeed, if the firm was already operating at its 'normal' capacity when devaluation occured, marginal cost would be likely to increase as output rose. For example, increased exports might mean that the firm had to accept a more than proportionate increase in labour costs, for overtime or shift working, or that it had to bring older and less efficient machinery back into operation.

5.5 Job-cost Firms

The job-cost firms needed the same sort of information as the rest of our sample. However, because they were 'job-cost' firms, no two orders they obtained were identical, and they had to work out the cost for each tender separately. As a result, they could always calculate marginal cost if necessary. The only decisions they had to take immediately after devaluation were for contracts already obtained and/or for tenders not yet awarded. Normally, these firms estimated the costs they would have to incur in meeting the particular order and added on the cost of components they had to buy. After devaluation, the cost of each such tender had to be recalculated, before the firm could begin to negotiate a new price with customers. Where components were imported, this often meant negotiations with overseas suppliers too. With tenders put in after devaluation, component suppliers' prices were then known.

To see what happened in these firms, we can divide the four in this group into two groups. Two firms recalculated the cost of each outstanding tender on a marginal cost basis at the time of devaluation, and two re-calculated total costs for each tender. The first two were Inverness Plant Builders and Quantox Construction, and the second two Cardiff Instruments and Oxford Furnaces. The first two firms require little comment. With depressed markets, they had become accustomed to making very careful calculations of variable cost, because they needed to discover the absolute minimum price at which they could afford to tender on each occasion. Indeed, Quantox Construction was even treating part of its labour costs as fixed, on tenders for plant of a new type for which it wanted to obtain experience. It had decided which of its employees it would *not* be prepared to dismiss, at any rate for a considerable period of time, however bad business became. Their wages and salaries were therefore treated as fixed costs.

The allocation of 'full' costs to each individual contract in Cardiff Instruments and Oxford Furnaces was known to be inaccurate. Not only was there the usual problem of how to allocate overheads to individual products; there were also doubts about the accuracy of the figures for overhead costs. In Cardiff Instruments, the costing system provided a figure for the cost of each component, including a 'cost' for each component produced by Cardiff itself. Cardiff was engaged on a major review of its prices at the time of devaluation, and this was sufficiently well advanced to show the likely effect of devaluation on the 'cost' of components. However, no detailed estimate of the effects of devaluation on costs was available when the devaluation decisions were taken.

5.6   Other Information

5.6.1   INVENTORIES

Several of our firms adjusted their cost calculations to take account of their inventory positions.

Where a firm's stocks were considerably above the desired level at the time of devaluation, it could allow them to fall before buying more at a higher price. So, for example, Durham Plates had a stock of an important material at the time of devaluation sufficient to last the whole year. In most of our firms, however, stocks were at or below the normal levels. Further purchases therefore had to be made almost immediately, at post-devaluation prices. Taking stocks into account in cost calculations was sensible enough when the objective was to calculate profit, but in one or two cases the calculations were used for pricing decisions. Where a considerable proportion of stocks held at the time of devaluation had been bought at pre-devaluation prices, there was a feeling that price increases should be delayed.

The most important example was Stratford Equipment. It had usually held stocks of its main raw material equal to three months' normal use and continued to do so after devaluation. The firm therefore believed that it was unnecessary to increase its prices for at least one and a half months. It is doubtful whether Stratford Equipment's customers realised that they were being given this benefit. If they did, it is doubtful whether Stratford's behaviour had a significant effect on their goodwill towards it. At the time of devaluation, Kendal Accessories also held stocks of imported raw materials equal to three months' use in production. Since devaluation occurred half way through its financial year, Kendal argued that only three months of the current year's business would be affected by the higher cost of these materials.

It would have been more logical to treat the increase in the value of stock as a windfall profit. While those concerned must have been well aware of this, there was sometimes a feeling that it was not right to 'take advantage' of devaluation in this way. There was also a feeling that the firm might gain in consumer goodwill if customers were told that account had been taken of the value of stocks when the firm decided on the size and/or timing of price changes.

As so often seems to happen with inventories, our firms probably paid too much attention to what their accounting systems told them. Too few of them made straightforward calculations of the gains and losses that they would obtain, whether in goodwill or in profit, if they raised prices to cover the increased cost of raw materials and components sooner rather than later.

5.6.2   CONSTRAINTS

The amount of capacity that a firm had was obviously important in its devaluation decisions. At the time of devaluation, most of our firms and their competitors had a good deal of spare capacity. Only three firms (Durham Plates, London Switches and Stratford Equipment) were producing at or near capacity at the time of devaluation.

5.6.3   PROFITABILITY AND LIQUIDITY

Our firms' decisions were influenced by their profitability and cash flow at the time of devaluation. Where either or both were low, firms were more likely to take devaluation decisions that would increase export profit rather than export volume.

5.6.4   TAX CHANGES

The tax changes announced at the time of devaluation also

affected our firms. The selective employment tax premium was withdrawn from all manufacturing firms outside development areas. This affected all our firms, except Acton Chemicals and Gatley Hosiery. Similarly, the export rebate, previously given on exports outside EFTA, was brought to an end. It was also announced there would be a rise in the rate of corporation tax in the 1968 budget. This was largely ignored in the decisions made at the time of devaluation, partly no doubt because it was unlikely to affect our companies for at least a year and a half after devaluation. But it is far from clear how a change in corporation tax would have been handled by our firms.

Many of our firms did not deal with the changes in SET and the export rebate in a strictly logical way. Strictly, they should have treated the changes as reducing their income. In fact, many of them regarded the loss of rebate as increasing production costs in much the same way as a rise in the price of materials or wages would have done. The change was seen as increasing costs—total or marginal. The point is not so much that this might have led to wrong decisions as that it suggests some laxity in thinking.

5.7 Standard Costing

A standard costing system is one where the firm sets a 'standard' cost at which it would expect the budgeted output of a given product to be produced. The firm then analyses variances between actual and standard costs and can take remedial action, if necessary, to bring actual costs back towards the standard if the two have diverged. Divergences result from volume variances, where actual output is different from budgeted output; from cost variances, where the cost of raw materials, labour etc. is different from what had been expected; or from efficiency variances, where products are made more or less efficiently than was expected.

Most of our firms had standard costing systems, though they concentrated their attention on the variable rather than the fixed-cost element in standard costs. Nevertheless, many of our firms ran into costing problems. Because calculating standard costs was usually a complex operation, it was often carried out infrequently, say, once a year. Standard costs were therefore often based on data from the previous year; they were historical rather than current. With the whole level of costs rising because of steady inflation in the UK, there was some danger that these firms might understate their costs as they took their devaluation decisions.

5.8   Classification

We now look at the information which our firms had. We have already looked at the four job-costing firms. We now look at the other fifteen firms. These fifteen firms each manufactured a standard combination of products and so were able to use standard costing systems. In a cross-classification, we shall find it useful to distinguish between the firms which took positive action to increase their exports after devaluation, usually by cutting the prices of exports, and firms which left foreign-currency prices unchanged and therefore obtained higher sterling receipts from an unchanged volume of exports.

The group of five firms that left both foreign-currency prices and sterling expenditure on marketing unchanged we shall describe as 'passive' decision takers. The remaining fourteen firms took decisions which gave a stimulus to exports. All but one cut foreign currency prices by the *net* amount of devaluation or used the extra sterling they received from *not* making such big price cuts to increase marketing or sales promotion expenditure, or to change the design or quality of the product. We shall describe these firms as 'active' decision takers. All the job-costing firms took 'active' decisions.

This gives us a double classification, in terms of the costing system used and the type of decision taken. We now look at our firms, using this double classification.

5.9   Standard Costing Firms: Active Decision-takers

Ten of the fifteen standard-costing firms took 'active' decisions after devaluation. Information about the effects of devaluation on incremental costs was therefore especially important for them. The ten firms were:

> Birmingham Cakes
> Durham Plates
> Ealing Electrical Appliances
> Gatley Hosiery
> Hertford Stoves
> Jarrow Furniture
> Kendal Accessories
> London Switches
> Stratford Equipment
> Tottenham Piping

5.9.1   CALCULATING THE EFFECT OF DEVALUATION ON TOTAL COSTS
Apart from Gatley Hosiery and London Switches, the ten firms regularly produced figures for variable cost and contribution.

As for the two exceptions, Gatley Hosiery allocated factory, general and administrative overheads separately to each product group and this obscured relevant costs. The effect of devaluation on the total costs of the manufacturing company was estimated by revising the cost figures, but not until some time after the devaluation decisions had already been taken by the overseas company. No tailor-made cost information was provided for its decision taker, who had to rely on his (good) general knowledge of the amounts of raw material that Gatley used and the effect that devaluation was likely to have on their prices.

In London Switches, the costing system was simple, there was little detail in the standard cost figures and overheads were allocated to individual products. The managing director claimed that he had a good 'feel' for London's cost structure and that prices were therefore set on the basis of 'experience'. After devaluation, London Switches saw no need to re-calculate its costs completely. Instead, it assumed (wrongly as it turned out) that the cost of its main imported raw material would increase by the full amount of devaluation.

With good standard costing systems, the remaining firms could easily calculate variable cost and contribution. Birmingham Cakes calculated the effects of devaluation on total costs not by using the output figures in its current budget, but figures for the volume of sales in the year ended March 1967, because these were readily available. In Durham Plates, although the effect of devaluation on total costs was calculated from the budget for the following year, the cost information available when the devaluation decisions were taken did not distinguish between the cost of producing for home and for export markets. Eventually, more-detailed cost figures were worked out for Durham Plates' 185 products, but by then the devaluation decisions had already been taken. Export costs were still not treated separately.

Ealing Electrical Appliances was content until several months after the devaluation decisions with the rough costings jotted down by its cost accountant, from memory, on the day after devaluation. Since this was a Sunday, it was not possible to get detailed figures from the filing cabinets, which were locked. Again, there was no attempt to discover whether devaluation would have different effects on home and export costs. A similar procedure was followed by Jarrow Furniture, where the cost information it collected after devaluation was a good deal less detailed than the market information it sought at the time.

Kendal Accessories did not revise its standard cost figures until March 1968, but these calculations were largely irrelevant to its decisions. While only the broad effect of devaluation on total costs was estimated, without any separation of home and export costs, Kendal Accessories was forced by keen competition to work out separately the variable cost of meeting each export contract. Stratford Equipment was well informed about the effect of devaluation on its total costs by the time its decisions were implemented, though not when they were taken. Moreover, Stratford was able to allow for the increase in productivity which it expected to obtain in the following year, when its new machinery could have been brought into use.

London Switches and Stratford Equipment could include figures for higher wages in their cost calculations because they had already negotiated new pay agreements, to come into effect at the end of 1967. The only other firm in this group which made even a rough allowance for wage increases was Jarrow Furniture. Ealing Electrical Appliances belonged to an industry where the trade unions were strong, but possible wage increases were not allowed for. Tottenham Piping also faced strong trade unions, but made no allowance for possible increases in labour costs.

Six of these firms treated the abolition of the export rebate and of the SET premium as reductions in income. Of the others, Stratford Equipment had never allowed for the export rebate when making its price calculations before devaluation. It treated the rebate as an undeserved general subsidy. Durham Plates, Ealing Electrical Appliances and Jarrow Furniture were uncertain how to treat the changes in the tax rebate, but finally decided to treat them as cost increases.

5.9.2 CALCULATING THE EFFECT OF DEVALUATION ON MARGINAL COSTS

The ten firms that took 'active' devaluation decisions realised that these were likely to increase output. They implicitly assumed that marginal cost would be roughly constant for any likely increase in exports. This was probably a good assumption for the firms with spare capacity. For example, Birmingham Cakes had recently installed enough new plant to be able to meet any likely increase in home and overseas sales, and believed that marginal cost was constant over this range of output. In addition, because Birmingham sold a very similar product both at home and abroad, and because its freight charges were low, it was able to assume that marginal cost would be similar for both home and export sales. Similar assumptions could be made by Ealing Electrical Appliances, Jarrow Furniture, Kendal Accessories and Tottenham Piping.

The remaining firms should perhaps have paid a little more attention to incremental costs. In Durham Plates, for example, output of its non-cartelised product was running at peak levels, and this suggests that the marginal cost of the product should perhaps have been studied in some detail. Similarly, in Gatley Hosiery the output of the manufacturing company we studied was running at peak levels, so that its marginal costs might also have been worth studying more carefully. For the current season, any extra sales would have pushed output above 'normal' capacity, though the same problem would not necessarily have arisen in the following season. In London Switches and Stratford Equipment, new capacity was due to be installed within a few months. In Stratford Equipment this was needed to allow the firm to meet increasing demand, while in London Switches it was expected to be fully occupied for some time in reducing the order book. Since both firms made some cuts in foreign-currency prices after devaluation, it might have paid them to look more carefully at marginal cost.

5.10   Standard costing firms: passive devaluation decisions

We now look at the five firms with standard costing systems which took no positive action to simulate exports at the time of devaluation. They were:

> Acton Chemicals
> Fulham Castings
> Nottingham Confectionery
> Peterborough Tubes
> Rugby Processing

Three of the five firms produced either basic raw materials or products where value added represented only a very small proportion of price. One other firm, Peterborough Tubes, produced components, and Nottingham Confectionery non-durable consumer goods.

Because they took 'passive' decisions, these firms could argue that there was no need to calculate the effect of devaluation on incremental costs. However, strictly, they should have looked at what marginal costs *would* have been if exports had been increased, in order to see whether they should take positive action to stimulate exports. Indeed, they did. What is not in doubt is that these firms needed to calculate the effects of devaluation on total costs.

All four firms enthusiastically based their management accounting systems on variable cost and on contribution. Each firm's cost information was excellent, so that the effects of devaluation on both total and incremental costs were calculated accurately. Acton Chemicals and Fulham Castings each used computers to link their own costs to those of their parent groups.

The firms which had to face the biggest cost increases after devaluation were Fulham Castings and Peterborough Tubes. In Fulham Castings, the most important raw material was imported and its price increased by the full amount of devaluation. By comparison, all other likely cost changes looked insignificant. Increases in costs of imported raw materials also represented the most important cost increase for Acton Chemicals. In Peterborough Tubes, value added represented a significant percentage of the cost of both the products we studied, but the main raw material was also an important element in cost. Its price rose by the full amount of devaluation, because there was collusion in pricing between the foreign suppliers. The immediate effect of devaluation on costs was therefore easily predicted. On the other hand, in Rugby Processing the cost of imported raw materials formed such a small proportion of total costs as to be negligible.

Our firms were uncertain how to deal with other costs which increased because of devaluation. The extra royalties that Acton Chemicals would have had to pay on its new production processes could not be calculated precisely, nor could its extra labour costs. Consequently, the possibility for error was considerable. In Peterborough Tubes, devaluation was seen as an opportunity to recover a number of cost increases which had accumulated since 1964, and this tended to obscure the effects of devaluation itself. Rugby Processing and Peterborough Tubes both treated the withdrawal of the export rebate as increasing variable cost, while Acton Chemicals treated the withdrawal of the SET premium as increasing marginal cost.

5.11 Conclusions

Because, in some of our firms, the cost information on which they based their devaluation decisions fell short of the ideal, one might be tempted to criticise the internal information they used in their devaluation decisions, even though all but four of them had accounting systems that worked in terms of contribution. While about half the ten standard costing firms which took 'active' decisions decided to consider the effects of devaluation on incremental costs, the other half made detailed calculations only of its effect on the total cost of producing the existing output. Two of the four job-costing firms based their decisions on figures for 'full' unit cost, including 'allocated' overheads. However, all five 'passive' exporters with standard costing systems calculated the effect of devaluation on marginal costs, and all worked in terms of contribution rather than profit.

While our impression is that the cost calculations made by at least half of the firms which took 'active' decisions were rather rough, we must try to see how far this really mattered. Since all our firms felt the need to take their devaluation decisions quickly, being able to calculate the precise size of the increase in cost, total or incremental, was less important to them than having a good idea of orders of magnitude. The decision taker would have information that was good enough for his purposes if he could estimate the effects of devaluation on total or marginal costs to within one or two per cent. Making the calculation more precisely might well mean missing some export opportunities, if only of obtaining greater goodwill from overseas customers. In any case, the effect of the devaluation decisions on profitability would be significant only if the increase in costs caused by devaluation turned out to be rather different from the initial estimate. Moreover, most of our firms allowed for such uncertainty in taking their decision. Because of this, where cost increases were likely to be small, the need for precision was reduced. We therefore brought the cost increases expected by all our firms onto a common basis, ignoring the effects of losing the SET and export rebates. We found that six of the fourteen 'active' decision takers expected to meet increases in total costs of 4%, or less, as a result of devaluation. For the remaining eight 'active' firms, the cost increases were bigger than 4%. However, for various reasons, these firms felt that they could assess the effect of devaluation on total costs quite accurately. For example, in Durham Plates raw material costs were especially important and Durham Plates could predict changes in sterling raw material prices quite easily. In London Switches and Stratford Equipment, the price changes were delayed for some months, which gave their accountants sufficient time to be certain what the increase in total cost due to devaluation would be, before the decisions were put into effect.

It would also be unfair to criticise the fourteen 'active' decision takers for taking little trouble to calculate the effects of devaluation on incremental costs. For eight of the fourteen firms, business was so depressed that output could easily be increased and the assumption that marginal costs were constant was reasonable. Indeed, in six of them—Inverness Plant Builders, Jarrow Furniture, Kendal Accessories, Oxford Furnaces, Quantox Construction and Tottenham Piping—the amount of surplus capacity they had was so great that obtaining extra export business might even have *reduced* marginal costs. Ealing Electrical Appliances was in a slightly different position. While it could hope to have some spare capacity once the 'pre-budget' boom in sales in early 1968 was over, its output could not be increased immediately, because it took time to arrange for the necessary increase in supplies of raw materials and components. We have already noted that Birmingham Cakes had just finished re-equipping a major part of its plant and so had spare capacity. In these eight firms, incremental costs could therefore be expected to remain constant, or even to fall, for any likely increase in export output.

It follows that only in one or two of the firms which sought to increase exports after devaluation could the failure to discover whether devaluation might effect incremental costs have been important. London Switches and Stratford Equipment both planned to install extra capacity at the end of 1967, so that figures for marginal cost in the new plant could have been helpful in deciding how to price its output. Similarly, Durham Plates was short of capacity for producing Product B and a more careful calculation of marginal cost might have helped it.

Nevertheless, we think that it would be difficult to demonstrate convincingly that any of our firms' decisions were based on defective internal information. With cost information, for example, a sound criticism would require being able to show that using, say, more accurate and detailed figures would have led to better decisions. It was obviously impossible for us to show that in our study. We have little hesitation in saying that, in general, the information used was reasonably adequate. Of course, there are two further reasons why we can be happy about the accuracy and quantity of the information used in taking the devaluation decisions. First, and most obvious, pricing decisions do not have to be taken in perpetuity. They can always be revised. Of course, there may be objections to changing prices too frequently, but such objections are usually weakest in a firm's export markets. The other reason is that where, as with most of our firms, the firm uses a standard costing system, it has an automatic check on how costs actually turn out. Remedial action is fairly easily taken, though perhaps only after some lapse of time.

Nevertheless, we feel bound to record the fact that, as economists looking at firms' actual pricing decisions often seem to have found, there was reluctance among our 'active' decision takers to look at marginal costs. Yet, paradoxically, all the four 'passive' exporters with standard costing systems could quickly and easily calculate marginal cost. The very firms which had no great need to calculate marginal cost at all after devaluation were in much the best position to calculate it.

CHAPTER 6

The Elements in a Devaluation Decision

In this chapter we prepare the way for a detailed analysis of the devaluation decisions that our firms took. First, we look at the main elements in any devaluation decision, so that we can have a better understanding of our firms' decision procedures. Second, we look at some problems in classifying devaluation decisions.

6.1 Devaluation Decisions

6.1.1 DEVALUATION OBJECTIVES

In taking devaluation decisions, the firm first needs to be clear about its objectives, as indeed most of our firms were. In Chapter 2 we assumed that firms seek to maximise profit. In Chapter 3 we saw that among our firms at the time of devaluation only Hertford Stoves did this unambiguously. We are not at this point arguing that firms need to have any particular kind of devaluation objective, but simply that good decisions require them to be clear what their objectives are.

6.1.2 DEMAND FACTORS

Having clarified its objective the firm should then respond to devaluation by discovering what changes in price, export volume, sales promotion expenditure, etc., will bring it closest to this objective. As we have already explained, our firms concentrated on price in their devaluation decisions, and we shall therefore look only at possible decisions about the price of exports.

In order to take good decisions on export prices, the firm needs information about the volume of sales that would be realised at each possible export price. In other words, it needs to know elasticity of demand at all points over the range of foreign-currency prices between the pre-devaluation foreign-currency price and the lowest foreign-currency price that might be worthwhile after devaluation. Unless costs fall very rapidly as exports increase, this will be the foreign-currency equivalent (at the new exchange rate) of the pre-devaluation sterling price. Thus, for a British product selling before devaluation in 1967 for £100, the range would have been from $2 80 to $2 40

If the price set after devaluation is expected to remain unchanged for a considerable period, and/or if the firm feels that it needs to consider the long-run effects on demand of a change in its price, it will also want to take into account the rate at which the demand for its exports is increasing over time. It will want to know how rapidly the demand curve for its export products, whose elasticity we considered in the previous paragraph, is shifting over time. While it is unlikely that it will have information that is precise enough to allow it to make anything like an accurate estimate of such general changes in demand conditions, the firm will realise that after devaluation it is less likely to be sensible to cut foreign-currency prices if demand is increasing very rapidly in export markets, and vice versa.

With information about elasticity of demand and about the rate at which general demand conditions are changing, it will be easy for the firm to take whatever decision is most appropriate, given the devaluation objectives the firm has, *except* in two circumstances. The first is where the amount of one of the firm's products that consumers will buy depends on the prices charged for one or more of the firm's other products. Where there are such complementary or competitive relationships between the firm's products, the amount of information needed and the complexity of the calculation required is increased.

Oligopoly also introduces complications. We have seen that, with perfect competition, all that the firm needs to do is to allow its output to adjust to the change in the world price. With monopolistic competition, also, the firm will find it has to adjust in whatever way its competitors allow. Unless British firms account for a significant proportion of sales in overseas markets, it is unlikely that there will be retaliation to foreign-currency price cuts by any British firm. The firm will therefore be able to choose whether to use devaluation mainly to increase sterling profits or mainly to raise the volume of exports.

However we have seen that problems arise in oligopoly—where there is a danger of retaliation to a foreign-currency price cut—especially if the overseas market is depressed and/or most competitors are also from the devaluing country. The firm must judge how likely retaliation is, how serious its effects are likely to be and how best to react if it takes place.

6.1.3   SUPPLY FACTORS

On the supply side, the firm needs information about its costs over the range of output between the existing one and that which would be reached if foreign-currency prices were cut by the full amount of devaluation. Ideally, the firm needs to be able to calculate marginal cost over this range. At worst, it must use some other method to discover what will be the cost of producing the volume of exports implied by the various devaluation decisions.

6.1.4   THE DECISIONS

Finally, the firm must take its devaluation decisions, given its objectives and the information it has. Some kind of calculation will be required. Indeed, if the decision relates to a number of products, or there is a complicated market situation for one product, some kind of mathematical model may be required. The important thing is that the decision should be taken in a logical way, and should flow from the objectives and the information. We shall be able to see how far our firms did this as we proceed.

We saw in Chapter 2 that if a firm wanted to maximise profit, an economist would reach any devaluation decision by equating marginal cost with marginal revenue. In practice, marginal revenue is difficult to calculate; moreover, many of our firms did not seek to maximise profit. Nevertheless, given its objectives, the firm is unlikely to take good decisions unless it takes account of demand and supply factors of the kind outlined above and unless it looks in a logical way at how it can best meet its objectives in its particular circumstances. While the firm may not use a mathematical model, and while the complexity of the decision may well not be sufficient to warrant using one, the decision must be taken logically if it is to be a good decision.

6.2   Some Classifications

We shall find it useful, later in this book, to look at our firms by classifying them in a number of ways. The three most important are the following.

6.2.1   TYPE OF DECISION

The first and most obvious classification is in terms of the kind of decision taken. We have looked so far at four main possibilities. First, firms could either make no reduction at all in their foreign-currency prices, or as small a reduction as the could get away with.

Second, they could reduce their foreign-currency prices by the full amount of devaluation or, more probably, by the *net* amount of devaluation. Third, firms could make across-the-board reductions in foreign-currency prices by less than the full gross (or net) amount of devaluation. If a firm does this, there is obviously a range of price cuts that could be made, ranging from no cut at all to a cut by the full (gross) amount of devaluation.

The fourth possibility is that firms could examine individually the position in each country or group of countries. They could then make appropriate changes in export prices according to competitive conditions in the individual country or group of countries. Even this does not strictly exhaust the possibilities. We have concentrated on price because this is what our firms did, but it is obviously possible to alter one or more other marketing variables as well as price. A complete classification would therefore have to allow for the possibility of changing these other marketing variables too. We have explained that we shall ignore them because our firms concentrated on price decisions.

On *a priori* grounds, one might imagine that all decisions after devaluation should be based on an individual examination of each market in turn. However, things are not quite so simple. The assessment of conditions in individual markets would not guarantee good devaluation decisions. Whether or not the decisions were proved right by events would depend on the decision taker's ability as well as on the method of decision taking. More important, perhaps, good devaluation decisions would require good market information. Where the number of export markets is large, we have seen that it is far from easy to obtain good information about all of them. The fact that few of our firms examined each overseas market separately, in order to take a separate decision for each, is not in itself a criticism of the way the devaluation decisions were taken.

6.2.2   BY SPEED OF DECISION

The second way of classifying the devaluation decisions is by the speed with which they were taken. About two thirds of our firms took their decisions within a few days of devaluation. The remaining third delayed them until they could obtain extra information. Obviously, the more quickly a decision was taken the less time there was for considering alternatives. However, some of our firms already had adequate information. Indeed two of them had contingency plans. Speedy decision taking was then more clearly justified.

In other firms, the decision to act quickly was dictated by the likely reactions the firm expected from competitors and/or customers. The apparent need for speed then had to be offset against the fact that some relevant information would not be available until after the decision was taken.

6.2.3   BY ORGANISATIONAL DECISIONS

The third way of classifying devaluation decisions is in terms of the organisational arrangements within the firm. In some of our firms, the decision was effectively taken by one man. In others, it was taken by groups of managers at one or more meetings, formal or informal. In some firms, the final decision had to be arrived at in consultation with other firms, either because all were members of an export trade association or because one or more of the competitors was so big that it seemed wise to agree a course of action with it in advance.

With these introductory comments we now proceed to consider the decisions that our firms took.

CHAPTER 7

The Decisions

In this Chapter, we look in detail at the devaluation decisions of our nineteen firms, using the classification from section 6.2.3. Detailed descriptions of the devaluation decisions are given in the case studies. Here we look at the decisions taken by the firms in each of the categories, to see what are the main generalisations that we can make.

7.1 One-man Decisions

The firms in this category were:
Birmingham Cakes
Cardiff Instruments
Gatley Hosiery
Nottingham Confectionery
Peterborough Tubes

7.1.1 ADMINISTRATIVE ARRANGEMENTS

In each firm, the devaluation decisions were taken effectively by one man, though there were varying degrees of consultation with and approval from equals or more senior management. In Birmingham Cakes, Gatley Hosiery and Peterborough Tubes, the decision was taken by the marketing manager concerned with the product in question. In Nottingham Confectionery, it was the finance director. In Cardiff Instruments, the effective decision-taker was the contracts manager. As in Nottingham Confectionery, the initial estimates of the effects of devaluation on cost were little altered by subsequent discussion. Cardiff Instruments obtained business by tendering, so that for every tender the estimating department always had to make a separate estimate. Because the sales managers were usually brought into any final decision meeting, both the estimates- and sales-managers were well placed to assess the effect of devaluation on costs.

In three of the five firms, Cardiff Instruments, Gatley Hosiery and Nottingham Confectionery, the decisions were taken almost immediately after devaluation, using existing information about markets and costs. Cardiff Instruments and Gatley Hosiery each decided to make an across-the-board reduction in prices, cutting them by a similar amount for all products in all markets. In Birmingham Cakes, while provisional decisions were taken at once, the final decisions were delayed until fuller cost and market information could be collected and until the provisional decisions had been discussed with Birmingham's agents in its four main markets. Birmingham assessed separately the situation it faced in each market. A similar procedure was followed by the marketing manager of Peterborough Tubes, for Product D. For X-ply, Peterborough's marketing manager saw no need for more market information, apparently because X-ply was in a monopolistic position in a rapidly-growing market. Nevertheless, the final decision on X-ply was delayed until more detailed cost figures were available.

7.1.2   THE DECISIONS

(a) *Birmingham Cakes*

The decisions about how to respond to devaluation were made by the vice-chairman, who was responsible for the group's export activities, on the advice of the export director. They were then discussed with Birmingham's overseas agents before being submitted to the Chairman for his approval.

As we have seen, Birmingham Cakes took a careful decision for each market. With its good accounting system, it was well equipped to calculate the effect of devaluation on marginal costs and its calculations allowed for the possibility that some supplying countries might devalue. Since output was currently well below capacity, Birmingham Cakes could reasonably assume that raw material and labour costs were constant over the relevant range of output. This calculation was treated as showing how far Birmingham Cakes could 'afford' to reduce prices or to increase marketing expenditure in any market. The aim after devaluation was to increase 'contribution' by expanding sales volume, although how big an increase in sales was required was not stated explicitly. Because the assessment of Birmingham's overall position carried out before devaluation showed that the firm's overall exports were expanding strongly and that they would continue to grow quickly, even without devaluation, it was felt unnecessary to 'give anything away across the board'.

The first conclusion was therefore that a separate decision should be made for each market, by the export director, mainly from his existing knowledge.

Rather more than 90% of Birmingham's exports went to nine countries and the remainder to a comparatively large number of small markets. As the case study shows, each market was considered separately in taking the devaluation decisions. Birmingham Cakes treated the gain in sterling receipts from devaluation in each market as a fund to be used to increase sales volume in that market. However, so that part of these proceeds would be kept as additional 'contribution', the foreign-currency price was nowhere allowed to fall by the full amount of devaluation. The policy was to 'reinforce success with success' on a selective, market-by-market basis.

The procedure followed is set out in the case study. Birmingham Cakes considered the rate at which its sales in each market were growing; the elasticity of demand there (at least in the general sense of the extent to which price changes were likely to alter sales volume); the attitude of consumers to Birmingham's products; and the way competitors were likely to react to its devaluation decisions.

(b) *Gatley Hosiery*

In Gatley Hosiery, we studied the devaluation decisions of manufacturing company A and of the overseas company, which was responsible for all Gatley's overseas activities.

In the manufacturing company, the devaluation decisions were taken by its own management. They were based on data collected by the chief accountant and discussed with the managing director before being circulated to managers. These decisions were provisional until the managing director approved them, which he had done in every case by 26 November. As the case study shows, the prices of all items in one range of products were to be increased by between 3 and 4% from 1 January 1968. All other prices were to be left unchanged.

For manufacturing company A, the only question was whether to begin to recover the extra costs resulting from devaluation before it issued its next price lists during 1968. For most products, the extra costs were so small that they could be absorbed until the new price list was brought out. However, at the time of devaluation, one product range had been produced for only three months out of its expected twelve-month production cycle. Since it contained an above-average amount of imported raw material, Gatley increased prices for this product range by between 3 and 4%.

The decision-takers in manufacturing company A had a good deal of cost information, showing how a whole range of possible devaluation decisions would affect profits. However, there was some guesswork, especially since the figures for raw material prices were regarded as maxima.

In the overseas company, the managing director would normally have taken the devaluation decisions himself. Since he was abroad at the time, most of the immediate decisions were taken by the marketing director on the morning of Monday 20 November. One decision, about products for the next season, was taken by consensus among senior managers later in the week.

The overseas company made the following decisions. First, it increased sterling prices to its American and Canadian subsidiaries immediately by 8%. Second, it left the existing sterling price charged to Russia unchanged. Third, it increased sterling prices charged to all other markets by 8%, from January 1968. For the products for the next season, senior management decided later in the same week that Gatley Hosiery would add a higher rate of profit per unit than in the past when calculating their prices. In general, Gatley would do this by aiming at the same foreign-currency prices as before devaluation.

All these decisions were taken before any cost calculations could be made by the manufacturing company. Despite having no detailed cost figures, the marketing director of the overseas company felt certain that increasing the sterling price of Gatley's exports by 8% would more than offset any likely cost increase resulting from devaluation. The first, rough cost figures came from the manufacturing company on Friday 25 November. Not for some weeks could it assess accurately the increase in total costs caused by devaluation, which it finally put at between 3 and 4%. The manufacturing company had decided to increase its home market prices sufficiently to recover these extra costs, so that all UK prices, including those charged to the overseas company, were increased by 4% in January 1968.

The main factors leading to the overseas company's decisions were as follows. First, there was a belief that Gatley's export sales would not be affected by price cuts of the size that devaluation made possible. But, second, there was a feeling that devaluation and the 'associated propaganda' had raised such hopes of price cuts among overseas customers that sales would fall if Gatley did not reduce its foreign-currency prices. Third, Gatley would gain a marketing advantage over its British competitors by taking its devaluation decisions immediately, so that there was no period of uncertainty. Special factors influenced the marketing director's decisions for individual countries and what happened is set out in the case study. For example, in North America sales had been growing rapidly without any price reductions, so that there was no case for cutting prices to increase sales. Gatley 'split the difference', increasing sterling prices by 8%.

With Russia, the price reductions were postponed until January 1968 to allow time for explanations and to carry out the necessary clerical work.

Since, for the next season, it intended to pursue its general philosophy of 'charging what the market would bear', Gatley feared that its sales might fall if local-currency prices were not cut on exports of product ranges already being sold. However, we have seen that it was decided that when future product ranges were designed and produced their prices, in local currency, would be roughly the same as before devaluation, giving higher sterling profits.

No written information was used by the marketing director of the overseas company in taking the decisions. He simply felt that a price increase of 8% would more than cover any likely effects of devaluation, and that nothing worthwhile would be gained from seeking extra information.

(c) Cardiff Instruments

Immediately after devaluation (on Sunday 19 November) the commercial manager recommended an increase in sterling prices to cover the increase in costs resulting from devaluation. This recommendation was amended by the sales manager and confirmed by the general manager, after discussion at a regular fortnightly meeting of senior managers already arranged for Monday 20 November.

Since these cost increases were put at 3%, Cardiff decided to increase the prices of its products by 3% in both the home market and most export markets. For the small number of imported accessories used with Cardiff's product, the aim was to raise prices by the full amount of devaluation, though we shall see that there were problems here. On exports to Eastern Europe, Cardiff Instruments continued to charge the UK prices, plus 10%.

The decision to cut foreign-currency prices on all exports outside Eastern Europe by the *net* amount of devaluation seems to have been strongly influenced by the fact that Cardiff's prices were not competitive for its cheaper machines. The fact that the same foreign-currency cuts were made on the more expensive items reflected a feeling that technological superiority alone would no longer sell them, now that technological developments were slowing. Cardiff was taking a longish view of its export position.

Apart from detailed information about the increases in costs which devaluation was likely to cause, Cardiff's decision takers had only the information normally brought to their fortnightly management meetings. This led to the conclusion that costs would rise by 3 %. In addition, the sterling prices of imported components were thought likely to rise by the full amount of devaluation. The problem of what to do if this did not happen was finally resolved by a decision to put the new sterling prices of imported components directly into tender prices.

Devaluation led to changes in Cardiff's forecasts of how much business would be available immediately after devaluation. In January 1968, when Cardiff reviewed the probabilities already assigned to its export tenders, they were reduced on five projects and increased on five others. We cannot say how far the increased probabilities resulted from devaluation and how far from the fact that Cardiff's understanding of what its customers were likely to do increased as time passed.

(d) *Nottingham Confectionery*

Since we are not able to write a detailed case study for Nottingham Confectionery, we here give the information which we did collect. This firm's policy was to treat the world as divided into two parts. 'Countries of the western type' included those in North America, Europe, Japan and two smaller markets in South Africa and Australia. In all these countries, Nottingham Confectionery began local manufacture at an early stage, because national policy instruments, like tariffs, made this essential. Some products which sold only in small quantities continued to be exported to these countries from the UK. However, Nottingham explained that once it had a factory in any country to produce any product, other products could be produced there at a lowish cost because some fixed expenses had already been incurred. Japan had so far been an exception. It had put various obstacles in the way of local manufacture, but this restrictive attitude was easing and local production would soon be undertaken in Japan.

In 'the rest of the world', Nottingham did not want to begin local manufacture, mainly because these countries controlled the activities of foreign firms (including their remittances of profits). The countries were also relatively poor and politically unstable.

Nottingham Confectionery was operating in very competitive markets. Its aim was to earn a given profit margin on all products. The price of any new product was initially planned to give this margin. If this gave a price above those of competing products, another look was taken to see whether a change in the product, or a lower price, was the answer. In most markets, Nottingham was currently selling products which gave the desired margin. These markets were ones where Nottingham's level of sales was roughly the one that it had assumed when allocating overhead costs. In some countries, products were sold at an 'accounting' loss with price not covering all the overheads allocated to the product. The hope was that the goods would become 'profitable' in these countries within a reasonable period of time. While this period varied, it was rarely more than five years.

When devaluation occurred, Nottingham Confectionery saw no point in looking at any individual product, or group of products, because its general rule held for everything it sold. Since all its products sold in markets where the price level was set by competition, Nottingham decided to take the whole benefit of devaluation in increased sterling profits, keeping prices constant in local currencies. The only situation where an exception might have been made would have been where overseas competitors had for some reason decided to react to devaluation in the UK by cutting their own local-currency prices overseas. While this did happen to some of our firms, it did not happen with Nottingham Confectionery.

Where Nottingham's products had not been competitive enough before devaluation to be sold in a given overseas country, devaluation sometimes persuaded Nottingham Confectionery to begin to sell in that country. However, this had not happened in a major market or to a significant degree.

An essential characteristic of Nottingham's activities was that its products could be manufactured efficiently even in relatively small countries. There was no barrier to local manufacture if Nottingham wished to undertake it. Nottingham told us that devaluation had not led to any decision to begin local manufacture. However, there were some markets in the Middle East or Africa where local manufacture was not contemplated but devaluation had allowed Nottingham to resume (or begin) exporting to them from the UK.

It had been decided to take as much sterling profit from devaluation as possible, because price elasticity of demand was thought to be low in overseas markets for Nottingham's products. As for sales promotion, Nottingham did not know how profitable a marginal increase in expenditure on sales promotion in any market would be. Expenditure on it was therefore set as a standard percentage of total sales receipts in local currency in each market. Since the aim had been to keep these local receipts constant after devaluation, there had been no change in sales promotion expenditure as a result of devaluation. However, this did mean that sales promotion cost more in sterling.

Nottingham's accounting system showed how much 'profit' each product was making. A standard schedule was produced at intervals showing price and 'profit margin' in each market. If a product was making a 'profit' (after deducting overheads) in an export market, Nottingham felt sure that it was profitable. Nottingham agreed that it should perhaps be shifting some of its energies away from its small export markets, but did not see any such shifts as worthwhile at the time of devaluation. Nottingham Confectionery was growing rapidly, and its main problem was how to recruit able people to deal with its major overseas markets. Devaluation apart No-one in the firm was advocating a change in overseas marketing expenditure. Since Nottingham Confectionery lacked neither cash nor profit, it was always able to spend any necessary amount on advertising. There was no change apart from that caused by devaluation increasing sterling equivalents.

Nottingham argued that, for each of its products, there was a range of prices which could be charged for such a product. What Nottingham tried to do was to discover the appropriate price bracket. It also argued that the frequency of price changes was important. A price change of 5 to $7\frac{1}{2}\%$ would make no difference to sales, but a larger change might reduce them. Nottingham therefore tried to make a series of small price changes rather than leaving prices unchanged so long that a big change was then necessary.

(e) *Peterborough Tubes*

Devaluation took Peterborough Tubes by surprise, but was immediately seen as an opportunity to increase export margins significantly. All devaluation decisions for the UK and Europe were taken by one of two marketing managers. Each was responsible for the sales of one of the two products we studied and each dealt with both the UK and Europe. For other overseas markets, the decisions were made jointly by these two men and the overseas marketing manager. The initiative lay with the marketing managers, who had general authority from their divisional general manager to suggest how to respond to changes like devaluation. No further instructions were issued by the divisional general manager or by anyone at a higher level in the firm.

Every market was considered separately. For example, in Latin America where Product D was competing on equal terms with products from the USA, the size of the price reductions made in each market was determined by its particular circumstances. In Europe, price reductions were bigger, because German competition was keen.

Peterborough decided to raise the price of Product D in the UK by the amount of the estimated cost increases accumulated since 1964, because it seemed only reasonable to use devaluation as the opportunity to offset the increases in cost which had occurred before devaluation as well as those caused by devaluation itself. Peterborough's senior management believed that all their British competitors were in roughly the same position and would also want to raise prices as far as government policy on prices would allow. It was not thought to be good tactics to raise prices by less than the maximum possible in the hope of gaining in competitive advantage over other producers, although this was apparently done by some competitors.

For sales of X-ply to Europe, the reasoning was that if sterling prices had been held after devaluation, the foreign-currency prices at which the output of the European plant was sold would have been correspondingly reduced. 'Such a loss of potential income was a risk....not justifiable in the particular circumstances', the firm thought. Peterborough Tubes was a monopoly supplier for X-ply in Europe, where demand for it was already greater than supply, and growing rapidly. Peterborough's EEC plant had also suffered substantial losses but was just beginning to earn a profit. Peterborough wanted to earn as much profit as it could in the short term, to recoup as much as possible of the losses accumulated before devaluation.

In other overseas markets, the American firm which licensed X-ply to Peterborough was a competitor. A cut in local-currency prices was therefore thought desirable. In the home market, for X-ply as with Product D, it was seen as necessary to raise prices by an amount equal to the total increase in unit costs since 1964.

Apart from the cost information described in the case study, no special data was collected for the devaluation decisions. There were no contacts with local representatives in any overseas market, because of the time, expense and effort it would require. The overseas marketing manager later said that, as it turned out, he and his colleagues felt that they had made unnecessarily big reductions in local-currency prices. The same results might have been obtained if smaller price reductions had been made. Perhaps consultation with local representatives would have led to better decisions.

7.1.3   THE RESULTS

(a) *Birmingham Cakes*

The export marketing director said that, in general, he thought the devaluation decisions had been about as successful as could reasonably have been expected, apart from difficulty in ending the special discount conceded under pressure from its agent in the USA. Birmingham Cakes saw some special factors at work. For example, it believed that the 40% increase in exports to Canada in 1967–68 was partly the result of over-ordering by their agent there, and so was not surprised when exports to Canada fell in 1968–69. Similarly, the fall in exports to Finland in 1968–69, by almost two-thirds, was mainly the result of successful competition from foreign firms.

Despite the overall increase in export sales volume in the first year after devaluation, Birmingham Cakes' total profits from exports were below those in the previous year, because of a substantial rise in the price of a major raw material. Birmingham Cakes thought that it would be harmful to 'goodwill' to raise prices immediately to recoup the increase. However, prices were raised in 1968–69 and the desired increase in profits achieved, without any apparent reduction in sales volume.

(b) *Gatley Hosiery*

The management of the manufacturing company was satisfied that its decisions led to the results they intended. In the short run, the cost increases caused by devaluation were recovered. Later, as new ranges of hosiery were introduced, foreign-currency prices were pushed back to roughly the pre-devaluation levels so that sterling profits increased.

For the overseas company, detailed figures are set out in the case study. The most striking individual changes are those in the proportion of sales to Russia and to EFTA. While Gatley's comments are given in the case study, the main factors seem to have been a switch in Russian purchasing policy, coupled with the fact that high and profitable sales in the UK led Gatley to quote higher prices and longer delivery dates to Russia. Improved sales in both EFTA and the EEC were said by Gatley to result from a decision, taken before devaluation, to increase sales in Europe. Because of the reduction in business with Russia, this policy was speeded up.

(c) *Cardiff Instruments*

Cardiff Instruments' export orders increased by 39% between 1 April 1968 and 31 March 1969, to reach £750,000, or 24% of total orders, as against 17% the year before. Cardiff did not think that much of this increase could be attributed to devaluation. Technical performance was seen as the main factor selling their most expensive products. Sales of the cheaper products, which *were* thought to be sensitive to price reductions, did not increase substantially. Devaluation was not a major short-term influence. Nevertheless, Cardiff Instruments believed that the effects of devaluation might still show themselves and was confident that its decision to cut the foreign-currency prices of its products was sound.

(d) *Nottingham Confectionery*

As we have seen, the objective of Nottingham Confectionery was to take the maximum sterling profit from devaluation, while maintaining sales promotion expenditure overseas constant in foreign currency. Since neither customers nor competitors reacted to Nottingham's decision in a way that reduced its export sales, Nottingham Confectionery felt that its objectives had been achieved.

(e) *Peterborough Tubes*

Peterborough Tubes' profits on its sales to Europe increased substantially in the year after devaluation, as did sales volume. Peterborough did not doubt that devaluation helped its overseas operations, especially outside Europe, enabling it to be more selective in taking business. Devaluation had made it easier to take a number of other decisions, about, for example, export pricing, overseas representation and overseas investment, as the case study explains. The most significant effect of devaluation was on some major marketing decisions, for example, for South Africa. However, Peterborough's senior management did not believe that devaluation itself made a significant difference to Peterborough's overseas profits.

In Europe, the devaluation decisions for X-ply were thought to be very successful, while with Product D they increased its competitiveness without provoking retaliation from competitors. 'Contribution' increased on all exports.

Unfortunately, the potential benefits of devaluation for Peterborough were reduced by the pricing policy adopted by the overseas producers of its main raw material. They raised sterling prices of the material by the full amount of devaluation, while reducing their domestic currency prices for finished products somewhat. So, while sterling prices of finished products rose, they did so by less than the amount of devaluation. This swing in the competitive balance in favour of foreign producers led to an increase in imports into the UK. Even so, Peterborough increased the volume of sales of both Product D and X-ply in the UK market by some 8% in 1968. Since Peterborough had also increased its home market prices, profit margins in the UK improved.

7.1.4   COMMENTS ON THE DECISIONS

In three of these firms, namely, Cardiff Instruments, Gatley Hosiery and Nottingham Confectionery, the devaluation decisions were taken almost immediately, with existing cost and market information. Cardiff Instruments and Gatley Hosiery each reduced its prices by the same amount for every product in every overseas market (outside the USSR for Gatley). Nottingham Confectionery decided to maintain foreign-currency prices.

In Birmingham Cakes, the decisions were delayed until more cost and market information could be obtained, and a separate analysis for each market carried out. A similar procedure was followed by Peterborough Tubes for Product D. For X-ply, Peterborough saw no need to seek extra market information, since the firm had a monopoly position in the rapidly growing UK and European markets. Here, the final decisions were delayed until the effects of devaluation on costs could be assessed more fully.

The task of collecting the necessary information was not so important for Birmingham Cakes since it exported to only a few markets, some with few customers. It was fairly easy to reach a decision for each market. Peterborough Tubes sold X-ply to many more markets, but had a well-developed distribution system and an elaborate export organisation which provided good information. For Product D, the number of customers was comparatively limited, and Peterborough quoted for individual orders. Here, too, assessing the position for individual markets, or rather customers, was relatively easy. Acquiring information was most difficult for Gatley Hosiery. It exported to a large number of markets, had a large product range and regarded the information available for most markets as far from adequate. We can, however, say that market information for these firms, except perhaps Gatley Hosiery, was reasonably good. Only Birmingham Cakes sought extra market information after devaluation.

On costs, the situation was less satisfactory. Only Birmingham Cakes worked consistently with marginal cost. Though Cardiff Instruments had been working in terms of fixed and variable cost for the machines it made, it did not do so for components. The other firms studied in this section had standard costing systems that used absorption costing.

The quality of the decisions varied equally. We would rate the decisions taken by Birmingham Cakes highly and those of Peterborough Tubes almost as highly. While Gatley Hosiery may well have taken good decisions, and while in any case these were only for the season, there was no careful analysis of the situation. Nottingham Confectionery's decision to take the maximum sterling profit from the existing export volume cannot be questioned, given its objectives, and the fact that it was selling in monolistic competition, but we were less sure about its decision to hold sales promotion expenditure constant in foreign currency. We also have some reservations about Cardiff Instruments, especially the usefulness of its cost information.

However, while we rated the decisions taken by Birmingham Cakes very highly, we found that the standard product which was re-costed after devaluation was manufactured in several stages. At each stage, a margin was included in the cost estimates to allow for a possible under-estimation of cost increases at the previous stage. The total size of these margins was big enough to cause a significant increase in the size of Birmingham's estimate of the rise in costs caused by devaluation, and may have influenced the devaluation decisions. So, while we were impressed by the decision taking in Birmingham Cakes, this criticism could be made even there.

There was little risk of making the wrong decisions in these firms. In Gatley Hosiery, the decision to cut prices affected only the remainder of the season's product range, due for early replacement, and was reversed for the next season. Birmingham Cakes knew there was a risk that price cuts would lead to little increase in sales and was therefore careful to try to balance price cuts against selling expenditure of various kinds. Nottingham Confectionery also took little risk. It made no change in either foreign-currency prices or sales promotion expenditure, hoping to take the maximum benefit from devaluation in increased sterling receipts. In Cardiff Instruments, on the other hand, while a price cut was likely to bring in extra business, this business might turn out not to be profitable. Apart from that, Cardiff's small price cuts were likely to have little effect on profit. In Peterborough Tubes, the situation was different for each of the two products we studied. Peterborough was a monopoly supplier of X-ply in Europe, and demand for it was growing rapidly. The decision not to reduce foreign-currency prices therefore involved little risk. For Product D, the risk of a wrong decision was much the same as in Cardiff Instruments.

7.2   Decisions by Cartel

The firms here were Durham Plates and Kendal Accessories.

7.2.1   ADMINISTRATIVE ARRANGEMENTS

In Durham Plates, for Product A and some grades of Product B, and for Kendal Accessories, the broad decisions about devaluation were taken at meetings of their export cartels. For Durham Plates, the trade association meeting was held within a week of devaluation, so that most of those attending it, from whatever firm, had only rough estimates of the effect of devaluation on costs. The meeting of Kendal Accessories' cartel was not held until three weeks after devaluation.

7.2.2   THE DECISIONS

(a) *Durham Plates*

For Durham Plates, the decisions about Product A were taken at a meeting of the export cartel on 23 November, attended by representatives of the three firms producing it. The Managing Director of Durham Plates took the chair, and the export manager and comptroller were also there. Opening the meeting, the Managing Director of Durham Plates suggested that while the cartel's prices in a number of markets were already 10 to 15% lower than those of its European competitors, devaluation could give lower prices still to overseas customers. Even before devaluation, the cartel had agreed that sterling prices should be increased by $7\frac{1}{2}\%$, because of an accumulation of cost increases. After devaluation, such an increase could be made and yet leave foreign-currency prices in most countries lower than those of competitors. One question was how and when to recoup the further cost increases which were bound to result from devaluation. Again, should there be a different price change in each country? Should any possible response to devaluation first be agreed with the cartel's European competitors? In the discussion which followed, some members of the cartel felt that an increase in sterling export prices by the full amount of devaluation would 'defeat the objective of devaluation'. Durham then suggested that the solution might be to make no increase at all in some sterling prices, but to increase other prices by varying amounts up to the full amount of devaluation. This would test the elasticity of demand in some markets and show what level of prices would best secure increased sales in each of them. To this, it was replied that it was essential to obtain an overall increase in sterling export prices in order to restore profits, and that in some countries there was little scope for increasing sales by foreign-currency price cuts.

The meeting went on to consider whether to treat differently countries which had also devalued, as well as the position of a large foreign customer with whom there were long-term contracts. The upshot of this discussion was an agreement that if profits were to be restored to the April 1966 level there would have to be an increase in prices of between 6½ and 10%, depending on the raw material content of each particular grade of Product A. The average was about 8%. However, it was then noted that the cost of packing materials would rise, partly because of price increases decided upon by suppliers before devaluation and partly because of the effects of devaluation itself.

It was finally agreed that selling prices for Product A would be increased immediately by 10% for all countries which had not devalued and by 7½% for all countries which had. A sub-committee was appointed to draft new terms for the large customer.

With Product B, Durham Plates took no decisions until the size of all increases in cost since April 1966, including those resulting from devaluation, had been worked out for the whole range of Product B, which was not done until the middle of December. It was then decided that prices within the UK would be increased by between 5 and 10% for most grades, and by 15% for a new grade, the increases being made in three equal, monthly stages. The precise increases for individual grades were very much determined by the amount of imported raw material used. Sterling export prices for all markets were brought up to exactly the same level as home market prices, which meant a slightly bigger price increase for one or two grades of Product B than for the remainder. However, for all grades except the new one, the effect of the devaluation decisions was to reduce foreign-currency prices, sometimes quite substantially.

The reason given for charging the same prices at home and overseas was that this would somehow improve Durham's chances of establishing itself permanently in export markets. It was thought unwise to take advantage of the opportunity that devaluation gave Durham to increase its sterling prices in export markets above the prices charged within the UK.

(b) *Kendal Accessories*

Kendal Accessories saw devaluation as a welcome opportunity to increase the profitability of exports, since it was expected that costs would increase by only 4% as a result of devaluation.

A meeting of Kendal's export cartel was held on 7 December, nearly three weeks after devaluation. At this meeting, the first suggestions about how to deal with devaluation were made by the chairman and sales manager of Kendal, namely that the cartel should make no immediate change at all in foreign-currency prices. It should then take several months to examine each market in detail and take a decision for each on its merits and at leisure. This attitude was not shared by everyone, and the meeting decided to revise the whole export price list there and then. As the case study shows, the meeting divided overseas markets into two groups.

The first group, containing 21 countries, included all those where exports were unimportant to the cartel or where its prices were already competitive. Here, the foreign-currency price was left unchanged, despite the fact that three of the countries had devalued by the same amount as the UK.

The second group contained seven countries, namely, those to which the cartel had significant exports and where it was not competitive. Here, no change was made in the sterling price, despite the fact that, here again, there were three countries which devalued by the same amount as the UK and two other countries which devalued by about 20%.

There were three exceptions. In the Sudan and Cuba, where competition from Eastern Europe was severe, the foreign-currency price was reduced by 6%. In Hong Kong, where there was keen Japanese competition, it was reduced by about $2\frac{1}{2}\%$.

7.2.3 THE RESULTS

(a) *Durham Plates*

The result of devaluation was that export prices of Product A were increased, on average, by 8%. We were not able to obtain comparable figures for Product B. At first sight, devaluation appears to have been successful in increasing Durham's exports of Product A. In 1968 they rose by 90% above the admittedly low level in 1967, the proportion of output exported rising from 8 to 13%. However, most of the increase in exports was the result of obtaining one, very large order from Eastern Europe. Durham Plates is convinced that this business was likely to be given to a British company, for political and balance of payments reasons. Since no other member of Durham's cartel was in a position to supply exactly the same product at a reasonable price, Durham took the contract.

Even in the rest of the world, where Durham's exports increased by about 30% in 1968, Durham argued that the reason was as much a general recovery in world trade in its products as the advantage given by devaluation. In 1969, Durham's exports of Product A fell by 20%, and the proportion of output exported declined again to 9%, though obtaining the large order in 1968 affected this percentage.

(b) *Kendal Accessories*

The results of devaluation for Kendal were also disappointing. Its industry's exports rose by less than 5% in the year ended March 1968, and fell by 32% in the year to March 1969. In the same two years, exports by Kendal Accessories fell by about 26 and 49%, respectively. Kendal's share in exports of its products from the UK fell to 28%.

Part of the decline in exports was due to technological changes and to the growth of local manufacture behind tariffs in some important markets. However, it was also due to Kendal's inability to match its competitors'prices in some markets, even where it ignored the decisions of the cartel and passed on the full exchange effect of devaluation. Japanese competition was especially difficult to meet, as the case study shows.

While he agreed with the decision to cut foreign exchange prices in most countries where Kendal was a serious exporter, Kendal's sales manager felt that, especially in New Zealand, customers could have been persuaded to pay a little more. By giving way to pressure from one other member, the cartel had prevented him from obtaining the best possible prices in New Zealand.

7.2.4 COMMENTS ON THE DECISIONS

(a) *Durham Plates*

As for the decisions themselves, we are not entirely happy that the meeting of Durham's cartel took the best decisions it could have taken, although we appreciate that decisions taken by a committee, especially one whose members are drawn from different firms, are always likely to be less satisfactory than those taken by one man or by a group from the same firm. Even so, we are surprised that no serious consideration was given to the possibility that European producers would make retaliatory price cuts. The European producers were already uncompetitive in some markets. The foreign-currency price cuts that the cartel was able to make after devaluation would make them even more uncompetitive, unless their own country devalued too. Given the depressed state of world demand for the product, it surprises us that

Durham's cartel implicitly assumed that the probability of retaliation was zero, and that the suggestion by the chairman that the cartel might agree to joint action with European competitors was ignored. It is true that the European producers did not retaliate, but this is not in itself a good reason for failing to take seriously the possibility of retaliation.

We are also unhappy that there was no serious discussion of whether differential pricing in different markets would have paid off. While the members of the cartel assumed that demand in most countries would not be very responsive to price cuts, the discussion was sketchy because the cartel had little detailed market information. It did not even try to discover which *were* the markets where price cuts might lead to substantial increases in sales. Again, the meeting concentrated on the effect that devaluation would have on total costs, with which its members were more familiar, rather than looking at the effect of devaluation on incremental costs. No doubt the difficulty of taking the devaluation decisions was increased because they had to be taken at the cartel meeting by people representing three firms. It would also have been difficult to discuss marginal costs, because the effects of devaluation, and indeed earlier price increases, on different products varied significantly. The effect on marginal cost would have been almost impossible to calculate, even if firms had been prepared to reveal the relevant information. It would also have been difficult to go at all deeply into the different firms' views of the profitability of making different price cuts in different markets. As a result of all these problems, it was much easier to agree to a simple, flat-rate increase in sterling prices in all markets in all countries.

The increases finally agreed on were therefore determined in a rough and ready way. The result was that while Durham Plates' 'contribution' from some products was increased by the devaluation decisions, 'contribution' on the products where the biggest cost increases occurred was little altered. Yet this cartel, which made a flat-rate increase in prices for all products in all markets, operated an elaborate pricing system. It grouped its export markets into a number of 'zones', and charged a different price in each zone.

It is perhaps surprising that the cartel's decision on export prices was taken so quickly when it was so long before price increases were agreed for the home market. A questionnaire on costs sent out by the cartel secretariat was not discussed by its members until the end of December. At an informal meeting then, separate cost and price increases were agreed for Product A in the home market, for each of four different raw materials and nine methods of processing. In most cases, these price increases were significantly bigger than the expected cost increases, which were themselves generous.

The decisions which Durham itself made for Product B were worked out in a more leisurely way, and the cost information which Durham used was quite detailed. However, as we have already noted, Durham was already producing to its normal capacity for making Product B and it was not reasonable to assume that marginal cost was constant. Since Durham did not work out marginal cost for Product B at greater outputs than the existing one, it was difficult to calculate the likely effects of different devaluation decisions. In any case, we have seen that Durham's new export prices for Product B were identical with its home market prices. It had become standard procedure to charge the same price at home and abroad, so that alternative marketing decisions were simply not considered. Nor was the reaction of European competitors to the decision, or the effect that it would have on the balance between demand and capacity in Durham's plants.

(b) *Kendal Accessories*

We feel that the same criticisms can be made of the decisions of this cartel as of Durham Plates'. There was no discussion in terms of marginal cost. Nor was there any attempt to recover the (small) increase in total production costs resulting from devaluation either in the seven markets where sterling prices were left unchanged or in the three markets where the country in question had devalued but there was no change in the foreign-currency price. It is true that each market was considered individually, but in most of them the cartel was unable to agree on anything other than one of the two extreme price decisions that were possible. The situation was not examined carefully enough to discover whether something between these two extremes would be acceptable except in the cases of the Sudan, Cuba and Hong Kong. Indeed, in those countries where special decisions were made, they reflected pressures within the cartel rather than the results of careful analysis. Again, whether the cartel reduced its foreign-currency prices or maintained its sterling prices where a country had also devalued, the reason given was fear of competition from Japan and Eastern Europe. As with Durham Plates' cartel, no thought seemed to be given to how likely it was that there would be competitive retaliation. In a sense, the decisions of the cartel were irrelevant to Kendal because in most of its important markets Kendal reduced its foreign-currency price by the full amount of devaluation, even though this went against the decision of the cartel. Nevertheless, the quality of the decision-taking procedures was not high.

One can therefore make three criticisms of this cartel's behaviour. First, there was no careful study of cost and demand conditions in individual markets. Second, the way the competitive situation developed meant that the whole export price list had to be effectively abandoned within a few months. It is not certain that more careful consideration of the position in individual countries would have led more quickly to the kinds of price change that overseas competition later forced on the cartel. However, it might have done. The third criticism also applies to Durham Plates, and indeed to most committee decisions, especially ones where the members of the committee represent different interests. It is usually impossible for a large number of people from different firms to reach good decisions. There are too many individual interests involved. There is too much reluctance to share information for fear of letting one's competitors learn too much.

7.3   Decisions by Collusion

7.3.1   ADMINISTRATIVE ARRANGEMENTS

The firms here were London Switches and Stratford Equipment. Both shared their UK markets with one other British producer, which also provided most of the competition they faced abroad. Neither company had a specialist marketing department and, in both cases, the devaluation decisions were taken by the managing director in discussions with the other British producer.

7.3.2   THE DECISIONS

(a) *London Switches*
London Switches believed that devaluation gave it an excellent opportunity to increase profits, and saw two reasons for doing so. First, with demand increasing rapidly both in the UK and abroad, only shortage of capacity was holding back sales. Second, demand was inelastic so that, even if the production capacity were there, sales would not increase significantly where foreign currency prices were reduced.

London Switches had no contingency plan for devaluation. Consequently, at the regular meeting of the Board already arranged for Monday 20 November, there was a discussion between the Board and the export and home sales managers. The meeting saw no immediate need to increase prices. The response to devaluation could be worked out at leisure. Since London Switches had only the one competitor in the UK, it seemed wise to press on it the desirability of leaving foreign currency export prices unchanged. However, for reasons of its own, the competitor was anxious to reduce foreign-currency prices and, in the end, London Switches reluctantly agreed to do the same.

Both firms agreed to maintain their prices in both home and export markets until 1 January 1968. After that, prices in the UK would be increased by 10%, while sterling export prices would be increased by 8% in all countries which had not devalued and by 5% in countries which had. Because the two firms would, in any case, have increased sterling prices of exports early in 1968, sterling prices were increased very little because of devaluation itself.

(b) *Stratford Equipment*

Stratford Equipment's initial reaction to devaluation was to conclude that there was now a national crisis and that it should therefore be prepared to give the national interest priority in taking its decisions, so long as sterling profit margins would not actually be reduced. Stratford was already exporting about 30% of its output and capacity was short. Despite this, Stratford's attitude to devaluation led it to seek only a modest increase in its export prices and profits.

Although such non-economic considerations weighed most heavily at the time of devaluation, Stratford's managing director also knew that his German competitor was trying to break into some markets at prices that Stratford could not profitably meet. While Stratford believed that the total market in which its product sold was fairly inelastic to price changes, its managing director took the view that devaluation offered a timely opportunity to 'stand up to the foreigner' by reducing foreign-currency prices.

After some argument with the other UK producer, which was of roughly equal size, it was agreed that sterling prices would be raised by 10%, reducing foreign-currency prices by about 6% in all countries which had not devalued. For countries which had devalued, and for the home market, a flat-rate increase in prices of $7\frac{1}{2}$% was agreed on. It was agreed to postpone these changes until January, effectively reducing foreign-currency prices by the full amount of devaluation in the intervening six weeks. Even before devaluation, it had been expected that raw material and labour costs would rise at the end of the year. It therefore seemed reasonable to wait until January 1968, and then increase prices sufficiently to cover all the cost increases.

By the end of the year, detailed cost calculations showed that the main result of devaluation would be to increase the price of the main raw material by about 13%. Allowing for the new wage award and productivity increases, costs of production were therefore likely to increase by 7%. By raising its sterling prices by 10%, Stratford increased its profitability somewhat, while still passing some benefits of devaluation on to export customers.

7.3.3   THE RESULTS

(a) *London Switches*

In London Switches, in 1967–68 (year ended September), total sales rose by 28%, home sales by 24% and exports by 40%. The sharp rise in sales, both home and export, was mainly due to the expansion of capacity, at the end of 1967, which enabled London Switches to begin to reduce its order books. In 1968–69, the rate of growth of both home and export sales fell sharply because the new capacity was now fully used. Total sales rose by 11%, home sales by 8% and exports by 18%.

(b) *Stratford Equipment*

In the two years following devaluation, there was a dramatic rise in Stratford Equipment's export sales. The proportion of its output exported rose to over 60%, compared with 34% in 1967, and this was entirely the result of Stratford's success in selling its new product in the American market.

The decision to move into the American market had been taken before devaluation. Indeed, it was included in the September 1967 budget plan. Moreover, the managing director claimed that his success in the USA had not been influenced significantly by devaluation. The sterling price for the new product in America had already been decided and was not altered. Indeed, the new product was so successful in the American market that Stratford felt able to impose a surcharge of 10% on its prices in the USA, to cover the cost of maintaining British technical staff permanently in the USA.

While devaluation does not seem to have helped Stratford Equipment in selling its new product in the USA, the fact that the sterling price had already been set meant that American customers obtained the full benefit of devaluation in a cut of about 14% in dollar prices. Though Stratford then imposed the 10% surcharge, there was still a small cut in dollar prices.

7.3.4   COMMENTS ON THE DECISIONS

London Switches did not analyse its position at all carefully at the time of devaluation. Perhaps this was inevitable, given the extreme buoyancy of both home and overseas markets and London's willingness to bow to the pressure from its rather larger competitor and agree to foreign-currency price cuts. After devaluation, the export objectives London Switches pursued were as nebulous as before it. There was a general feeling among London's senior managers that it should make a greater effort in export markets, but what exactly should be done was not spelled out. With the shortage of capacity, it is difficult to see what more London Switches could have done. There was a series of meetings between the managing director and the managers concerned with selling and exporting, but there was no attempt to obtain fuller information about either external or internal factors. However, London Switches' managing director was having discussions with his counterpart in the rival firm and this added to London's supply of information.

No detailed predictions were made of the effect of devaluation on costs. It was assumed that the cost of the main raw materials would increase by the full amount of devaluation.

Since Stratford Equipment and *its* only UK competitor both made much the same reductions in their foreign-currency prices, their competitive situations relative to each other were little changed. However, the value of the marketing advantage each gained relatively to foreign competitors was doubtful. First, by far the most important competition abroad came from each other. Second, a foreign-currency price reduction of around 6%, even if passed on in full by agents (which was not certain) was unlikely to make much difference in a market where demand was inelastic. In Norway and Austria, while Stratford Equipment's prices were being seriously undercut by its German competitor, the price disparity was so big that a 6% reduction in prices would not be significant. Again, even if price reductions were necessary in these two markets, there was no obvious reason, other than administrative convenience, for making the same price reduction in all other markets, where Stratford Equipment's prices were competitive. Even so, in these markets Stratford went out of its way to persuade its overseas agents to cut prices to final customers, although the agents had no obvious commercial reason for doing so.

The decision to cut prices is also a little surprising since we know that Stratford Equipment was about to launch its new product, which was virtually certain to be readily accepted by customers and, indeed, to give Stratford a major competitive advantage over all competitors, including the other British producer. Finally, even if demand for the old product had proved elastic to the foreign-currency price reductions, Stratford Equipment was suffering from a shortage of capacity which would have restricted its output once the new product was introduced. Much of the capacity which would become available in 1968 was designed to produce only the new product.

In overseas markets other than the USA, Stratford Equipment reduced its prices substantially, although not by the full amount of devaluation. However, unlike London Switches, the opposition to Stratford's wish to reduce prices came from its main UK competitor. While Stratford Equipment felt that it would be 'patriotic' to cut foreign-currency prices, it could not overlook the fact that its German competitor had been undercutting its prices greatly in Norway and Austria. Although Stratford Equipment believed that the total demand for its existing product was inelastic to price cuts, where all producers reduced their prices similarly, in this case, where it wanted to regain business from the individual German producer whose prices already seemed to be very low, 'patriotism' coincided with Stratford's commercial interests. However, no consideration was given to an alternative pricing policy, of cutting prices only in the markets where the German producer was active. Indeed, when told that Stratford wanted to cut its foreign-currency prices, the other British producer protested that there was no need to reduce prices in any export market except Norway and Austria. The other producer would have preferred *not* to cut export prices, because it was having difficulty in meeting current demand, as indeed was Stratford Equipment.

The decision in both these cases seems somewhat surprising. Since shortage of capacity was the main factor limiting output and since demand was both inelastic to price cuts and likely to continue to grow rapidly, there seemed little scope for increasing exports by cutting prices. For a year or two at least, both London Switches and Stratford Equipment would have earned bigger profits, and lost few sales, if they and their British competitors had taken more of the benefit of devaluation in increased sterling profits. And the UK balance of payments would have benefitted too. It is true that London Switches had little choice in this decision, since its slightly larger competitor was determined to cut foreign-currency prices whether London did or not. However, Stratford Equipment had greater freedom of action.

7.4   Immediate Group Decisions

7.4.1   ADMINISTRATIVE ARRANGEMENTS

The three firms here were: Acton Chemicals, Ealing Electrical Appliances and Hertford Stoves. All three firms reached their decisions at meetings of their senior executives within two days of devaluation.

7.4.2   THE DECISIONS

(a) *Hertford Stoves*
Since it had two or three months in which to work out its contingency plan, Hertford Stoves was able to look in detail at the position in each of its markets. Because there were about a hundred of them, the marketing and finance departments provided the data needed for drawing up the contingency plan by concentrating on what the marketing department saw as a 'typical' product for each market. The finance department provided a figure for the variable cost of producing this 'typical' product; the marketing department then worked out the best price to charge. The most important decision was for the USA, where it was decided to leave dollar prices unchanged. Although there was strong Japanese competition in America for its cheaper products, Hertford Stoves was not meeting significant Japanese competition in its own more expensive product range, in the American market, at the time of devaluation.

(b) *Acton Chemicals*
Acton Chemicals held a meeting on Monday 20 November to discuss its response to devaluation. The general manager was chairman and the divisional managers and their main colleagues also attended the meeting. Since Acton produced a basic chemical, it did not need to take a decision on anything except price. The meeting discussed separately the price of each product produced by Acton, and a general memorandum on pricing after devaluation was distributed on the next day. For the product we studied, new home and export sales targets were drawn up by the marketing manager by January 1968, and increased in July 1968.

By the time the meeting was held on 20 November, preliminary estimates had already been made of the effects of devaluation on the prices of Acton's principal raw materials. Price increases were expected to increase Acton's costs by about $3\frac{1}{2}\%$, so the firm decided to seek approval from the Government for price increases in the home market of 9%. However, Acton soon had second thoughts. Although devaluation put its competitors at a disadvantage, reducing their foreign currency receipts at current sterling prices, Acton felt that a 9% rise in its UK prices might lead to increased imports. In addition, the cost figures turned out to be over-estimates. Acton therefore asked for a price increase in the UK of only 6%. In export markets, however, Acton decided to try to increase its sterling prices by the full amount of devaluation, maintaining the foreign currency-prices of its exports where it could.

The only exceptions to this were Denmark and Ireland. Since Denmark had devalued by 7%, local currency-prices there were increased slightly, to compensate Acton for the supposed $3\frac{1}{2}\%$ increase in sterling costs. Ireland had also devalued by the same amount as the UK and it was thought necessary to recover some of Acton's extra production costs from its Irish customers. Since one of Acton's biggest export customers was based in Ireland, it was thought wise to negotiate with him. It was finally agreed that Acton's sterling price to Ireland would be slightly increased.

As it turned out, all Acton's other overseas customers insisted on negotiating new prices. The result was that the overall increase in Acton's sterling price was not 17%, but between 8 and 10%. Customers insisted on lower prices, pointing out that while prices charged by firms in countries like Germany had not altered, Germany had not devalued Britain had, so that British firms should give some of the benefits of devaluation to their customers.

(c) *Ealing Electrical Appliances*

In Ealing Electrical Appliances, the devaluation decisions were taken by a Special Board Meeting on Sunday 19 November. A further (regular) Board Meeting was held on Thursday 23 November. The main decisions on export pricing were taken on the Sunday, clarified on the Monday and Tuesday, and approved at the Board Meeting on the Thursday. The decisions, set out in detail in the case study, may be summarised as follows. First, for countries which had not devalued, Ealing's sterling export prices were to be increased by $4\frac{1}{2}\%$; or by $6\frac{1}{2}\%$ if the country was one where the export rebate had previously been received. Second, in countries which had devalued, but by less than the UK, sterling prices were to be increased by $6\frac{1}{2}\%$. Third, for countries which had devalued by the same amount as the UK, there was no decision at the time. Half way through 1968, sterling prices for these countries were also increased by $6\frac{1}{2}\%$. Fourth, there was to be a temporary surcharge of $6\frac{1}{2}\%$ on prices of spare parts. Fifth, the prices of all extras supplied when the caravan was originally bought were increased, by an average of 5%, in all countries where there had been no devaluation. No change was made in prices within the UK until the middle of 1968.

What Ealing did was to increase the sterling prices in countries which had *not* devalued by the expected increase in costs, thus making the maximum possible reductions in foreign-currency prices.

The main marketing information used at the meeting was Ealing's forecasts of export sales for the period to October 1968. They showed that overseas dealers' stocks had been run down, while they were waiting for new models. Ealing therefore knew that it was likely to be short of production capacity as overseas dealers' stocks were built up again. If the cuts in foreign-currency prices did stimulate sales, they could not increase output for some months.

As for costs, once the accountant, who was on the Board, had given his rough calculations of the effects of devaluation, it was quickly agreed that his cost figures would be used as the basis for the devaluation decisions. However, those at the meeting thought that it would be too difficult to make a different price change in each overseas market. Similarly, exactly the same sterling price increases were made for the USA as for other countries that had not devalued, although Ealing's competitive position there was strong. For EFTA countries, although the export rebate on sales to these countries had been lost some months earlier, the meeting felt able only to recover the increases in costs resulting from devaluation itself.

(d) *Oxford Furnaces*

Devaluation took Oxford Furnaces by surprise. As a result of listening to broadcasts by leading politicians and industrialists over the devaluation weekend, there was general agreement among Oxford's senior managers that the right reaction to devaluation would be to cut export prices by as much as possible in order to increase export volume. Indeed, there was a feeling that Oxford should be prepared to absorb some of the extra costs resulting from devaluation, in the national interest.

Proposals for reacting to devaluation were worked out over the weekend by the deputy chief executive. He calculated its effects on total costs on Sunday 19 November, and drafted and circulated a memorandum setting out his proposals on the next morning. The marketing manager and divisional cost accountant were not consulted until later. These calculations and proposals were widely discussed during the next few days by the chief executive and senior managers in Oxford Furnaces. There was no special meeting about devaluation, but managers were approached informally as and when they were available.

After looking at the big contracts it was negotiating, Oxford decided to follow two strategies. When tendering for business against foreign competition, the aim would be to reduce foreign-currency prices by half the net amount of devaluation. Where competitors were mainly British, and also in the Far East, prices would be reduced by the net amount of devaluation. This decision was taken despite the fact that, earlier in the week, the deputy chief executive had telephoned Oxford's main British competitors, and found them very reluctant to cut the foreign-currency prices of exports.

By the end of the week, under pressure from the majority of managers, who took the view that in the national interest foreign-currency prices ought to be reduced as far as possible, this decision had been changed. The final decision was to increase the sterling prices of all products in all markets, including the UK, by 5%, cutting foreign-currency prices by approximately 9%. Since the cost estimates made by the deputy chief executive showed that devaluation would raise the total costs of exports by about 7·5%, this implied that exports would bring in about 2½% less sterling than before devaluation.

Oxford's reaction was described to us by its next managing director as a case of 'devaluation hysteria'. It resulted from the strong feeling, already mentioned, that Oxford Furnaces' patriotic duty was to reduce export prices by the net amount of devaluation, or even more. So, the initial decision to charge different prices was altered.

The need to reduce the amount of spare capacity that Oxford currently had was one factor leading to its decision, but making maximum price cuts was not necessarily the best way of doing this. Having a good deal of spare capacity, Oxford was already in a strong competitive position over export business.

A few weeks later, Oxford's British competitors announced that they would raise their sterling prices by the full amount of devaluation. This led to an outcry from their overseas customers, and much of the announced increase was then cancelled. Oxford saw this incident as confirming its own decision on export prices. However, it is likely that the other British firms would not have been forced to cancel so much of their intended increases in sterling export prices had overseas customers not been able to quote Oxford's own decision. They took this as implying that there was no need to raise sterling export prices by more than 5%.

Oxford's decision is surprising because the firm told us that both before and after devaluation it had been opposed to cuts in sterling prices in the UK and in foreign-currency prices overseas. Indeed, before devaluation, price cutting was seen as a 'last resort', with Oxford taking work as a sub-contractor, in slack times, rather than cut prices. The speed, extent and uniformity of its price cuts after devaluation are perhaps best explained as the result of a temporary change in attitudes caused by the shock of devaluation.

7.4.3   THE RESULTS

(a) *Acton Chemicals*

In Acton Chemicals, home sales in 1968 expanded by 21%, compared with a 3% rise in 1967. Exports increased by 39%, but Acton found it difficult to say how much of this increase was due to devaluation. More than half of the increase represented sales to Acton's two biggest overseas customers, and Acton inclined to the view that they would probably have increased their purchases in any case. What is clear is that Acton's sterling export prices did not benefit much.

Before devaluation, Acton had estimated that during 1968 its average prices in the UK would be 4% lower than in 1967. By the end of 1968, UK prices were actually $2\frac{1}{2}$% higher on average than a year before, although this was a smaller increase than the expected rise in costs. As we have seen, the attempt to increase sterling export prices was unsuccessful. The average increase in sterling export prices was only $3\frac{1}{2}$% in 1968. There was a fall in foreign-currency prices of about 11%. Perhaps the most important effect of devaluation was to reinforce Acton's decision to remain a permanent exporter, if only on a small scale.

(b) *Ealing Electrical Appliances*

Ealing Electrical Appliances increased its exports by about 30% in each of the two years after devaluation. However, the full impact of devaluation on exports was not felt until March 1968. A marked increase in home market demand in early 1968, as consumers anticipated the 1968 budget, restricted the number of caravans available for export. Even so, over the two years, restrictive economic policies in the UK, designed to switch resources to exporting, led Ealing to do just this.

While Ealing was certain that the increase in its exports was mainly a result of devaluation, its profit margins improved only slightly. With sales to the more-profitable home market falling and with only a 3% increase in home market prices in June 1968, Ealing's cash flow worsened.

(c) *Hertford Stoves*

Hertford felt that its devaluation decisions were good ones. In most of the world, they did appear to maximise contribution. However, though it had no regrets over its decision in the USA, Hertford's position there deteriorated shortly after devaluation because of restrictions on credit. Instead of doubling, 'contribution' from the USA halved in the financial year ended March 1969. However, the corollary was that Hertford was very satisfied with its decision to hold dollar prices. This decision brought in approximately £750,000 more sterling than would have been earned had there been no devaluation.

(d) *Oxford Furnaces*

The amount of business that Oxford obtained in the UK more than doubled in 1968–69, and its exports quadrupled, because Oxford was actively seeking business in markets which it had previously treated as too unprofitable. Most of the big increase in export orders came from Canada, where Oxford was well placed, because it had finished establishing an export selling company just before devaluation.

However, Oxford was little more profitable; some of the extra export business seems to have been taken at little more than marginal cost. While the reduction of foreign-currency prices by 9% at the time of devaluation was probably too big, because Oxford's exports were not sensitive to price changes, by announcing that it would reduce its prices as far as possible, Oxford limited its bargaining power.

Oxford seems to have drawn the correct conclusion. In discussions at the time of a scare over a possible further devaluation in 1969, the conclusion was that, if sterling were devalued again, Oxford would make only marginal reductions in its foreign-currency prices.

7.4.4 COMMENTS ON THE DECISIONS

Acton Chemicals had based its devaluation decisions on the detailed report on export strategy, drawn up a month before devaluation, although this had not taken the possibility of devaluation into account. The report had considered using price cuts as a way of increasing exports, but had concluded that cutting prices in overseas markets would only provoke retaliation from foreign competitors. When devaluation took place, Acton felt that these considerations still held and its decision to try to maintain foreign-currency prices was almost automatic. Indeed, at the devaluation meeting, it was assumed that everyone had so recently been considering the report on export strategy that they understood the relevant market factors. The meeting therefore concentrated on the effect of devaluation on costs.

Acton Chemicals took few risks. Because it tried initially to maintain foreign-currency prices, it left itself with considerable flexibility. In any case, Acton's production capacity was limited while it was modernising its production plant, so there was every reason to make the smallest possible price cuts.

As for Ealing Electrical Appliances, its devaluation meeting was notable because it was held on the Sunday after devaluation. As a result, information from filing cabinets was not available. Ealing's Board had to rely entirely on their experience and judgement, in the absence of any documents. Ealing Electrical Appliances may have taken some risk in deciding to cut its prices by the maximum possible amount, while making no careful calculations of the likely effect on sales.

In the whole of the discussion at the Sunday meeting, it was implicitly assumed that there was no practicable alternative to reducing foreign-currency prices by the maximum amount that the expected increase in UK costs would allow. No allowance was made for the possibility that this might lead to a price war with foreign manufacturers, even in Europe where price competition was keenest. The alternative of reducing foreign exchange prices in Europe by a smaller percentage was not seriously considered. Nor, as we have seen, was it thought worth making any other distinction between different markets in deciding what price to charge.

Hertford Stoves had made detailed analyses of individual markets, as well as rough estimates of price/sales-volume relationships. The firm was a model of good decision-taking. It made its decisions at leisure and in advance, while drawing up the contingency plan, and so could look at all relevant factors. It worked entirely in terms of contribution.

In Oxford Furnaces, the problem was not so much the decisions, which were basically worked out by the deputy chief executive, but whether the objectives pursued were sensible. Unlike the decisions, which were essentially formulated by one man, the discussion about objectives seems to have involved a good deal of argument within the whole senior management team. The decisions not only seem to have lost profit for Oxford Furnaces, they also seem to have reduced prices available to the whole industry on exports from the UK. Given Oxford's view of its objectives, the decisions followed naturally. However, one wonders whether the objectives were sensible—a view which Oxford itself now appears to share.

7.5   Postponed Group Decisions

7.5.1   ORGANISATIONAL ARRANGEMENTS

Three of our firms are in this category: Inverness Plant Builders, Jarrow Furniture and Quantox Construction. All postponed their decisions until they could obtain extra information. In addition, they made separate decisions, either for each market or for each contract. With Inverness Plant Builders and Quantox Construction this was inevitable, because they had to tender separately for each contract.

7.5.2   THE DECISIONS

(a) *Inverness Plant Builders*

Inverness Plant Builders had no contingency plan for devaluation. It was in a difficult position because most of its foreign contracts were negotiated at fixed sterling prices and included contingency clauses against exchange rate changes, so that, in most cases, the devaluation of sterling automatically resulted in reduced foreign-currency prices. While contracts with the USA were normally negotiated at fixed dollar prices, so that devaluation did give a windfall gain, there was no possibility of any gain with most of the contracts outstanding in November 1967.

Some weeks before devaluation, Inverness's sales manager had informal discussions with his senior colleagues about how overseas competitors were likely to react if Britain devalued, and how these competitors were likely to expect Inverness itself to behave if there were a devaluation. The conclusion was that the foreign competitors would probably match any reduction in foreign-currency prices that Inverness was able to make, unless the devaluation was very large, say, 25 %. It was also feared that if Britain devalued some of Inverness's foreign competitors might take the initiative and reduce their own tender prices in anticipation of reductions by Inverness. Inverness did not attempt a similar assessment of the reactions of its British competitors to a devaluation, seeing them as likely to do exactly what it did itself.

Devaluation had therefore been discussed to some extent in advance, so that the devaluation decisions were made informally by the sales manager, who consulted his subordinates at regular management meetings. Hurried calculations, later confirmed, suggested that total costs would increase by around 7% as a result of devaluation. This gave the sales manager an estimate of the maximum reduction in foreign-currency prices that he could make. However, in view of the earlier discussions, he saw no point in making any price reduction. Accordingly, for all outstanding contracts, it was decided that Inverness would try to increase its sterling prices by at least $7\frac{1}{2}\%$.

Each outstanding tender was re-examined to see whether its probability of being accepted would be increased by raising its sterling price by only $7\frac{1}{2}\%$, in order to cover only the estimated increase in costs. In most cases, the conclusion was that this would simply lead to retaliatory cuts by foreign competitors. Only in one case did such an 8% reduction in the foreign-currency price seem likely to make any difference. This was a contract being negotiated in New Zealand against Italian competition. Inverness offered a small price reduction and the Italian competitors felt unable to match its new price. In view of this success, Inverness's sales manager told his salesmen to be more active in looking for business in marginal export markets. However, the sales manager suspended Inverness's usual process of delegating tendering for three months after devaluation because he felt that the situation was too fluid for delegation to be safe.

(b) *Jarrow Furniture*

Jarrow Furniture's devaluation decisions are set out in detail in the case study and are rather complicated. Because Jarrow felt it necessary to collect more information, its devaluation decisions were not finally taken until almost two weeks after devaluation. There were three stages. First, a 'basic principle' was defined which was 'to be followed in export pricing ... unless there is good reason for acting otherwise'. This principle was that foreign-currency prices should not be reduced. In the second stage, Jarrow Furniture worked out which were 'special situation' markets where price reductions were necessary. Third, decisions were taken for these 'special situation' markets.

The 'basic principle' was agreed by the chairman, the director of resources and planning and Jarrow's export managers on Monday 20 November. It was then set out in the pricing policy document, dated 4 December 1967.

The second stage was a meeting held on 27 November. This was attended by all who had attended the meeting on 20 November and by other senior executives. At this meeting, every country was formally classified as either 'special' or standard. In the third stage, a week later, the decisions were taken by the chairman and the financial and export managers.

The decisions were as follows: First, Jarrow reduced its dollar prices in the USA by 4·5% from the level they *would have* reached in January 1968, had a planned price increase of about $1\frac{1}{2}\%$ been made. Second, Jarrow raised its sterling prices by 8% for all European markets. Third, Jarrow left its sterling prices unchanged for all countries which had devalued. Fourth, sterling prices were increased by $12\frac{1}{2}\%$ in Canada, as well as in a large number of other countries, each of which was a rather insignificant market in itself. Fifth, in the UK it was decided to make no price increases for at least six months.

The only reason why prices were reduced slightly in the USA was 'almost a price reduction hysteria' in the USA, caused by the American press. Since Jarrow had already trebled the promotional budget for the USA, it decided that the smallest possible price reductions should be made, in order to increase profits. It sought an increase in sales as a result of the increase in the promotional budget, with the cut in price of only marginal significance.

In Canada, Jarrow's objective was also to persuade its agents to allow sterling prices to increase by at least enough to cover those increases in Jarrow's costs which were the result of devaluation. The $12\frac{1}{2}\%$ increase actually made was easier to introduce than it would have been in the USA, because the Canadian press had conditioned the Canadian public to expect British costs, and therefore sterling prices, to increase.

In Europe, Jarrow's sales were largely of furniture for assembly. The choice of 8% for the increase in sterling prices in all European markets (except Denmark which had devalued by 7%) was somewhat arbitrary and was based on a notion of 'splitting the difference' over the benefits of devaluation. It was not until much later that any estimate was made of the likely effect of this price change on sales. It was vaguely felt that because price competition was particularly severe in Europe, price might be a more important marketing variable than elsewhere, but no-one considered the possibility that Jarrow's European competitors might retaliate to a cut in sterling prices. In the countries which had devalued, the decision to maintain sterling prices resulted from Jarrow's lack of competitiveness there. The possibility of making price increases, just big enough to offset the increase in costs, on exports to countries which had devalued by smaller percentages than the UK, does not seem to have been looked at in detail.

In most of Jarrow's remaining markets, prices had been increased by a small percentage in October 1967. Jarrow felt that if there was no reduction in local-currency prices there, so shortly after this increase, customer resentment might reduce future sales, but there was no attempt to predict the size of such effects. In the few remaining markets where no price increase had been made in October, there did not seem to be much to be gained from price reductions; Jarrow held a very dominant position.

As for the UK, Jarrow believed that the deflationary measures introduced by the Government at the time of devaluation were likely to depress sales, and that this decline could only be accelerated if it made substantial price increases. At the same time, devaluation gave Jarrow a major advantage over the foreign suppliers of some accessories which it made and sold to customers to add to their furniture, and this advantage seemed worth preserving, at least until the situation could be studied more fully.

(c) *Quantox Construction*

In Quantox Construction, it was not easy to find a direct connection between the general principles on which its devaluation decisions were based and the tender prices it finally submitted. However, we did study two tenders submitted soon after devaluation.

With the first, the immediate reaction of Quantox's European competitors to Britain's devaluation was to reduce the prices they were quoting by between 10 and 15% in the customer's local currency. They feared that, with devaluation, Quantox would be able to reduce its tender prices by this percentage. Since Quantox had previously been given an order with similar specifications by the same customer, it believed that it would obtain this contract, even at a rather higher price. Initially, then, Quantox made only a marginal reduction in its tender price. Later, Quantox decided to reduce its foreign-currency price to 10% below the level it had been quoting before devaluation, but no more. The result was that a big European firm took the contract. In retrospect, Quantox saw this as perhaps a blessing in disguise. The competitor was now so busy that it was difficult for him to take further business and he became much less active in seeking new contracts. As the market improved, Quantox later obtained business at much more attractive prices. Although Quantox did not see any clear relationship between devaluation and its ability to obtain this business, we feel confident that devaluation did help.

The other order we studied was one where Quantox was prepared to make a short-term sacrifice in order to obtain the contract, because it was for one of a new generation of plants in whose construction Quantox was anxious to build up experience. Quantox therefore carefully studied the marginal cost of producing this plant, distinguishing between 'key' and 'non-key' workers in order to charge the minimum possible price. 'Key' workers were those which Quantox was determined to keep on, for a time at least, even if the contract was not obtained, and whose wages and salaries could therefore be regarded as fixed costs. In this case, Quantox did obtain the contract and felt its action fully justified. In particular, the same customer later placed another order at a much better price. Quantox did not doubt that the experience it gained in supplying the original plant gave it a decisive competitive advantage for taking the later business. Devaluation may well have helped it in obtaining the first contract.

7.5.3 THE RESULTS

(a) Inverness Plant Builders

In 1967–68, the performance of Inverness Plant Builders was disappointing. Home orders fell by more than 20%, and export orders by 59%—a drop in total orders of about 43%.

The fall in home demand was largely a result of the deflationary measures with which the British Government supported devaluation. Looking back, the sales manager felt that his firm had not been aggressive enough in its export pricing because it had feared bringing about competitive price cutting. Inverness hoped that the high level of orders recently obtained in the USA would continue. Indeed, to be more certain of obtaining this business, Inverness held back its sales effort in less-profitable markets. While this left Inverness with enough spare capacity to offer early delivery dates to the American customer, he also reduced the amount of business he was offering.

(b) Jarrow Furniture

In Jarrow Furniture, profits in the year ending July 1968 were more than three times as big as in the previous year. About 30% of this increase represented a once-for-all gain from the conversion of money balances Jarrow held abroad at the time of devaluation and of foreign currency owed to Jarrow by its customers. In general, Jarrow thought that its decisions had satisfactory effects on its volume of sales. Total exports rose by $2\frac{1}{2}$%. However, Jarrow did not feel able to give credit for much of the increase to the price cuts made at the time of devaluation.

In the USA, the extra sales volume and sterling profits aimed at in the devaluation decisions materialised, but the small reduction in prices had 'no effect at all' on sales. Similarly, while Jarrow achieved a 37% rise in its sales in Canada in 1968, its new marketing policy may well have had the main effect on sales.

In Europe, the results were rather disappointing. The 7·5% cut in foreign-currency prices was accompanied by an increase in sales volume of only 2–3%, partly because there were retaliatory price cuts by competitors. In other export markets, Jarrow's experience was varied, but there was an overall fall of 10% in its sales volume.

(c) *Quantox Construction*

As for Quantox Construction, we have already seen that the nature of its activities was such that no-one could see the effect of an event like devaluation quickly. However, the way that its main European competitor behaved meant that it took business at unprofitable prices. This increased the length of its order book and probably helped Quantox to take business at more profitable prices later.

7.5.4   COMMENTS ON THE DECISIONS

In all these firms the first meeting to discuss devaluation was held on Monday 20 November. In general, they decided to make the minimum possible reductions in foreign-currency prices.

Most of the outstanding contracts of Inverness Plant Builders and Quantox Construction were covered by exchange rate clauses which made it virtually impossible for them to increase sterling prices to their export customers, even to the extent required to cover the effect of devaluation on their sterling costs. For tenders not yet accepted, detailed cost calculations led the firms to reduce their prices only marginally. In doing this, they were influenced as much by the fear of competitive retaliation as by a wish to maintain profit margins. As we have seen, with one very large contract, the European competitors of Quantox Construction took the initiative and cut their own prices substantially. On the other hand, the marginal reductions in price that Jarrow Furniture made in North America reflected the need to avoid retaliation by customers or competitors. In Europe, where competitors did retaliate, Jarrow's prices were cut, but export sales increased only marginally, although there was at least a recovery in sales of completed furniture.

Since there was this competitive retaliation in Europe, one wonders whether Jarrow should have made smaller price reductions, in at least some countries, in the hope of avoiding retaliation.

All three firms examined each market separately. None could afford to make a serious mistake, since no firm's financial position was satisfactory. For Jarrow Furniture, the immediate effect of devaluation, in increasing sterling profits in 1968 from the conversion of foreign-currency balances and debts outstanding, was very important.

7.6 The Basic Material Firms

7.6.1 ORGANISATIONAL ARRANGEMENTS

This group contains three firms, namely: Fulham Castings, Rugby Processing and Tottenham Piping. As we shall see, for various reasons, they all decided on their prices after devaluation in a largely automatic way.

7.6.2 THE DECISIONS

(a) *Fulham Castings*
In Fulham Castings, a document written in July 1966 had explained what action was to be taken if the pound were devalued. All export contracts should be quoted in US dollars except, in some cases, for the freight component. This recommendation was put into effect soon afterwards.

There was therefore no decision to be taken at the time of devaluation for contracts with countries which had not devalued. The marketing director simply checked that all contracts were adequately protected. For countries that had also devalued, the appropriate product group manager was asked to increase the price charged in order to recover the increase in Fulham's import costs. Because of Government pressure, an increase in Fulham Castings' home market price was postponed for several months. The increase then made was very small.

(b) *Rugby Processing*
The Board of Rugby Processing decided to take the biggest possible sterling profit if there were a devaluation. No explicit instructions were given to anyone; top management saw devaluation as a purely operational matter.

As a result, when it did happen, there was no special meeting to discuss devaluation; and no detailed instructions were given to the export sales manager. He simply continued to use Rugby's existing foreign-currency price list as the basis for all price negotiations. He sought no more market information than he already had.

While Rugby sought to leave foreign-currency prices unchanged, after detailed negotiations with its customers Rugby had to be satisfied with smaller sterling price increases. Rugby was able to increase sterling prices by only about 12%.

(c) *Tottenham Piping*

The detailed devaluation decisions are set out in the case study. As we have seen, export prices of the processed raw material (Product M) were automatically adjusted for changes in the prices of imported raw materials, by changing the variable element in price. To this extent, no further action was called for. Prices to customers, in countries that had devalued, automatically rose by the amount of devaluation. The other component in price was intended to cover Tottenham Piping's own costs. Its size was discovered by looking at Tottenham's price list and allowing for appropriate extras. However, since early in 1966, each price had effectively been set in discussion with the individual customer.

When devaluation occurred, some orders for Product M had been taken at fixed sterling prices. With the large amount of imported raw material it contained, the result of devaluation was to increase sterling costs substantially without any corresponding increase in sterling prices. This was why the meeting on Monday 20 November decided that the suppliers of the raw material, with whom Tottenham had excellent relations, could perhaps be persuaded 'in their own long-term interests' to make concessions 'to help the company out'.

With Products A and B, there was no immediate decision on prices. Because the Product M they contained made up a large percentage of their cost, and because the part of price reflecting the price of M was automatically adjusted, their prices fluctuated with changes in the balance between supply and demand for Product M in world markets. For Tottenham Piping's purposes, it was unnecessary to separate out the effects of devaluation on the price of Product M, and probably impossible. The right time to change the other elements in the prices of Products A and B would be when, for whatever reason, there appeared to have been a permanent rise in the price of Product M.

With Product C, Tottenham Piping took the view that, since the raw material costs of this product were little affected by devaluation, and since there was no reason to suppose that devaluation would quickly have much effect on the price of labour, there was no obvious reason for increasing sterling prices. The decision after devaluation therefore centred on whether the marketing advantage that Tottenham Piping would get from keeping the sterling price of Product C constant would lead to greater profit, in the longer run, as a result of increased sales, than holding local-currency prices constant and earning an increased amount of sterling. This, in turn, depended on how far reducing foreign-currency prices would increase sales of Product C. After some discussion, it was decided that holding sterling prices constant would be the best course. It was thought that the local-currency price reductions which this would allow would lead to a significant increase in sales. A further factor was that, in November 1967, significant productivity increases were being obtained in the production of Product C.

7.6.3 THE RESULTS

(a) *Fulham Castings*
Since there was a world price for Fulham Castings' product, the only possible effect of devaluation would have been to switch some production from Europe to the UK, and organisational considerations ruled this out. Nevertheless, Fulham Castings believed that devaluation did allow it to be marginally more competitive. The main effect of devaluation on Fulham was to improve its liquidity. All funds remitted by overseas subsidiaries, from countries that had not devalued, now increased in sterling terms.

(b) *Rugby Processing*
In Rugby Processing, the year ended March 1968 saw exports rise by 37% in volume and by 46% in value, though the home market remained stagnant. Almost all the extra exports went to Europe. In the year ended March 1969, there was a further increase of 13% in the volume of exports. The year ending March 1969 was also good for the home market, with an increase in sales volume of 20%.

Rugby Processing saw devaluation as a painless way of restoring its profit margins, and profit did increase. Rugby felt that devaluation emphasised how important it had been to treat Europe as an extension, though up to this point a relatively small extension, of its home market. It was therefore happy with the decisions it took at the time of devaluation.

(c) *Tottenham Piping*
Tottenham Piping believed that the only identifiable effect that devaluation had on its operations was to increase costs. It seriously under-estimated the effect that devaluation would have on labour

costs for all products. Wage rates rose sharply during 1968. Because Tottenham Piping devoted so much of its capacity to producing the raw material and because the prices of Products A and B depended on the price of that material, it could see no clear marketing advantage there from devaluation. For Product C, where foreign-currency prices were reduced by the full amount of devaluation, Tottenham Piping did not feel able to judge the effects of its devaluation decisions.

7.6.4   COMMENTS ON THE DECISIONS

As we have seen, Fulham Castings perhaps demonstrated the extreme case of 'non-decision'. There was a world price for its product, and therefore no point in making a unilateral price reduction. This would either have lost profit for Fulham Castings, or would simply have set off a general price war without increasing Fulham's sales significantly. Because its policy for dealing with devaluation had been worked out more than a year earlier, there was no devaluation meeting. Also, because of the earlier decisions, prices were now quoted in dollars.

Similarly, in Rugby Processing, the Board had discussed the possibility of devaluation informally several months before it happened. Rugby had agreed that there would be little point in reducing foreign-currency prices, partly because of the danger that competitors would retaliate, partly because Rugby's prices were already competitive and partly because it had little spare capacity. No Board Minute was issued, because the devaluation decisions were seen to be operational matters, to be dealt with by the export sales manager, who was assumed to be aware of all the relevant facts. After devaluation, the export sales manager issued no special instructions on pricing to subordinates and made no special report to his superiors.

In Tottenham Piping, the important question for Products M, A and B was how big a mark-up to add to the cost of raw material, which fluctuated from day to day on the world market. Value added represented a small proportion of price. It could have been argued that a small increase in price to cover it was unlikely to have a significant effect on Tottenham's sales. Despite this, there was no attempt to increase the mark-up, not even by the amount of devaluation. It was calculated in the same way as before devaluation, even though the reduction in the foreign-currency price that this gave was so small that it was unlikely to give Tottenham a noticeable marketing advantage. For Product C, where the mark-up represented a larger proportion of price, the decision to reduce the foreign-currency price was made after careful consideration of the long-term marketing advantages of doing so.

Tottenham's price negotiators were given no specific set of rules about how big the permitted reductions in sterling price after devaluation could be. Tottenham Piping also told us that no *general* decision had been taken about how to set export prices. What seems to have happened is that those responsible for negotiating prices with overseas customers did their best to increase sterling prices. We are rather puzzled by this, since it appears to suggest that a general rule *was* being applied, despite Tottenham Piping's denial that there was one.

CHAPTER 8

The Findings

In this chapter we comment on the case studies.

8.1 Speed of Decision-taking

In general, we think that the decisions that were taken relatively slowly, say over a week or two rather than over a day or two, were better decisions. For example, Ealing Electrical Appliances would almost certainly have benefitted from waiting until at least 20 November when the filing cabinets with cost information in them would have been open. Of course, the firms with contingency plans had the best of both worlds. They were able to take their decisions at leisure and yet to put them into effect immediately after devaluation. It certainly seems that, where a firm wishes to take a different decision for each individual market, a period of at least two weeks is necessary for good devaluation decisions. It may take longer if the firm wishes to consult its foreign agents.

8.2 Organisational Arrangements

In this study, there was no clear evidence that organisational arrangements of one kind were superior to others for taking the devaluation decisions. In most firms, the decisions were taken either by one man or by a small group of people. The decisions were fairly straightforward, in the sense that almost all of them were concerned only with price. Moreover, different interests in the firm rarely participated. This study suggests that, with what the firm regarded as a rather technical decision, relatively few people became involved. With few people concerned, organisational factors did not prevent good decisions being taken. In the one case where there was confusion, this was caused by many managers taking part in deciding on the objectives which Oxford Furnaces was to follow in its devaluation decisions. Almost the whole management team was drawn into the discussions on precisely what the objective after devaluation should be, and especially whether the firm should consider the national interest rather than its own. The implication is that if more people had taken part in the decisions, in other firms, there might have been greater confusion there too.

8.3   Types of Decision

We have seen that one way of classifying our firms is by the type of decision they took. We have therefore distinguished those firms which took no action to expand exports after devaluation from those which did. The former group of firms, which left unchanged both foreign-currency prices and sterling expenditure on marketing, we have described as 'passive' exporters. The remaining firms took decisions that gave a stimulus to exports. Some cut foreign-currency prices by the full *net* amount of devaluation. Others limited the cuts they made in foreign-currency prices after devaluation, but used the extra sterling thus received to increase marketing and sales promotion expenditure, or to change the design or quality of the product. We have described these as 'active' exporters.

While we have emphasised that this distinction has been made solely for the purpose of this study, it is an important one to us because all but four of our 'firms' took one of the two extreme courses of action open to them. Once again there are twenty-one 'firms' with Tottenham and Peterborough each counted twice. Of the other seventeen 'firms', about half left foreign-currency prices unchanged and about half cut them by the full (usually net) amount of devaluation. Two of the four 'firms' described as exceptions used some proportion of the sterling profit the firm obtained, by limiting cuts in foreign-currency prices, to increase marketing expenditure in some way.

Our classification is given in Table 8.1, though all the firms in any cell did not display exactly the same characteristics. The interesting fact that Table 8.1 reveals is that all five firms we have classified as 'anti-cyclical' exporters took 'active' decisions. The 'regular' exporters were about equally divided between seven 'active' and nine 'passive' firms, although all nine firms which were 'passive' were regular exporters.

In other words, all nine 'passive' firms were regular exporters. And all the anti-cyclical exporters were 'active', though seven regular exporters also took 'active' decisions. Why did we get this pattern?

8.3.1   ANTI-CYCLICAL EXPORTERS

As we saw in Chapter 3, all five anti-cyclical exporters were selling in depressed home markets; they were at the stage in the cycle

TABLE 8.1

Type of firm	Type of decision	
	Passive decisions	Active decisions
Anti-cyclical exporters	—	Durham Plates Ealing Electrical Appliances Inverness Plant Builders Kendal Accessories Quantox Construction
Regular exporters	Acton Chemicals Fulham Castings Gatley Hosiery* Hertford Stoves Jarrow Furniture Nottingham Confectionery Peterborough Tubes (X-ply) Rugby Processing Tottenham Piping (Products M, A and B)	Birmingham Cakes Cardiff Instruments Oxford Furnaces London Switches Peterborough Tubes (Product D) Tottenham Piping (Product C) Stratford Equipment

*Gatley Hosiery is included among the 'passive' firms, despite the fact that it cut its foreign-currency price immediately. It did so only on the current season's product and raised foreign-currency prices for the next season's range to pre-devaluation levels.

where they were anxious to export. Ealing and Inverness, in particular, were finding that their low sales volumes were leading to high unit costs, because overheads could not be spread over big enough outputs. Devaluation offered them the chance to expand their sales volumes and so to achieve the economies of scale needed if they were to reduce costs and earn acceptable (or in Ealing's case minimal) profits at the prices being received in the UK and overseas. However, while Ealing Electrical Appliances went almost to the limit in its 'active' policy, Inverness Plant Builders was more cautious. It continued to charge the highest foreign-currency prices it could for each of its tenders. What Inverness was now prepared to do was to tender seriously, though at prices that gave little contribution, for business which before devaluation it would have seen as 'unprofitable'.

To include Kendal Accessories among the 'active' decision takers is somewhat misleading. Its immediate reaction to devaluation was an attempt to leave its foreign currency prices unchanged—

to adopt a 'wait and see' attitude. We have seen that this was not acceptable to its cartel, whose members feared losing sales to foreign competitors, especially in countries like Hong Kong and New Zealand, more than they hoped for higher profits. Kendal Accessories ultimately accepted the cartel's view and made significant foreign-currency price reductions in most of its markets, hoping that this would reduce its spare capacity. However, Kendal Accessories would have preferred to make smaller reductions in prices, if the cartel had agreed.

The decision of Durham Plates for Product A were also taken by its cartel, though here sales expansion was put before profits. The cartel thought that it should take the national interest into account and its members believed that the government's objective was to increase the volume of exports, rather than export turnover or profitability. However, the price cuts that Durham Plates made for Product B resulted from an independent decision to go for increased sales, based on its convention that the price for Product B in overseas markets had always been the same as in the UK.

8.3.2 'ACTIVE' REGULAR EXPORTERS

Among the seven 'active' regular exporters, Cardiff Instruments reduced export prices, not so much to increase export sales, as to prevent competition, especially for its cheaper HEMS, from actually reducing exports. Tottenham Piping (for Products M, A & B) reduced its prices somewhat, almost automatically, but because it held constant the sterling mark-up which it charged to cover the costs it incurred in producing the products. Its main raw material represented Tottenham's biggest cost and this material had a dollar price, determined in a world market. Both companies went to the limit in pursuing an 'active' policy, because both aimed at increasing exports as much as possible, provided only that a desired rate of profit was earned. Oxford Furnaces, on the other hand, deliberately decided to treat devaluation as providing an opportunity to increase sales volume rather than profits. Its decision was affected by the uncomfortably large amount of spare capacity it had. However, we have seen that its management also believed, after listening to the first reactions to devaluation by businessmen and politicians in the press and on radio and tele-vision, that a major objective of devaluation was to secure sub-stantially lower foreign-currency export prices.

Similarly, Stratford Equipment felt that it would be 'wrong' to earn too much profit from devaluation, despite the fact that its sales were out-running its available production capacity. Even so,

Stratford Equipment did take the opportunity to improve its profit margins somewhat. London Switches also increased its profit margins to some extent, but by less than it would have done if its principal competitor had taken the same view as itself.

Birmingham Cakes is perhaps the best example of a firm which tried to use devaluation both to increase its sales in the short-term and to improve its long-term market position. Nevertheless, it did take the opportunity to improve its short-run profit margins somewhat.

8.3.3 'PASSIVE' REGULAR EXPORTERS

We now turn to the nine 'passive' regular exporters. Fulham Castings was forced to charge the world price, set in dollars, for its basic raw material. Had it made any price cuts, these would probably have simply lowered the world price without giving Fulham Castings a compensating increase in sales. Its decision to adopt a passive policy after devaluation was almost automatic. Because its profit margins were under pressure at the time of devaluation, Fulham gratefully accepted the opportunity to take bigger sterling profits from its existing volume of sales. However, it would perhaps not have dared to reduce export prices in any circumstances, because that would have risked retaliation by competitors.

Profit margins in Peterborough Tubes were also under pressure, but sales of X-ply, at least, were rising rapidly. It therefore seemed sensible to Peterborough to use the fact that it was a monopllist for X-ply within Europe to avoid making any reduction in its foreign-currency prices. Even though Peterborough had to make some price reductions for Product D, its sterling profit margins were bigger after devaluation. More than this, Peterborough believed that any profit which mght have been lost because of these foreign-currency price cuts could be recouped on repeat orders.

Gatley Hosiery, outside the USSR, was in a similar position. It tried to keep the goodwill of its customers immediately after devaluation by 'splitting the difference' with them on the export prices of its existing product range. Yet Gatley knew that the amount of business affected by the cuts was very small. Moreover, it hoped that when its new brands were introduced in a few months' time, it could benefit from the goodwill its price cuts had given it and restore foreign-currency prices to their pre-devaluation levels. It could then take the whole of the benefit of devaluation in increased sterling prices, while suffering no fall in sales volume.

The remaining 'passive' firms, Hertford Stoves, Jarrow Furniture and Rugby Processing, had all been anxious to increase profit even before devaluation. Partly because of this, before devaluation they had already taken various steps to expand sales, such as increasing expenditure on various kinds of sales promotion. At the time of devaluation, these measures were successfully increasing exports. It therefore seemed desirable to continue them in order to maintain, or increase, sales volume, but simultaneously to maintain foreign-currency prices in order to make more profit.

8.3.4   SOME CONCLUSIONS

What seems to emerge from this is that the 'active' firms were anxious to use devaluation to increase sales, mainly because they were finding it difficult to keep their capacity occupied and their labour forces employed. Those that were anti-cyclical exporters did not have established export businesses, so that they were forced to take export business at relatively low prices. Devaluation made it more profitable to do this than it would have been before. The regular exporters did not need to cut prices quite so severely, though for differing reasons Oxford Furnaces, London Switches, Stratford Equipment and Tottenham Piping (Product C) did.

What of the passive firms? The regular exporters which sought increased profit on existing sales were already well established in export markets. For example, Peterborough Tubes was successfully exporting X-ply, but was anxious to earn more profit from these exports. Gatley Hosiery was in a similar position. As we have just seen, Hertford Stoves, Jarrow Furniture and Rugby Processing had all made major changes in their marketing activities before devaluation, in order to increase exports. They saw devaluation essentially as providing an opportunity to do what they had already planned to do, but much more profitably than they had dared to hope when they took their various decisions aimed at stimulating exports. We believe that the emphasis that the regular exporters put on profit stems from the fact that, simply because they *were* regular exporters, they had already been trying to increase their exports before devaluation, at a time when costs in the UK were out of line with those in the rest of the world. Perhaps they felt that they had sufficient marketing facilities, and enough expertise, to increase exports, even before devaluation, in a way that the anti-cyclical exporters did not. We have seen that some regular exporters did cut prices by varying amounts, but in several cases (especially Oxford Furnaces, London Switches and Stratford Equipment), we regard these decisions as somewhat unsatisfactory.

The fact that the regular exporters put so much emphasis on profit may simply reflect the timing of devaluation. It came after a period when the government had been deflating the British economy, for long enough to have led regular exporters to take the kinds of step we have described to increase exports, even though export profits were not very attractive.

Few of our firms adopted a policy anywhere between the two extremes of holding foreign-currency prices constant and reducing them by the maximum possible amount. One of those that did, Gatley Hosiery, simply 'split the difference' with its customers.

8.4 The Use of Agents

At an early stage in our studies, we concluded that the role of agents was an interesting one and worth looking at in more detail. Our conclusions are as follows.

For various reasons, few of our firms consulted their overseas agents, or indeed their overseas offices, before making their devaluation decisions. Of our nineteen firms, only two had detailed discussions with their overseas agents at that stage. Both of them, Birmingham Cakes and Jarrow Furniture, manufactured consumer goods. One reason why other firms did not consult their agents was that most of them saw their devaluation decisions essentially as solving limited and technical short-term marketing problems. This did not seem the occasion to re-examine their whole export strategy. It was therefore logical to pay little attention to overseas agents, or indeed to their own colleagues overseas. The expense and delay that consultation would have caused did not seem worthwhile.

Moreover, the way our firms did their business often meant that it was unnecessary to consult overseas agents or colleagues. For example, the four capital-goods manufacturers made their products to customers' specifications. When an initial enquiry had been received by their overseas agents, the firms dealt directly with their clients, through their headquarters staff. As a result, agents in these firms were less well-informed than were headquarters staff about how negotiations on outstanding tenders were proceeding in November 1967. Those at headquarters saw little point in consulting agents about what tactics to pursue over particular tenders after devaluation. Again, the basic-material firms produced identical, or nearly identical, products to those of their competitors. They also had little choice but to accept the ruling price for these products after devaluation and saw no point in consulting agents. Durham Plates and Kendal Accessories were bound to abide by the decisions of their export cartels in pricing a substantial proportion of their export business so that here, too, there was little point in consulting agents about how to respond to devaluation.

The prices the other firms charged also departed little from their price lists. For London Switches and for Stratford Equipment, the main competitor in the home market was also the main competitor overseas. The devaluation decisions resulted from negotiations with these competitors, carried out directly by their managing directors who were their main export marketers. Bringing in agents would have added little to the success of the negotiations and would almost certainly have complicated them. Stratford Equipment had not consulted its agents when drawing up its budget plan about two months before devaluation and London Switches had no budget plan at all. While it is true that Hertford Stoves did not consult its agents after devaluation, its contingency plan, completed about a month before devaluation, had taken their opinions into account. Since all that Hertford did at the time of devaluation was to put the contingency plan into effect, there was no need to consult its agents again.

In three firms, Ealing Electrical Appliances, Gatley Hosiery and Peterborough Tubes, overseas representatives and agents might have been able, if consulted, to provide it with useful information. However, none of the firms consulted agents. Ealing Electrical Appliances was anxious to take its decisions rapidly, for commercial and public relations reasons, and so did not have time to consult agents. It asked them for their views on the implications of the devaluation decisions for export sales, only after they had been put into effect. Since Gatley Hosiery's decisions affected only a few months' business before the new season's brands were introduced, it seemed less important to have more information than to take the devaluation decisions rapidly, in order to impress overseas customers with Gatley's wish to reduce prices. There were protests later from Gatley's North-American offices about the decision, but they were over-ruled by the marketing manager. Since Peterborough Tubes' X-ply was the only product of its kind in Europe, and since demand there was growing very rapidly, the decision to maintain its foreign-currency price was not difficult to take. It did not need extra information from agents. However, in other markets, the position was not so simple and Peterborough's agents might have been able to make a useful contribution.

One argument put to us by all three firms was that their agents had little idea of the level or behaviour of the firms' production costs in the UK or how these costs were likely to be affected by devaluation. The firms felt that if they consulted their overseas agents the latter would simply press for bigger reductions in foreign-currency prices than would be optimal, because this would make the agents' own selling jobs overseas easier. They would simply 'sub-optimise', doing what seemed right when viewed from their positions, well away from the centre of the firm and so of the decision-taking process.

We have seen that one or two agents did not fall into line with their firm's decisions. For example, one of Ealing Electrical Appliances' European distributors immediately reduced its foreign-currency prices by the full amount of devaluation without Ealing's approval, causing Ealing considerable embarrassment, because it was anxious to recoup as much as it could of the increase in costs in the UK which devaluation caused. Ealing therefore had to countermand the agent's decision and persuade him to put his reduced prices up by about 12%.

8.5 Contingency Planning

Obviously, the difficulty a firm has in discussing with its agents how it should respond to devaluation is much reduced if they can be consulted at leisure, when the firm is drawing up contingency plans for changes in marketing policy, before any devaluation takes place. In 1967, it had been obvious for some time, if only from reading the press, that devaluation of sterling was likely. Why did so few of our firms think it worth making contingency plans?

Undoubtedly, the best prepared of our firms was Hertford Stoves, with its detailed contingency plan which assumed a 15% devaluation. Since Hertford exported over 90% of its output to more than a hundred countries, the preparation of this plan was bound to take time and Hertford must have been well satisfied to have completed it during the summer of 1967. Fulham Castings had also taken precautionary measures, in 1966, by beginning to quote for all foreign business in dollars. Of course, Fulham was an extreme case, with its products being sold in a world market at a dollar price. Devaluation was likely to lead to little change in Fulham's direct exports, which were aimed only at meeting temporary shortages of capacity in its European plants. Hence, there was no real decision to take. All that Fulham needed to do was to continue to charge the highest dollar price it could.

We have seen that the sales manager of Inverness Plant Builders had considered with his senior colleagues, some weeks before devaluation, how Inverness's foreign competitors were likely to react to devaluation. They had also considered what assumptions these competitors were making about Inverness's own response to devaluation, as well as what assumptions the foreign competitors were making about how Inverness would respond to their own moves. While Inverness did not work out a detailed contingency plan, the meeting had agreed that, for a devaluation of less than 25%, any price cut made by Inverness was likely to be matched by its overseas competitors. Similarly, Rugby Processing's top management had decided in the summer of 1967 that it would take all possible sterling profit if there were a devaluation, though it had issued no specific instructions to its more junior managers.

Only these firms had any kind of contingency plan. What of the others ? Some argued that contingency planning was impossible because they did not know how much the pound would be devalued, or how far other countries would devalue in turn. Yet Hertford Stoves proved that it was possible both to make a very good guess and to time its contingency plan very well. Only Birmingham Cakes, which was able to take its decisions rather slowly after devaluation, looked at all its overseas markets in an equally relaxed way, though it did have only four major overseas markets. Yet firms could have planned their reactions to a range of possible amounts of devaluation, lying between the biggest and smallest that was likely. It is true that such proposals made, say, in 1965 or 1966 would have needed periodic revision, but this might have been worthwhile.

8.6 Considering Alternatives

An important factor determining how good any firm's decisions are will clearly be the ease with which it chooses between the alternative courses of action open to it. To make this section easier to read, Table 8.2 shows the types of decisions that our twenty-one 'firms' took, classified according to the organisational arrangements the firms had for dealing with devaluation. (Again Tottenham and Peterborough are counted twice.)

In general, the firms which decided to reduce their prices gave little or no attention to alternative courses of action. Yet a decision to reduce export prices always meant a greater degree of risk. There was always some uncertainty whether it would increase sales volume sufficiently to pay off. On the other hand, a decision to hold foreign-currency prices meant an increase in gross sterling

TABLE 8.2 *The decisions taken*

| | All or most markets | | | | Differential policies | |
| | Minimum price reductions | | Maximum price reductions | | | |
	Immediate	Postponed	Immediate	Postponed	Immediate	Postponed
One-man decision	Nottingham Confectionery Gatley Hosiery*	Peterborough Tubes (X-ply)	Cardiff Instruments			Birmingham Cakes Peterborough Tubes (Product D)
Decision by cartel			Durham Plates (Product A) London Switches Stratford Equipment			
Decision by collusion						Kendal Accessories
Group decision	Acton Chemicals		Ealing Electrical Appliances Oxford Furnaces	Durham Plates (Product B)	Hertford Stoves	Inverness Plant Builders Jarrow Furniture Quantox Construction
Basic material firms	Fulham Castings Rugby Processing		Tottenham Piping			

*See footnote about Gatley Hosiery on Table 8.1

receipts equal to the full amount of devaluation, except from sales in countries which had also devalued. If for some reason—like the reactions of customers or competitors—it did not, the firm was still able to cut prices later, to whatever extent seemed desirable as the situation facing it became clear. It also minimised the likelihood that competitors *would* react.

8.6.1   FIRMS MAKING MAXIMUM PRICE REDUCTIONS

Of the firms that reduced foreign-currency prices by the maximum (usually net) amount of devaluation, only London Switches could be said to have seriously considered the alternatives facing it. The course taken by the conversations with the managing director of its main rival (both at home and overseas) forced the managing director of London Switches to consider both his own alternative of keeping foreign-currency prices unchanged and his rival's suggestions for cutting them by various possible amounts. In the end, the managing director of London Switches was forced to agree to a price reduction, but only against his better judgement.

It is true that at first Oxford Furnaces tried to work out a way of making a number of different price reductions, according to the nationalities of the firms competing with it in each market. However, this was quickly abandoned in favour of the decision to reduce all prices by rather more than the net amount of devaluation. Because Oxford's management became concerned about the objectives of devaluation, and argued that it would be against the national interest for Oxford Furnaces to make 'excessive' profits out of devaluation, the possibility of pursuing a differential pricing policy was abandoned. Yet, Oxford could point to no commerical reason for its final decision to reduce prices by the same amount in every market, with the size of this reduction determined by cost, rather than demand, factors.

Durham Plates' representatives went to the cartel meeting for Product A suggesting that the cartel should pursue the pragmatic policy of making a different price cut in each market according to conditions there. This suggestion was not discussed in detail. Only the effect of devaluation on total costs was allowed for. Even Durham Plates' own pricing decision for the non-cartelised grades of Product B accepted, without considering alternatives, the established practice of charging the same price at home and overseas. In both cases, the effect of devaluation on total costs was the main factor considered.

In Cardiff Instruments and Stratford Equipment, the devaluation decisions were effectively made by one man. It is therefore difficult to determine how far alternatives were seriously considered. Our researches suggest that the decision-taker in Stratford Equipment looked mainly at the size of price reduction that was needed if Stratford's overseas agents were to be able to pass on some price reductions to their customers. The possibility of leaving foreign-currency prices unchanged, or of making different price reductions in different countries, does not seem to have been studied, despite Stratford's strong competitive position overseas.

The decision-taker in Cardiff Instruments claimed to have hit on the 'right' price intuitively, even though he did not consider either holding the foreign-currency price constant, or making a different price reduction in each market. The size of price reduction was determined simply by estimating the likely rise in costs.

The two other firms which decided to reduce their prices in all markets were Ealing Electrical Appliances and Tottenham Piping. Tottenham Piping was one of the firms where the decision was largely a matter of routine, because it was tied fairly closely to world prices. However, it is not clear that enough account was given to the possibility of increasing the amount that Tottenham Piping charged for processing its material. The effect of devaluation on raw material costs was the only factor seriously considered. In Ealing Electrical Appliances, the size of the price reduction was arrived at by looking at the effect of devaluation on costs. The possibility of making smaller price reductions in some countries was not considered, although that might have been profitable. For example, although the meeting to discuss devaluation recognised that competition in the caravan market was less keen in the USA than elsewhere, there was no serious discussion of the possibility that a smaller price reduction might be made there.

In Gatley Hosiery, the effect of devaluation on costs was not known. Outside the USSR the price was therefore set simply so as to 'split the difference', on the assumption that the marketing director's private guess at the effect of devaluation on costs was correct.

8.6.2 FIRMS MAKING MINIMUM PRICE CUTS

The need to consider alternative courses of action was obviously less urgent for the firms which decided to make no reduction, or the smallest possible reduction, in foreign-currency prices. They could lower prices later if that seemed best. However, in most cases they saw no obvious alternative course of action. For example, Fulham Castings and Tottenham Piping had little control over prices, because they sold homogeneous products in world markets. Any unilateral price reduction by them would have brought about immediate retaliation by competitors. Acton Chemicals had considered, and ruled out, alternatives to the decision to hold prices unchanged, when making its market assessment just before devaluation. There had also been pre-liminary discussions of the possible alternatives by the Board of Rugby Processing some months before devaluation. On the other hand, Peterborough Tubes did not consider any alternative policy for X-ply. Its sales were expanding rapidly at the existing price and there was no direct competition. Moreover, profits from X-ply before devaluation had been regarded as too low. Nottingham Confectionery was concerned to obtain the maximum sterling benefit from exporting the same amount as before devaluation and did not seriously consider alternatives to this.

8.6.3 FIRMS MAKING DIFFERENT PRICE CUTS TO DIFFERENT MARKETS

It goes without saying that all the firms which adopted differential pricing policies had to consider at least some alternative courses of action when arriving at their decisions. Kendal Accessories' cartel, however, looked only at the two extreme possibilities in each overseas market—either to leave the foreign-currency price unchanged or to reduce it by the amount of devaluation. In Inverness Plant Builders, Quantox Construction and Peterborough Tubes (with Product D) the market situation meant that there was no real alternative to price cuts. However, since Inverness Plant Builders and Quantox Construction had to tender separately for each contract, they were able to look at possible alternatives on each occasion when a tender was put in. With Jarrow Furniture, cash flow was so inadequate that there was no real alternative to making the smallest possible price reductions but 'special' overseas markets were identified and singled out for careful study to see what the best decision there would be. Because they really did look in detail at each market, Birmingham Cakes and Hertford Stoves appeared to us to have looked at all relevant alternatives.

8.6.4 SOME COMMENTS

Most of our firms looked only at two alternatives. They considered holding foreign-currency prices constant or they considered cutting them by the net amount of devaluation, or sometimes even more. When settling on one of these alternatives, our firms usually treated all countries in the same way. We were struck by the extent to which firms saw themselves faced by this stark choice between no reduction at all in foreign-currency prices and reducing prices by the full amount (more usually the full *net* amount) of devaluation. Hardly any firm cutting prices considered the possibility of reducing prices by less than the net amount of devaluation. Similarly, few firms made significant changes in other marketing variables at the time of devaluation, though here it is not clear whether the firms simply did not consider them at all or whether they were selling products where such marketing factors were not important. Our firms certainly included more than a representative proportion of firms selling to other businesses rather than to wholesalers or retailers. Again, we have seen that because devaluation came at the end of a long period of 'squeeze' on the British economy, several of our firms had increased expenditure on various forms of marketing activity, other than price cutting, before devaluation, and saw no need to make another increase at the time of devaluation. However, it is still possible that our firms put too much emphasis on price cuts and too little on changes in other marketing variables when taking their devaluation decisions.

8.7   Market Factors

Since our firms made price changes rather than changes in other marketing variables after devaluation, an economist would expect four factors to be particularly important in the devaluation decisions. The first is elasticity of demand. The second is the rate of growth of sales in relevant overseas markets, whether single countries or groups of countries, at the prices already being charged. The third is the amount of spare capacity the firm has and the fourth the way it expects its costs to alter if it increases sales above the pre-devaluation level.

Elasticity of demand is important because a low elasticity of demand would mean that the firm would benefit from increasing rather than reducing prices; a high elasticity of demand would imply that a price cut might pay. As we have seen, the rate of growth of sales would be important only if the price were being set with long-run objectives in mind. However, if it was, then, if sales were growing rapidly, there would be less justification for reducing prices than if they were growing slowly.

In general, the firms which decided not to reduce foreign-currency prices faced either low elasticity of demand or rapidly growing sales in overseas markets, which is what an economist would expect. The firms which decided to make different price changes for different markets or groups of markets also took such factors into account. However, no explicit estimates of elasticity of demand were made by any of these firms.

While this did not surprise us, we were surprised that so few of the firms which decided to reduce foreign-currency prices by the same percentage in all export markets looked with any care at either elasticity of demand or potential market growth in each export market before making their decisions. In this group of firms, only London Switches and Tottenham Piping (and the latter only for Product C) looked carefully at how sales might respond to their price cuts. Neither firm calculated elasticity of demand, but their decision takers felt fairly certain that they knew how demand would respond to price cuts. London Switches' own view was that the increase in demand resulting from a cut in price would be very small, though its main competitor forced it to cut prices all the same. Moreover, with demand growing rapidly, its biggest problem was to provide enough production capacity. In Tottenham Piping, the consensus of opinion was that, for Product C, the price cut which devaluation allowed would be big enough to improve Product C's long-run market position significantly, but how long the long-run was expected to be was not made clear.

What of the other firms which made the same price cuts in all markets? Because Stratford Equipment and Oxford Furnaces took their decisions, at least to some extent, on non-economic grounds, they can be correspondingly absolved from the need to calculate elasticity of demand carefully. Again, the decision-takers in Ealing Electrical Appliances may well have taken elasticity of demand implicitly into account, though it was certainly not considered explicitly and in detail. Nor is there any reason to suppose that it would have been considered if Ealing's devaluation meeting had been held on a weekday, when all the relevant documents would have been accessible. There was no detailed discussion of elasticity of demand for any market at the cartel meeting attended by Durham Plates. Indeed, Durham's suggestion that the cartel should be pragmatic, and should change its prices in an experimental way in each market to discover what was the best price, was not taken up. Finally, in Cardiff Instruments, elasticity of demand and the rate of growth of sales in overseas markets do no seem to have been considered at all, either implicitly or explicitly.

Our firms do seem to have looked carefully at the level of capacity at which they were operating. All five anti-cyclical exporters took 'active' decisions. They regarded the need to keep capacity and men employed as being at least as important, in leading them to these decisions, as the need to keep profits from falling too far. Similarly, while a large number of our regular exporters took 'passive' decisions, this does not mean that they ignored capacity. Indeed, we have already suggested that the most important reason why these firms put so much emphasis on profit, at the time of devaluation, was that they had already begun to take steps to increase exports, in order to keep capacity more fully employed, before devaluation occurred.

Finally, of the seven regular exporters that took active decisions, Cardiff Instruments, Oxford Furnaces and Tottenham Piping were keen to keep capacity employed. Only London Switches and Stratford Equipment were short of capacity.

As for the behaviour of costs, we saw in Chapter 5 that there were some cases where our firms could usefully have looked more carefully at incremental costs. All firms looked at the effect that devaluation would have in increasing the total costs of producing the existing output. With the 'passive' decision takers, once they had decided to *be* passive, this was all that mattered, though strictly marginal cost should have been looked at before doing so. With the 'active' ones, it was important to look at the likely behaviour of costs, after devaluation, over the relevant range of output. While we have seen that few of the 'active' decision takers did this, we have also seen that for most of them output was so low that it was reasonable to assume that marginal cost would be constant over any likely increase in exports, though it is not clear whether this marginal cost was always balanced against possible revenue. Total cost calculations were too often given preference. Nevertheless, in only two firms (Cardiff Instruments and Durham Plates), does it seem at all likely that the failure to calculate the effect of devaluation on marginal cost was important.

8.8   Goodwill and Customer Pressure

Several of our firms told us that their devaluation decisions were influenced by the effect that they thought it would have on their customers. This was most important where an overseas country could import very similar products either from Britain, which had devalued, or from third countries which had not. Devaluation meant that even a British firm that decided to leave its foreign-currency prices unaltered was not facing an unchanged situation. The UK *had* devalued; the countries where the other suppliers were located had not. In many overseas countries, press, radio and television led the customers of British firms to expect substantial reductions in the foreign-currency prices of British goods. Because of this, several of our firms, which did not cut their foreign-currency prices at once, were told by customers that they should cut them. This put them in a difficult position. They not only had to estimate what effect a price cut would have on sales and profits. They also had to consider what effect *not* reducing prices would have on sales and profits. Some firms felt compelled to make at least token price cuts in some overseas markets, in order to defend their long-term sales and profits there, even if they believed that demand in these markets would not increase quickly after such price cuts.

Jarrow Furniture faced this problem in the USA. In normal circumstances, the $4\frac{1}{2}\%$ price reductions which it made there would not have had much effect on its sales. However, the USA was Jarrow's most important single market, and the American press, radio and television had led Jarrow's customers and distributors there to expect significant price reductions. If Jarrow had made no price cuts, there would certainly have been disappointment, perhaps resentment. The difficulty was that the consequences of such resentment could not be predicted at all precisely. Jarrow had put a great deal of effort into expanding its sales in the USA, because that was where it saw the main scope for future growth. If its reputation in the USA had suffered because of disappointed expectations, its long-run growth objectives in the USA might have been more difficult to achieve. But how much more? In the end, only the small price cuts of $4\frac{1}{2}\%$ were made, and Jarrow's management had to argue strongly with customers and distributors to avoid having to make bigger ones. It was felt that these cuts were a reasonable price to pay to maintain Jarrow's position in the USA.

Gatley Hosiery faced a similar problem. Most of the orders for its product range for the current season had already been placed before devaluation. Cutting prices for the remainder of the season was unlikely to bring in many extra orders. However, this meant that any loss in 'contribution' from cutting prices for the current season, was also likely to be small. Gatley's marketing manager was less concerned with this season's sales than with the next season's. He feared that Gatley's sales in the next season would be reduced if its customers thought that it had been unfair to them after devaluation. Gatley therefore did not risk keeping the whole sterling benefit of devaluation for itself, leaving foreign-currency prices unchanged. Its quite substantial price cuts of about 8% were made immediately, and were intended by Gatley Hosiery to show its customers how fairly they were treated. Yet Gatley not only lost little revenue. It also felt free to increase its foreign-currency prices for the next season's product range, back to the level that they would have obtained had there been no devaluation, without losing either goodwill or sales. The immediate cut in foreign-currency prices was an investment in goodwill, aimed at making the next season's product range more profitable. This kind of behaviour, which in other industries might seem devious, was acceptable because it conformed to the conventions of a fashion trade.

Peterborough Tubes also faced problems of maintaining goodwill, particularly for Product D, which was sold by tender. Although keeping the customer's goodwill was probably less important to Peterborough than increasing its chances of obtaining particular contracts, the combined influence of these two factors significantly affected the size of the price cuts Peterborough made. In particular, this was the reason why Peterborough's management quickly agreed that no sterling tender price for Product D would be increased by the full amount of devaluation. As with Gatley Hosiery, the main pressure to take decisions aimed at maintaining customer goodwill came from within Peterborough itself. They were seen as 'an investment' to safeguard future business.

In Ealing Electrical Appliances, goodwill was also important, though here the main factor behind the decision to reduce prices by the full net amount of devaluation was the need to improve market share overseas. One reason for Ealing's foreign-currency price cuts was that it was afraid of unfavourable press publicity abroad if it did not make them.

Acton Chemicals and Rugby Processing also had to take their customers' feelings into account. Rugby Processing was in a strong position, with its export prices already below those of its main overseas rival. Even so, it felt the need to make some small price cuts, as a gesture to customers.

Acton Chemicals is an interesting case. Its original decision was to leave its foreign-currency prices unchanged, even though this might antagonise some customers. However, the resentment felt by these customers was much stronger than Acton had expected, and they threatened to take their business elsewhere. They argued that while the prices that suppliers from other countries were charging them were no lower than before devaluation, these countries had not devalued. Britain *had* devalued and therefore British firms ought to cut their prices. The result was that, in 1968, instead of increasing sterling export prices by 17%, Acton could increase them by only some 10%. At the same time, its total costs rose in 1968 by about $3\frac{1}{2}$%, because of devaluation and of other factors. Because of the way customers reacted, the increased profit Acton obtained from devaluation was much smaller than it had hoped.

A big problem for all these firms was that it was almost impossible to obtain an accurate estimate of what effect on sales or profit customer resentment might have. Acton Chemicals, Jarrow Furniture and Rugby Processing all waited until they were able to talk to their overseas customers and agents before cutting their foreign-currency prices. However, Ealing Electrical Appliances, Gatley Hosiery and Peterborough Tubes cut prices not because of actual complaints from customers but because they felt that customers would be antagonised if they did not. It will be remembered that one of Ealing's agents cut the prices of Ealing's products without obtaining its agreement. This kind of incident may have led those we interviewed to magnify the importance of goodwill as they looked back on devaluation. This agent was only one among many, and his market was a particularly competitive one. Even there, despite the embarrassment, he was persuaded to cancel the cuts. Gatley Hosiery's North American executives criticised the smallness of the price cuts after they had been made, claiming that to meet their customers' expectations they should have been bigger. However, Gatley's central management saw this simply as an attempt by the North American management to make its own selling task easier, and not as showing a genuine concern for Gatley's overall profitability. Those who took the devaluation decisions in Peterborough Tubes had no clear evidence to show them how much importance to attach to goodwill, but felt that some foreign-currency price cuts had to be made to maintain it.

It may be important that Ealing Electrical Appliances decided to make once-for-all, and substantial, changes in its complicated price lists to avoid having to make a series of small changes over a period. Where goodwill is seen as important, the firm may well be wise to aim at a single, substantial price change big enough to allow for future changes in costs. Both Ealing and Gatley saw price stability as an important factor in maintaining consumer goodwill; experience after devaluation in 1949 had shown that customers were irritated if devaluation was followed by a series of small price changes over a period.

8.9   Retaliation

Where there is oligopoly in an overseas market, each firm selling there is likely to fear that its competitors will retaliate if it makes changes in its marketing variables. Most of our firms which decided to reduce their prices substantially in export markets were oligopolists, facing few foreign competitors. Yet they were apparently unconcerned about the possibility of retaliation, even where they faced competition from a few other British firms in export markets. Because the latter also had the benefit of devaluation, and could reduce foreign-currency prices without reducing profits proportionately, this is rather surprising. British competition overseas was especially important for Cardiff Instruments, Inverness Plant Builders and Oxford Furnaces, but they did not look carefully at the likely reactions of their British competitors. Cardiff Instruments did not consider them at all. Inverness Plant Builders concluded, somewhat casually during discussions before devaluation, that its British competitors could be ignored since they were all operating in the same economic environment as Inverness. Admittedly, the fact that Inverness had to put in a separate quotation for each tender meant that it could adjust its policy as time passed, in the light of what its competitors actually did, but its initial view is clear. Oxford Furnaces did discover, by making telephone calls, how its British competitors were going to behave in export pricing, but this did not seem to affect its devaluation decisions. Indeed, by reducing its own prices by rather more than the net amount of devaluation, in most export markets, Oxford almost certainly precipitated a general reduction in export prices by all its British competitors.

Most of the firms which made across-the-board price cuts in export markets faced only a few competitors—at least in some of these markets. Cardiff Instruments, Durham Plates and Tottenham Piping were selling to export markets that were depressed and were likely to recover only slowly. Oxford Furnaces' export markets were also depressed, though here an early upturn was hoped for. We should have expected Cardiff Instruments, Durham Plates and Tottenham Piping, at least, to take the danger of retaliation by competitors explicitly into account before making price cuts.

The decision-taker in Cardiff Instruments knew that the firm could not compete on price for its cheaper machines, but the possibility of retaliation by foreign competitors, if Cardiff reduced its prices, was not considered. Nor did the likely behaviour of competitors seem to influence the decision to cut the prices of all the more-expensive machines by exactly the same percentage.

Possible competitive reactions were mentioned by the Chairman at the beginning of the meeting of Durham Plates' export cartel, but then ignored. This may not have been entirely unrealistic.

The only serious competition came from two European firms and, although the world market was depressed and business hard to obtain, the British firms' prices were already well below those of the two European producers. However, our feeling is that the cartel might have spent some time considering whether this meant that the European firms simply could not afford to cut prices further or whether the enormous gap, between their prices and those of the cartel, meant that they would be forced to reduce prices, however unprofitable this might be. As we have already seen, Durham Plates' export price for Product B was set by precedent, rather than by explicit decision, and no account was taken of the danger of foreign retaliation.

In Oxford Furnaces, the implications of the price reductions decided on were not discussed until the decision had been both made and implemented. Its decision-takers were confident that, if they had made a significant mistake, this would become apparent when the prices of outstanding tenders were re-examined, as was to be done soon after the decision was made. However, we are not convinced that there was enough market information for Oxford Furnaces to be absolutely sure that the review had considered all relevant factors. Since Oxford Furnaces had more spare capacity than its competitors, it is not surprising that it should have felt able to ignore the reactions of competitors, because they were therefore less likely to retaliate. Even so, our impression is that Oxford cut prices more than it needed. This impression is strengthened by Oxford's own belief that it had reduced prices too far.

In Ealing Electrical Appliances, which also reduced its export prices by the full net amount of devaluation, the possibility that price reductions might spark off a price war with foreign competitors was aired in a very general way at the decision meeting. Indeed, because it made such big price reductions, Ealing could hardly ignore the possibility of retaliation completely. The main reason why the meeting did not consider it more fully was that no one felt confident that he could predict exactly what would happen. Certainly, when Ealing's export sales forecasts were increased soon afterwards, the possibility of retaliation was left out of account.

In general, the firms that made the smallest possible foreign-currency price cuts, or which made different price cuts in different markets, showed more awareness of the dangers of retaliation than those making big ones. What is not clear is whether this means that the firms making big price cuts were less careful (or more anxious to increase exports) than the other firms; or whether the fact that they had been able to make such large foreign-currency price cuts made them feel that the most competitors were likely to be able to do was to match them; or indeed whether the firms in question made these cuts as a *result* of the fear of retaliation.

8.10 Non-economic Factors Affecting the Decisions

8.10.1 'DEVALUATION HYSTERIA'

Oxford Furnaces referred to 'devaluation hysteria' in the company. Senior managers thought that speeches by prominent politicians and industrialists implied that the maximum possible price cuts should be made. They felt that it was Oxford's duty, as a patriotic British business, to cut export prices even though Oxford's market appeared to be inelastic to price cuts. Indeed, we have seen that Oxford probably forced general price reductions for the exports of all the other firms in its industry. Oxford's management saw the fact that the rest of its industry in the UK cut prices as proving the soundness of their own decisions. Yet Oxford could almost certainly have obtained higher foreign-currency prices, both for itself and for the rest of the industry, had it wished to do so.

Other firms mentioned 'devaluation hysteria' in the USA. They blamed this on the American press, radio and television, which was said to have led American customers to expect British firms to make substantial cuts in their dollar prices after devaluation. Several of our firms felt that this 'hysteria' was to blame for at least part of the price cuts they had to make in the USA.

'Patriotism' was also important for Stratford Equipment, which reduced its foreign-currency prices despite the fact that demand for its products was growing rapidly, and likely to continue to do so, and that its competitive position was very strong. 'Patriotism' also influenced the decisions of Durham Plates' export cartel, even though its export prices were generally lower than those of overseas competitors.

The conclusion seems to be that devaluation decisions, and perhaps all business decisions, are more difficult to take if the firm tries to consider the national interest rather than its private interest. It is not so much that pursuing the national interest requires altruism. It is rather that, with an event like devaluation, businessmen apparently find it difficult to know what the national interest *is*. Yet in our firms, and especially in Oxford Furnaces, national and private interests coincided much more closely than its management supposed. The UK balance of payments would have benefitted more, with a product with an inelastic demand, if Oxford had maintained rather than cut its sterling prices. We feel that there are lessons here for Governments. Our study suggests that economic policy measures are likely to be more successful if they require the firm to follow its own, rather than the national, interest. If, on some occasions, Governments feel that they have to ask firms to pursue the national, rather than their private, interests they should make it abundantly clear to firms what the national interest requires.

8.10.2 OTHER NON-ECONOMIC CONSIDERATIONS

Some of the firms that reduced their foreign-currency prices substantially, and for all overseas countries, were influenced by the idea that it would be 'morally wrong' to take advantage of devaluation to improve profit margins by as much as possible. The feeling here does not seem to have been that increasing sterling prices was against the national interest.

We have the impression that, in firms where scientists and technologists are dominant, there is often a feeling that prices ought to be 'fair'. [This was certainly the case with Wensum Engineering, referred to in *Pricing in Business*, D. C. Hague, London (1971). We have found it in other 'technological' firms too. However, the experience of firms like Ferranti and Bristol Siddeley in Government contracting makes one wonder whether the attitude to Government is different!] For example, until 1967, Cardiff Instruments had found it easy to earn the short-term profit required by its parent firm. It had been more concerned with maintaining its technical lead over competitors, even if this meant sacrificing opportunities for immediate profit. It linked its pricing decisions to 'cost', rather than to charging what the market would bear. If the 'cost-plus' price was too high to allow Cardiff to win a contract, it then aimed at an acceptable 'contribution' over marginal cost. After devaluation, this general policy seems to have influenced the way in which Cardiff arrived at its new prices. Its sterling prices were adjusted upwards by the percentage that total cost had increased, but there was no suggestion that it might be worth going further. While it is true that Cardiff was finding it difficult to earn an acceptable contribution to profit from its cheaper products, so that there can have been little scope for increasing their prices, the same was not true of its more expensive units. Yet Cardiff did not consider increasing their prices by a bigger percentage. It worked on a 'cost-plus' basis. It is true that Cardiff feared that its competitors would soon develop more effective alternatives to its own more-expensive products, but there must have been a case for making profit before the competition appeared.

At least one firm which made differential price changes, namely Peterborough Tubes (for Product D), believed that it should charge 'fair' prices. Peterborough therefore reduced all its prices after devaluation, even though it knew that for much of its business this would not increase the probability of obtaining orders. Peterborough did have an eye on the effect of this policy on future sales, but it was very much concerned to make no more than 'fair' profits.

8.11   Sterling Price Quotations

Despite fears of devaluation during the early part of 1967, and indeed during 1965 and 1966, most of our firms continued to quote export prices in sterling. Sometimes, this was because customers were reluctant to accept prices set in other currencies. In most cases, it was simply because firms had always quoted prices in sterling and simply continued to do so. These firms had to justify the sterling price increases they made to foreign customers. They often had to do this even though the foreign-currency price had not been increased, and might even have been reduced. Had more of our firms quoted their prices in foreign currency, as Fulham Castings did, they might have been able to make smaller price reductions.

There was some evidence of a change in attitude to quoting prices in sterling as a result of devaluation. Some of our firms felt that their bargaining position had been weakened by doing so and were trying to quote foreign-currency prices instead. However, one difficulty was that the obvious alternative to sterling was the dollar, and its weakness in 1968 made quoting prices in dollars seem undesirable.

8.12   Internal Factors

8.12.1   CASH FLOW

We have seen that several firms used devaluation to make their existing volume of exports more profitable, rather than to expand it. This was especially the case with firms whose overall profits were too low at the time of devaluation, and for whom short-term profitability was therefore very important, but we have seen that these firms had often already taken steps to increase export volume and were now concerned to increase export profitability.

Jarrow Furniture was a typical example. Its overall profits had been falling for some years, largely because its home market was not growing. Exports took a large percentage of output and its export markets had not been as large or profitable as it had hoped. Moreover, when devaluation took place, Jarrow was worried over what its long-term effect on Jarrow's costs, especially raw material and labour costs, would be. Jarrow concluded that over the next eighteen months they would rise quickly enough to offset the initial advantage that devaluation gave. Not only had Jarrow's profits from both home sales and exports been seen as too low before devaluation, Jarrow feared that rising costs after devaluation would cancel out most of the extra profit it gave. This was why Jarrow tried to maintain its foreign-currency prices after devaluation. Its predictions of cost increases in 1968 and 1969 may well have been too high; Jarrow may also have looked at the situation in too static a way. Nevertheless, the decision-takers assumed that their predictions were correct. The pressure on Jarrow's cash flow and the fear that, at best, this pressure would continue, was the most important single factor influencing their decisions.

Acton Chemicals was also in difficulty with its cash flow, because it was not introducing its new production process as quickly as it had hoped. However, while profit margins were low at the time of devaluation, they were not low enough to be the only factor considered in the devaluation decisions. The most important pressures on Acton Chemicals came from outside the firm, especially from its customers.

Peterborough Tubes had been losing money on X-ply because output from its new plant in the EEC was well below capacity. While the profitability of the EEC plant had improved during 1967, the parent company still did not feel that it was getting an adequate return on its investment. Leaving the foreign-currency price of X-ply unchanged enabled Peterborough to obtain the maximum profit from devaluation.

While its cash flow was adequate, Rugby Processing had decided before devaluation that the margins it was earning in Europe were too narrow. It saw devaluation as an excellent opportunity to widen them.

For these firms, then, inadequate cash flow was an important influence leading them to try to maintain foreign-currency prices. By contrast, at least two of our firms reduced their prices even though their profit margins were under pressure. Durham Plates, and the export-pricing committee of its trade association, had been considering making substantial price increases in January

1968, in order to recoup all the cost increases that had accumulated over the previous two years. After devaluation, the cartel decided to make significant reductions in the foreign-currency prices of all its products. Tottenham Piping was in a similar situation to Jarrow Furniture, with the market for its main product very depressed. The increase in sales likely to result from the very small price reductions that Tottenham could make, especially for Products M, A, and B, given the small percentage of value added in its total costs, were likely to be negligible. Despite this, Tottenham did not use devaluation to increase sterling profit margins on most of its products.

8.12.2   CAPACITY AND EMPLOYMENT

Shortage of capacity was a significant factor at the time of devaluation for only a few of our firms. Indeed, in seven of them the overriding objective was to reduce the uncomfortable amount of spare capacity that they had as a result of very depressed home and export markets.

Their positions differed. For example, Jarrow Furniture saw its problems as due mainly to the secular fall in world demand. Cutting prices was thought likely to give only limited, transitory benefits, even if Jarrow had been able to afford to do so. In Inverness Plant Builders, Kendal Accessories and Quantox Construction, at least, some of the lack of sales was a result of a cyclical fall in orders. These firms set the price for each tender according to the circumstances at the time, trying to achieve a satisfactory balance between profitability and turnover. Quite apart from their desire not to lose skilled labour which might be hard to attract back, they felt a moral obligation to keep well-established work forces together and to prevent unemployment increasing in their areas.

Ealing Electrical Appliances and Oxford Furnaces blamed their low levels of sales at least in part on the fact that they were uncompetitive with overseas firms. Their policy of making general price reductions must have been partly the result of the wish to reduce spare capacity, but this fact was not explicitly discussed when their decisions were being taken.

Some of our firms could not increase output significantly at the time of devaluation because they were short of capacity. One might have expected them also to be reluctant to cut foreign-currency prices. Acton Chemicals, Peterborough Tubes (for X-ply) and Rugby Processing were certainly reluctant to cut prices. On the other hand, London Switches and Stratford Equipment both cut foreign-currency prices somewhat although they were short of capacity. It is true that London Switches would have made no reductions in foreign-currency prices had not its competitor led it to do so. However, while Stratford Equipment also had little spare capacity, and its new product was about to be launched, it thought reducing prices the 'patriotic' thing to do. Gatley Hosiery and Durham Plates were also likely to experience some shortage of capacity, but both firms reduced their prices. Because export sales were dealt with by Gatley Hosiery's overseas company, and because this was organisationally separate from the rest of the firm, the overseas company ignored problems of capacity. Durham Plates' decision to reduce the prices of both its cartelised and non-cartelised products was taken partly on non-economic grounds and capacity problems were not explicitly discussed.

Largely because so many of our firms had a good deal of spare capacity, devaluation led them to do little investment during the period of our study—1967 to 1970. As we have seen, London Switches and Stratford Equipment had already decided to increase capacity, even before devaluation. While Rugby Processing did decide to build a large new plant soon after devaluation, partly to meet European demand, for most of our firms the big problem was how to keep existing capacity employed rather than how to increase it. However, devaluation does seem to have led to an increase in investment in manufacturing industry as a whole in 1968 and 1969 so that, in this respect at least, our firms do not seem to have been typical.

8.13 Import Substitution

8.12.1 BY OUR FIRMS

None of our firms thought that the increase in import prices caused by devaluation was big enough to make it worth switching to the use of home produced rather than imported raw materials, components or capital equipment. A major reason was that few foreign suppliers increased prices to the UK by anything approaching the full amount of devaluation.

Where our firms imported capital equipment, this was usually more efficient than its British counterpart, by a margin that devaluation did not cancel out. Indeed, some of our firms simply could not obtain the plant they wanted from the UK at all. Thus, after devaluation, Acton Chemicals decided to introduce another new process, under licence from a foreign firm, because it could not find an equally attractive British one.

While none of our firms substituted British for imported raw materials, Durham Plates, Gatley Hosiery and Jarrow Furniture each worked through its list of imports to see whether there were any items where import substitution seemed worthwhile. They found none. Similarly, before devaluation, Peterborough Tubes and Tottenham Piping had each been putting into effect a long-term plan to reduce their imports of raw materials, which came from only a few overseas producers. While these firms were increasing their purchases of British raw materials, even here the main decisions had already been taken before devaluation.

With these exceptions, our firms had all convinced themselves, without making special studies, that there was no case for importing fewer raw materials. For most of them, the main materials they used were bought in an international commodity market. Since their prices were usually set in dollars, the sterling equivalent was automatically increased by the full amount of devaluation. In some cases, the materials were simply not available, in the required quantity or quality, from within the UK.

Most of our firms were not looking enthusiastically for ways of using British rather than imported materials. This may be explained by the fact that it was not difficult, after devaluation, to pass on the increased costs of materials and components to customers both within and outside the UK. The ease with which such costs were passed on may have been partly the result of the fact that foreign producers seemed to go out of their way to keep down the prices of the raw materials and components they exported to the UK, after devaluation, if necessary by reducing profit margins.

In general, it seems that there was little import substitution in our firms. Two further points need to be made. First, our firms may not be typical in this respect, because we considered so few firms making final consumer goods. Second, and going against this, we have already seen, in Chapter 1, that there seems to have been relatively little, if any, import substitution in the UK economy as a whole.

8.13.2 BY THEIR CUSTOMERS

Having now looked at the extent to which our firms themselves switched from overseas to British suppliers of materials, components and equipment, we now look at how far devaluation induced the British customers of our firms to switch business to them and away from foreign suppliers. Again, devaluation had little effect. One reason seems to be that the particular firms we studied faced relatively little competition from imports in 1967. The firms which were significantly affected by competition from imports were Acton Chemicals, Cardiff Instruments, Ealing Electrical Appliances and Jarrow Furniture.

A priori analysis suggests that British customers would be more likely to switch their orders to our firms, and away from foreign competitors, the more homogeneous the product. Among the firms whose products were effectively homogeneous was Acton, producing basic chemicals. There had been considerable imports of chemicals into the UK before devaluation, and there was little to choose in quality between Acton's products and imported substitutes. Prices before devaluation were low. Indeed, shortly before devaluation Acton Chemicals had convinced the Board of Trade that some foreign competitors were 'dumping' chemicals in the UK. Acton Chemicals believed that this meant that its foreign competitors would find difficulty in accepting the reduction in foreign exchange earnings they would suffer if they did not increase their prices in the UK after devaluation. Having initially decided to increase its UK prices by 9%, Acton later scaled this increase down to 6%, which was just big enough to compensate for the increase in its total costs caused by devaluation. Acton hoped that its foreign competitors would have to charge increased prices after devaluation, and would then find difficulty in competing in the British market. In the event, the foreign producers decided to accept the loss of foreign-currency earnings caused by devaluation rather than withdraw from the British market. Indeed, they increased their volume of sales in the UK in 1968, although this represented a slightly smaller share of a growing British market. One reason why there was no move by British customers to substitute Acton's product for imported products seems to have been that foreign firms were keen to keep down prices, in order to maintain their sales in Britain, at a time when there was world wide excess capacity in the chemical industry. Another was that Acton Chemicals' own output was held down by its difficulty in bringing in its new production process.

Ealing Electrical Appliances was in an industry where the products of each producer were carefully differentiated, and where British firms were protected by a tariff. Nevertheless, foreign manufacturers had been increasingly successful in selling caravans in the British market before devaluation. While Ealing predicted that devaluation would increase its costs, for caravans sold in the UK, by between $3\frac{1}{2}$ and $4\frac{1}{2}\%$, it did not increase the UK prices of its caravans until July 1968, and then by only 3%. Apart from government supervision of prices, an important reason for the delay seems to have been that Ealing wanted to see what would happen to imports. It hoped that British consumers would buy substantially more British and fewer foreign caravans. They did not. Imports of caravans into Britain increased sharply in 1968. Moreover, this happened despite the fact that foreign firms increased their sterling prices by roughly the amount of devaluation. The rather wide gap between British and foreign prices, caused by devaluation and by Ealing's decision to hold down its UK prices, was accompanied by a significant increase in imports.

The main products competing with those of Jarrow Furniture were also 'differentiated'. Imports accounted for only a small fraction of total UK furniture sales in 1967. Nevertheless, when deciding its pricing policy in the UK after devaluation, Jarrow set its prices at a level which it hoped would persuade customers to switch from imported to British products. It decided not to increase its prices in the UK until the middle of 1968, largely in order to avoid damping down a rise in demand within the UK, which had begun just before devaluation. Nevertheless, imports of furniture into Britain doubled in 1968, mainly because of successful marketing by one European firm, which decided to absorb the reduced profit from exports to the UK which devaluation caused.

Substantial numbers of the machines made by Cardiff Instruments had been imported into the UK before devaluation. Nevertheless, price was by no means the most important factor which customers took into account when deciding whether to buy from Cardiff or its competitors. Technical performance, delivery dates and after-sales service were also important. As a result, devaluation apparently did not lead to a sufficiently big change in the relative prices of British and overseas machines to cause British customers to buy from Cardiff Instruments rather than from abroad. Cardiff did not expect devaluation to lead to much import substitution; so far as they were able to judge, little took place.

8.14 Home Market Prices

The price increases that our firms made in the UK were usually 'cost-plus' increases, closely linked to the increases in total costs that were expected to result from devaluation. One advantage that a firm does have after a devaluation is that most of its customers, whether individuals or firms, expect it to raise prices in its home market. Yet they do not know what would be a 'fair' increase, because they know too little about the firm's cost structure, and, especially, the proportion of its raw materials and components that are imported. In 1967, the most important factors working in the opposite direction within the UK were that many British firms were subject to the 'early-warning system' for notifying price increases, and that price increases could be reviewed by the Prices and Incomes Board, if the Government thought that desirable. Our firms were therefore more anxious than usual to increase prices by only as much as costs had risen. The fact that there was Government supervision of prices is probably the most important reason why, at the time of devaluation, our firms tied their price increases so closely to costs. However, while there was undoubtedly a great deal of 'cost-plus' pricing in the UK in 1967, there was probably less enthusiasm for it than our study suggests. Nothing is more likely to lead to 'cost-Plus' pricing than Government intervention of this kind.

Some of our firms did use devaluation as an opportunity to increase profit margins on sales within the UK. For example, Durham Plates and Peterborough Tubes both knew only too well that their profit margins were shrinking. Both had found it difficult to increase prices in the UK before devaluation, because their home markets were depressed and because the Government was anxious to keep prices down. At the same time, costs were increasing, largely for reasons beyond their control. After devaluation, both firms increased their prices in the UK by more than their estimates of increased total costs. They aimed to recover the cost increases that they had accumulated over a longish period. London Switches and Stratford Equipment also raised their home market prices by more than they estimated that total costs had increased because of devaluation. Part of this was to cover cost increases caused, not by devaluation, but by wage awards. They were keen to increase profit margins in Britain, if they could do so without antagonising customers. Birmingham Cakes and Jarrow Furniture behaved in the same way. Acton Chemicals would have liked to increase its prices by more than the increase in total costs, in order to improve its profitability, but did not do so because of competition from imports.

While the prices charged by Durham Plates, Birmingham Cakes and Jarrow Furniture were covered by the early warning system, it is far from clear that this had much effect on the size of the price increases they made in the UK. Again, while the early warning system may have led Acton Chemicals to limit its price increases in the UK, the fear of competition from overseas was much more important. Almost all the other firms kept their price increases in the UK to the bare minimum required to cover increased costs, even where there was no obvious competitive pressure on them.

All the firms subject to the early warning system (namely, Acton Chemicals, Birmingham Cakes, Durham Plates, Ealing Electrical Appliances, Fulham Castings, Jarrow Furniture, Peterborough Tubes and Rugby Processing) delayed price increases in the UK for eight months, and the other firms for about three. Although London Switches and Stratford Equipment were not subject to the early-warning system, they also waited for three months before increasing prices in the UK.

8.15   The Results of Devaluation

8.15.1   EXPORT MARKETS

A striking feature of this study was the reluctance of our firms to attribute improved export sales or profits in 1968 and 1969 to devaluation. Indeed, we began almost to sense a 'conspiracy' to deny any credit for the improved performance of the UK to devaluation. One senses a similar attitude during casual discussions with businessmen just before the floating of the pound in June 1972. Businessmen tend to assert, as many did in May and early June 1972, that British export volume, and even more, British import volume, are too insensitive to price changes for devaluation to 'work'. Similarly, when we visited our firms in 1969 and 1970, they argued that devaluation by a 'mere' 15% was too small to stimulate exports significantly.

(a) *Increased Exports*
Most of our firms whose export performance improved after devaluation were reluctant to attribute this improvement to devaluation itself. Of the firms that took positive action to increase their exports, only three were convinced that devaluation had a significant effect on export volume. They were: Birmingham Cakes, Ealing Electrical Appliances and Jarrow Furniture (in Europe).

For Ealing Electrical Appliances and Jarrow Furniture, the price reductions which devaluation made possible (particularly in Europe by Jarrow), brought a long period of declining exports to an end. The upturn in Jarrow's sales in Europe was only marginal, but it did follow the long period of steady decline. What is more, the fact that Jarrow made only small cuts in prices in the USA and Canada, led to a big increase in the total sterling profits Jarrow earned from its exports. There was a big increase in export volume in Ealing Electrical Appliances, but Ealing's profits continued to be extremely low.

(b) *Increased Export Profits*

Eight firms (again including Birmingham Cakes) were convinced that devaluation made a significant difference to the profitability of exports. Six of them were: Birmingham Cakes, Fulham Castings, Hertford Stoves, Nottingham Confectionery, Peterborough Tubes and Rugby Processing. Hertford Stoves argued that other British firms were being unreasonable when they described a fall in the exchange rate of 15% as 'too small'. In what other circumstances, Hertford Stoves asked, could a firm be given an overnight competitive advantage of, say 10% (after allowing for increased costs caused by devaluation) against its overseas competitors? We rank the quality of the devaluation decisions taken by two of these firms (Birmingham Cakes and Hertford Stoves) very highly.

Hertford Stoves believed that its devaluation decisions helped to improve its sales in those markets where it cut prices, namely, outside North America. However, North America had previously accounted for most of Hertford's export sales and the firm did not foresee a sudden fall in the demand for its products there, which took place in 1968, when credit restrictions were imposed in the USA. Sales to North America in 1968 were considerably less than had been expected. Even so, because Hertford left its dollar prices to the USA unchanged, it earned significantly more sterling than it would have done without devaluation.

In Birmingham Cakes, exports continued to rise. The careful way it chose a combination of marketing changes for each export market at the time of devaluation seems to have helped.

We may add here two firms, Gatley Hosiery and Quantox Construction. While, as we have seen, Gatley reduced its foreign-currency prices for exports immediately, the aim was to raise currency prices again to pre-devaluation levels for the next season's range of products and so increase sterling profit margins by the net amount of devaluation.

There was a small increase in its European sales in 1968–69, which Gatley attributed mainly to the reorganisation of its European distribution network, already planned at the time of devaluation. However, devaluation did increase Gatley Hosiery's profits, not least because it was able to increase the profitability of its next season's product range as planned. Gatley continued to argue that this increase depended on the immediate price cuts it made after devaluation.

We ourselves are similarly convinced that Quantox Construction increased profits after devaluation, though the firm itself is not equally certain. It is true that the short-term effects of devaluation were disappointing for Quantox Construction. We have seen that for the first tender we studied, foreign competitors cut their prices by about ten per cent immediately after devaluation, in anticipation of a substantial price reduction by Quantox. Yet Quantox had not intended to make such a cut unless it was absolutely necessary. As we also saw, despite later making a similar price cut, Quantox lost the business. Only after obtaining the second tender at an unprofitable price, largely to get experience of producing the new type of plant, did Quantox obtain a profitable order. However, the most important foreign competitor, which cut its prices initially, then found its plant heavily committed to relatively unprofitable business. This may have been why Quantox was then able to take further orders at much more profitable prices. In the long run, we think that devaluation *did* help Quantox.

(c) *The Other Firms*
What of the other firms? While Acton Chemicals increased its exports somewhat after devaluation, the intention had been to increase export profitability rather than export volume. Yet we know that, because it sold in a market where a small number of producers faced a large number of purchasers, its customers were able to use the bargaining power they had to reduce Acton's foreign-currency prices.

Although Cardiff Instruments reduced its export prices by the net amount of devaluation, the increase in the probabilities that it assigned to the likelihood of being awarded outstanding tenders after devaluation was very small. Cardiff doubted whether even this small difference owed anything to devaluation itself. The probabilities were increased only marginally, and then on only five of the twenty-one tenders outstanding in November 1967. Cardiff attributed even this increase mainly to the fact that, as time passed, it obtained more information about its customers' requirements. At the same time, the probabilities assigned to six tenders were reduced. Together, these represented much more business. Only two of the twenty-one tenders outstanding in November 1967 had been accepted by January 1968. Both had been assigned high probabilities of acceptance, even before devaluation.

In Durham Plates, the dramatic rise in exports of its non-cartelised product was largely a result of one very large order from an Eastern European country. Although devaluation allowed Durham Plates to quote a slightly lower price than it would otherwise have done, it argued that this order was almost certain to go to a British company, for political and balance of payments reasons. Moreover, no other British firm could supply the specialised product, required by the Eastern European country, at a reasonable price. Nevertheless, Durham Plates' exports to the rest of the world also increased by 30% in 1968. While Durham Plates argued that this also owed more to rising demand abroad than to devaluation, there can be no certainty about the true reasons. On the other hand, it is certainly true that exports of Durham's cartelised product fell slightly in 1968, because of depression in the industry which used it. While Durham Plates is convinced that the very substantial increase in its exports was in no way a result of devaluation, we think that devaluation may have had some effect.

Inverness Plant Builders and Kendal Accessories were operating in depressed markets. Despite the substantial price cuts they made, export sales for both fell sharply in the year after devaluation. For Kendal, at least, this was mainly because even devaluation did not make its export prices competitive.

London Switches, Stratford Equipment and Oxford Furnaces linked the sharp increase in their exports to various factors, none of them directly connected with devaluation. In London Switches and Stratford Equipment, demand for their products before devaluation had been rising so rapidly that capacity was short. Even if they could have attributed any increase in exports to the cuts they made in foreign-currency prices after devaluation, those cuts were hardly necessary. These firms would almost certainly have been wiser to keep up prices.

The improvement in exports by Oxford Furnaces followed large price cuts but, again, Oxford argued that most of the increase would have occurred in any case. In Canada, it attributed gaining a series of very large orders mainly to the reorganisation of its selling arrangements before devaluation. In the rest of the world, Oxford had more spare capacity than most of its competitors, and so could quote keener delivery dates. Oxford was not certain how far its increased exports were the result of spare capacity and how far of price cuts.

Tottenham Piping was in a difficult position because there was a good deal of spare capacity in its industry. In addition, a large percentage of its price represented what it had to pay for the imported raw material, whose price increased automatically after devaluation. Devaluation therefore had little effect on Tottenham Piping.

(c) *A Summary*

In total, it is not easy to be certain what effect devaluation had on our firms' exports. For some it certainly increased the volume of exports; for others it certainly increased their profitability; for some it did both. Only in a few firms did it obviously do neither.

Let us list the firms in each category. First, there were ten firms, where devaluation did appear to increase export volume and/or export profitability. They were:

Birmingham Cakes
Ealing Electrical Appliances
Fulham Castings
Gatley Hosiery
Hertford Stoves
Jarrow Furniture
Nottingham Confectionery
Peterborough Tubes
Quantox Construction
Rugby Processing

There were four firms where devaluation seems to have had very little effect. These were:

Cardiff Instruments
Durham Plates
Inverness Plant Builders
Kendal Accessories

Indeed, if anything, the devaluation decisions of all four firms reduced their profits.

Third, there were five firms where devaluation did bring benefits, but for various reasons they were not as big as they might have been hoped. These firms were:

Acton Chemicals
Oxford Furnaces
London Switches
Stratford Equipment
Tottenham Piping

Despite all the qualifications, we find it somewhat puzzling that our firms were so reluctant to attribute improved export performance, whether in terms of sales volume or profit, to devaluation. No doubt other factors helped to increase our firms' exports in 1968 and 1969. Above all, the amount of excess capacity they had at the end of 1967 was substantial. Nevertheless, we are convinced that ten of the nineteen firms obtained a clear benefit from devaluation and at least a further five a qualified benefit, though it is true that five of these fifteen firms themselves argued that devaluation gave them little or no benefit. Perhaps we are right in our general feeling that devaluation had more effect on our firms than they were ready to admit. What does seem to be true is that devaluation had more effect on export profitability than on export volume. We shall look at this point in more detail in section 8.15.

It also seems clear that if a country is going to devalue, doing so at the end of a period when home demand has been held down and when firms have already begun to take steps to increase their exports, is likely to ensure that devaluation has the maximum effect. The price advantage given by devaluation is then supported by improved export marketing arrangements of various kinds and the improved export marketing arrangements are supported by higher profitability, in domestic currency.

Another lesson for governments seems to be that they should not pay too much attention when businessmen explain why devaluation cannot possibly improve the balance of payments by increasing export volume or profitability. What matters is what businessmen do, not what they say.

While not all our firms did what was best either in the national interest or in their own interests, what happened after devaluation, for whatever reasons, *did* improve the balance of payments. The fact that many businessmen predicted that devaluation could not 'work' is beside the point, though their anxiety, after the event, to give credit for improved export performance to any factor *except* devaluation may be more worrying. Businessmen may well be able to tell civil servants what factors influence their decisions when there is a devaluation, but they usually look too narrowly at the interests of their own firms to predict accurately what effect a change like devaluation will have on the balance of payments.

8.15.2 THE HOME MARKET

As we have seen, there seems to have been little import substitution within our firms. Devaluation does not seem to have caused our firms to switch their purchases from foreign to British suppliers in a significant way. Nor do the British customers of our firms seemed to have switched from foreign suppliers to our firms.

8.16 Some Reflections

We have seen that, in 1967, all the 'passive' exporters, all of whom were also 'regular' exporters, were anxious to hold foreign-currency prices unchanged after devaluation. The 'active' exporters all cut foreign-currency prices in some degree. We suggested a rationale for this behaviour in section 8.3.4. Let us now put our suggested explanation in terms of the analysis used in Chapter 2.

We there looked at the way the firm would respond if it were maximising profits both before and after devaluation. We saw that in most cases the firm would increase both output and sterling prices. The reason why our 'regular' exporters were more anxious to increase sterling prices than to increase export volume may be that they were *not* maximising profits at the time of devaluation. Consider the firm in Figure. 8.1.

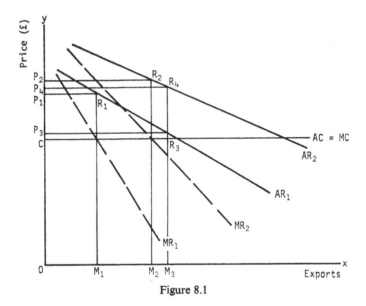

Figure 8.1

We assume that this firm is producing in conditions of monopoly. While the point we are making is a more general one, it can be made most easily in this situation. Before devaluation, the average and marginal revenue curves in an export market are AR_1 and MR_1. The profit-maximising export price and volume are therefore OP_1 and OM_1. Suppose there is now a devaluation, so that the average and marginal revenue curves, expressed in domestic currency, become AR_2 and MR_2. The profit-maximising export price and volume are now OP_2 and OM_2. Prices are higher, and exports bigger, than before devaluation.

However, if the firm is a 'regular' exporter, it could well have been exporting, say, OM_3 before devaluation. There are various reasons for this. Low demand at home may have led the firm to seek more business abroad to keep up employment and profit-ability, even though prices overseas may have been relatively low, as was certainly the case in the UK in 1966 and 1967. The firm may have felt that, in due course, the government would be forced to take some step, like devaluing, to improve the profitability of the country's regular exporters, though we have seen that Jarrow Furniture, in particular, saw the benefit of devaluation as rather temporary. Alternatively, simply because it *was* a 'regular' exporter, the firm may have been pursuing a long-term plan for expanding exports without paying too much attention to their profitability. For such reasons, it seems quite likely that, in the circumstances of Britain in November 1967, our 'regular' exporters were exporting more than the profit-maximising amount of output.

Suppose that there is now a devaluation, and that the firm shown in Figure 8.1 feels that this gives it an opportunity to move closer to the profit-maximising position. As most of our regular exporters did, it may leave its foreign-currency price unchanged, increasing its sterling price from OP_3 to OP_4. The assumption that exports remain at OM_3 is a sensible one. Since the firm has left the foreign-currency price unchanged, there is no reason why exports should alter. The firm has moved from a position at R_3 where profits were *not* maximised to a new position at R_4, where they are *still* not maximised. Nevertheless, R_4 is closer to the profit-maximising position (R_2) than R_3 was. By leaving foreign-currency prices unchanged, the firm is both better off and closer to the optimum position.

The reason why R_4 lies to the right of R_2 is that we are assuming that initially the firm's exports were not only bigger than the profit-maximising amount before devaluation (OM_1) but *also* bigger than the profit-maximising amount after devaluation (OM_2). Had OM_3 been bigger than OM_1, but smaller than OM_2, the firm could have set its prices so as to obtain some increase in exports after devaluation and moved itself closer to the profit-maximising position at R_2 by a rise in exports.

Put simply, all we are saying is this. If, for any reason, firms are selling before devaluation more than the profit-maximising volume of exports and, *a fortiori*, if they are selling before devaluation more than the volume of exports that would have maximised profits *after* devaluation, it would be entirely rational for them to make no increase in export volume, but maximise the increase in sterling export price. What is more, we have suggested why a 'regular' exporter in November 1967 might well have been in this position. Simply because he was a regular exporter he could well have been pressing ahead with increasing export volume while the home market was depressed, trusting the government sooner or later to ensure that exports were again made acceptably profitable. If this argument is correct, the decisions of our 'regular' exporters who decided to increase export profitability rather than export volume in November 1967 may have been entirely sensible. As the case studies show, a number of our 'regular' exporters *had* been taking serious steps to increase export volume during 1966 and 1967. Having already begun to increase export volume in this way, they may now have been doing all they could to make those exports profitable.

Nor does the fact that most of our other firms, including all the anti-cyclical ones, concentrated on increasing export volume subject to there being no fall in profit per unit of exports, mean that they were not interested in increasing profit at the time of devaluation.

We have seen that the general export objectives of most of our firms was to increase export volume, subject to earning a given rate of return. This implies that over longish periods of time these firms were more concerned with export volume than export profit. It seems that, as the firms grew, and as they installed extra capacity to produce goods for export, these firms were content to earn a roughly constant rate of return on each extra unit of capital employed. However, devaluation was not concerned with long-run growth, but with the firm at a particular moment of time. Since in all our anti-cyclical firms, and in most of the others, there was a good deal of surplus capacity, an increase in exports resulting from devaluation could provide an increase in the total profit earned on a given amount of capital, even if the *rate* of profit per unit of exports remained unchanged. All would depend on the effect of devaluation on total receipts and total costs. In the longer run, a sustained increase in exports would lead sooner or later to a shortage of capital assets. The firm would have to invest extra plant.

Of course, as we have seen, whether making the various price cuts which our firms did make was wise, depended on how elastic the demand for their exports was. They may well have made unnecessarily large price cuts, so that they did not *maximise* the profit of the firm. Nevertheless, these firms may have been acting so as to *increase* profit by their devaluation decisions. Just as we have argued that the 'passive' exporters that held foreign-currency prices constant after devaluation may have been producing more than the profit-maximising output before devaluation, so the 'active' exporters may have been producing less. The apparently different responses they made may have brought *both* types of firm closer to the profit-maximising position. Before devaluation, both types of firm may have been in non-optimal positions, but the 'passive' decision-takers may have been exporting too much, and the 'active' decision-takers too little.

8.17 Conclusions

Our view is that, in general, the firms that reduced their foreign-currency prices as little as possible after devaluation and, even more, those that altered prices by different amounts in different countries took better devaluation decisions than those reducing their prices by the maximum possible amount.

The five firms that tried to reduce foreign-currency prices by as little as possible were: Acton Chemicals, Fulham Castings, Nottingham Confectionery, Peterborough Tubes (X-ply) and Rugby Processing. Apart from Fulham Castings, they delayed their decisions. With the exception of Peterborough Tubes with X-Ply, for which it was technically a monopolist, and Nottingham Confectionery, they were selling relatively homogeneous products in oligopolistic markets. They feared that reductions in price might evoke immediate price cuts by their competitors. By taking no action, they received an automatic increase in sterling receipts while still keeping open the possibility of reducing prices later, in at least some countries, if the situation changed. Because of its monopoly position, Peterborough Tubes was able simply to leave the price of X-ply unchanged.

We think that the four firms that looked carefully at each country or group of countries, in taking their devaluation decisions, took very satisfactory ones indeed. They were: Birmingham Cakes, Hertford Stoves, Inverness Plant Builders and Quantox Construction. By examining each market (or group of markets) separately, they made efficient use of the market information they had. At the same time, they could easily look at relevant costs, because they were all firms which calculated variable cost and contribution. For each market, the question was a simple one. In the case of Hertford Stoves, it was what price changes would maximise contribution. For the other three firms, it was what price change would give the best balance between increased 'contribution' from that market, increased sales volume and increased market share.

We would rank less highly the decisions of the three firms that made different price changes for different groups of countries, but which did not look carefully at the situation in any individual country. These firms were: Jarrow Furniture, Peterborough

Tubes (Product D) and Kendal Accessories, or more accurately, its trade association.

Some criticisms can be made of the eight firms that made price cuts across the board. They were: Cardiff Instruments, Durham Plates, Ealing Electrical Appliances, Gatley Hosiery, London Switches, Oxford Furnaces, Stratford Equipment and Tottenham Piping. Ealing Electrical Appliances, Gatley Hosiery, London Switches and Tottenham Piping had little or no alternative, because of pressure from competitors or customers. Nevertheless, apart from London Switches, which was under pressure from its equal-sized competitor, all these firms might have achieved more satisfactory results if they had made somewhat smaller price cuts, though we admit that there were strong pressures for big price cuts. Cardiff Instruments, Durham Plates, Stratford Equipment and Oxford Furnaces probably all cut prices by more than they need have done. Certainly, Stratford Equipment and Oxford Furnaces seem to have sacrificed profit in an attempt to pursue what, perhaps wrongly, they regarded as the national interest.

None of these eight firms seemed to pay much attention to elasticity of demand. Again, while Ealing Electrical Appliances, in particular, believed that price cuts would maintain goodwill, there was no clear evidence to support this view. Perhaps these firms were also too ready to assume that there would be no retaliation, by their foreign competitors, to any price cuts they made. Indeed, Cardiff Instruments and Tottenham Piping, which made the maximum possible price reductions, did not consider possible retaliation at all. They may have been right in assuming that they would not meet serious price cutting overseas by British firms; they argued that all British firms were likely to react as they themselves did, because circumstances of all British firms had changed similarly. At the same time, several of the firms engaged in collusion with British competitors in determining export prices after devaluation, either through export pricing associations or in other ways. In a similar way, Cardiff Instruments had no close links with other exporters in its industry, but assumed that they would not retaliate if it made price cuts.

Of the four firms that made the maximum possible price reductions, only one (Cardiff Instruments) was in a buoyant market, where demand was satisfactory. Ealing Electrical Appliances, Oxford Furnaces and Tottenham Piping were all selling in depressed markets at the time of devaluation. Ealing and Oxford were having difficulty in remaining competitive with foreign firms. While all these firms were unhappy about their cash flow, their need to maintain sales, output and employment led them to reduce foreign-currency prices. These factors, plus Oxford's desire to be 'patriotic', meant that devaluation led to little improvement in profitability. Even Cardiff Instruments was also suffering from a fall in orders at the time of devaluation, though its cash flow position was still satisfactory.

The remaining four firms which made smaller price cuts, namely, Durham Plates, Gatley Hosiery, London Switches and Stratford Equipment were more profitable, though Durham's profit margins had been narrowed by cost increases. The need to increase capacity utilisation and employment did not seem to be important here. Indeed, we have seen that in London Switches and Stratford Equipment capacity was already under severe pressure.

To sum up, the eight firms that made generally maximum price reductions paid little attention to elasticity of demand, although several of them thought price reductions were necessary to maintain customers' goodwill. They paid little attention to the danger of retaliation by competitors and were little influenced in their decisions by problems over capacity or cash flow.

As we noted earlier, we are surprised that most of our firms concentrated almost exclusively on changing prices rather than other marketing variables. However, the firms whose decisions we rate most highly did look at all marketing variables. In particular, Birmingham Cakes and Hertford Stoves considered them carefully. Similarly, a number of firms, including Jarrow Furniture, had made significant increases in expenditure on other forms of sales promotion, or had reorganised their export organisations, shortly before devaluation. They saw no need to make further changes in November 1967. Part of the reason for the emphasis on price changes may be that our sample contained few consumer-goods firms, but many firms producing basic products whose prices fluctuated on a world market; or intermediate goods, where prices were open to negotiation; or goods sold by tender. Few of our firms had price lists to which they adhered strictly over longish periods, as appears to happen with consumer goods. On the other hand, it is clear from a study of the structure of British exports that the UK still relies heavily on exporting goods where consumer marketing techniques are rarely needed.

CHAPTER 9

Economic Theory and our Findings

In Chapter 2 we saw what predictions economic theory would make about the reactions to devaluation of a firm in each of the competitive situations that economic theory usually distinguishes. We did so, assuming, as economic theory often does, that all firms seek maximum profit. In this chapter, we see how far our firms did what the analysis of Chapter 2 would lead one to expect.

9.1 Perfect Competition

None of our firms was selling overseas in conditions of perfect competition. In one sense, this is of no importance, because we know what a profit-maximising firm selling in a perfectly competitive market would do. It would have no choice but to sell at whatever price competition had established in that market after devaluation. With a homogeneous product, the market is likely to be world-wide. (We follow the normal procedure of economic theory and treat tariffs as incompatible with perfect competition. In practice, a tariff would tend to make prices in different national markets differ by the amount of the tariff. In practice, too, transport costs would differ, and prices would reflect differences in these costs as well.) Even if the firm does not seek maximum profit, to charge less than the price that perfect competition set, in this world market, would be foolish. Since everyone is prepared to buy at the competitive price, it would mean that the firm was taking less profit than it could without securing any competitive advantage in return. Indeed, it would be likely to be overwhelmed by a rush of orders. (Both students and teachers of economics tend to be a little sceptical about this argument. However, Professor Hague's work with the British Price Commission has convinced him that a firm selling a homogeneous product can experience a very considerable rush of business if its price is below those of its competitors, even for a relatively short period.) To charge more than the competitive price would be impossible. It is therefore certain that a firm selling in perfect competition in an overseas market will sell all (or most) of its output at the foreign-currency prices ruling after devaluation. However, it was suggested in Chapter 2 that the world price level is likely to be lower the bigger the percentage of world output sold by firms from the country that has devalued.

9.2   Monopolistic Competition

Three of our firms—Birmingham Cakes, Gatley Hosiery, and Nottingham Confectionery—sold most of their output in overseas markets where there was monopolistic competition, though some of these markets, mainly in smaller countries, would perhaps be better described as oligopolistic.

In general, our case studies for monopolistic competition bear out our predictions in Chapter 2. In all cases, the level of prices in overseas markets was influenced more by the actions of overseas than of British firms. The analysis in Chapter 2 would therefore lead us to predict that the level of foreign-currency prices charged by our firms would alter little after devaluation. They would raise their sterling prices by the full amount of devaluation, or something approaching it. This is what seems to have happened with Gatley Hosiery and Nottingham Confectionery, though the position with Birmingham Cakes is less clear.

It is true that Gatley Hosiery announced, immediately after devaluation, that it would cut foreign-currency prices by about half the amount of devaluation, for exports to all overseas countries, except Russia. However, these cuts were more illusory than real. Since the products and prices for the next season were soon to be announced, very little business could be done at the reduced foreign-currency prices. For the next season, Gatley aimed to charge the same foreign-currency prices as before devaluation. In other words, as Chapter 2 would predict, Gatley decided to accept the level of foreign-currency prices which competition established in overseas markets, with Russia as a special case. Since most firms in these overseas markets were from countries which had *not* devalued, there was no reason for them to change their prices.

As the case study of Birmingham Cakes shows, what happened there was more complicated. The firm decided to alter its price, and the other elements in its marketing mix, so as to give what it saw as the best result in each overseas market. However, this meant that Birmingham Cakes was taking the existing competitive situation in those markets as given, and this situation was largely determined by competition between non-British firms. As with the other two firms in this category, Birmingham Cakes was adjusting to the situation in each of its monopolistically-competitive overseas markets as seemed best in that individual case, but with the competitive situation mainly influenced by foreign firms.

9.3 Oligopoly

Most of our firms were selling in oligopolistic markets both within the UK and overseas. However, to give an accurate account of our findings, we once again need to divide some of our firms into two parts, because they took different decisions for different products. If we do this, we have twenty-one 'firms' selling in oligopolistic markets overseas.

9.3.1 A SUMMARY

A small majority of these 'firms', to be precise eleven out of twenty-one, were selling in depressed overseas markets. Eight were selling in overseas markets that were buoyant. The remaining two 'firms'—Fulham Castings and Tottenham Piping—were selling in markets with a world price, expressed in dollars.

The way that our twenty-one oligopolistic 'firms' reacted to devaluation is shown in Table 9.1.

TABLE 9.1 *Summary of reactions of oligopolists*

Conditions in export markets	Total number of firms	Number of firms that cut foreign-currency price	Number of firms that held (or tried to hold) foreign-currency price
Depressed	11	6	5
Buoyant	8	6	2
World price	2	0	2

What does Table 9.1 show? We saw in Chapter 2 that, unless overseas markets were dominated by British firms, which was not true in any of our cases, then, in a depressed market, one would expect firms to maintain foreign-currency prices. Table 9.1 shows our firms as being about evenly divided between those which held, or tried to hold, foreign-currency prices and those which cut them. One more firm cut foreign-currency prices.

Where overseas markets are buoyant, the kinked average-revenue curve analysis of Chapter 2 suggests that devaluation is likely to be followed by a change of foreign-currency prices, upwards or downwards. Of our eight firms in this category, six cut foreign-currency prices and two held them. No firms increased foreign-currency prices. However, we shall see that the reactions of two of the four firms which cut prices may have been misguided.

The two 'firms' selling in markets where there was a world price behaved as our theoretical analysis would predict. In both cases, sterling prices were increased by the full amount of devaluation, to keep them in line with the (foreign-currency) world price.

Our conclusion must be that about half our 'oligopolistic' firms did what the analysis of Chapter 2 predicted. It will pay us to look in more detail to see whether this first impression is correct. The individual firms in each of the categories we are considering are listed in Table 9.2. We denote each firm by the first letter of its name.

TABLE 9.2   *Reactions of oligopolists*

Condition of market	Firms in category	Firms which cut foreign-currency price	Firms which held (or tried to hold) or increased their foreign-currency price
Depressed	A, D (Product B$_1$), D (Product B–), E,I,J (Europe), O,Q,R,T (Products A, B), T (Product C).	D (Product B$_1$), D (Product B$_2$), E, J (Europe), O, T (Product C).	A,I,Q,R,T (Products A & B).
Buoyant	C,H (North America), H (outside North America), J (North America), L, P (Product D), P (X-ply), S.	C, H (outside North America), J (North America), L,P (Product D), S.	H (North America), P (X-ply)
World price	F, T (Product M).	—	F, T (Product M)

9.3.2   DEPRESSED OVERSEAS MARKETS

We first look at the firms selling in depressed overseas markets at the time of devaluation, beginning with the firms which cut foreign-currency prices after devaluation.

(a) *Firms cutting foreign-currency prices*

For Durham Plates we have distinguished in Table 9.2 between Products B_1 and B_2. All we are doing is to separate off one product (Product B_2), which had recently been introduced, from all other types of Product B, here denoted as B_1. We here look first at Product B_1.

Foreign-currency prices for every grade of Product B_1 were cut by between about 5 and 10%. This decision does not seem to have been based on a careful analysis of elasticity of demand. It was taken simply because Durham's practice had always been to charge the same price for Product B_1, both at home and overseas. After devaluation, the established procedure was continued.

It is not easy to discover whether Product B_1 faced a kinked average revenue curve or not. Despite the cut in its foreign-currency price, exports of Product B_1 fell by 5% in 1968. But this may have been because the whole demand curve for Product B_1 shifted, not because it was 'kinked'. All that one can say is that there is no definite evidence that demand for Product B_1 overseas was elastic. The demand curve may have been kinked, but the firm did not believe that it was.

With its newly introduced Product B_2, Durham Plates decided to increase its sterling price by roughly the full amount of devaluation. The new product was selling well and Durham believed that its sales volume was almost completely inelastic to changes in its prices. Here, the decision to reduce the product's foreign-currency price, but only slightly, resulted from Durham's belief that the sterling price of the product had previously been too low. Before devaluation, Durham Plates had not been maximising its profits from Product B_2. Since we assumed profit-maximisation in Chapter 2, the theory does not pretend to fit.

While Ealing Electrical Appliances faced a depressed demand for caravans in many export markets, its prices were already competitive in most of them, so that there was no compelling reason to reduce export prices. However, Ealing thought that it would be too complicated to make a separate price change for each overseas market. As a result, the firm does not seem to have given serious consideration to any action, except reducing foreign-currency prices, in all countries which did *not* devalue, by about $8\frac{1}{2}$%. It is true that there was some discussion with Ealing about whether this would lead to a price war with foreign manufacturers, especially in Europe. However, since no one was certain whether the demand curve for Ealing's products was kinked or not, the decision was to reduce prices in Europe, as well as everywhere else, by $8\frac{1}{2}$%. In the event, there does not seem to have been any significant retaliation from any competitors in Europe. The firm's assumption that there was no 'kink' in its demand curve seems to have been justified.

Jarrow Furniture (in Europe), although operating in relatively depressed overseas markets, felt that any danger of retaliation by overseas competitors was worth facing. There was severe competition in Europe, and Jarrow found that price was there the most important determinant of sales. Here, the theory lying behind the kinked average-revenue curve describes what happened. Jarrow took the risk of reducing foreign-currency prices by 7·5%, but this led to an increase in sales volume of only 1%. A major reason was that competitors retaliated, cutting their own prices. The situation postulated by the kinked demand curve for a depressed market occurred; a cut in price led to little increase in sales.

In Oxford Furnaces, as we have already pointed out, the firm's decision may well have been misguided. The evidence is that there *was* here a kinked demand curve for Oxford Furnace's products so that, when Oxford cut its export prices, its British competitors were compelled to cut theirs equally. Indeed, we have seen that, had Oxford Furnaces been forced to take a similar decision later, it would almost certainly have held its prices, as economic theory would have predicted. The demand curve was apparently kinked: the decision to cut export prices therefore led competitors to cut their own prices equally, and Oxford Furnaces now sees its decision as wrong.

Tottenham Piping, with Product C, seems to have been a special case. As we have seen, Tottenham was hoping to replace its 'traditional' product by Product C because of the latter's technical superiority. No other British firm produced an identical product, but about 30 American firms, at least three in Europe and one in Japan did so. Tottenham Piping therefore saw a market for Product C 'everywhere in the world' and its sales were growing very rapidly. Tottenham Piping regarded devaluation as providing it with an opportunity to reduce foreign-currency prices, and so obtain a significant increase in sales, in a situation where significant increases in productivity were reducing Tottenham Piping's costs of making Product C. After the event, Tottenham Piping felt that the decision to cut the foreign-currency prices for Product C by the whole amount of devaluation had been very successful, increasing both sales volume and profit.

To sum up, the number of firms selling in depressed overseas markets which cut their prices was perhaps greater than economic theory would have predicted. But this does not mean that the theory itself is wrong. Of the six firms, only two (Jarrow and Oxford) seem, fairly certainly, to have faced kinked demand curves. Despite this, they cut their prices. With Product B_2 of Durham Plates and Product C of Tottenham Piping relatively new, and therefore perhaps special cases, this leaves only two 'firms'— Ealing Electrical Appliances and Durham Plates with Product B_1. While there is no doubt that Ealing's export markets were depressed at the time of devaluation, its price cuts do not seem to have led to retaliation, despite the serious concern within Ealing over whether this would happen. The demand curve for Ealing's products was apparently *not* kinked. For Durham Plates (Product B_1) there is no clear evidence whether it was or not.

(b) *Firms seeking to maintain foreign-currency prices*
We must now consider whether the kinked average-revenue curve analysis explains the decisions of the five 'firms' which tried not to reduce their foreign-currency prices.

Acton Chemicals attempted to hold its foreign-currency prices because it believed that to cut them would simply reduce its profits without increasing its sales, which is what the theory says will happen in a depressed oligopolistic market. We have seen that Acton was unable to sustain its position. But this was the result of pressure from its customers, not its competitors, and does not seem to have led retaliation by competitors, conceivably because the latter were not certain what prices Acton was actually charging. Perhaps to avoid being dependent on one supplier, or a supplier from one country, these customers continued to take the product from a number of firms. All that seems to have happened is that Acton's customers obtained from Acton the same quantity of chemicals as they would have taken in any case, but at lower prices. There is no evidence that this led these customers to substitute British for foreign goods on a significant scale.

Inverness Plant Builders also believed that it faced a kinked demand curve. Indeed, because of this, Inverness was extremely cautious about cutting its prices after devaluation. Its sales manager told us that he believed Inverness had consequently missed some export opportunities. Being so afraid of precipitating a price war, Inverness refused to cut prices at all after devaluation, even though the sales manager later came to believe that small price cuts might have been worthwhile. Inverness took its decisions in the belief that it *did* face a kinked oligopoly demand curve though it now doubts whether, at least for small price cuts, the danger of retaliation was as great as that implies.

Quantox Construction also tried to hold its foreign-currency prices after devaluation. It was Quantox's foreign competitors who felt certain that Quantox would take advantage of devaluation to cut its prices, and attempted to forestall this with price cuts of their own. Quantox was right in believing that it faced a kinked demand curve; it was wrong in believing that it would be able to keep its foreign-currency prices constant. Its competitors simply could not believe that Quantox would be able to resist the opportunity to cut prices. The result, as the kinked oligopoly demand curve predicts, was simply that, in the short run at least, roughly the same amount of business was obtained by the industry as a whole, but at lower prices. As the theory predicts, Quantox feared the results of cutting prices and tried to hold them, but its competitors were more afraid of losing business than of producing a further round of price cutting.

It is not clear exactly what assumptions Rugby Processing was making about the shape of its demand curve. Rugby certainly operates in an oligopolistic industry. However, not only is this an industry where both output and prices fluctuate significantly. It is also one where, in the second half of 1967, output was beginning to recover from depressed levels. Rugby Processing saw no need to test the demand conditions facing it by altering its prices. Had it done so, it might well have discovered that it faced a kinked demand curve.

As for Tottenham Piping's Products A and B, no decision at all was made at the time of devaluation. Because their prices fluctuate with changes in the balance between supply and demand for Product M, Tottenham Piping found it both unnecessary, and perhaps impossible, to separate out the effects of other influences on the price of Product M from that of devaluation. The right time for making changes in the prices of Products A and B would have been if the price of Product M had changed significantly, whether because of devaluation or for some other reason. This decision does not seem to have resulted from fears of retaliation by competitors, but simply from the fact that conditions were too uncertain for a quick decision to be sensible.

It follows that three of the five firms which held, or tried to hold, their foreign-currency prices after devaluation did so because they believed that they faced kinked demand curves. They are: Acton Chemicals, Inverness Plant Builders and Quantox Construction. They reacted in the way that the theory in Chapter 2 would predict. Rugby Processing may well have done so too. Only Tottenham Piping (Products A and B) does not seem very certain what shape of demand curve it faced.

(c) *Conclusions*

The conclusion for our eleven oligopolistic firms selling in relatively depressed overseas markets must therefore be this. While not all behaved in the way that economic theory would predict, five of the eleven appear to have faced kinked oligopolistic demand curves. While only two of the six firms that cut prices seem to have faced kinked demand curves, it is possible that as many as four of the five firms that held them did so.

Our feeling is that the notion of the kinked demand curve comes out of this part of the study rather well. We must emphasise again that the kinked demand curve analysis is only one method for predicting what will happen with pricing decisions under oligopoly. We have insisted that such decisions are difficult to predict because the possible reactions of competitors are rather more numerous than this simple device implies. We therefore find the number of our 'firms', selling in depressed markets, which appear to have been thinking explicitly or implicitly in these terms gratifyingly large.

9.3.3 BUOYANT OVERSEAS MARKETS

We now look at the firms that were selling in buoyant overseas markets. As we have seen, in such conditions the kinked average-revenue curve analysis predicts that foreign-currency prices are likely to be changed after devaluation. The raw data suggests that this prediction is borne out. Six firms out of eight cut their foreign-currency prices, and only two held them. However, examination of the individual decisions themselves does not suggest that they often resulted from the kind of situation postulated by those who developed the concept of the kinked average-revenue curve.

(a) *Firms which cut foreign-currency prices*

Cardiff Instruments seems to have cut its prices mainly because it felt that, technologically, it was falling behind its competitors and therefore needed to boost sales of its products. Like most economic theory, that of the kinked average-revenue curve assumes that technology is constant. It would not claim to deal with a situation where it changed. As for Jarrow Furniture in North America, the firm did not intend to change its foreign-currency prices. It did so only because of intense pressure from its North American subsidiary. This situation, also, was not assumed by the theory.

Nor is the kinked average-revenue curve theory relevant to the decisions taken by London Switches and Stratford Equipment. With rapidly growing overseas demand in both cases, the theory of Chapter 2 predicts that prices are more likely to be raised than to remain stable. It would certainly not suggest that they would be reduced, for neither firm had spare capacity. In the event, London Switches cut export prices because it was persuaded to do so by its competitor. Stratford Equipment did so because it believed that this would be a 'patriotic' gesture, an eventuality that, again, economic theory normally ignores.

With Hertford Stoves, its market, both inside and outside North America, was reasonably buoyant at the time of devaluation, but there was strong Japanese competition outside North America. Hertford Stoves did not cut its prices wholly in order to take advantage of the fact that it had spare capacity, as the theory suggests. It did so rather to meet this competition. However, demand was sufficiently buoyant to allow Hertford Stoves to make these cuts without fearing significant retaliation. Within North America, Hertford Stoves felt able to maintain its foreign-currency prices, because the Japanese were not at the time competing effectively in that part of the total product range for Product H where Hertford Stoves was concentrating.

For Peterborough Tubes, with Product D, sales were growing rapidly. However, as with Hertford Stoves, the firm felt that, to meet competition, it would pay to cut prices. Having enough spare capacity, Peterborough felt that since it was selling in a buoyant market it could safely cut prices and obtain a competitive advantage. This is what the theory says.

With X-ply, Peterborough Tubes, like Hertford Stoves in North America, was in a strong market position through the world and felt that it could safely hold prices because demand was reasonably buoyant. For neither firm did there seem to be any justification for increasing prices. The position of their foreign competitors was unchanged, and there was therefore no apparent incentive for those competitors to follow our firms if they increased their prices. But there seemed to be equally little reason for cutting prices.

The correspondence between the theory of Chapter 1 and what happened, therefore, seems to be less in the case of the firms in buoyant markets than with those in depressed ones. While the two firms which held prices were behaving in line with the theory, only two (Peterborough Tubes and perhaps Hertford Stoves) among the six firms which cut prices seemed to be doing so.

9.3.4   FIRMS SELLING AT A WORLD PRICE

We have seen that the two 'firms' in this situation were Fulham Castings and Tottenham Piping (Product M). They both behaved as our theory would predict. Sterling prices were increased by the full amount of devaluation, to keep them in line with the world price, expressed in both cases in dollars. However, especially with Fulham Castings, where the firm felt it could take extra business by setting a price slightly lower than the world level, without suffering retaliatory price cuts, it did so. Devaluation gave both firms increased incentives to do this. This situation for a price increase was similar to that in perfect competition, in the sense that if the individual firm increased its price above the world level it would lose a very great deal of its custom. However, the situation was different for a significant price cut. Any significant reduction was likely to lead to retaliatory cuts by competitors, so that it would not attract extra business in the way that it would in perfect competition. These firms were selling in the special situation of oligopoly with homogeneous products.

9.4   Firms in Cartels

Economic theory finds prediction very difficult where decisions are taken by cartels. Provided that its members obey its rules, a cartel will behave like a monopolist and, as we saw in Chapter 2, a monopolist has great discretion in pricing. With both Durham Plates (for Product A) and Kendal Accessories, the cartel was a monopolist only within the UK. Outside the UK, each cartel was competing with a number of firms, though the number was smaller for Durham Plates than for Kendal Accessories. This may explain why, while the decision of Durham Plates' cartel does not seem to have taken demand conditions seriously into account, it experienced little difficulty in putting its decision into effect. In the case of Kendal Accessories, the decision of the cartel does not seem to have taken sufficient account of competitive conditions in world markets. The cartel's whole price list had to be revised about a year after devaluation.

9.5   Conclusions

What our firms did seems to have been fairly close to what economic theory would predict. The firms belonging to export cartels found that they had the degree of freedom that a monopolist in their position would have had, as the theory would suggest.

The three firms operating in monopolistic competition obviously had little choice in the decisions they took. So did the two oligopolists selling products that had world market prices. However, we think that the remaining oligopolists behaved more in line with the predictions in Chapter 2 than many economists would have expected. Economists are prone to say that 'the solution to the oligopoly problem is indeterminate'. We think that many of them would see the kinked average-revenue curve analysis as simply a brave attempt to solve an insoluble problem. The fact that a significant number of our oligopolistic firms selling in depressed markets behaved in the way that the theory would suggest is gratifying, though one can be less satisfied about the way the decisions of the firms selling in buoyant markets fitted the theory.

CHAPTER 10

Summary and Conclusions

In this Chapter we summarise the main findings of our study.

10.1 The Study

We looked at the way that nineteen British firms responded to devaluation. We considered how far they anticipated devaluation; what their objectives were at the time and whether devaluation changed them; whether they took advantage of new opportunities for exporting or for import substitution; and how the devaluation decisions were taken.

All the firms were manufacturing businesses. Six produced consumer goods on a large scale; five produced components; four processed basic materials; and four sold capital goods. Most firms met more major competitors in export markets than in the UK. Three had no competition in the UK for the products we studied; four more had only one effective competitor. The numbers of competitors met in the UK, and the extent to which the firms' own capacity was producing for the UK, influenced attitudes towards exporting. In export markets, the number of competitors varied from country to country. The capital-goods manufacturers usually faced a small number of competitors for each tender they submitted, and the component and basic-material firms also usually met a few competitors in each overseas country. The consumer-goods manufacturers faced more.

In all but two of the firms, a study of confidential information about the devaluation decisions, including papers circulated at the time, was supplemented by interviews with both senior and middle management.

We found the concept of 'contribution' an important one. If one splits a firm's total costs into their fixed and variable elements, then to make a profit the firm must cover both its variable and fixed costs and have something left over. However, while it is usually possible to identify the variable costs incurred in producing different amounts of a given product, this is not possible with fixed costs. The most one can say about the profitability of any individual product, and *a fortiori* about any individual unit of output that is exported, is usually that it has covered the variable costs incurred in its production and contributed a certain amount towards fixed costs and, hopefully, profit.

Contribution is defined more fully in Chapter 2. Briefly, we may define 'unit contribution' as the difference between the price of a unit of output and the average variable cost incurred in producing that unit. This is often known also as the 'contribution margin'. 'Total contribution' is the difference between the total receipts from selling a given quantity of output and the total variable costs incurred in producing and selling it.

Contribution from a unit of output exported is therefore the amount of money received from the sale of that unit of output abroad minus the variable costs incurred in producing it and getting it to the customer.

10.2   Objectives

Five of our firms were 'anti-cyclical' exporters which saw exports as something of an expedient, to be given priority only when the home market was depressed. Fourteen of our firms were 'regular' exporters, which saw exports as an important and permanent part of their activities. At the time of devaluation, the UK markets of all five anti-cyclical exporters were depressed and they had therefore been increasing their export effort, but from necessity rather than choice. Their success had been limited.

All the regular exporters had marketing organisations in their important overseas markets and five had production plants overseas. A major reason for the emphasis that the regular exporters put on exports was that most of them could see only limited opportunities for increasing their sales of existing products at home, not only in the short run as with the anti-cyclical exporters, but even in the medium or long run. Nor, because they lacked the necessary expertise and/or experience, did they see profitable opportunities for moving into the production of new products. Several of our firms already dominated the home market for their products and so saw the best hope for growth in exporting.

The firms whose home sales were growing rapidly had less coherent export policies, but still exported a good deal because demand in overseas markets was also growing rapidly. The anti-cyclical exporters were not satisfied with profits on exports, but the regular exporters were in a better position, though at the time of devaluation few were earning as much on overseas sales as at home. We are confident that this is true despite the difficulty of identifying 'profit' on exports as distinct from home sales.

Of our nineteen firms, fourteen had general objectives that required them to increase market share or sales volume in varying degrees, subject to earning a required rate of profit. Two more firms sought to maximise sales, subject to earning a required rate of profit. Only three firms (Hertford Stoves, Birmingham Cakes and Fulham Castings) aimed at maximising contribution, though Jarrow Furniture aimed at the maximum profit from budgeted sales and Quantox Construction at the maximum 'contribution' from the business which the firm believed it could obtain.

Export objectives were similar. All firms, except Hertford Stoves and Birmingham Cakes, were more concerned with export volume than export profits.

Nine of our firms had specific, quantitative objectives for each major market overseas, and altered these only marginally at the time of devaluation. Three firms sought to achieve a budgeted total amount of sterling export turnover. Seven firms found it too difficult to draw up export targets for individual overseas markets because demand in them fluctuated too much.

In responding to devaluation, eight 'firms' sought to increase sterling profit on their existing exports by the full amount of devaluation, and not to increase export volume. Nine 'firms' aimed at increasing export sales, subject to there being no reduction in profit per unit of exports. Hertford Stoves sought to maximise contribution, while Durham Plates and Stratford Equipment sought 'modest' increases in profit. No 'firm' saw devaluation as requiring it to re-think its export objectives completely. (We have a total of twenty 'firms' here, because Peterborough Tubes appears twice. On X-ply, it sought to increase profits from the existing export volume; on Product D, it sought to increase export volume.)

10.3 Market Information

In general, our firms had enough information to take good devaluation decisions. They were well-informed about their own sales and prices in export markets and reasonably informed about those of competitors. This information appeared to be more detailed the bigger the percentage of the firm's total sales turnover coming from exports.

An economist would expect a firm deciding how to respond to devaluation to want information about elasticity of demand. In November 1967, none of our firms had tried to work out elasticity of demand in any market with rigour. This was true even where the firm had reliable and detailed statistical information. After devaluation, Jarrow Furniture began to estimate elasticity of demand and found doing so worthwhile. Two other firms had tried to measure elasticity before devaluation but found it too difficult. Nevertheless, this kind of information *is* important. To take good decisions, a firm must form a judgement about the relationship between price and quantity sold especially where, as our firms did, it responds to devaluation by changing price rather than other marketing variables. More information about elasticity of demand would have been especially helpful to the five of our nineteen firms which examined the situation separately in all, or most, of their individual markets. However, they did try to sense what it was.

Where the market was oligopolistic, it was important for the firm to assess the likely reactions of its competitors. This is something to which both business men and economists have probably paid too little attention, despite the interest of the latter in the phenomenon of oligopoly. Of our fifteen firms where competitors' reactions were important at the time of devaluation, we think that only six looked with sufficient care at what these reactions were likely to be. However, only two of these found the actual reactions embarrassing.

To take good devaluation decisions, then, our firms needed information about market size and market shares, elasticity of demand and competitors' reactions. In principle, they also needed information about the way sales were likely to respond to increased expenditure on other forms of sales promotion. However, few of our firms sold products where such expenditure was relevant. We think that seven of our nineteen firms had good information on market factors and six moderate information. Six had information which did not impress us. We cannot say that the last six firms had inadequate information. Our studies were not detailed enough to allow us to give a judgement.

Moreover, information about export markets was often difficult to obtain, especially for markets in less-developed countries. It was also expensive, because many of these markets were small and most of our firms exported to a large number of them. The cost of obtaining *all* the information that would have been useful in making decisions about exports would have been prohibitive. In general, it seemed to us that our firms were sensible in the way they sought information about export markets.

Perhaps more of our firms should have used probability analysis, assigning probabilities to the likelihood that possible business would be obtained, and so calculating an expected value for the business they were likely to take in each relevant future period. Cardiff Instruments and Inverness Plant Builders were already finding it useful to do this and Quantox Construction had made substantial progress towards doing so.

10.4   Cost Information

Of our nineteen firms, four had to set a price for each individual contract, while fifteen based their prices on a general price list. Sixteen of the nineteen said they worked in terms of contribution. Of the fifteen firms that based prices on price lists, ten found it difficult to calculate the increases in cost which devaluation was likely to cause. They found it hard to identify which raw material and component costs would increase; they found it difficult to predict the size of such increases and to make the necessary calculations quickly enough.

However, we must emphasise that this task was not as easy as it may sound. In a world where costs were rising or falling because of other factors than devaluation, it was difficult to decide which cost increases were the result of devaluation and which of the other factors. More important, our firms did not have the same interest as we did in keeping the two kinds of cost increase separate. The important thing for them at the time of devaluation was to charge the right prices, whether the cost increases they had to allow for in doing so were a result of devaluation itself or of other factors. What is clear is that, though most of our firms worked in terms of variable cost and contribution, many gave marginal (or variable) cost little weight in their devaluation decisions. They argued that marginal costs were more relevant when quoting prices for individual customers than when taking decisions about the whole of their export sales.

However, we did find some cases where we felt that the cost calculations were misleading. For example, while we have rated the decisions taken by Birmingham Cakes very highly, we found that the standard product which was re-costed after devaluation was manufactured in several stages. At each stage, a margin was included in the cost estimates to allow for a possible under-estimation of cost increases at the previous stage. The total size of these margins was big enough to cause a significant increase in the size of Birmingham's estimate of the rise in costs caused by devaluation and may have influenced its devaluation decisions. So, while we were impressed by the decision-taking in Birmingham Cakes, this criticism could be made even there.

The methods that our firms used to calculate the size of cost increases were sometimes very simple. In Cardiff Instruments,

Ealing Electrical Appliances, Inverness Plant Builders and Kendal Accessories, the effect of devaluation on costs was worked out 'on the back of envelopes'. They relied heavily on the predictions of individuals, especially cost accountants. These were firms where the devaluation decisions were taken very quickly, although we could see no pressing commercial reasons for doing so. The rough, hurried costings used were not formally revised later, and the devaluation decisions, once made, were adhered to.

10.5 The Decisions

Every one of our nineteen firms made an explicit decision about what to do after devaluation. They concentrated more on deciding what export prices to charge than on whether to change other marketing variables. Birmingham Cakes, Hertford Stoves and Jarrow Furniture were the exceptions. This is a statement of fact, not a criticism. Many of the firms we studied sold products where price was the only relevant marketing variable.

In seven cases, the decision about export prices was taken on the initiative of an individual manager or managing director within a day or two of devaluation. These decisions were effectively worked out by one man, though after discussions with other managers. In two cases, the decisions were taken by the pricing committee of an export association. In eight firms, the decision was taken by a group of managers, usually small. In three of these firms, Acton Chemicals, Ealing Electrical Appliances and Jarrow Furniture, a special meeting was called under the chairmanship of the managing director or general manager within a few days of devaluation. Finally, there were three firms which were selling raw materials. Two of them were selling products whose prices were wholly, or almost wholly, set in world markets.

There were three main types of decision. Either foreign-currency prices were held in all markets; or they were cut in all markets; or different decisions were taken for each individual market or group of markets.

Of our twenty 'firms' (here, again, Peterborough Tubes has been counted twice), thirteen made the same decision for all markets. Of these thirteen, six held prices and seven cut them. In four of the thirteen 'firms', the need to take a decision as quickly as possible was seen as justifying them in taking across-the-board decisions and in three of the four the wide geographical spread of their export activities was given as an additional justification. The other firm, Fulham Castings, increased export price in all markets, because its price was closely linked to a world price set in dollars.

Some or all of the firms which made across-the-board price cuts spoke of 'devaluation hysteria' among their customers or colleagues.

The remaining seven 'firms' took individual decisions for some, or all, overseas markets. Because it took its time in drawing up a contingency plan, Hertford Stoves was able to do this even though it sold in about 100 countries. Birmingham Cakes made no contingency plan but had significant overseas markets only in the USA, Canada and seven European countries. Its decisions took about three weeks.

There was uniformity among our firms, in the sense that all but one were able to increase exports after devaluation, both in volume and value (turnover), although only eight were convinced that devaluation increased the profitability of total exports. There was considerable reluctance to attribute the increases in either export volume or export profit to devaluation. Unfortunately, the relative effects of devaluation and of other changes in overseas markets are difficult to disentangle, so we cannot prove or disprove the view our firms took.

Whether or not sales promotion expenditure was changed depended on the product being sold. All four capital-goods producers cut their sterling export prices substantially. Partly because this left a relatively small margin for increased expenditure on sales promotion, but partly because they were selling to experts so that other forms of sales promotion were unimportant, they made very small increases in sales promotion expenditure. The nine firms producing components and other intermediate products behaved similarly. Among the six consumer-goods manufacturers, only three increased sales promotion expenditure more than marginally.

Even where a significant change was made in total sales promotion expenditure, there was little or no increase in the amount spent per unit of export sales. In all firms where an increase in the volume of export sales depended on sales promotion expenditure, if only the cost of tendering more seriously for business in a country, there was an increase in such effort in all countries where the firm was already selling. In some cases, firms also began to tender seriously for business in countries where they had not previously sold. However, there was no case where devaluation caused a firm to establish a new marketing organisation in a foreign country.

After devaluation, one might have expected that there would be a general move towards import substitution. However, none of our firms switched to British suppliers on a significant scale because devaluation had increased import prices. The reason most commonly given was that the products in question were not produced in sufficient quantities in the UK. With a basic raw material, there was usually a 'world' market for the product. British suppliers of such products therefore usually maintained foreign-currency prices, raised sterling prices within the UK, and so removed any advantage to British firms from import substitution. At the same time, most of our firms were operating within the UK in market conditions that were buoyant enough to allow them to recover from their customers any increase in costs caused by higher import prices. This reduced the pressure to look for cheaper, home-produced substitutes. All our firms could pass on the costs of raw materials and components to customers and continue to operate reasonably profitably. It must be emphasised, that these conclusions apply only to our firms, though the evidence given in Table 1.3 (p. 25) suggests that there was little import substitution in the UK as a whole after devaluation.

In our firms, the incentive to replace imports was not seen as strong enough to justify any break with traditional foreign suppliers or any effort to look systematically for new suppliers within the UK. Despite the small number of firms we studied, we think this finding is of more general significance. There were high hopes, both inside and outside government, of substantial import substitution after November 1967. These were not realised, as Table 1.3 shows.

Some of our firms appeared to reduce their foreign-currency prices because they believed that not to do so would in some sense defeat the Government's objective in devaluing. London Switches, Stratford Equipment and Oxford Furnaces, in particular, apparently reduced foreign-currency prices for this reason, despite a conviction that demand in their export markets was price inelastic. The most important factor introducing confusion into our firms' decision taking at the time of devaluation was the attempt to pursue the national interest rather than their private interests. Our firms found it difficult to work out what the national interest required.

Ministerial statements do not seem to have helped. While there was mention of reduced prices in the speeches of some Ministers, there was no clear injunction to British firms to cut export prices. Indeed, perhaps the lack of any clear advice on this point was the problem. Firms were far from certain what the national interest *did* require. One difficulty was that most of our firms were operating in oligopolistic markets, so that if one British firm cut its prices after devaluation its British competitors were usually forced, by the complaints of customers, to do the same. For example, the fact that Oxford Furnaces cut its prices appears to have enabled foreign customers to force all its UK competitors to make similar cuts.

Some of our firms referred to an atmosphere of 'devaluation hysteria' induced in colleagues, customers and overseas agents by the pronouncements of British ministers and industrialists. Abroad, it was the result of comment in newspapers, radio and television, particularly in the USA. Such factors were important in some of the decisions we studied. Apart from 'devaluation hysteria', there was the desire to pursue the 'national interest' and bargaining factors. For example, negotiations between Acton Chemicals and its customers led to price reductions because the customers threatened to take their business elsewhere if Acton did not reduce its prices. Economists predicting the effect of a devaluation perhaps assume too readily that what happens after that devaluation is determined by impersonal economic forces.

Apart from Fulham Castings and Hertford Stoves, none of our firms tried to work out a contingency plan before devaluation. Most of the firms realised that devaluation was likely during 1967 but, apart from these two firms, did not think that drawing up a contingency plan would be worth the effort it entailed. Many firms stressed the informality of the relationships between their executives, claiming that the latter would 'know what to do' if there were a devaluation.

We would certainly not argue that a firm which did not make contingency plans for devaluation was wrong. However, Hertford Stoves benefitted from having a contingency plan and the other firms may have been too ready to dismiss the idea. Some, at least, of their decisions would have been more satisfactory if they had been made at greater leisure. The fact that Hertford Stoves accurately predicted the amount of devaluation, and so had several weeks in which to work out at leisure how to respond to it, was the main reason why its decisions were among the best we studied.

The particular set of firms we chose to consider included several examples of bilateral oligopoly—where small numbers of British firms were selling to small numbers of foreign customers—and where these customers forced the firms to reduce prices by more than they wished to do. We do not know how frequently such a market situation is met, although we certainly did not take it into account when we chose our firms. We doubt whether the fact that firms like this were selling under conditions of bilateral oligopoly in 1967 had much influence on the way devaluation affected the UK balance of payments. Nevertheless, the fact that such a market situation can occur should be borne in mind by those responsible for similar changes in British economic policy.

What happened in bilateral oligopoly is linked to another factor. Unlike the devaluation in 1949, Britain's devaluation in 1967 was followed by very few other countries. Our firms stressed that British export prices therefore became the focus of world-wide attention. Many foreign customers expected an immediate reduction in the foreign-currency prices of British goods and the fact that Britain was the only major trading country to devalue may have increased the size of the export price cuts that British firms had to make.

Early in our research, we discovered that the overseas agents in one or two firms, especially Ealing Electrical Appliances and Jarrow Furniture, had put considerable pressure for export price reductions on these firms, pointing out that foreign customers expected British prices to be reduced. Indeed, we have seen that one of Ealing's agents decided to make the price reductions on his own initiative, without consulting Ealing. Later in the study, we therefore looked with some care at the effect that our firms' agents had on their devaluation decisions. While we found one or two interesting examples of the roles that agents play we did not, in the end, feel that they had very much influence on the reactions of our nineteen firms to devaluation.

One slightly odd fact is worth recording. We rated the decisions by Birmingham Cakes and Hertford Stoves highly Both firms looked at devaluation in terms of the effect it could have on 'contribution'; both looked at conditions in each export market separately; and Hertford Stoves drew up a contingency plan. Yet both firms did very badly in export markets in 1968. Because of credit restrictions in the USA, the overseas sales and profits of Hertford Stoves fell substantially. In Birmingham Cakes, while exports increased a good deal, profits fell because of an increase (over which Birmingham had no control) in the price of an important raw material. However, this does not affect our view of their decisions. While devaluation was followed by low profits in 1968, profits in both firms would have fallen even further if the devaluation decisions had not been taken so well.

10.6   Conclusions

10.6.1   FOR THE COUNTRY

From a national point of view there seem to be three conclusions from our study.

First, if a country is going to devalue, doing so after a long 'squeeze' on the economy appears to be the best possible time. Having found business difficult to obtain at home, firms have already begun to seek ways of increasing exports. Devaluation gives them the opportunity to cut export prices, to increase export marketing expenditure or simply to find greater profit in and therefore greater enthusiasm for, export activities that they have already begun to expand.

Second, it seems that in November 1967, and for a year or more afterwards, our firms found the very idea of devaluation so unpalatable that they were prepared to go out of their way to give credit for what happened after devaluation to *anything* except devaluation itself. Governments should not pay too much attention to what businessmen *say* about the effects of devaluation. What they do is what matters.

Third, much of the economic advice given to governments assumes that markets are perfectly competitive, or nearly so. As our study has shown, in some situations there is competition between small numbers of buyers and small numbers of sellers— bilateral oligopoly. What will happen to export prices and volumes after devaluation in bilateral oligopoly is much more problematical than in most other situations and there may be government policy decisions in which this is important.

10.6.2 FOR THE FIRM

For a firm facing devaluation there seem to be six lessons.

First, if at all possible, the firm should not rush its decisions. Many of our firms would have taken better decisions had they done so more slowly. Cost calculations would not have been so rushed; agents and other overseas colleagues could have been consulted; individual markets could have been studied separately. As what Hertford Stoves did shows, there really is a lot to be said for drawing up a contingency plan when devaluation looks likely.

Second, the firm must look in enough detail at individual markets or groups of markets in taking its decisions. Doing this, if only for its major markets, can be rewarding.

Third, as with all pricing decisions, it is important for the firm to look at its response to devaluation in marginal terms. It should work in terms of variable (or marginal) rather than average (unit) cost.

Fourth, our firms, at least, seemed to have had rather strange ideas of what the national interest required. Unless the firm is absolutely clear what the national interest is, it should realise that its devaluation decisions may well be bad ones if they aim at satisfying the national interest rather than the interest of the firm.

Fifth, the firm must carefully watch the reactions of customers and competitors. In particular, it should beware of being stampeded by 'devaluation hysteria' into cutting prices, either at home or in other countries, further than is profitable.

Sixth, if devaluation is likely, the firm should set its export prices in a stable (or appreciating) foreign currency rather than in its own.

Part II
The Case Studies

Acton Chemicals

A.1 General Background

Acton Chemicals was the British subsidiary of a large inter-national chemical group and manufactured basic chemicals. The one which was most typical of Acton's output, Product A, was both cheap and widely used. Competition in the industry was keen, because most industrialised countries were largely self-sufficient in Product A. As a result, profits were low both in the UK and overseas. The main manufacturers, including Acton, had been forced to find ways of reducing their costs in the hope of reducing the pressure on their profits.

A.1.1 THE INDUSTRY

Consumption of Product A in the UK had more than trebled in volume between 1961 and 1968; it had risen by about 240%. The percentage growth rate was consistently high, but there had been a period of relative stagnation in 1965 and 1966, when Govern-ment economic policy was restrictive. Rapid growth was resumed in 1967 (with output up 13%) and in 1968 (19%), but these percentages must be compared with increases of 35% in 1964, and 49% in 1962.

Acton Chemicals had only two British competitors in the UK at the time of devaluation and they accounted for about 50 and 4%, respectively, of home market sales of Product A. Imports represented a major source of supply, and foreign firms had a share of the UK market that had varied between 15 and 25%. In the years before 1967, the trend in imports had been downwards. There were eight identifiable foreign firms selling in the UK market, of which only two were of significance.

Exports of Product A were important to the industry; in 1961, and again in 1963, more than half its output was exported. Later, the proportion dropped, and in 1967 it was only 25%, although precise figures are not available.

The price of Product A was determined by supply and demand in world markets; one could speak of a world price. Although this price fluctuated considerably, the products of different firms were virtually identical. However, because of tariffs, prices in individual countries differed. In any country, however, no firm could charge even a slightly different price from the others for long, without either losing almost all custom or being swamped with orders. Moreover, so long as the appropriate price was charged, business could be obtained by providing reliable supplies and by establishing friendly relations with customers.

The price of Product A had been falling steadily since the early 1950s, with the biggest fall in the period 1958–62. Prices fell less quickly in the next three years, but in 1966 the downward trend was resumed, and prices were still falling at the time of devaluation. Between 1960 and 1967 the average price per ton had fallen by about 32%. These price falls were a result of considerable excess capacity in the rest of the world. Before devaluation, Acton Chemicals and the other major British producer had submitted a joint application to the Board of Trade for an anti-dumping duty to be imposed against some imports. This had been approved just before devaluation.

A.1.2 THE FIRM

Between 1960 and 1967, home sales by Acton Chemicals rose by 175%, so that its market share was declining over the period. In volume, Acton's share of the British market fell from a peak of 37% in 1962 to a low of 25% in 1964. It then rose steadily to 28% in 1967. We have seen that this was a market containing two significant British firms, but where imports represented a major source of supply.

Exports by Acton Chemicals rose by 37% in volume in the period 1961–64, and then stagnated for three years. Exports represented a relatively small proportion of total sales, accounting for 16% by volume in 1967. Export prices were much lower than those at home. Since 1961, the realised export price had never been less than 11% lower than the home market price. In 1963, a sharp rise in the volume of exports (32%) was achieved at the cost of a difference between home and export prices of about 20%. These low overseas prices do not include the extra cost of transport on exports, which effectively limited the export market to Western Europe, although small amounts of Product A had been sold, at times, to Eastern European countries. Sales to countries outside Europe were virtually ruled out by high tariffs

A.2   Export Position

Traditionally, Acton Chemicals had regarded its export business as unimportant because of the relatively low profitability. Whenever the home market had expanded, Acton had reduced exports. However, this policy had been changed after a review of Acton's sales strategy undertaken a month before devaluation. The reason for the review was that Acton Chemicals was converting its production plant to use a new process, and progress in doing so was very slow, because of technical snags. The parts of Acton's plant that had not yet been converted were consequently having difficulty in meeting demand. There was no immediate crisis, but it seemed likely that productive capacity would fall short of demand for the next few months. It was therefore necessary to decide how to ration output between customers.

Acton Chemicals decided that it would remain permanently in the export market, though the proportion of its output to be exported would be relatively small. This was a deliberate change from its previous policy, and was partly due to a close and profitable relationship which Acton Chemicals had recently built up with two major overseas customers. Between them, they accounted for half of Acton's export volume. One was in Sweden and the other in Eire. Acton Chemicals thought that it would be in its own best long-term interests to increase its sales to these customers, whose purchases were likely to grow rapidly. Negotiations were therefore begun, and informal understandings were reached with these customers. They promised to remain loyal to Acton Chemicals in return for being given priority in supplies of Product A and assurances that the price they paid for it would be reasonably stable. Sales to all other export customers were to continue on an 'anti-cyclical' basis, with the aim of using up the small amount of capacity that Acton expected to have left after supplying its home market. When devaluation took place, Acton Chemicals felt wholly justified in having taken these decisions.

A.3   Objectives

Acton Chemicals' main objectives were reviewed only a month before devaluation. The target rate of return on total capital employed was set at 20% before tax. However, this was not a realistic figure. Acton had *lost* 15% on capital employed in 1965–66; in earlier years the return had usually been well below $7\frac{1}{2}$%. For the home market, the objective was to increase market share beyond the 28% held in October 1967. Indeed, by 1972, it was hoped to regain the 37% market share held in 1962 by introducing an improved grade of product and by bringing extended and more efficient plant into operation. There was no intention to cut prices, since they were expected to drift downwards in any case.

As for exports, it had been agreed with the two customers in Sweden and Eire that they would be given priority in supplies of Product A provided that they remained loyal to Acton Chemicals. These customers had been chosen after a study of the likely growth of the markets for their final products. As we have seen, sales to other export customers were to continue on an anti-cyclical basis. Devaluation strongly reinforced Acton's decision, taken in October 1967, to remain permanently in the export market but to concentrate its sales on the two main customers. However, the other export markets looked more encouraging after devaluation, though the emphasis of Acton's overseas selling effort was switched from the EEC to EFTA.

A.4 Market Information

Until a year before devaluation, Acton Chemicals had been content to obtain rather haphazard information about its export markets. However, it had recently been taken over by another firm, whose management had made a study of each of Acton's export markets while preparing the annual budget for the whole group.

As we have seen, for logistic reasons, Acton's export markets were mainly in European countries close to the UK. For these, Acton had just analysed trends in consumption of Product A over the previous four years and had projected them for the next four. This analysis was carried out by the parent company and was very sketchy for some markets. Nevertheless, Acton was able to persuade its two major export customers, whose consumption seemed likely to grow more rapidly than that of any other customers either at home or abroad, to help in this forecasting exercise. These two firms provided detailed information about the growth prospects for their own products and hence their requirements from Acton. Acton's management felt confident that the two firms would continue to take their supplies from Acton.

Acton Chemicals offered standard discounts for individual orders, depending on the quantity of product bought and on delivery terms. However, Acton found it very difficult to discover what discounts were being offered to its customers by competitors, since customers often bluffed in order to obtain more favourable treatment.

As we have seen, Acton had made a detailed study of its export markets only a month before devaluation, in order to discover how best to ration Product A while it modernised its plant. In this review, besides forecasting trends in consumption, Acton had investigated the demand and capacity position of its European and British competitors and had concluded that they would quickly match any price changes it made. At the same time, the likely effects of the 'Kennedy round' reductions in EEC tariffs were examined.

When devaluation took place, Acton Chemicals was therefore quite well-informed about its export market position.

A.5 Internal Factors

Acton Chemicals was acutely embarrassed by the production difficulties, which limited the number of courses of action open to it at the time of devaluation. Because the price of Product A had been falling steadily, Acton had decided that the best way to prevent a further fall in profits would be to cut production costs by introducing the latest production technique. Accordingly, Acton Chemicals invested in a new, foreign production process at the beginning of 1967. It hoped that the quality of Product A would then be more acceptable to its customers, enabling it to increase its market share. However, we have seen that the change from the higher-cost process did not take place as smoothly as had been hoped. The cost of solving the technical problems was so great that profits were reduced still further. By October 1967, it was recognised that these difficulties were unlikely to be over-come before the end of 1968. During this period, Acton's output would be too small to allow it to meet all the demands of its customers. However, at the time of devaluation Acton still had enough capacity to be able to increase output somewhat.

Acton Chemicals had a standard costing system based on contribution. Prices, both at home and overseas, were worked out from this system. In the period before 1966, the downward trend in Acton's export prices had meant that they were sometimes below unit cost, which included allocated overheads, though we have seen that Acton did not normally allocate overheads.

Within six days of devaluation, its effect on the costs of Acton's main raw materials had been worked out in detail. Since most of these were already available on favourable terms from the parent group, the detailed cost increases were then worked out in a special computer study of all the parent company's costs. This study was completed towards the end of December 1967. The increase in total costs, for the output budgeted for 1968, was put at $3\frac{1}{2}\%$.

A.6 The Decisions

On Monday 20 November, a meeting was held to discuss export prices after devaluation. The general manager of Acton Chemicals was chairman, and the meeting included Acton's divisional managers, and their main subordinates. There was a separate discussion about the price of each product sold by Acton. A general memorandum on pricing policy, signed by the general manager, was distributed on the same day. For Product A, a revised set of home and export sales targets was drawn up by the marketing manager on 8 January 1968. These increased the budgeted volume of exports slightly, and revised their (sterling) unit values by the full amount of devaluation. In July 1968, these sales forecasts were increased again, mainly because there was now more information about the amounts of Product A that the two main export customers were likely to buy. These amounts did not seem to be significantly affected by devaluation. The expected increase in purchases was mainly due to rapid growth in these customers' domestic markets.

The preliminary cost estimates had been made before the meeting on 20 November, but only for the main raw materials. Increased raw material prices were expected to increase Acton's total costs by about $3\frac{1}{2}\%$, but it was decided to seek approval for price increases of 9%, within the UK, in order to cover other cost increases. These included the 'cost' of losing the SET premium and the export rebate, as well as extra sterling royalty payments that Acton would have to make to its foreign licenser. These increased 'costs' represented about a fifth of Acton's total cost increase of $3\frac{1}{2}\%$.

Acton realised that the information on which its cost estimates were based was not complete. In particular, it had so far made no plans for dealing with the extra sterling cost of the royalty payments, which would have to be made for the new production process and which were calculated in dollars. Since their amount would depend on the speed at which modernisation took place, and this was uncertain, no definite figure could be arrived at. It was also recognised that wage and salary costs would increase by much more than $3\frac{1}{2}\%$. A final guess at the likely increase in Acton's total costs ranged between 6 and 9%. It was therefore decided to seek approval for home market price increases of 9%.

Acton Chemicals soon had second thoughts. It feared that a rise in the UK price of Product A by 9% would make it difficult to keep out imports, which had recently been substantial. Perhaps unrealistically, Acton began to argue that these costs would rise by more than 9%. The price increase in the home market was therefore reduced to 6%.

On export pricing, the 20 November meeting decided to attempt to increase sterling prices by the full amount of devaluation, maintaining local-currency prices in most markets. Competitive conditions in these markets were not considered explicitly at the time, although all the managers at the meeting knew the details of the market assessment carried out a month before, which had assumed that no price changes would be made after devaluation. However, those at the meeting agreed that export margins on Product A were too narrow, so that an increase in 'contribution' was desirable, not least because of the loss of profit being suffered while the new process was being installed. They also accepted that some export customers would insist on lower prices after devaluation. This reinforced the decision to try, initially, to increase sterling prices by the full amount of devaluation. Otherwise, there would be no margin for bargaining.

Exceptions were made for Denmark and Ireland. Since Denmark had devalued by 7%, it was decided to raise the price of Product A in Danish currency slightly, to compensate for the supposed 9% extra sterling costs. Ireland had devalued by the same amount as the UK, but Acton wanted to recover some of its extra production costs from its Irish customers. One of the two main export customers with whom Acton had understandings was based in Ireland, and it was accorded special treatment. Two of Acton's executives were sent to Ireland to negotiate with the major customer. In the end, the sterling price to Ireland was slightly increased.

In March 1968, Acton Chemicals increased its prices in the UK by 6%, and its UK competitor immediately did the same. Until then, overseas firms exporting Product A to Britain had kept their prices unchanged. Now they also increased them by at least 6%. In view of this, Acton decided that although it had announced the increase of 6% in the UK price of Product A, it would be unwise to impose the same price increase on all UK customers. Instead, selective price increases were made. A similar procedure seems to have been followed by Acton's main UK competitor.

A.7 The Results

Before devaluation, Acton had forecast that the average UK price of Product A in 1968 would be 4% below the 1966 level. At the end of 1968, the prices actually being charged in the UK were some $2\frac{1}{2}$% higher than those a year earlier—a smaller increase than the estimated increase in total costs. During 1968, the volume of home sales rose by 21%, as compared with a 3% rise in 1967. This was possible because no shortage of capacity was now expected before August 1968.

There was a 39% rise in exports in 1968. More than half of this represented increased sales to the two major customers. In a market where demand was growing so quickly, the question is how far these customers would have increased their purchases even if Britain had not devalued. In other overseas markets, the export price decisions could not be put into effect. While the decision on 20 November 1967 had been to try to maintain local-currency prices, individual customers insisted on renegotiating the prices they paid. As a result, over the next few months the expected rise in sterling prices was reduced from the intended 17% to about 10%. This implies a fall in foreign exchange prices of around 7%. Had there been no devaluation, Acton believes that sterling and foreign exchange prices would both have fallen by around 4%. If so, the net effect of devaluation was to reduce foreign exchange prices by 3% more, and sterling prices by 6% less, than would have happened without devaluation.

'Contribution' per unit on home and export sales together had fallen by an annual average of about 4% between 1961 and 1967. Because prices in the UK were increased from March 1968, the average gross margin obtained by Acton Chemicals in the UK actually increased by 1% of price in 1968, with three months at the old price and nine months at the higher one.

While devaluation made Acton Chemicals a little more competitive in export markets, most of its overseas customers insisted on cuts in foreign exchange prices for Product A, though not promising to buy any more than they would otherwise have done. Rather, there were threats that if export prices were not reduced, these customers would transfer their business to third countries. While the effects of devaluation on Acton Chemicals' sales is hard to estimate, devaluation did confirm its decision to continue exporting on a permanent basis.

Birmingham Cakes

B.1 General Background

Birmingham Cakes was concerned with the production, wholesale distribution and marketing of consumer goods. It was the parent company of a small group, built up mainly during the decade before 1967, which consisted of a few manufacturing companies (including the parent) and a group of wholesalers. Birmingham's main product was a speciality that competed with a wide range of more or less close substitutes.

B.1.1 THE INDUSTRY

If the home market was defined to include all competing products, it was slowly becoming even more fragmented. Total demand in the UK had been increasing very little, roughly in proportion with the growth of population. To overcome the results of slow growth in home sales, the industry had been increasing its exports. The volume of exports in 1963 was 46% up on that in 1960; between 1963 and 1967, exports had levelled off.

The UK market for all the products of the industry taken together was rather inelastic to price changes. Indeed, complete saturation of the market seemed to be approaching. There was keen competition for market share between British and overseas firms. The main competitive weapons used in the UK were product differentiation and various forms of sales promotion, but not price changes. Perhaps because of this, profit margins on turnover were comparatively high.

B.1.2 THE FIRM

Birmingham Cakes had performed more satisfactorily than the industry as a whole. Since 1960, its gross trading profits had almost quadrupled, although its rate of return on capital had declined somehwat while it had expanded and diversified. It had done this both by acquiring a number of competitors and by re-equipping its plant. Like the industry, Birmingham faced a static home market for its main products. Consequently, its main sales growth had been in export markets.

Birmingham Cakes had for some time taken the view that it must steadily increase its exports if its output and profits were to grow at the desired rate. It believed that, in most markets, it had still not reached the sales level it was capable of attaining and that this was especially true of North America and EFTA. Despite this, Birmingham's export record before devaluation was impressive. Table B.1 gives export indices for Birmingham Cakes, and for all UK producers, in the period 1960–67, to put Birmingham's export performance in context. In this period, Birmingham's exports had doubled and, as a result, in 1967 it accounted for more than 9% of the total exports of its industry.

TABLE B.1   *Export volume indices for Birmingham Cakes and its industry*

Year	All UK producers	Birmingham Cakes	Birmingham Cakes' percentage share of total UK exports
1960	100	100	6·7
1961	104	110	7·0
1962	(N.A.)	114	(N.A.)
1963	146	138	6·2
1964	146	159	7·2
1965	143	168	7·7
1966	143	178	8·2
1967	151	212	9·3

As we have seen, Birmingham Cakes operated in markets where competition through product differentiation and sales promotion was more important than price competition. There was little difference between the product sold in the home market and that going to the various export markets. Where there were differences, these were in pack sizes and in the proportion of imperfect goods sold. Birmingham's export sales were very concentrated, with two countries accounting for half of them, and three more for a further 30%. In all export markets, the number of direct competitors for Birmingham Cakes was very small, although there was the great variety of products that competed indirectly. Its product was sold to customers through wholesalers, and in some markets the number of potential wholesale customers was very small.

The company's pricing philosophy in export markets was to earn the biggest 'contribution' judged to be consistent with its sales-volume objectives. Birmingham Cakes was prepared to negotiate special export prices on a 'marginal' basis if this was thought wise at any given time.

At the time of devaluation, the day-to-day management of exports was in the hands of the export marketing director and it was his job to recommend what action was to be taken in each export market. In most cases, his recommendation became the decision. The vice-chairman, who was in charge of the group's exporting, gave advice and was formally the final decision-taker. In a few cases, the company's local overseas representatives came to the UK to give advice. Other employees supplied information, for example, cost data. The final decisions were submitted to the chairman for approval.

Devaluation had no effect on Birmingham Cakes' purchasing pattern for raw materials. They were all products that were not produced in the UK.

B.2   Export Position

With the slow growth of home market, by the time of devaluation the proportion of Birmingham Cakes' output exported had risen to 30%. However, the size of this proportion owed a good deal to the personalities in the firm. Senior management appeared to enjoy exporting.

Birmingham Cakes had been increasing its sales as planned during 1967, and had no major problems over capacity or cash flow. However, its margins were shrinking in both home and export markets, because of rising raw material costs. The firm had been reluctant to make compensating price increases in export markets, for fear of reducing exports at a time when the volume of overseas sales was exceeding budgeted levels in most countries.

B.3   Objectives

Birmingham Cakes' nominal export objective was 'to maximise total contribution'. The management of Birmingham accepted that, in some circumstances, this might conflict with other objectives. For example, Birmingham Cakes also aimed at keeping the most mechanised part of the plant running continuously. When such conflicts between objectives arose, agreement on what to do was reached through informal discussion between those concerned. Prices could be reduced almost to marginal cost, if that seemed desirable. In other words, Birmingham Cakes did not aim unambiguously at maximising contribution. Sales volume, and

therefore employment and capacity-utilisation, were also important objectives. Because agreement on how to adapt the objective
of achieving maximum contribution was reached informally, there
was no explicit ruling on the relative importance of sales-volume
and profit objectives.

Birmingham's objective over devaluation was to use it as an
opportunity 'to increase sales volume by the maximum amount
compatible with earning an acceptable level of profit' (chairman).
This emphasis on expanding export volume was characteristic of
the Board's enthusiastic approach to exporting, which had earned
the company a high reputation as a dollar earner. However, it was
clearly in danger of conflicting with the general objective of
'maximising total contribution' on exports. How this conflict was
to be resolved had not been fully clarified between those concerned even when the devaluation decisions were taken.

B.4 Market Information

With few export markets, and a small number of export customers
and competitors, it was relatively easy for the small export
department (effectively the export director himself) to keep itself
well informed about market developments, through *ad hoc*
reports from agents. Although the agents were not exclusive ones,
they were mostly of long standing and were considered 'part of
the family'. The export director had frequent personal contacts
and consultations with the agents and the latter helped in working
out the detailed annual export targets. Recently, some agents had
carried out research which had helped to determine what would
be the best package design and had shown differences in consumer
purchasing habits between countries.

Birmingham Cakes paid close attention to the market statistics
that were available, and received detailed export statistics from its
trade association. However, the sector of the overall export market
in which Birmingham operated was so narrow that general
statistics, even for its own industry, on overseas consumption,
etc., were of little use.

At the time of devaluation, Birmingham Cakes was in a good
position to examine general trends in each major export market
and to discover its own competitive position in each. Although no
explicit attempt was made to work out elasticity of demand for
Birmingham's products in each market, agents were asked for
their advice on the best marketing policies to pursue in their own
countries.

B.5   Internal Factors

Birmingham Cakes carefully broke down its costs into their fixed and variable elements. No attempt was made to allocate overheads, which were shown separately in its internal accounts. Productive capacity could be used flexibly between products and, because of its re-equipment programme, Birmingham Cakes had enough spare capacity to allow a substantial increase in exports. Because of the seasonal nature of its trade, it had not hesitated to recruit extra labour, mostly female, when required and to dismiss it if demand fell again. Marginal costs were roughly constant, even for considerable increases in output. For each product and market, a standard cost was calculated at regular intervals. This was made up of direct variable costs, namely, raw materials and labour. Variances from standard were analysed. It was quite easy to allocate variable labour costs to any product. because of Birmingham's recruitment policy. The company used more than twenty raw materials and these were included in the standard cost calculation. Because the prices of several raw materials were rather volatile, this part of standard cost was frequently revised.

As required by the early-warning system, Birmingham Cakes had submitted detailed costings to the Board of Trade in July 1967, to justify a claim for a small price increase in the home market. This claim was based on a rise in the world price of Birmingham's principal raw materials. There was little difference between raw material and labour costs for home and export products; home and export costs had increased similarly. This application was still *sub judice* at the time of devaluation, so that Birmingham's profit margins in the home market were being squeezed. While fully compensating price increases had not been made in export markets either, the reduction in margins caused by higher production costs was less severe there. The main raw material for export products was obtained under a marketing arrangement which provided it more cheaply than for the home market. However, margins on exports to some countries, especially in the EEC, had been reduced because of tariff changes.

B.6   The Decisions

B.6.1   CALCULATIONS

Birmingham Cakes was well-equipped to calculate the effect of devaluation on total costs. A rough figure was worked out over the week-end by the financial planning officer and discussed with the purchasing officer on Monday 20 November. The likely effect of devaluation on the cost of each raw material was estimated separately by the financial planning officer, in the light of his general experience. He allowed for the possibility that some supplying countries might devalue. In this way, by the end of the week after devaluation, the increase in costs of the main raw materials going into the standard export product (which accounted for a very large proportion of export sales) had been calculated at an extra $3 \cdot 7\%$ per unit; this was increased to $4 \cdot 5\%$ to allow for uncertainty. Extra packaging costs were estimated as adding a further 3%. This increase in the cost of the standard unit was then multiplied by the sales volume in each market during the year ended March 1967 and an estimate of the net effect of devaluation obtained. It was known that output was currently running considerably above the budgeted levels, but it was assumed that the raw material and labour cost elements in variable cost were constant up to the current output level, and beyond.

This calculation was seen as indicating the extent to which Birmingham Cakes could 'afford' to reduce prices or to increase promotional expenditure in any market. The aim was to increase contribution by an appropriate expansion in sales volume, although the sales volume required was not set down explicitly, and the only requirement for contribution on export sales was that it should be 'acceptable'.

B.6.2   THE DECISION PROCESS

The decisions about how to respond to devaluation were made by the vice-chairman, who was responsible for the group's export activities. He was advised by the export director. The decisions were then discussed with Birmingham's overseas agents, before being submitted to the chairman for his approval. The decisions were made in the light of an assessment of the company's overall export position, carried out before devaluation by the export director. The conclusion had been that Birmingham Cakes' total exports were expanding strongly. It followed that they would have continued to grow quickly, even without devaluation. After devaluation, it was therefore agreed by the vice-chairman and export director that it was unnecessary to 'give anything away across the board'.

The first conclusion was therefore that the decision in each export market should be taken individually. The market assessments were made by the export director, whose main source of information was his existing knowledge of each market. In some major markets, provisional decisions were made immediately and then discussed face-to-face with the company's agents. In more than one instance, these discussions led Birmingham to alter its decisions.

The EFTA countries had been a particularly good market for Birmingham Cakes, and took about 50% of its total exports in 1967. Sales to EFTA had more than doubled since 1960, and growth in the previous year was particularly rapid. While the company considered its performance in these markets satisfactory, it noted an increase in competitive pressures from other firms. Price concessions, in some form, seemed prudent, Historically, the most important EFTA markets had been Sweden, followed by Norway, Denmark and Finland in that order.

B.6.3 THE DEVALUATION DECISIONS

Rather more than 90% of Birmingham's exports went to nine markets, and the remainder to a comparatively large number of minor markets. In taking the decisions after devaluation, each major market was considered separately. The final decisions were as follows:

1 *EFTA Markets*

SWEDEN — Local price for all grades of product to be reduced by 5%.

NORWAY — (a) All local prices to be reduced by the amount previously included in the cost calculation, and so in prices, to cover sales promotion

(b) Local prices of the main grade to be further reduced by 9%, and remaining grades by smaller amounts.

DENMARK — Both company agents' promotional allowances to be increased. (The company had two agents here.)

FINLAND — The unit-quantity of the standard grade to be increased without a change in the local price.

2 *EEC Markets*

WEST GERMANY — Agent A. Landed, i.e. pre-tariff, sterling prices to be restored to the pre-June 1967 levels.

Agent B. A reduction in local prices by 14%.

HOLLAND   Landed prices to be maintained.

BELGIUM   An alteration in the quality of product offered, to provide a more expensive product (believed to be more in line with consumer tastes) at an unchanged local price.

3 *North American Markets*

UNITED STATES (a) The promotional budget to be increased by 40%;

                   (b) Local prices, as invoiced to the Agent, to be subject to a special *ad hoc* discount for a period of one year.

CANADA   (a) The promotional budget to be increased by 33%;

                   (b) Packaging to be improved, at the same price in local currency.

OTHER   Local prices to be reduced 'across the board' by 5%.

B.7 The Logic of the Decisions

Birmingham Cakes' general approach was to treat the expected gain from devaluation for each market as a fund to be used to increase sales volume in that market, by whatever competitive measures seemed most promising. However, an unspecified part of these proceeds was to be retained, by ensuring that prices did not fall by the full amount of devaluation. This approach was conditioned by the history and circumstances of the export trade. In particular, Birmingham knew that its exports were 'in a strongly expansionist phase, which would have continued to develop even without devaluation' (export marketing director). This led them to a policy of 'reinforcing success with success' on a selective, market-by-market basis.

The procedure to be adopted was this:

Step 1   Re-calculate the unit costs of the 'standard export product', which made up a very high proportion of total exports.

          This calculation was made by the management accountant, who consulted the buyer for an estimate of changes in raw material prices resulting from devaluation. The buyer provided cost figures for all significant materials, based on his general knowledge.

Step 2   Calculate, for each main market, the 'net monies available'. First, the previous year's quantity sold was multiplied by the pre-devaluation foreign-exchange price (at the post-devaluation exchange rate). From this was deducted the previous year's quantity sold, multiplied by the unit cost calculated in Step 1.

Step 3   Assess each market's situation. Look at all relevant variables to decide what would be the most effective deployment of a proportion (no specific percentage) of the 'net monies available'.

The market assessments were made by the export marketing director, whose main source of information was his own knowledge of each market, derived from close personal contact with them all. For a few major markets, provisional decisions were made immediately and later discussed with the company's agents. The latter persuaded Birmingham Cakes to alter its decisions in several instances.

With the cost calculations, the main uncertainty was not knowing how the prices of inputs would change. The procedure was:

1   To over-estimate the increase in the cost of each individual input.
2   To round-off all estimates upwards.
3   To add a percentage to each estimate, as a safety margin.

The main uncertainty about demand was how the quantity sold in each market would respond to the various possible changes in the set of decision variables that Birmingham could alter in order to influence demand. This problem may have been increased by the management's view that it was important to take action as soon as possible, but Birmingham Cakes did not think that anything significant was lost by not lengthening the period of search for information. The response to this uncertainty was that there was no market where Birmingham planned to spend the whole of the 'net monies available'. There would therefore be some increase in profit, from higher sterling prices, even if the 'net monies' spent had no effect on demand whatever.

B.7.1 SWEDEN

An example of the information used in one market assessment is as follows:—

MARKET ASSESSMENT

Sweden

'Competition from (a certain named UK producer) with certain customers. This producer expected to reduce prices by 10% at end December 1967. This should be tackled selectively. No general price reduction but more trade deals to be mounted. Consider raising quantity allowance at top end of scale to maintain customer loyalty. Further sales growth tied up with increasing product range.'

This was the original assessment and recommendation. The *final* decision was to reduce all Swedish prices, in local currency, by 5%.

The EFTA countries had been a particularly good market for Birmingham and took about 50% of its total exports in 1967. Sales to EFTA had more than doubled since 1960, and growth in the previous year was particularly rapid. While Birmingham Cakes considered its performance in these markets satisfactory, it noted that there had been an increase in competitive pressures from other suppliers. Price concessions, in some form, seemed prudent. Historically, the most important single market had been Sweden, followed by Norway, Denmark and Finland in that order.

Sales in Sweden had risen by 70% in the period 1960–67. However, Birmingham felt that the rate of growth was likely to diminish once consumption per head of its products was clearly above that in the UK, which would imply that saturation point was near. There was only a small number of important wholesale buyers in Sweden and their purchases were not very responsive to price changes. Birmingham's market intelligence was good and the firm was well informed about its one German and one British competitor in Sweden, who were both thought likely to reduce prices by about 10% at the end of 1967. The initial recommendation was that there should be no general price reduction. Future growth was seen to depend on increasing the range of products sold in Sweden rather than selling more of existing products. A selective increase in discounts was proposed, to maintain customer loyalty. After discussions with its local agent, however, Birmingham Cakes changed the decision to making a price reduction of 5% for all customers and products. A small price cut was thought most likely to maintain sales, and therefore profits, while leaving room for further selective price cuts if the other firms made the anticipated price reduction of 10%.

B.7.2 NORWAY

Birmingham Cakes' exports to Norway were only a quarter of those to Sweden. However, Norway had been Birmingham's most rapidly growing market in EFTA since 1960, with sales increasing sixfold. Despite this rapid increase, consumption per head was still very low, so that Birmingham Cakes saw scope for considerable further growth in sales, at roughly the same rapid rate. The initial recommendation was therefore that prices should be reduced only by the amount of promotional expenditure previously included in prices. However, after discussion with the local agents, it was concluded that sales of Birmingham's main products in Norway were likely to face increasing competition from the same German producer as in Sweden. The local price of the main product was therefore reduced, beyond the cut in promotional expenditure, by a further 9% and smaller reductions were made in the prices of less important products.

B.7.3 DENMARK

In Denmark, sales had remained roughly constant since 1964, at less than half the level for Norway. They were expected to continue at this level and were thought to be almost completely unresponsive to price changes. In any case, the scope for price reductions was limited by Denmark's own decision to devalue by 8%. Accordingly, it was decided only to make a slight increase in the Danish agent's promotional allowances.

B.7.4 FINLAND

Finland was a very small market, entered very recently, but thought to have good growth potential. Research undertaken there by Birmingham's agents some months before devaluation had shown that consumers regarded Birmingham's pack as inferior to that of local manufacturers. Further growth in sales was therefore seen as linked to the introduction of an improved pack, which Birmingham Cakes had already decided on. The extra cost of the new pack, combined with the earlier devaluation by Finland, had led before devaluation to a decision to reduce the weight of product sold in Finland at the existing price. The devaluation of sterling provided an opportunity to increase the pack weight instead. It was decided to divide the extra revenues offered in Finland by devaluation between an increase in the amount of product in the new pack and an increase in margins. The weight of the new pack was raised by $7\frac{1}{2}$%, but its foreign-currency price left unaltered.

B.7.5 THE EEC

(a) *Germany*

The EEC had never been as important a market for Birmingham

Cakes as EFTA, but sales there had nevertheless grown sixfold between 1960 and 1967. The most important market was Holland, where total sales in 1967 were about half of those in Sweden. Substantial amounts were sold in Germany, but Belgium was an unimportant market. Birmingham Cakes had been reasonably happy about sales to the EEC until there was an effective increase of 18 % in the common external tariff in June 1967. With strong competition from the German producer, Birmingham Cakes had been forced to reduce its sterling prices for Germany and they now gave an inadequate return. Devaluation was seen as providing the opportunity to restore margins in the EEC.

Sales to Germany had been depressed for two years, after a period of rapid growth. There were two representatives there. One was an agent who dealt largely with small retailers and wholesalers. In 1967, he had successfully persuaded Birmingham to absorb the increase in the tariff. Since that time, the market situation had improved and Birmingham now considered that wholesale and retail margins in Germany were too high and its own margins too low. The decision for this agent was therefore to raise sterling prices to the same level as before June 1967. The second agent dealt with larger customers, whose demand was fairly unresponsive to price changes. For various reasons, Birmingham's prices to this agent had not been reduced significantly after the tariff increase in June 1967. Consequently, he was encountering severe competition from the big local producer. Devaluation enabled Birmingham Cakes to reduce the foreign-currency prices charged to him by 14 %.

(b) *Holland*

Holland was Birmingham Cakes' largest EEC market, and sales there had increased sevenfold between 1960 and 1967. However, Birmingham considered that its main product line would face increasing competition in Holland, so that future growth in sales there would depend on extending its product range. Although demand was to some extent responsive to price cuts, Birmingham Cakes was reluctant to reduce its prices after devaluation. It had already narrowed its margins to an unacceptable level by absorbing the EEC tariff increase in June 1967. Birmingham Cakes estimated that, if the local price in Holland was kept constant after devaluation, this would offset about 80 % of the reduction in margins caused by the tariff increase. Accordingly, it was decided to maintain foreign-currency prices in Holland.

(c) *Belgium*

As we have seen, Birmingham's sales in Belgium were very small. They were also subject to sharp fluctuations. It was difficult to increase sales because of consumers' attitudes. Moreover, Birmingham's business with its local agent represented only a small proportion of his total activities. Although Birmingham Cakes had not been under pressure from its agent to change prices after the increase in the tariff in June 1967, the firm believed that without some positive action on their part the market would 'fade away to zero'. Accordingly, it was decided to bring the quality of the product more into line with the local market's preferences, but to maintain the foreign-currency price.

B.7.6 NORTH AMERICA

In the USA, Birmingham's sales had been both very small and static for some years; yet the market was considered to have much potential. Some increase in sales had been achieved in 1966, following an improvement in local representation. Birmingham Cakes believed that the growth of sales in the USA could be stimulated by a further increase in expenditure on sales promotion. Accordingly, it was decided to make a significant increase in the promotional budget for the USA, improve the pack, but leave prices unchanged. After strong protests from its agents, however, Birmingham agreed to reduce its dollar prices by 6%, subject to a review after a year.

On the other hand, sales to Canada had doubled in the last five years. The Canadian market was both much larger than the American one and much more profitable. Growth prospects were especially good, and a month before devaluation Birmingham had substantially increased its Canadian promotional budget. Being under no pressure from the Canadian agent to reduce prices, Birmingham decided to spend some of the extra revenues from devaluation on increasing sales promotion even further, while leaving its foreign-currency prices unchanged.

B.8 The Results

Table B.2 sets out indices of export volume (1966–67 = 100), for each market where a separate devaluation decision was made.

The export marketing director said that, in general, he was satisfied that the devaluation decisions had been about as successful as could have been expected. An exception was that granting

TABLE B.2 *Export volume indices 1966–67* to *1968–69 (years ended in March: 1966–67 = 100)*

	1966–67	1967–68	1968–69
Sweden	100	122·5	133·3
Norway	100	117·5	108·0
Denmark	100	108·5	162·5
Finland	100	140·0	47·5
West Germany	100	104·5	131·5
Holland	100	111.5	127·0
Belgium	100	74·0	134·0
United States	100	123·0	190·0
Canada	100	140·0	94·0
Other	100	126·0	129·0
TOTAL	100	119·0	128·0

the special *ad hoc* discount, conceded under pressure from the United States' agent, was seen as a mistake. Unfortunately, it proved difficult to end the concession, and Birmingham Cakes did not finally do so until 1969.

Commenting on its figures for export volume, Birmingham Cakes said that the very large increase in sales to Canada, in 1967–68, had been partly a result of over-ordering by their agent. They had thought that this was probably happening at the time and so were not surprised when exports to Canada fell in 1968–69. The large fall in exports to Finland in 1968–69 was mainly the result of successful competition from other (mainly non-British) firms. The Finnish market was abnormal, because there were only five buyers of any size in the country. A significant change in sales to any one of them therefore led to a relatively large change in exports to Finland.

Despite the overall rise in its exports after devaluation, Birmingham Cakes' total profits from exports in 1968–69 were below those in 1967–68. This was not what the devaluation decision had been intended to achieve and was due to an unexpected factor. This was a substantial rise in the price of one major raw material, which accounted for about 30% of the cost of the 'average' product. Once it was known that this cost increase would occur, Birmingham Cakes immediately calculated its effect. However, it was decided that it would be unwise to raise prices immediately, given that the changes associated with devaluation had only just been made. Prices were, however, raised in 1968–69 and the desired increase in profits achieved, without any apparent reduction in sales volume.

CASE STUDY C

Cardiff Instruments

C.1 General Background

Cardiff Instruments was a newly established division of a large firm producing a wide range of capital equipment. It operated fairly independently and specialised in producing heavy machinery (HEMs).

C.1.1 THE INDUSTRY

The figures for the number of HEMs installed or on order in the UK had increased dramatically since 1962, and especially since 1965. The number installed in the UK quintupled between 1962 and 1965; it quadrupled again between 1965 and 1968. While figures for the most recent years were not strictly comparable, because the coverage of the statistics had been widened, the market had obviously grown very rapidly. Figures for sales value were not available. However, since the price of HEMs had risen steadily, total sales turnover must have increased even faster than sales volume.

Figures for the whole industry's exports were not available, but Cardiff believed that the export market had grown roughly as fast as the home market, with the UK industry becoming extremely export conscious. While HEMs had become steadily more expensive, their quality and performance had also improved sharply. There was no representative price for an HEM because each machine was built to the customer's individual specification. At the time of devaluation, there were five UK producers of HEMs, as well as Cardiff Instruments. All Cardiff's British competitors belonged to large industrial groups, whose average size was much greater than that of the parent group of Cardiff Instruments. Only three foreign firms were selling in the UK at the time of devaluation, and all were based in the USA.

C.1.2 THE FIRM

The sales record of Cardiff Instruments in the home market was certainly impressive. Its sales amounted to £200,000 in 1961–62, year ending in March. They rose to £360,000 in 1963–64, jumped £900,000 in 1964–65, and rose again to £3,960,000 in 1966–67, though the 1966–67 figure was for seven orders only. Home sales then fell to £2,590,000 in 1967–68. A general review of prices was begun in mid-1967 and was not completed for a year. It resulted in an increase in the price at which Cardiff sold some components, while the prices of others were reduced mainly as a result of advances in technology. In 1967, Cardiff Instruments accounted for about 30% of sales of HEMs in the UK, a slight increase on its market share in 1966.

C.2   Export Position

Cardiff had been exporting for only about four years before devaluation, yet it had become the largest single exporter of HEMs from the UK, accounting for about 40% total UK exports. Because its sales turnover was so volatile, the proportion of output exported had fluctuated sharply from year to year. However, there was an upward trend in 1967.

TABLE C.1   *Value of export orders* (index Numbers: 1963–64 = 100)

Years to March	Export index	Percentage of total orders obtained abroad
1963–64	100	20
1964–65	111	10
1965–66	334	25
1966–67	800	15
1961–68	600	18

Cardiff's main marketing effort was in Germany, where the HEM market had been expanding rapidly, despite strong competition from three local producers and two overseas firms. By the beginning of 1969, Cardiff Instruments had sent forty-one HEMs abroad. Of these, fourteen went to Germany, nine elsewhere in Western Europe, three to Eastern Europe, ten to the USA and five to the rest of the world. The ten installations sold to the USA exaggerated Cardiff Instruments' strength in that market. One very large order for HEMs had been placed by a British firm, which then sent some of them to its American subsidiaries.

As with the home market, in any given price range technological superiority seemed to be the most important factor in selling the bigger HEMs. However, in both home and export markets Cardiff

Instruments seemed to be uncompetitive on price, at the cheaper end of the market, before devaluation. Cardiff's export prices were much the same as its home market prices, for comparable items, after allowing for extra installation charges.

C.3   Objectives

Cardiff Instruments set down its objectives formally, in writing. When new objectives were necessary, they were established by consensus at regular, fortnightly meetings of senior managers. The basic objectives were 'to get more orders than last year; to keep capacity fully occupied; and to take advantage of any market opportunity which may arise'. Cardiff Instruments had no detailed profit objectives, but aimed at a return of 15% on capital employed. At the time of devaluation, the home market objective was to supply one-third of the UK market, as against the currently estimated 30%. Cardiff's non-operational objectives included achieving technical superiority. This objective probably weighed more heavily than that of achieving the 15% return on capital.

The objectives for exports were general and undocumented. At the time of devaluation, the export objectives were to consolidate Cardiff Instruments' competitive position in Germany, to set up marketing facilities in other European countries, especially Czechoslovakia, and to consolidate recent sales growth in South Africa and Australia. There was no major change in any of these objectives after devaluation, but it was decided to use devaluation to try to increase exports of Cardiff's less-expensive HEMs. As with Cardiff's general export objectives, these new objectives were not set out in detail. There was no conscious attempt to change the balance between home and export sales.

C.4   Market Information

Information about its customers was obtained by Cardiff's sales manager through *ad hoc* reports by representatives and from studying the trade press. Each year, Cardiff's sales managers forecast sales by listing the contracts which they were going to try to obtain in the next year in each market, and assigning probabilities of success in order to obtain an expected value of sales. These forecasts were brought up to date each quarter. Information about the main markets in Western Europe, particularly Germany, was satisfactory. Information about the less important markets in Eastern Europe, the USA, Australia and South Africa was much less plentiful.

With the market for HEMs growing rapidly, Cardiff Instruments had relied heavily on its reputation for technical excellence in selling its products. It was reluctant to compete on price. When technological progress had been rapid, this policy had succeeded. At the time of devaluation, however, sales were running about one-third below the peak of the previous year, because of a 35% fall in sales to the home market and one of 25% in export markets.

Although the industry was already accustomed to considerable volatility in its sales, Cardiff was concerned that the general slowing of technological development might lead to increasing price competition. It feared that in turn this might erode Cardiff's technological lead and cause profit to fall so far that the lead was reduced still further. Indeed, we have seen that Cardiff was already unable to compete on price for the cheaper HEMs. Yet Cardiff had no systematic information on these trends, and had made no detailed studies of the capacity available to its main competitors.

No extra market information was collected after devaluation.

C.5 Internal Factors

Cardiff's management calculated the prices at which it would tender from its internal price list for its standard components. It then made an allowance for the costs of bringing these together. (This included markups for overheads, warranties, royalties, etc.). Cardiff had an elaborate costing system, which distinguished between direct and indirect costs for each tender, but did not allocate overheads to individual HEMs. Cardiff used an elaborate cost coding system which enabled it to isolate any cost element immediately.

About the middle of 1967, Cardiff Instruments had begun a detailed review of the internal prices for each of about 700 standard components, but this was not completed until the middle of 1968. Besides estimating changes in material and labour costs, this review had tried to take account of changes in technology. These not only meant that the performance of some components had improved, but also that components could be combined more economically. In making its decisions after devaluation, Cardiff did not examine the costs of each outstanding tender separately.

C.6 The Decisions

While devaluation was not wholly unexpected, Cardiff Instruments had not made any contingency plans. Cardiff's first reaction was to try to estimate what extra sterling costs would result from devaluation. As the import content of an average HEM was very small, the cost increase resulting from devaluation was put at 3%. This figure was agreed in informal discussions between Cardiff's executives.

Immediately after devaluation (on Sunday 19 November) the commercial manager recommended an increase in sterling prices. This recommendation was amended by the sales manager and confirmed by the general manager, after discussion at the regular fortnightly meeting between senior managers. This took place on Monday 20 November. It was there decided to raise the sterling price for all 'British' elements in the price of Cardiff Instruments' HEMs in both the home market and most export markets by 3%. This reduced their foreign-currency price by about 11%. For the imported components used in Cardiff's HEMs, prices were raised by the full amount of devaluation, by including the sterling prices of components at the new exchange rate in all HEMs. On exports to Eastern Europe, Cardiff Instruments continued to charge the UK (sterling) price plus 10%.

The decision to cut foreign-currency prices on all exports outside Europe by the net amount of devaluation (after deducting the estimated 3% cost increase) seems to have been influenced by the feeling that Cardiff's prices for the cheaper machines were not competitive. The fact that the same foreign-currency price cuts were made on the more expensive items reflected a vague feeling that technological superiority alone would no longer be enough to sell them, now that the pace of technological development was slowing. Cardiff saw a danger that its technological lead might be eroded and feared that price competition would become increasingly severe. It was taking a longish view of its export position.

Apart from some extra information about the effect of devaluation on costs, Cardiff's decision takers had the information which they were normally given for their fortnightly management meetings. But they had no document setting out in detail the increases in cost which would be caused by devaluation. The main cost factors emerging from the regular meeting on November 20 were as follows:

1 Costs would be increased by the amount of extra taxation (the increase in Corporation Tax). In addition, the SET and export rebates would be lost.
2 Additional export finance would be required to meet higher insurance premiums, interest charges and credit terms.
3 Warranty charges would increase.
4 Travel by executives and technical experts would cost more.

5 The sterling price of imported components (unobtainable in the UK) would rise by the full amount of devaluation. Although the 'average' HEM contained few imported components, in the larger HEMs imported components accounted for about 20% of cost. As we have seen, this problem was resolved by introducing the new sterling price of imported components directly into the tender price.

Devaluation led to some changes in Cardiff Instruments' forecasts of how much business was likely to be available in the period immediately after devaluation. As we have seen, Cardiff used probability analysis in its sales forecasting. Each potential order was assigned a subjective probability in order to arrive at an expected value for its amount, timing and the likelihood that the order would be obtained by Cardiff Instruments. In January 1968, Cardiff reviewed the subjective probabilities it had assigned to its export tenders. Of £3.2M of export business thought to be available, the (mainly low) probabilities were left unchanged on nine projects, valued at just over £2M. They were reduced on five projects worth £450,000 and increased on five other projects. With two HEMs already ordered, this gave an expected value for exports in 1968 of £750,000. What is not known is how far the increased probabilities were the result of devaluation and how far they were the result of the increased understanding of what customers really needed which was always gained as any negotiation proceeded.

C.7 The Results

Cardiff's outstanding export orders increased by 39% between 1 April 1968 and 31 March 1969; they reached £750,000, or 24% of total orders, as against 17% the year before. Cardiff doubted whether much of this increase could be attributed to devaluation. Technical performance was still more important than price for the expensive HEMs. Sales of the cheaper ones, which *were* thought to be sensitive to price reductions, did not increase substantially in this period. Indeed, out of £750,000 worth of export orders obtained in the year ended 31 March 1969, four alone accounted for £670,000. Again, some £400,000 out of £540,000 of export orders obtained in the year ended 31 March 1968 were placed before December 1967. Devaluation was not a major short-term influence.

Nevertheless, in 1969 Cardiff Instruments believed that the effects of devaluation might still show themselves. It was confident that its decision to cut the foreign-currency price of its HEMs was sound.

Durham Plates

D.1 General Background

Durham Plates manufactured industrial raw materials. Its products were differentiated from competing substitutes by technical characteristics, which might or might not be important for any given order or market. To satisfy customers, Durham had to provide expert technical salesmen and a reliable after-sales service. Selling costs were correspondingly high, particularly for new and overseas customers. Partly for this reason, well over 50% of sales had been made within the UK. Durham Plates was the parent company of a group which had expanded considerably since 1950, mainly by increasing its own output in the UK and by taking-over or merging with other British firms.

D.1.1 THE INDUSTRY

Output and sales figures were not available for the industry, but the pattern of output was cyclical and the trend rate of growth of sales was low. In 1967, overseas demand was depressed. There were only four firms in the UK, of which Durham Plates was the biggest. There had been a long history of friendly co-operation between these firms, and before the Restrictive Trade Practices Act ended their pricing agreements in the UK, in the early 1960s, prices in the UK were set by their trade association. Trade association pricing continued in export markets, and for some grades of product there had to be agreement between all British producers before a price was quoted. The export cartel set minimum prices for one of the products we studied (Product A), but Durham Plates was effectively the only producer of Product B. The export cartel only set prices for one or two grades of Product B.

Sales of the industry's product were not particularly responsive to changes in its price. There was more competition in providing technical sales service than in price. The two major European producers, in particular, emphasised competition on service. With both products, there was a list price for standard specifications.

However, small quantities of both products were occasionally made to the specifications of individual customers, and prices were then closely related to unit costs. In general, export prices were lower than home market prices, although the difference was bigger for Product A than for Product B. For Product A, the cartel had divided the world into a number of price zones, and it agreed minimum export prices for each. In some markets, the prices that British firms quoted for given grades of product were considerably below those of the European firms. In no market were British prices higher than European ones.

D.1.2 THE FIRM

The figures for Durham Plates' sales, by volume, in the period before devaluation are given in Table D.1. In each case, the index number for 1963 is 100.

TABLE D.1   (1963 = 100)

Years	Product A			Product B		
	Home market	Exports	Percentage exported	Home market	Exports	Percentage exported
1964	124	106	11	117	79	36
1965	131	131	11	129	71	27
1966	110	89	9	148	99	22
1967	100	75	8	136	125	27

It will be seen that, for Product A, sales had been declining since 1964. This decline, affecting both home and export markets, was cyclical rather than secular. For Product B, sales at home had been tending to increase, though there was a small fall in 1967. Sales in export markets had been rising strongly since 1965. Table D.1 also shows that Durham Plates exported about 10% of its output of Product A, but nearer 30% of Product B. The most important markets for these products were in Western Europe and Australia, but both products were sold in about forty other countries.

Product B was sold in a variety of qualities. On the cheaper grades, which still accounted for the bulk of most users' needs, value added was relatively small and it was correspondingly difficult to earn attractive profits. On the more expensive grades, selling costs were high; potential buyers had to be convinced of the technological superiority of these grades of Product B and of its reliability. On average, the price of Product B had risen by about 3% between 1963 and 1967.

D.2   Export Position

As Table D.1 shows, exporting had never represented a very important activity for Durham Plates. Even so, Durham Plates estimated that British producers between them accounted for about 6% of world exports of Products A and B. It believed that there was considerable scope for expanding British exports and was putting into effect plans to increase its export effort, despite the problems of high selling costs.

Apart from the other British producers, Durham Plates' main competitors in export markets were the two big European manufacturers. It was tacitly agreed that the European producers' domestic markets 'belonged to them', so that all producers met little competition in their home markets. However, there was no agreement on what prices were to be charged in third countries.

Durham Plates' export pricing was affected by the fact that export prices for one or two grades of Product B were determined by the export pricing committee of the Trade Association. In 1967, all four British producers belonged to this. The committee's policy was to set a different price for each grade of Product B; it also set different prices for each grade in several groups of export markets, each group of countries having similar competitive structures and other marketing characteristics. For those grades of Product B where Durham Plates could choose its own price, its policy was to keep export and home prices as alike as possible. However, Durham Plates was quite prepared to bid for large-scale export business on a marginal basis if this seemed sensible in particular circumstances. More generally, Durham Plates adopted a fairly opportunistic approach to export pricing.

D.3   Objectives

D.3.1   GENERAL

At the time of devaluation, Durham Plates' activities in all markets were to be aimed at targets set in its seven-year plan. We were not given details of this plan, which was not yet in operation. However, the plan was already influencing what Durham Plates did and an important objective was to reach and maintain a considerably higher level of exports than in the early 1960s. Durham's idea was to change the status of its export business by becoming a regular supplier to certain export customers who would be given the same, or nearly the same, treatment as domestic customers when problems of priority of supply arose. It was hoped that this would go some way to cushioning

Durham Plates against the fluctuations in demand in the UK market, which were considerable. Variations in consumption by its customers were exaggerated by the building-up and running-down of inventories. Although the seven-year plan was not yet in operation, in November 1967, Durham Plates was already 'building towards the objectives defined in it'.

D.3.2 DEVALUATION OBJECTIVES

The objectives of Durham's devaluation decisions were as follows.

(a) *Home market pricing*
To recover, on average, the cost increases resulting from devaluation, and from all other cost changes in the period from April 1966, the date of the last previous price change, to November 1967.

(b) *Export pricing*
If possible, to set such prices as would:
  1 recover the cost increases resulting from devaluation;
  2 restore profit per unit of sales to a level considered 'acceptable';
  3 reach a minimum percentage of profit per unit sold, which Durham sought for all its business. For those product grades and markets where profit margins had fallen below this level in the period before devaluation, the aim was to restore them.

(c) *Increasing sales volume*
An increased sales volume in the long term, by encouraging potential customers to take an interest in 'trial lots' as a prelude to ordering on a larger scale was attempted. The amounts to be sold on this basis were to increase over time, but no more specific objectives than this were set.

D.4 Market Information

Durham Plates was the largest company in the export cartel and probably the best informed. Even so, its information was rather poor. Its export organisation consisted effectively of only one man, assisted by a team of technical experts who spent a good deal of their time with customers. Durham Plates' statistical information was little more than the figures for its own exports and for those of the cartel. Information from agents came infrequently and irregularly, and tended to be inadequate, perhaps reflecting the low status of its agents. The export manager relied heavily on his personal experience and on his 'feel' for overseas markets. He was on good terms with Durham's European competitors and therefore considered himself well-informed about their general marketing policies. Yet he was uncertain how far, with the low prices they were able to charge in a depressed world market, they would be able to meet any price cuts he was able to make after devaluation. Despite this, Durham Plates made no real effort to collect more market information before the devaluation decisions were taken.

Exports of Product B were bigger and were also rising. The product was technically very advanced and its sales seemed to be less responsive to price changes than those of Product A, despite the fact that the two products were in competition to some extent. Again, the main competition in export markets came from the same two European producers.

D.5 Internal Factors

In contrast to its market information, Durham Plates' cost information was unusually detailed. The firm had a system of quarterly budgeting for each of about two hundred grades of product, covering every category of production and administrative costs. Variances were analysed in detail after the quarterly figures had been received. There was no attempt to allocate overheads to individual products and the budgetary control system clearly distinguished between fixed and variable costs.

Costs had increased substantially in the year before devaluation, particularly labour costs. Apart from its own increased wage bill, Durham Plates had been seriously affected by the de-casualisation of the docks in 1966, because its product was both bulky and heavy. Since then, material and shipping costs had increased with the closure of the Suez canal. As a result, shortly before devaluation, the export pricing association had decided, in principle, to increase sterling prices for Product A by $7\frac{1}{2}\%$ in January 1968, in both home and export markets. Similar changes were planned for Product B. The aim was to restore profit margins.

Within a day or two of devaluation, the buyer had made 'off the cuff' estimates of the increases in sterling prices that devaluation was likely to cause for Durham's twelve main raw materials. These estimates were set out in a document giving the expected cost increases for the levels of output assumed in the 1968 raw material budgets, which had just been prepared. They also included a generous allowance for freight-rate increases. The managing director had this document when he attended an export pricing meeting of the trade association on 23 November, which was to decide what changes should be made in the export price of the cartelised product. The document dealt only with the effect of devaluation on costs in general; there was no attempt to separate out the effect on export costs. The managing director felt confident about most of the estimates, if only because Durham had long-term contracts for many of its imported raw materials. The impact of devaluation on these was easy to predict.

As had been intended, the decision on export prices for cartelised products was taken at the meeting on 23 November. A few weeks later, on 21 December, Durham supplemented the information in its original cost document by adding estimates of the effects of the tax changes announced at the time of devaluation, and of increases in the price of fuel, minor raw materials, packaging and transport. This gave an overall estimate of the extra costs Durham Plates expected to incur because of devaluation. The figures for budgeted output for 1968 were used to allocate these costs to Durham's various plants, in order to show the effect of devaluation on each. This was the key cost information used in deciding on new export prices for the non-cartelised product.

Meanwhile, a special study was made by Durham's comptroller to assess the effect on unit 'contribution' if sterling prices were left unchanged, the budgeted output for 1968 was produced and devaluation led to the expected increase in costs. These calculations of the effects of devaluation on 'contribution' were made separately for about 485 products and grades and divided between the plants in which they were manufactured. The document was ready by 12 December though the managing director challenged the price change calculated for one raw material, claiming to have better information than the buyer. About the same time, the secretary of the cartel sent out a circular asking member firms to estimate, on a percentage basis, the total of the other cost increases they had suffered since April 1966, for each grade of product, home or export. Like Durham's own more-detailed figures, these included the effects of the closing of the Suez canal and the de-casualisation of the docks. The results were discussed at a further cartel meeting, but only in terms of averages and percentages. They formed the basis for a decision, early in 1968, to increase the home market prices of cartelised products; these prices had to be submitted to the Board of Trade for approval.

Durham Plates was therefore fairly well informed about the general effect of devaluation on costs, though the cartel took its decisions on export prices before all of this information was available. None of the documents we saw purported to calculate marginal cost at the expected levels of export output. This was partly because the expected increases in export sales had not been worked out at all precisely, and partly because some marginal costs were themselves difficult to calculate. There was a good deal of spare capacity for producing the cartelised Product A, so that marginal costs could reasonably be assumed to be constant over any likely range of output, which is what Durham Plates implicitly did. However, the assumption was not equally reasonable for Product B, whose output was at peak levels.

D.6 The Decisions

The decisions about the export price of Product A were reached at the meeting of the export cartel on 23 November. We have seen the minutes of this meeting. The managing director of Durham Plates was in the Chair and his export manager and comptroller were also there. In opening the meeting, the Chairman emphasised that devaluation would cause an immediate increase in the costs of all imported raw materials and would also affect the cost of fuel oil and other materials. He suggested that as the cartel's delivered prices in several markets were already 15 to 20% lower than those of its European competitors, devaluation could be used to give their customers even lower prices. We have already seen that it had been agreed, in principle, to increase prices by $7\frac{1}{2}\%$ because of the cost increases accumulated before devaluation. In many countries, even an increase of this size would have left British prices competitive. Now that devaluation had occurred, it was thought unlikely that the European producers would be able to reduce their prices sufficiently to embarrass the British firms. The chairman argued that the problem for the cartel was how and when to deal with the further cost increases resulting from devaluation. Should the cartel's approach differ from country to country? Should any action which was taken be agreed in advance with the Europeans?

In a general discussion, some members of the cartel argued that an increase in sterling export prices by the full amount of devaluation 'would, of course, defeat the object of the devaluation'. Durham then suggested that a solution might be to make a range of increases in sterling prices, ranging from zero up to the full amount of devaluation. This would enable the cartel to test out demand conditions in its various markets and then to select for each whatever price was most likely to give the cartel increased sales. In response to this, it was pointed out that all export prices would have to be increased to some extent if profit margins were to be restored; if devaluation had not taken place, the cartel would almost certainly have increased prices across-the-board by $7\frac{1}{2}\%$. In some countries, there was little scope for increasing sales by cutting prices, although there might be more scope in others.

The meeting next considered the problem of countries that had also devalued and whether there should be differential price increases for them. It went on to consider how likely it was that the country with the two big European producers in it would also devalue in due course. It was pointed out that one large foreign customer had been given guarantees against devaluation, so that it would be some time before the prices he paid could be increased.

A discussion of cost increases, both before and after devaluation, followed and it was generally agreed that, to meet them, selling prices ought to be increased immediately by between $6\frac{1}{2}$ and 10%, depending on the raw material content of the product. The average would be around 8%. It was then noted that packing material would also cost more, partly because of devaluation and partly because the producers of this material had themselves been planning to increase prices before devaluation.

It was finally agreed that sterling export prices should be increased immediately by 10% to all countries which had not devalued, and by $7\frac{1}{2}\%$ to those which had. A sub-committee was asked to work out new terms for the large overseas customer.

We may note that there was no discussion on how likely it was that the European producers would make retaliatory price cuts. Nevertheless, they were already uncompetitive in some markets and the cartel's decision would make them even more uncompetitive there, unless their own country devalued. In its discussions, the cartel implicitly assumed that there would be no retaliation. The suggestion by the chairman that the cartel might consider the possibility of working out a joint response to devaluation with the European competitors was ignored.

Similarly, the cartel did not pursue the possibility of making differential price increases in different countries, although it was fully agreed that the possibility of increasing sales was smaller in some markets than in others. It was thought that the extra time and effort required to work out separate pricing policies for each market would not yield a worthwhile return.

The meeting concentrated on the effect of devaluation on total costs, with which members were more familiar. Because the estimated increase in costs due to devaluation and to other factors differed markedly between the various grades of Products A and B, it was much easier to agree on a flat-rate increase in sterling prices for all grades than to work out a different price for each of a large number of grades. The price increases finally agreed therefore improved the profitability of many grades. But it left margins unaltered, or even reduced them, for grades where cost increases were high.

There was no discussion of the home market prices of Product A until the end of December, after a questionnaire had been sent out by the cartel secretariat. At an informal meeting of the cartel members then, figures were worked out for the increased costs of producing Product A for the home market. The cost figures distinguished four types of raw material and nine methods of processing. Early in 1968, it was finally agreed that the price of each grade was to be increased by a different percentage. This was arrived at by taking the increase in raw material costs caused by devaluation, adding the increases in all other costs since April 1966 and adding a further margin. The price increases, expressed as percentages, ranged from 6 to 12·5%. They were rather greater than the allowances for increased costs, which were themselves probably generous.

Durham Plates did not take its own decisions about those grades of Product B whose export prices were wholly under its own control until detailed figures for the cost increases, both before and after devaluation, had been worked out, around the middle of December 1967. At that time, home market prices for Product B were raised by between 5 and 10% for most grades but by 15% for one that had only recently been introduced. The increases were made in three equal monthly amounts. The size of the price increase for each grade was determined very much by the size of the increase in its raw material costs. However, the 15% increase for the new grade was influenced by the realisation that demand for it was almost completely inelastic to changes in its price.

Export prices in all markets were raised to the same level as home market prices. For most grades, this meant the same percentage increase, but there were two grades where the percentage increase was marginally bigger. For all but the new grade, these decisions reduced foreign-currency prices by from 4% to 9%. In no case were export prices considered separately. They were always the same as prices for the home market. Durham Plates' objective had always been to try to charge the same price for Product B at home and overseas. After devaluation, no-one suggested that export markets, either as a whole or in individual countries, should be treated differently from the home market. Nor were the reactions of European competitors, or the implications for the balance between demand and capacity, considered.

D.7 The Results

The net effect of the decisions was to raise the average price that Durham Plates received from its sales of Product A on the home market by an average of 8%. The average increase in export prices was 5%. Figures for Product B were not available.

Durham Plates argued that the devaluation decisions seemed to have had only a limited effect in increasing exports. Exports of Product A increased by 90% in 1968, though admittedly from a low level in the previous year. The proportion of the output of Product A exported rose from 8 to 13%. However, much of this increase was accounted for by one very large order from an Eastern European country. While devaluation allowed Durham Plates to quote 'a slightly lower price than it would otherwise have done', it is not clear how big an influence this had in giving Durham the business. Political and balance of payments factors may have been important too, and no other British firm was in a position to supply this type of product at a competitive price. As for exports of Product A to other countries, there was here an increase in sales of 30%. Again Durham Plates saw this as due at least as much to a general recovery in world demand for its product as to the advantage given by devaluation. In 1969, exports of Product A fell by 20% and the proportion of Durham Plates' output that was exported fell to 9%.

For Product B, the results were more disappointing. Despite some reduction in foreign-currency prices, a continuing depression in the industry which used Product B resulted in a fall in exports in 1968 by 5%, although the proportion of Durham's output that was exported rose from 27 to 35%. Home demand fell even more sharply. In 1969, there was a dramatic recovery in home demand and sales rose by 36%. Because of the consequent pressure on capacity, export sales fell by 47% and the proportion of output exported fell to 17%.

Ealing Electrical Appliances

E.1 General Background

Ealing Electrical Appliances was a relatively autonomous subsidiary of a large caravan group, and made luxury caravans. It had been acquired in 1965, when the parent company was seeking to diversify its activities.

E.1.1 THE INDUSTRY

Home sales of caravans by British firms rose to a peak in 1964 when they were 93% above the 1961 level. Most of the increase occurred in 1963, when sales rose by 37%. In the three years to 1967, sales dropped by 15% and rose only slightly in 1968. Exports had also increased sharply in the period up to 1964, but since then sales had been declining. By 1967 they were less than in 1964.

Imports catered for only a small proportion of home demand for caravans but the share of the UK market held by foreign caravan producers had more than doubled since 1960, to reach 8% in 1967. The rise in imports was especially steep in 1967; they rose by 37%. Since imported caravans were mainly luxury models, they competed directly with the products of Ealing, but only indirectly with the products of other UK manufacturers.

Prices of caravans in the UK had risen gradually, reflecting both increases in the quality of caravans and rising costs. Even so, despite these improvements in quality, the average price of caravans in the UK rose by only 9% between 1961 and 1967, compared with a 22% rise in the index of retail prices. In real terms, the price of caravans had almost certainly fallen.

E.1.2 THE FIRM

Ealing Electrical Appliances had only four major competitors in the UK. Two of them accounted for about two-thirds of British caravan output. Table E.1 shows Ealing's sales volume figures for 1960–61 to 1966–67 (years ending 31 March). In this period,

Ealing had performed rather better than the industry as a whole. Since 1963–64, it had increased its home sales by 22%. On the other hand, its export performance was disappointing, with export sales falling by 22% (or by about the industry average) between 1963–64 and 1966–67. There was a 9% fall in exports in 1966–67. As a result, the proportion of Ealing's output that was exported fell from 48 to 38% between 1963–64 and 1966–67. Over the whole period since 1963–64, Ealing's total sales volume had increased by only 1%. At the same time, while its costs had risen, its prices had remained stable. Profit margins had therefore been squeezed. The increase in Ealing's export prices over the period 1961–67 was only $5\frac{1}{2}$%, and it was Ealing's normal practice to set its sterling export prices 20% below its home market retail prices before tax. Even so, additional cuts in Ealing's prices often had to be made, frequently to meet competitive situations in particular overseas markets.

TABLE E.1 *Volume sales index (1959–60 = 100)*

Years	Home	Export	Percentage exported
1960–61	74	49	38
1961–62	46	71	55
1962–63	80	85	49
1963–64	95	98	48
1964–65	99	94	46
1965–66	110	83	41
1966–67	116	76	38

E.2 Export Position

Ealing Electrical Appliances had always exported a substantial proportion of its output although this proportion had been bigger in years, like 1961 and to a smaller degree 1962 and 1963, when home sales were very depressed. Ealing's sales were not concentrated in any particular overseas country. Because it had a small share of the UK market, Ealing found difficulty in increasing its exports further. The volume of home sales was too small to allow it to achieve the spreading of overhead costs which it needed in order to keep unit costs at a competitive level. Although exports were substantially less profitable than home sales, with ex-works prices 20 to 25% lower, a large volume of export business was needed to keep down unit costs. Nevertheless, there was some room for switching at the margin so that Ealing's export effort tended to vary inversely with the level of demand for caravans in the UK.

Even so, the sharp decline in exports sales in the three years before devaluation was not primarily due to this. Much more important was Ealing's inability to charge competitive prices in most foreign markets. The exception was North America, where price competition for caravans was less keen. At the time of devaluation, there was general agreement among Ealing's senior managers that to maintain both market share and profit, Ealing's export volume would have to be substantially increased, though it was also felt that the chances of doing so were poor. As 'contribution' from exports was already small, there was great reluctance to lower export prices still further.

E.3 Export Objectives

At the time of devaluation, Ealing's main operational objective in the home market was to maintain, and if possible exceed, the existing 8% market share. This 8% share was actually achieved in 1967–68.

In the year ended October 1967, Ealing's exports were 9% below their level in the previous year, and considerably less than had been forecast. In view of this, the export target for the year ending October 1968 had been rather pessimistically set at the level actually reached in 1965–66. Even so, it was not expected that it would be achieved. After devaluation, it was decided that the new competitiveness in prices which this gave would allow Ealing to raise its export target for 1967–68 by 20%.

An important objective was to make a single, substantial increase in sterling export prices. Ealing's older managers still had unpleasant memories of the 1949 devaluation, which was followed by a series of smallish price increases as costs rose, that had caused considerable loss of goodwill among export customers. The feeling in 1967 was therefore that making a single price increase big enough to cover all likely contingencies would be much better than making a small initial price increase, followed by a series of further small increases as the cost position became clear.

E.4 Market Information

The statistical information about its overseas markets available to Ealing was very good. It relied on its parent firm for general economic analyses of overseas markets, as well as for background statistics on changes in consumer expenditure and in international trade patterns. These were readily available. In addition, Ealing's trade association provided detailed figures of exports, by country, for all Ealing's UK competitors. Ealing was also given the results of the parent firm's continuing research into how acceptable to British customers particular designs of caravan were, but there was much less information of this kind for export markets.

Consequently, Ealing relied on its overseas agents for much information about overseas markets. The agents sent in regular, monthly forecasts of the numbers of caravans they would need for the next three months, and these forecasts were used to help in production planning. In theory, they were to provide Ealing with information about price and discount trends in each agent's territory, together with reports on the competitiveness of Ealing's caravans, both in terms of general acceptability and of the effect that optional extras had in making each basic design more attractive to consumers. In practice, the information agents supplied was usually sketchy. Since most of Ealing's caravans were luxury models, most of its overseas distributors sold relatively few of them, so that they had to be allowed to sell competitors' caravans as well. Although this put Ealing's agents in a good position to assess the respective advantages and disadvantages of all the competing products, Ealing felt unable to insist on detailed market reports from its agents, since they devoted only a limited part of their time to selling Ealing's products. It was vaguely felt that demand for Ealing's products was rather elastic in response to price cuts, but there were no precise estimates of price-elasticity of demand.

In October 1967, Ealing had completed its sales budget for the year ending October 1968, though the main figures in it had already been worked out in June and the bulk of the work done in March and April. Ealing therefore had an up-to-date market assessment available to it when devaluation took place. No extra market information was obtained before Ealing took its decisions, though after they had been taken Ealing's agents were asked to assess their likely effects on sales.

E.5 Internal Factors

Ealing Electrical Appliances had a standard costing system which distinguished clearly between fixed and variable costs, and was based on 'contribution'. Indeed, Ealing was selling to many export markets at prices only a little above marginal cost. Prices in these markets covered variable labour, materials and component costs, but made only a small contribution towards fixed costs.

As we have seen, unit costs had been rising somewhat, mainly because the depressed state of both home and export markets meant that overheads had to be spread over smaller outputs than in more prosperous times.

While variable cost per caravan produced was roughly constant as output increased, the industry was capital intensive and the scale of production large. Increased output, even when sold at a relatively small unit contribution, gave worthwhile increases in total contribution.

The cost information available to Ealing's management when the decisions on devaluation were made was very rough. A hurried meeting was held on the day after devaluation (Sunday). Estimates of the effects of devaluation on costs were made there and then by the cost accountant, on the basis of his experience and intuition. These costings formed the basis of the pricing decisions which were reached on the next day. The cost accountant assumed that devaluation would raise the cost of the imported materials and components in each caravan by (approximatety) 17% of devaluation. This 'import content' was estimated for an 'average' product, giving an increase in total costs of $3\frac{1}{2}\%$, and then rounded up to $4\frac{1}{2}\%$ to allow for uncertainty. A further 2% was added to cover the 'cost' of losing the export rebate, which brought the increase in the total cost of producing the existing output up to $6\frac{1}{2}\%$.

The range of models that Ealing exported was large. The range sold in different markets varied, partly because of differences in consumer tastes and partly because of different safety regulations in individual countries. So, the figure for 'import content' varied somewhat between countries. However, it was several months before Ealing Electrical Appliances was able to calculate the increased cost for each model and market at all precisely. Similarly, no precise figures for marginal cost, over the range of output which Ealing would reach if the hoped-for increase in exports took place, were worked out until much later. Since Ealing had some spare capacity at the time it was implicitly, and reasonably, assumed that marginal cost would remain constant over any likely range of output. As we shall see, prices in the UK remained unchanged until the middle of 1968. In view of a desire to take the devaluation decisions quickly it was not thought worth collecting more information before they were taken.

E.6   The Decisions

The decisions were made at the special Board meeting convened on the day after devaluation, even though this was Sunday. No non-members were brought into this meeting. A further (regular) Board meeting was held on the Thursday 23 November.

The main decisions on export pricing were taken on the Sunday, clarified on the Monday and Tuesday, and approved at the Board meeting on the Thursday. They were as follows:

1 For countries that had not devalued, and for which it was expected that Ealing Electrical Appliances would lose the export rebate of 2%, there was to be an increase of 6½% in sterling ex-works prices.

2 For countries that had not devalued, but where the export rebate had no longer been available even before devaluation (the EFTA countries, excluding Norway) there was to be an increase of 4½% in sterling ex-works prices.

3 For countries that had devalued less than the UK, there was to be an increase of 6½% in ex-works prices.

4 Dealers in countries that had devalued by the same amount as the UK were told that there would be no change in price for the time, but that the situation would be reviewed when Ealing was in a better position to judge the effect of devaluation on costs. In mid-1968, sterling prices to those countries which had also devalued at about the same time as the UK were increased by 6½%.

5 There was to be a temporary surcharge on prices of spare parts of 6½%. Distributors were told that this might have to be increased later. Much would depend on what changes in retail prices individual distributors made in their own markets.

6 The prices of all extras provided when the caravan was originally bought were increased by an average of 5%, in all countries where there had been no devaluation.

Because of the 'early-warning system' of price control, then in force in the UK, no price change for the home market was made until the middle of 1968. By that time, the effects of devaluation on costs had been worked out fully.

So far as markets in countries that had *not* devalued were concerned, what was done was basically to increase sterling prices by the expected increase in costs—including the effect of losing the export rebate where this was still received. In other words, after allowing for the expected cost increases, the maximum possible reductions in foreign-currency prices were made.

The main information used about external factors was the export sales forecast for the period to October 1968. Most of the work on this had been done in March and April 1967. Besides suggesting that Ealing's prices in overseas markets were too high before devaluation, this forecast showed that overseas dealers' stocks had been run down. The reason was that Ealing's models had recently been slightly modified and dealers had allowed stocks to fall while waiting for the new models. Production capacity was therefore likely to be short as overseas dealers' stocks were re-built. If the cuts of 9 to 12% in foreign-currency prices in countries that had not devalued stimulated sales, they could not lead to increased output for some months. On the cost side, once the cost accountant had given his rough calculations of the effect of devaluation on costs, it was quickly agreed that these provided the basis on which the devaluation decisions would be made.

It was agreed that Ealing's prices were already competitive in many export markets so that changes were not needed there, but it was also thought to be too difficult to make a separate price change for each overseas market. So, although the fact that Ealing's competitive situation was stronger in the USA was mentioned during the meeting, exactly the same sterling price increases were made to the USA as for other countries that had not devalued. The only factors leading to different sterling price increases between countries were whether, and how far, the country had devalued and on whether exports of that country had previously qualified for the export rebate. In EFTA countries, although revenues from exporting to these countries had been reduced by the loss of the export rebate some months before, it was decided that Ealing could not raise sterling prices after devaluation sufficiently to recover the revenue lost, only to cover the increased costs resulting from it.

In the whole discussion in the Sunday meeting, it was implicitly assumed that there was no feasible alternative to reducing foreign-currency prices by the maximum amount that the expected increase in costs would allow, although there was some uncertainty over whether this would lead to a price war with foreign manu-facturers, especially in Europe where price competition was keenest. The alternative of reducing foreign exchange prices in Europe by some other percentage was not seriously considered.

One factor influencing Ealing's decision was the feeling that its overseas agents would object to paying the foreign-currency prices Ealing had been charging before devaluation for orders placed before devaluation, but not met until afterwards. The sums of money involved were substantial because of the low level to which overseas agents' stocks had fallen. The agents were likely to press for the maximum possible price cuts, since they had little idea what Ealing's production costs were. In any case, they were more concerned with their own problems than with those of Ealing. Indeed, one European distributor reduced his foreign-currency prices by the full amount of devaluation immediately after devaluation and without Ealing's approval. His action caused Ealing considerable embarrassment over several months.

Sterling prices for all countries that *had* devalued by the same amount as the UK were increased in June 1968, by an average of $6\frac{1}{2}\%$. For seven months, therefore, Ealing had felt unable to recover its extra costs in these markets.

No attempt was made to contact Ealing's overseas agents before the devaluation decisions were taken in order to ask their views on what should be done. However, after the decisions were reached, all the biggest agents were asked to send in forecasts, within a month, of the extra sales they thought they would be able to make as a result of the foreign-currency price cuts. This information was considered at a Board meeting on 22 December and appeared to confirm the correctness of the devaluation decisions. The information was not systematically built into Ealing's budgets until March 1968, when the export targets for 1967–68 were increased by 20%, an increase of 30% over the 1966–67.

No increase in home market prices was made until July 1968, when they were raised by only 3%.

E.7 The Results

Figures for Ealing Electrical Appliance's caravan sales are given in Table E.2.

TABLE E.2 *Ealing's sales, by volume, 1966–67 to 1961–69* (1966–67 = 100)

Year ended October	Home sales	Export sales	Percentage of output exported
1966–67	100	100	38
1967–68	100	129	42
1968–69	75	168	48

The volume of Ealing's exports rose by about 30% in each of the two years after devaluation so that, by 1969, the proportion of output exported was again 48%—the 1963–64 percentage. However, the full impact of devaluation on exports was not felt until after March 1968. Between November 1967 and March

1968 there was a marked increase in home market demand, as consumers increased their purchases in anticipation of purchase tax increases in the 1968 budget. This restricted supplies for export. Even so, the rise in exports in 1967–68 was impressive. The fall in home market sales in the financial year 1968–69 was mainly the result of restrictive economic policies in the UK, designed to switch resources to exporting. In Ealing's case, this is what happened.

Ealing did not doubt that the increase in export sales was mainly due to devaluation, which allowed it to cut foreign-currency prices and so improve its competitiveness in overseas markets. However, while exports increased dramatically, Ealing's profit margins improved only marginally. The sharp decline in sales to the more profitable home market, and the fact that it was thought wise to increase home market prices by only 3% in June 1968, led to a worsening of Ealing's cash-flow position. Profits were poor in both 1969–70 and 1970–71.

Fulham Castings

F.1 General Background

Fulham Castings was a large international group. It produced and marketed a wide range of semi-manufactured goods of varying complexity, as well as raw materials. The prices at which these sold were related to a world commodity price. While Fulham had a number of manufacturing and selling companies overseas, the whole group operated as a highly integrated concern. This study is concerned with Fulham Castings' production and marketing activities within the UK.

F.1.1 THE INDUSTRY

The product we studied was a basic material. The amount sold in the UK had been rising by about 9% per year since 1962. Export sales had not increased so quickly, rising by only 14% in the period 1962–67. The proportion of output exported had therefore been declining; it was about 25% at the time of devaluation. The world price for the material was unusually high in 1967, largely because of increased freight charges resulting from the closure of the Suez Canal. Before the Six-day War, prices had been falling and the market was rather weak.

Apart from Fulham Castings, only two other big UK firms made the same product. Imports had always accounted for a significant proportion of consumption in the UK; it was 28% in 1967. Nine identifiable firms were exporting the product to the UK and two of them were very large. Although the market was still concentrated, there had been a significant influx of small firms in recent years, which had reduced both the price of the product and the market shares of all the big firms.

We studied Grades 1 and 2 of the product. Sales of these rose by 55 and 34%, respectively, between 1963 and 1968, implying average annual growth rates of 9 and 6%. After falling slightly in 1964, the industry's exports of Grade 1 and Grade 2 rose in 1965 and 1966, but fell in 1967 to a level only 14 and 34%, respectively, above the 1963 level. World prices had traditionally been quoted in US dollars. The price of Grade 2 had been more stable than that of Grade 1. The price of Grade 1 fell steeply in 1964 and remained depressed until 1967. In 1967, the Six-day War and the closure of the Suez Canal increased freight charges and so caused prices of both grades to rise sharply.

F.1.2   THE FIRM

Fulham Casting's sales of Grade 1 in the UK rose sharply in 1964, and continued to rise until 1966, when they were 26% above the 1963 level. They declined sharply in 1967 (by 29%) and rose by only 5% in 1968. For Grade 2, sales in the UK were more stable, and in 1968 were some 22% above the 1963 level. Through its UK marketing company, Fulham imported a significant quantity of both grades of the product in order to supplement supplies from its UK plants. Thus, in 1967, the marketing company imported 31% of total UK imports of Grade 1 and 25% of those of Grade 2.

F.2   Export Position

Fulham Castings exported more of both Grade 1 and Grade 2 of the product than the rest of the UK industry. While the industry's total exports, as a percentage of total production, fluctuated in the period from 1961–1967 between 24 and 28% for Grade 1 and between 15 and 19% for Grade 2, comparable figures for Fulham were from 55 to 65%) for Grade 1 and (from 33 to 40%) for Grade 2. This was mainly because the other UK manufacturers had more plants in Europe. In Europe, Fulham's most important market in 1968 was Sweden (42% of Fulham's total exports to Europe), followed by Denmark (24%), Holland (12%), Norway (11%) and Germany (7%).

Exports of Grade 2 followed much the same pattern, rising to a peak in 1966, 51% above the 1963 level. They fell by 13% in 1967. Again, Fulham's largest European market was Sweden (26% of Fulham's total exports to Europe in 1968) with Denmark (17%) and Norway (11%) also important. Exports to the USA rose dramatically, by 77%, in 1967. This erratic behaviour of exports reflected the need to balance the Group's overall output against demand in various markets. Exports can therefore be seen as 'topping up' the output available from Fulham's European plants.

F.3   Objectives

In the period before devaluation, Fulham's activities were constrained by its production technology and by high freight costs.

It was cheaper to produce locally than to export from the UK. Exports from the UK were limited to making up any difference between demand for the product of Fulham's plants in Europe and their production capacity. There was no specific export objective, in the sense of aiming to supply particular markets from the UK.

Fulham Castings did not consciously seek to maximise exports from the UK. It was interested in the most economic operation of the whole group. Fulham's plants, both in the UK and overseas, were usually built to manufacture only a fairly inflexible mixture of products. More than marginal changes in this product mix could be made only at relatively high cost. For this reason, the production of the group was highly integrated. It was more economic to use a temporary surplus of capacity in one plant to relieve a temporary shortage in another plant, even if it were in a different country, than to try to increase output significantly in the plant where demand had run ahead of supply. It should be noted that value added was rather small.

Overall marketing objectives, both for the UK and overseas countries, were drawn up for each country. From the expected balance between demand and supply in each country, an export market objective was set for each year and each country, with varying degrees of precision for different products. As we have seen, there was no conscious distinction between home and export sales. Since the world price for the product was beyond Fulham's control, the aim was to minimise costs within the Group by supplying each market from the cheapest source, while attempting to ensure that no sale failed to cover its marginal cost.

F.4 Market Information

Fulham Castings was well-informed about its sales at the time of devaluation. There was detailed information about its sales in Europe. Since there were few active competitors in any major European market, and since the same competing firms were met in each European country, Fulham was well informed about their marketing policies. Each overseas plant made its own detailed market assessments and sent these to Fulham's headquarters for correlation and analysis. Fulham made extensive use of a computer in handling this information, and could predict fairly accurately what demands were likely to be made on its UK plants.

At the time of devaluation, the price of Fulham's main raw material was high because of the Middle East crisis. Its head-quarters staff were receiving daily reports on prices and sales,

so that no extra market information was sought before making
the decisions after devaluation.

F.5   Internal Factors

Fulham Castings' costing system worked on the basis of contribution. All elements in cost were kept under continuous and
separate review by the computer, and marginal production costs
for each product were circulated each month to help individuals
concerned with pricing (especially bulk pricing) and investment
appraisal.

At the time of devaluation, the computer was quickly able to
estimate the effect of devaluation on costs. It appeared that while
import prices of the raw material would increase by the full
amount of devaluation, other costs would be little affected. The
computer also showed that little benefit would accrue to the Group
if it switched more business towards its British plants and away
from its European ones. The computer analysis also implied that
it was not worth making the changes in organisation and routines
which such a switch would require.

F.6   The Decisions

A nine-page document had been drawn up in July 1966 to explain
what action should be taken in the event of devaluation. Fulham's
experience after the 1949 devaluation was taken into account. The
main recommendation (put into effect later in 1966) was that
henceforth all export contracts should be quoted in US dollars,
except for the freight component which could in some cases be
quoted in sterling. It had therefore become standard practice to
ensure that all Fulham's contracts gave protection against devaluation, about a year before devaluation occurred. The result was
that when it did occur there was no pricing decision, as such, for
countries that had not devalued; the decision had effectively
been taken when all contracts were made in dollars from 1966.
Fulham merely verified that the required procedure was being
followed. When devaluation took place, the marketing director
was told that all export contracts were adequately protected,
being quoted in dollars. For countries that *had* devalued, the
main recommendation was that immediate action should be
taken by the appropriate product group manager to recover
increased import costs. Since the practice of charging the dollar
price merely continued existing practice, and since the main
competitors in export markets were international companies likely

to pursue the same policy, there was unlikely to be any effective complaint by customers against this action.

On 27 November, a case was put to the British Government which set out the effects of devaluation on the cost of Fulham's imports into the UK. However, because of governmental pressure, prices in the UK were left unchanged for some months. The subsequent rise was very small.

F.7 The Results

In 1968, exports recovered from the low level of 1967, rising by 9%. This increased the proportion of Fulham's output exported from 64 to 65%. Since there had been no change in export policy at the time of devaluation, this rise can be attributed mainly to influences unconnected with devaluation that were affecting the Group's activities. Exports from the UK industry as a whole rose by some 32%, but again it is unlikely that much of this increase could be attributed to devaluation. As had been expected, the world price of the product declined during 1968, as the world market adjusted to the closure of the Suez Canal and as demand continued to be weak.

Fulham Castings considered that devaluation had enabled it to be marginally more competitive, giving it the opportunity to offer small price reductions for its products, below the world price level. However, Fulham Castings emphasised that more aggressive price cutting would have invited swift retaliation. It would simply have helped to accelerate the decline in world prices, without giving Fulham a long-term advantage. The main effect of devaluation was to improve Fulham's profitability, through an increase by the full amount of devaluation in the sterling value of the remittances received from its overseas subsidiaries.

CASE STUDY G

Gatley Hosiery

G.1 General Background

Gatley Hosiery was a large group with manufacturing and trading subsidiaries and sold branded and unbranded hosiery. It was an old-established firm, well known in its industry. In Britain, the group had two manufacturing companies, Companies A and B, both of which made finished products. It also had one company in the UK producing components and plant as well as a retail company. There was also an overseas company (holding and trading), responsible for various manufacturing, trading and distributive activities overseas. This study deals with the devaluation decisions of the UK manufacturing company A and the overseas company.

G.1.1 THE INDUSTRY

The industry contained a large number of firms, producing differentiated products. There was what economists called monopolistic competition. While the industry's market was secure in the sense that it supplied a necessity, growth in the industry had been unexciting, at least for UK producers. Table G.1 gives the figures. As can be seen, sales in 1967 were about 6% below those in 1964. The fall was mainly the result of a steady rise in imports, which now dominated the cheaper end of the market.

TABLE G.1 *Volume of sales by UK producers, 1960–67*

Years	Sales volume, thousand units
1960	183
1961	184
1962	170
1963	190
1964	202
1965	198
1966	194
1967	190

They had ranged between 6 and 30 % of total UK sales (by volume) and 6 and 7 % (by value) over the previous ten years. However, exports represented only a small percentage of output. Profit margins were low.

G.1.2 THE FIRM

Gatley Hosiery sold a wide range of products, all in higher-quality parts of its industry's product range. Gatley was the largest producer in its industry but the industry was made up of so many firms that Gatley accounted for only 8 % of the industry's total sales. Two other firms had market shares of about 7 and 5 %, respectively, and about a dozen firms had market shares of 2 %. The remainder of the market was supplied by a multitude of very small firms. Gatley's performance had been much better than that for its industry. Its home sales in 1967 were about 50 % up on those four years previously. Even so, they were down 15 % on 1965. Export sales had risen steadily since 1963, at an annual rate of some 17 %. The proportion of Gatley's output exported was 7 % in 1967, as Table G.2 shows.

TABLE G.2 *Gatley Hosiery, home and export sales volume* (1963 = 100)

Years	Home sales volume	Export sales volume	Percentage of sales exported
1963	100	100	4
1964	108	107	5
1965	176	148	5
1966	135	162	6
1967	147	186	7

Profits in 1967 were a record, so that liquidity was not a serious problem. However, as in the rest of the industry, profit margins were low, particularly in export markets. Competition in Gatley's section of the market was largely through product differentiation and advertising. To the extent that Gatley's own sales were directed at the more expensive end of the market, the effect of this competition was hard to measure.

Most of Gatley's export business was indirect, conducted by local companies overseas. Gatley's UK management believed that the effect of devaluation on its various overseas activities could not be estimated precisely. The remainder of its overseas activities were carried out by the overseas companies. The pattern of (group) turnover is given in Table G.3, which also shows the share of exports in group turnover.

TABLE G.3   *Sales of Gatley Hosiery's products: 1963–67*

Years	(a) Total group turnover, £M	(b) Export turnover, £M
1963	31	1·476
1964	36	1·572
1965	40	2·071
1966	43	2·392
1967	49	2·748

Table G.4 shows the distribution of Gatley Hosiery's exports, as in the column (b) of Table G.3, between its general market, the EEC, EFTA, the USSR and the USA and Canada.

TABLE G.4   *Gatley Hosiery's exports (£M): 1963–67*

	1963	1964	1965	1966	1967
General	—	—	502	507	543
EEC	831	923	166	245	250
EFTA	—	—	246	399	463
USSR	360	329	707	888	985
USA and Canada	285	320	450	353	507
TOTAL	1·476	1·572	2·071	2·392	2·748

Gatley Hosiery's overseas company was treated as an independent profit centre in its parent company's accounts. At the time of devaluation, the overseas company had its own managing director, to whom its marketing director, chief accountant and services manager were directly responsible. Two sales managers, one covering EFTA and EEC markets and the other the remaining markets, reported to the marketing director.

At the time of devaluation, the structure of manufacturing company A was as follows. There were three divisions, each with a general manager. Each general manager, in turn, had a sales manager, a marketing manager, a development manager, a financial analyst, a chief accountant and a buyer responsible to him.

Each division in company A produced a complete product range, that is, a large number of different kinds of stockings, each type aimed at a particular segment of the market. Each product range was divided into four main sub-classes. The overseas company bought finished products from the three divisions of manufacturing company A, from manufacturing company B (unbranded products) and on the free market, according to its requirements. Manufacturing company B did not export directly.

G.2 Export Position

While Gatley Hosiery was a major exporter, it set up its own manufacturing subsidiaries overseas whenever this seemed advantageous. Most of its overseas activities were carried out by local manufacturing subsidiaries in Eire, South Africa and Australia. These local subsidiaries were controlled by the overseas company, based in the UK, which determined the pattern of Gatley's exports from overseas countries within a global policy. This was why direct exports from the UK were so small. The overseas company controlled them, too, within the global policy. The overseas company did not manufacture in the UK, but purchased the goods it exported from the UK from Gatley's UK factories. These were controlled by the group headquarters in the UK, which was also responsible for all sales in the UK.

We are concerned in this study mainly with exports from the UK, since the activities of the overseas manufacturing companies were not affected significantly by devaluation. The overseas company's short-run objective for its exports from the UK was to earn maximum profits, since export margins had previously been unsatisfactory. Partly because home sales had been falling since 1965, Gatley had been prepared to export at marginal prices, particularly to the USSR where the size of individual orders was very large. Sales to the USSR accounted for over a third of Gatley's total exports in 1967. While the overseas company wanted to increase export margins, it wanted to do so without reducing sales volume.

Manufacturing company A had two objectives. The first was to recover the extra costs caused by devaluation. The second was to keep to a minimum the fall in sales, or loss of customer goodwill, which Gatley felt certain would arise if it made 'unscheduled' changes in prices, namely, outside the 'normal' arrangements of the hosiery trade.

The profits Gatley Hosiery earned from exports to the EEC and EFTA had been uncomfortably low recently and Gatley had just embarked on a major re-organisation of its sales and marketing activities in these areas.

G.3   Market Information

Gatley Hosiery made considerable changes in the whole of its product range every few months. These changes reflected seasonal and fashion changes in the kinds of stockings bought. Gatley Hosiery had always sold its products more by advertising and fashion elements than by price competition. Although no formal calculations of elasticity of demand had been made, Gatley believed that the market in each country was divided into a number of price ranges, corresponding in the consumer's mind to quality ranges. Experience suggested that demand was normally unresponsive to price changes within a given price range, quality remaining unaltered. However, if price moved outside that of any given quality range there was a significant increase or decrease in the quantity sold, according to whether price had been reduced or increased.

We have seen that less than one-fifth of Gatley's exports went to the USA and Canada, because Gatley had its own selling subsidiaries there. The information Gatley received from its North American offices was both regular and detailed. There were weekly and monthly sales reports, together with a six-monthly assessment of the position in the whole North American market, including an evaluation of Gatley's own competitive position. This information was supplemented by periodic visits to North America by Gatley's senior executives. Gatley also had good market information on the USSR, its largest single market, and one where Gatley had exported, through tendering, for many years.

Information about Gatley's other export markets was much less detailed. With its small European sales, Gatley Hosiery found it sufficient to rely on irregular, *ad hoc* reports on its competitive position from local agents, supplemented by fairly frequent fact-finding trips by senior executives. However, there were background statistics on imports and consumer expenditure for Gatley's major markets, from which Gatley could work out broad market trends. Nonetheless, Gatley saw the information it had about Europe as inadequate. This worried Gatley, because sales to Europe seemed likely to increase most rapidly in future. Accordingly, in 1966 Gatley had set about re-organising its arrangements for obtaining information about Europe, but the process was still not complete at the time of devaluation. The information Gatley had about its other export markets was even more defective.

At the time of devaluation, then, Gatley was fairly well informed about the pattern of demand as well as the competition it faced in its North American and Russian markets. Together, North America and the USSR accounted for just over half of Gatley's direct exports. However, the firm had too little information about its competitiveness on price and fashion in other markets, although it did have some statistical information about general trends.

Gatley did not seek any further market information before making its devaluation decisions.

G.4 Internal Factors

The overseas company bought directly from the UK manufacturing companies most of the goods it exported and the accounting information it had from these companies was fairly detailed. However, while the direct labour and material costs for each individual product range were shown separately, Gatley had an absorption costing system, allocating overheads to each range. Separate allocations were made for central, divisional and factory overheads. We shall see that, after devaluation two sets of decisions were taken by the overseas company. One was for its current products. The other was for the new season's products which were not due to be introduced to the market for some months. During this time, Gatley worked out detailed cost figures. The pricing decision for the current season's products shows us how the company operated. This decision was taken on the Monday after devaluation; the first document showing the effect of devaluation on costs was circulated by the manufacturing company five days later. There appears to have been little consultation between the managers of the overseas company and the cost accountants in manufacturing companies A and B. Instead, the export marketing director relied almost entirely on his own knowledge of the behaviour of the costs of raw materials used by the manufacturing companies.

The first cost document prepared by manufacturing company A set out the expected aggregate increase in the total cost of thirty-five grades of raw materials. A few days later, this was supplemented by new figures for unit costs, calculated on the assumption that the budgeted outputs would actually be produced. As usual, these unit cost figures included separate allocations for central, factory and divisional overheads. A supplementary study was made later to work out the cost of one raw material.

G.5 The Decisions

G.5.1 MANUFACTURING COMPANY A

The devaluation decision for manufacturing company A was taken by its own managers, who used data collected by the chief accountant, which he had discussed with the managing director before giving it to them. The decisions were provisional until approved by the managing director. All were approved by 26 November.

The decisions were as follows:

A1   The prices for all items in one particular range were to be increased by between 3 and 4% from 1 January 1968.

A2   All other prices were to be unchanged.

Manufacturing company A could cover the cost increases resulting from devaluation, at the latest, when it issued its next set of price lists, due in 1968. The only question was therefore whether to try to begin to recover the extra costs resulting from devaluation before the new price list came into effect. Decision A1 related to a product range which, by November 1967, had been produced for only three months out of an expected twelve-month production cycle. It also contained an above-average amount of imported raw materials. It was therefore decided to increase the price of all stockings in this range by 3 to 4%. With the other products, it was decided that the extra costs were sufficiently small to be absorbed until the new price lists were introduced.

Manufacturing company A produced a good deal of cost information, so that its decision-takers had detailed figures showing them the effect of devaluation on profits, etc. for a whole range of possible decisions about prices. A certain amount of guesswork was needed in preparing this cost information. For example, there were no accurate figures for the effect of devaluation on factory overheads, divisional overheads or central overheads, which had to be estimated by the chief accountant from his own knowledge. He felt that the degree of uncertainty in the figures was small enough to be ignored in the estimates. Figures for raw material prices were provided by the buyer, who regarded these estimates as maxima. 'In my own view the prices quoted are a maximum, and when the dust has settled I would hope and expect to do better.' (Buyer's memo to the managing director, chief accountant and other managers.)

G.5.2   THE OVERSEAS COMPANY

Normally, its managing director would have taken the decisions about devaluation himself, but he was abroad at the time. In his absence, most of the immediate decisions were taken by the marketing director on the morning of Monday 20 November.

One decision (see B4 below) was reached by consensus among senior managers later in the same week. The devaluation decisions for current products were as follows:

B1   To raise sterling prices charged to the American and Canadian warehousing and subsidiary companies immediately by 8%.

B2   To leave the sterling price for Russia unchanged.

B3   To raise sterling prices for all other markets by 8%, from January 1968.

All these decisions were for current products. For the next season's products, a decision was taken by consensus among the company's senior management, later in the same week. That decision (B4) was that Gatley would include a high enough rate of profit per unit when computing prices for the next season's products to maintain profit at pre-devaluation levels.

All these decisions were taken before the first cost information was produced by the manufacturing company on the Friday after devaluation. It was not until some weeks later that the manufacturing company was able to assess the increase in total costs caused by devaluation reasonably accurately at between 3 and 4%. As we have seen, the manufacturing company had decided to increase its home-market prices sufficiently to enable it to recover these extra costs. All UK prices, including those to the overseas company, were raised by 4% in January 1968. The marketing director had felt, from his knowledge of Gatley Hosiery's cost structure, that if he increased the sterling price of Gatley's exports by 8% this would more than offset any likely increase in costs resulting from devaluation.

The marketing director said that his decisions were based on his belief that Gatley's exports markets were not sensitive to price reductions of the size made possible by devaluation. However, he felt that in view of the expectations raised abroad by devaluation and the 'associated propaganda' Gatley's sales would fall if local-currency prices were not reduced at all. He also felt that Gatley Hosiery could gain a marketing advantage over its competitors if its pricing decisions were made immediately so that there was no period during which Gatley's overseas agents, representatives and associates were uncertain about what Gatley's prices would be. The marketing director explained that the special factors affecting each decision were as follows:

Decision B1: USA and Canada

(a) Sales here were growing rapidly, without the help of price reductions. Turnover in 1967 was more than 40% up on the previous year. Indeed, the two North-American subsidiaries actually did argue that the proposed (sterling) price increases would lead to a fall in sales, but this view was rejected.

(b) The decision would result in an immediate and substantial increase in revenue from North America, which had provided a 'relatively unsatisfactory' contribution to it in the period before devaluation.

(c) For various reasons, the management of the Overseas Company wanted most of the extra profit from devaluation to accrue in the UK, i.e. to itself, rather than to the two North-American subsidiaries, each of which was a profit centre.

(d) The management of the overseas company could issue instructions to these wholly owned North-American subsidiaries. In fact, it acted quickly, before there was time for any protest from the local management.

Decision B2: USSR

There were two reasons for postponing the price increases to Russia until January 1968.

(a) Gatley Hosiery wanted to give its overseas agents and representatives time to tell their customers what was going to happen.

(b) A considerable amount of clerical work was required in reducing Russian prices, and this took time.

Decision B3: Other Overseas Markets

Firms selling in these markets had to be prepared to supply for a year at a time, against the customer's specification. Once the business was obtained, the price was fixed in sterling for the remainder of the contract. The 8% increase in sterling prices therefore only came into effect for a few new contracts for the existing product range.

Decision B4: Profits

Gatley Hosiery's general pricing philosophy was 'to charge what the market will bear'. As we have seen, Gatley felt that sales might be reduced if local-currency prices were *not* cut on product ranges already being sold. However, when future product ranges were designed and produced, their prices, in local currencies, could be at roughly the same levels as before devaluation. This would mean that sterling profits would be higher.

No written information was used by the marketing director of the overseas company in taking the devaluation decisions. From his existing knowledge of costs, and of the amounts of imported material in Gatley's products, he felt certain that a price increase of 8% would more than cover any likely effect of devaluation. As for market information, he was convinced that nothing worth-while would be gained from seeking a greater understanding of the relationships between prices and sales in Gatley's overseas markets.

G.6 The Results

G.6.1 THE MANUFACTURING COMPANY

Its management were satisfied that the decisions led to the desired results. In the short run, the cost increases were covered by increased prices. As new ranges of hosiery were introduced, foreign-currency prices were pushed back to roughly the pre-devaluation levels so that sterling profits increased.

G.6.2 THE OVERSEAS COMPANY

Figures for Gatley's sales (in units) in 1967, 1968 and 1969 are given in Table G.4:

TABLE G.4   *Gatley Hosiery: sales (units) 1967–69*

	1967	1968	1969
General Markets	328	366	511
EEC	111	122	287
EFTA	168	177	338
USSR	441	576	168
USA and Canada	279	332	271
TOTAL	1327	1573	1575

Turnover figures for the same markets are given in Table G.5.

TABLE G.5   *Gatley Hosiery: sales (£000s) 1967–69*

	1967	1968	1969
General Markets	543	659	950
EEC	250	321	667
EFTA	463	490	944
USSR	985	1155	394
USA and Canada	507	684	604
TOTAL	2748	3309	3559

Apart from the continuing growth they show, the most striking feature of these figures is the changing proportions of sales to the USSR and to Europe. Between 1967 and 69, turnover doubled in the EEC and EFTA and was more than halved in the USSR. Gatley Hosiery's comments are as follows:

1 During 1969 the Russians purchased less hosiery from the whole British hosiery industry and more from France.

2 The overseas company's principal supplier was the manufacturing company, which had a particularly busy year in the UK in both 1968 and 1969. This lengthened its delivery dates and, together with the fact that home sales were more profitable, led Gatley to quote both higher prices and longer delivery dates to the USSR.

3 'The significant increase in turnover in our European markets during 1968 and 1969 arose from a management decision to improve our market penetration in this area. Because of the drop in business with the USSR, we accelerated this course of action by about six months.'

Previously, Gatley had been represented in Europe by commission agents, responsible to a manager who had other responsibilities as well. This situation was changed in 1967. From that date, a number of managers were appointed with the sole responsibility of stimulating exports to Europe. One of the changes they made was to replace sales agents working on commission by salaried employees of Gatley. Other factors, like the development of products that were tailor-made for local markets, improved service and increased advertising, all helped to increase market share in Europe.

Gatley Hosiery made other changes after devaluation. They told us: 'We have made changes in our policies concerning overseas representation and the marketing of our products since devaluation. However, none of these decisions resulted from devaluation. All arose in the course of the development of specific market plans.'

G.7 Import Substitution

Gatley Hosiery used a large proportion of one type of material, available from both British and foreign sources. The structure of the market for this product was such that its price was closely tied to the 'world price'. Movements away from the world price were rapidly eliminated by arbitrage. After devaluation, British producers of the material immediately raised their sterling prices to the new equivalent of the international dollar price. There was therefore no financial incentive for Gatley Hosiery to alter its buying policy, though it continued to shop around the various markets for the material in order to obtain its supplies at the lowest possible prices. Its actual purchases were determined by short-term needs for particular qualities of material.

With other materials, Gatley's buyer emphasised that the determining factor was availability rather than price. Gatley imported many goods for which there was no exact UK substitute. Devaluation therefore did not lead to any switch from imported to home-produced supplies. Dollar and sterling prices remained in line.

Hertford Stoves

(We obtained less information from Hertford Stoves than from most of our other firms. However, we feel that this is an especially interesting case study and therefore include it, although it is less detailed.)

H.1 General Background

Hertford Stoves was a division of a large firm in the engineering industry, and made a rather expensive durable consumer good, Product H. In 1967, Hertford exported about 90% of its output to more than a 100 countries. However, the USA provided the biggest amount both of turnover and of profit for the division. The UK was the least profitable market.

H.1.1 THE INDUSTRY

Hertford Stoves effectively *was* the UK industry for Product H, accounting for over 90% of UK output in 1967. Since Hertford exported about 90% of its output of Product H at the time of devaluation, it accounted for most British exports. A major problem in export markets was Japanese competition. There had been few governmental impediments to sales of Product H in Japan. In the UK, high rates of purchase tax and hire-purchase restrictions had held back demand. With a large home market and substantial exports to the USA, Japanese producers had found it easier to keep down prices than had British firms. One problem in the American market at about the time of devaluation was that Product H was subject to very rapid increases or decreases in consumer demand. Consumers would use money previously saved to buy much more of Product H; later they would withdraw their spending. Apart from these fluctuations in consumer spending in the USA, Hertford also faced keen Japanese competition in that market. Japanese producers accounted for more than half of sales of the product in the USA. There were about 1500 franchise dealers in the USA but only a small proportion of them dealt on any scale with the type of product made by Hertford. There was a very large number of very small dealers. Sales in the USA were highly seasonal, with the lowest sales at the end of January, and the peak in April. Sales in April were often ten times those in January.

Japanese competition was also keen in other parts of the world. At the time of devaluation, Japanese products accounted for about 10% of total sales in the UK. In the rest of the world, excluding the USA, they accounted for about 35%.

As we have seen, 90% of Hertford Stoves' sales were made abroad. Because there were virtually no other British firms in the Industry, Hertford was mainly worried by Japanese competition. There were five major Japanese competitors. The biggest was a large firm specialising in the production of Product H. The next three were multi-product firms. These were only medium-sized producers of Product H, but big firms when their other production was taken into account. The fifth Japanese producer was small. Japanese sales of Product H were growing rapidly, not least because the Japanese could afford to undercut British prices throughout the world by an average of about 10%.

H.1.2   THE FIRM

The particular range of Product H sold by Hertford was rather expensive. In the USA the firm had concentrated on the more expensive end of the market, which meant that Hertford's range of Product H covered only about 50% of the total range bought by American consumers. While the Japanese had previously concentrated on the cheaper 50% of the market, at the time of devaluation they were moving into the dearer end. However, this was offset to some extent by the fact that an increasing share of the expenditure of US consumers was also going into the more expensive products.

H.2   Objective

At the time of devaluation, Hertford was thinking basically in profit terms. Its aim was to respond to devaluation in such a way as to increase 'contribution' to profit by the maximum possible amount.

H.3   Information

Hertford had reasonably good sales information, not least because about half of its output went to the USA where trade statistics were extremely good. However, Hertford's understanding of the relationship between the price of Product H and consumer purchases of it was less reliable than it would have liked.

Hertford's cost information was also good. Because, at the time of devaluation, it was concentrating on increasing 'contribution', the finance department was able easily to provide cost figures which clearly identified the variable cost of producing each of Hertford's products.

H.4 The Decisions

Hertford was an interesting firm in that, alone of all those we studied, it made detailed contingency plans before devaluation. In the Summer of 1967, Hertford decided that devaluation was likely. Its chairman took the view that, if it occurred, the amount of devaluation would be 15%. The marketing and finance departments therefore worked together for several weeks to produce a contingency plan, assuming a 15% devaluation. This plan had been worked out in detail by September 1967. It was never formally approved by the Board, although the Board knew that it existed. The Board regarded the response to devaluation as an operational matter, mainly in the hands of the marketing department.

Those who worked out the contingency plan looked first at the American market. They felt that a reduction in the dollar price of Product H would not increase sales in the USA, though they felt that an increase in the dollar price would reduce them. Hertford had been quoting prices to the USA in dollars for years, and the contingency plan provided that these prices would be left unchanged.

At the time when the plan was being drawn up, Hertford was suffering little loss of sales because of Japanese exports to the American market in the more expensive product range. Since Hertford's more-expensive products were nevertheless selling well, Hertford felt that there was no point in competing with the Japanese by matching their prices. Because there were relatively few important dealers for Product H in the USA, and because Hertford did not advertise on American television, the only change in the USA was a small increase in advertising expenditure. It seemed more sensible to concentrate on convincing customers that Hertford's product was better.

In Canada, where the position was similar, the retail price was also held. There was no change in the rate of commission paid to agents or dealers either in Canada or the USA.

In the rest of the world, the situation was different. Competition still came from the Japanese, but in many countries there was also competition from local manufacturers. Hertford therefore lowered its foreign-currency prices by an average of $7\frac{1}{2}\%$. It thought hard about reducing prices farther, but took the view that costs were likely to rise in the UK.

Because its objective was to maximise 'contribution', Hertford looked in detail at the situation in each country, even though these markets numbered about 100. In looking at any country, Hertford took the retail price of the particular types of product it sold in that country and compared them with the prices of competing products. It also looked at the tariff position for itself and its competitors. Since most of Hertford's European competitors were based within the EEC, tariffs were important.

Using what impressions it did have about the relationship between price and quantity sold, Hertford tried to see how it should change prices after a 15% devaluation in order to increase contribution to profit from each country by the maximum amount. Hertford insisted that there was nothing sophisticated about its calculations. Since it sold a large number of products in a large number of countries, it would have been very time-consuming to look at all products in all countries. Hertford therefore chose a typical design of product in each country. Having discovered from the marketing department what was the typical product for each market, and looked at the relationship between its competitive position and that of the closest competing product, the finance department then calculated the variable cost of producing that particular product and the marketing department used this information to decide what action to take. Hertford's prices were altered by what seemed the best percentage for each country.

As we have seen, the whole contingency plan had been worked out in detail by September 1967, on the assumption of a 15% devaluation. After devaluation, it was quickly agreed that since the devaluation was one of approximately 15%, the decisions set out in the contingency plan should be put into effect at once.

H.5   The Results

Hertford felt that its devaluation decisions were good ones. In most of the world, the decision did appear to maximise contribution. However, though it had no regrets over its decision in the USA, Hertford's position in the US market deteriorated sharply soon after devaluation. Because of restrictions on credit in the USA Hertford's contribution to profit on sales of its whole product range in the USA in the financial year ended 1969 was not much more than half the figure for the previous year. If sales had grown as had been expected, it would have doubled. However, the corollary of this was that Hertford was very satisfied with its decision to hold its dollar prices constant. Although the volume of sales had fallen, because dollar prices were unchanged the level of sales achieved actually brought in about £750,000 more sterling than it would have done had there been no devaluation.

CASE STUDY I

Inverness Plant Builders

I.1 General Background

Inverness Plant Builders was an important division of a large
group producing capital equipment. It specialised in producing
heavy plant, which could take up to two years to build. Usually,
only a few competitors were tendering for the same business at
any time, either in the home or the export market. Inverness
operated in a fairly autonomous way, with its divisional manager
directly responsible for profitability to the Chairman of the group.
Within Inverness, profit margins varied from division to division,
the larger ones being the more profitable. However, for several
years profits in all divisions had been very low.

I.1.1 THE INDUSTRY

Information about demand for the product and total capacity for
producing it within the UK was not reliable, but overall sales in
the UK had been falling since they reached a peak in 1965. The
industry had expanded its capacity substantially in that year,
expecting higher sales as the National Plan took effect. When
these did not occur, Inverness Plant Builders was left with considerable excess capacity and this led to a general decline in
prices and margins, especially for business within the UK. At the
same time, customers both at home and abroad were ordering
more and more of the bigger units that the industry produced,
and whose manufacture needed special-purpose machinery.
Consequently, the world market was contracting in terms of
numbers of units of equipment sold, while the average size of a
unit was increasing. Competition was keen and profit margins
were low.

There were only six other producers of this type of plant in the
UK, and just before devaluation none of them exported more than
about 10% of its output. Nor did each firm compete over the
whole range of products sold by Inverness Plant Builders. In
export markets, the number and identity of competitors varied
from tender to tender, but was usually small.

I.1.2   THE FIRM

Inverness Plant Builders normally accounted for about a fifth of the UK industry's output. Before devaluation, its sales had been as shown in Table I.1.

TABLE I.1   *Inverness Plant Builders: home and export sales, 1961–62 to 1967–68* (1961–62 = 100)

Year ending 31 March	Total sales	Home sales	Export sales	Export sales as a percentage of total sales
1961–62	100	100	100	6
1962–63	146	135	278	12
1963–64	157	145	335	14
1964–65	156	162	76	3
1965–66	175	178	149	5
1966–67	157	156	184	7
1967–68	152	68	1410	60

After rising steadily until 1965–66, home sales had been falling for two years. At the time of devaluation, they were less than 40% of their amount in 1965–66. As Table I.1 shows, in the period up to 1966–67, exports had never been more than 14% of home sales and were often less than 7%. However, with the sharp fall in home demand after 1965–66, Inverness's sales effort was switched to exports, which increased nearly seven-fold in 1967–68. Even so, this success was mainly a result of obtaining a series of large orders from one customer in the USA.

Inverness Plant Builders' prices to its UK customers had fallen with those of the rest of industry after 1965. Product A was the one with the biggest sales in the home market, so that A can be taken as the standard product. If its price is expressed as a ratio to the total of labour and raw material costs, then its home-market price fell from 1·6 in 1965–66 to 0·9 in 1967–68. In other words, by 1967–68, with the ratio at 0·9, price was below the aggregate of labour and raw material costs. At this point, the Sales Manager deliberately began to quote high prices to home customers in order to divert production to exports.

It is difficult to say much about export prices, since these varied not only between customers but between countries as well. Typically, export prices were lower than home market prices and the difference was especially marked for Inverness's more expensive products, though this was not so true in 1967–68.

In 1967 there were six competitors in the UK, two of which have since merged; for the bigger units there were only two or three competing firms. Inverness produced about 20% of the British output of its type of plant. Not all companies, competed seriously for every order, because each was using a different proportion of its capacity. Indeed, we should note that gaining or losing one large order could have a significant effect on a firm's output. Normally. Inverness would submit tenders for about ten times as many contracts as it actually expected to take. Large swings in the size of order books were usual.

The more complicated and expensive the equipment being tendered for, the smaller was the number of competitors in export markets. Excluding British firms, there were 30 or 40 competitors for Product A in export markets, but there were only six to eight competitors for Product C. It was rare for all firms to be competing for any one contract. Imports into the UK of the type of plant produced by Inverness had not been significant. However, there was increasing concern about potential import competition at the time of devaluation, partly as a result of the creation of EFTA.

I.2 Objectives

The general objective was to earn profits of 15% on capital employed, while trying to increase the rate of capacity utilisation. In the years immediately before devaluation, Inverness had not been successful in reaching either objective. As to market share, Inverness aimed to supply between 20 and 25% of the home market and some 10% of what the Sales Manager regarded as the 'available' export market. Inverness was also very concerned to maintain its image as a technological leader. At times when market prices were high enough to give a 15% return, Inverness put the emphasis on developing its technological superiority.

I.3 Market Information

Inverness had a satisfactory system for obtaining market information. At the time of devaluation there were plans for improving the way information was collected and presented, though these had not yet come to fruition. Few managers were accustomed to thinking in terms of market shares, bidding strategies, etc.

The most important set of information was provided for regular meetings of the marketing department. This gave managers information about prices, enquiries and the number of tenders accepted. Information about competitors' policies, the amount of capacity they had available and, in particular, about their delivery dates was less detailed, especially for export markets. However, Inverness felt that it could assess the general position in its most important markets reasonably accurately. Further information could be obtained if required, but this required a great deal of effort. For example, Inverness could estimate how far bids, orders or prices were likely to reach, or fall short of, the budgeted levels and what the recent sales performance of major competitors had been. However, this information was not presented regularly or systematically. There was a good deal of reliance on the experience and 'feel' for the market of the sales manager responsible for each group of customers. Although every outstanding tender was re-examined by Inverness after devaluation, there was no attempt to obtain extra market information.

I.4 Internal Factors

The profits of Inverness Plant Builders had been well below the desired rate of 15% on capital employed for several years, so that Inverness had considerable spare capacity. The fact that Inverness's competitors also had a good deal of spare capacity had forced Inverness to work out its marginal costs when calculating tender prices. Those in Inverness who were responsible for calculating tender prices began by working in terms of a standard mark-up over direct labour and material costs. The desired amount of 'contribution' to overheads and profit was then easy to calculate. When the price for a particular tender was being agreed, those concerned took into account the desired amount of contribution. However, at the time of devaluation this was largely irrelevant, because prices were not high enough to give the desired return of 15% on capital. Inverness could only try to get the best rate available in a depressed market. Prices rarely reached the desired levels.

As this suggests, cost information within Inverness was plentiful and relevant, not least because the depressed conditions in Inverness's market had forced those who worked out tender prices to base them on variable costs. Arrangements had been made to supply the sales manager with weekly reports giving the percentage of capacity already committed and the amount of work in progress, and with monthly reports on labour and material costs. In practice, the cost system was kept under continuous review, because it was re-examined every time a bid was submitted, and this happened frequently. Immediately after devaluation, the estimates department calculated that devaluation would cause an overall increase in costs of about 7 %, mainly because of increased material costs.

I.5   The Decisions

No contingency plan had been made for devaluation. While most overseas contracts were negotiated in sterling, they included clauses by which any devaluation of sterling automatclally reduced Inverness's foreign-currency prices. Inverness Plant Builders realised how vulnerable these contracts made it and had succeeded in introducing cost-escalation clauses into some contracts to protect it at least against the cost increases resulting from devaluation. However, these arrangements did not apply in the USA, where contracts were normally taken at fixed, dollar prices. The result was that, with most of Inverness's outstanding contracts, there was no possibility of making a windfall gain from devaluation.

Some weeks before devaluation, Inverness's sales manager had discussions with his senior subordinates to try to predict the reactions of overseas competitors to devaluation, and to decide how Inverness itself should react. They agreed that Inverness's foreign competitors were likely to match any reduction in Inverness's own tender prices if sterling were devalued, provided that the devaluation was by not more than 25 %. Inverness expected that some foreign competitors would attempt to forestall Inverness, reducing their own tender prices before Inverness was able to do so. There was no detailed assessment of the likely reaction of Inverness's British competitors to devaluation; all were seen as being in roughly the same position as Inverness itself.

Devaluation had therefore been anticipated to some extent. When it took place the necessary decisions were made by the sales manager himself, after informal discussions with his subordinates at the regular management meetings. His first step was to have the costs of outstanding contracts and of tenders already submitted or about to be submitted recalculated. The estimates department's immediate calculations showed that the costs of meeting Inverness's existing tenders would rise by about 7 %. This was confirmed as soon as there had been time to make more-detailed calculations. Inverness's sales manager therefore knew roughly what were the maximum permissible reductions in foreign-currency prices. Given the low level of profits then being earned, and the earlier discussions in the marketing department, there was no intention to reduce prices generally. The decision was that Inverness would attempt to increase the sterling price of each outstanding contract, whether within the UK or overseas, by at least $7\frac{1}{2}\%$. This would enable it to recover the expected increase in costs. However, with export contracts outside the USA, Inverness had little hope of doing this. Most contracts included an exchange rate clause, keeping foreign exchange prices constant. However, for contracts with the USA where prices had been negotiated in dollars, there was no change in the dollar price. Inverness reaped the full benefit of devaluation in increased sterling prices.

With the tenders still outstanding, there was a possibility of altering the price. Each tender was therefore re-examined to see whether the probability that it would be accepted was likely to be increased by making a price reduction within the acceptable range. In most cases, it was concluded that such a price reduction would result in an immediate price reduction of the same amount by Inverness's competitors, so that there would be no significant increase in the number of contracts that it obtained. On only one outstanding tender was it thought that the small reduction in price that devaluation would allow would alter the probability that Inverness would obtain it. This was a contract being negotiated in New Zealand, against Italian competition. The Italian competitors were unable to match the price advantage given to Inverness by devaluation. The order therefore eventually went to Inverness. The New Zealand market was one where prices had been exceptionally low and, before devaluation, both Inverness and its Italian competitors had been tendering at prices close to marginal cost. However, because of this success, Inverness's sales manager instructed his salesmen to seek business more actively in marginal markets.

The sales manager himself decided all tender prices for three months after devaluation. He withdrew all delegation of price setting because he saw the situation as very fluid. The general principle of making the smallest possible reduction in foreign-currency prices was maintained.

I.6 The Results

Inverness Plant Builders' performance in the year after devaluation was disappointing. The number of contracts obtained from customers in the UK continued to fall—in 1968–69 by more than 20%. However, the ratio between price and raw material plus labour costs in the home market rose to $1 \cdot 3$, compared with the $0 \cdot 9$ of 1967–68, and the export effort was reduced somewhat.

Partly as a result, export contracts fell by 60%. The net effect was an overall reduction in new orders of about 45%. The continuing fall in home demand was largely a result of the deflationary measures which accompanied devaluation and the depressed export market could not make up for this fall. Looking back after the end of 1968, the sales manager felt that Inverness had not been as aggressive in its export pricing as it should have been, and he thought that Inverness had been unnecessarily fearful of starting a world-wide price war, through its own price cuts.

Inverness had hoped that the high level of orders in the USA would continue, because prices there were comparatively high. To be sure of getting its share of this business, Inverness had been keeping available a substantial amount of the capacity that was designed to produce products that sold well in the USA. As a result, Inverness did not make the maximum possible sales effort in less profitable markets, even though several of them became more attractive to Inverness after devaluation.

In the event, Inverness's forecasting was wrong, and its biggest American customer failed to provide the expected amount of business. Instead, it cut back sharply on its investment programme. This was the main reason for a dramatic fall in new export business available in 1968–69.

The sales manager also deliberately refrained from tendering to potential customers in South Africa, where export prices were very low. He thought Inverness was likely to take over a competing firm in the UK which was in difficulties because it had taken on large amounts of export business, particularly in South Africa. Had the take-over gone through, the competitor's plant would have been closed down and the export orders completed in Inverness's own plant. Consequently, the sales manager reduced Inverness's export sales effort somewhat, for this reason also, particularly in South Africa. His aim was to have capacity available to meet the accumulated South African business after the merger, as well as the business expected from the USA. The South African situation affected Inverness's export strategy for about three months immediately after devaluation. In the event, Inverness's intended prey merged with another competitor.

Inverness's exports performance was disappointing, although it is true that, because orders took so long to complete, the level of production in Inverness was more stable than what is said above might suggest.

Nevertheless, the sales manager's main conclusion was that some opportunities had been missed because of Inverness's concern to avoid beginning a price war.

CASE STUDY J

Jarrow Furniture

J.1 General Background

Jarrow Furniture was a large firm by any standards; exports had always been important to it. They represented 73% of its total output in 1967, although this was a lower figure than for previous years.

J.1.1 THE INDUSTRY

Home sales of the industry had been static for decades; demand for the product was very income-inelastic so that total UK consumption actually *fell* as consumers' incomes rose. In 1967, total home sales were 15% below the 1965 level. Jarrow was much the largest British producer in the industry. The remainder of UK output came from two medium-sized firms and about six small ones. None had significant exports.

J.1.2 THE FIRM

Figures for Jarrow's sales and those of the rest of its industry are given in Table J.1.

Jarrow Furniture had performed rather better than the industry as a whole. It had increased its sales volume by 11% in 1967, bringing its UK market share to almost two-thirds. In part, its

TABLE J.1   *Indices of sales volume 1963–67* (1963 = 100)

	Home sales	Percentage of total UK sales	Export sales	Percentage of total UK exports	Percentage of Jarrow's output exported
1963	100	54	100	98	83
1964	101	55	78	97	79
1965	112	55	72	95	76
1966	99	59	62	96	75
1967	111	64	63	97	73

better performance in the home market was the result of take-overs; it was also due to the successful introduction of new designs. Jarrow usually earned higher profits than its UK rivals since its products sold at a premium, because of their well-known brand name. Even so, various substitutes had for some time been encroaching upon Jarrow's market, as consumers' tastes had changed. Thus, in 1967, the number of units of furniture that Jarrow sold in the UK was some 30% below the figure for 1960.

With little prospect of sustained growth in the British market, Jarrow had been exporting most of its output for many years. As can be seen from Table J.1, it exported about three-quarters of output in the period 1963–67. Indeed, over the whole period, it accounted for almost all exports of its product. This decline had, of course, focussed attention on export markets to an even greater extent than before. However, sales in overseas markets had been affected by forces beyond Jarrow's control. In particular, there had been a steady increase in the number and size of local production plants in overseas countries, because Jarrow's was a relatively labour-intensive industry. Tariffs were high in many of these countries and the initial investment required to set up a local plant was quite small. Jarrow Furniture had tried to anticipate this competition, wherever possible, by concluding agreements to allow local manufacturers to assemble its products. However, Jarrow's export sales had been declining rapidly, and by 1967 they were only about two-thirds of the 1963 volume.

Jarrow's main export markets in 1967 were the USA, Canada and Europe, which took 43% of its total exports. The balance went to a large number of smaller countries, mainly in the Commonwealth. In most of these Jarrow had achieved a dominant market position by negotiating assembly agreements with local manufacturers. The way exports to these areas had changed is shown in Table J.2.

TABLE J.2 *Jarrow Furniture: exports by area* (Index numbers of export volume, and percentages of Jarrow's total output going to each area: 1963 = 100)

	Total exports	USA	%	Canada	%	Europe	%	Other	%
1963	100	100	50	100	5	100	8	100	37
1964	78	57	36	72	5	98	10	103	49
1965	72	45	32	66	5	93	10	102	53
1966	52	34	36	76	6	97	12	89	47
1967	63	36	29	82	7	87	11	92	54

The deterioration in Jarrow's export performance was mainly due to the dramatic fall in sales to the USA. This was the fastest-growing market in the world, with sales rising at around 9% a year during the 1960's. Moreover, in contrast to other markets, consumption in the USA tended to rise as consumer incomes rose because, to American consumers, Jarrow's furniture was an expensive status symbol. Nonetheless, competition at the cheaper end of the market had increased sharply. The American market was enormous relative to Jarrow's existing and planned production capacity. It was expanding, and American consumers tended to buy imported rather than home-produced goods. Indeed, Jarrow supplied 20% of all furniture imported by the USA. In addition, the American market was sufficiently fragmented for a far-sighted firm to be able to develop a quasi-monopoly position for itself. At the same time, these quasi-monopoly markets were not big enough to attract competitors into them.

In 1963, Jarrow decided to move into the more-expensive end of the American market in a search for higher profit margins. At the same time, it reorganised its distribution system and set up a local selling company. Unfortunately, there was a sudden contraction of demand in the more expensive part of the US furniture market in 1964. Jarrow's sales in the USA fell by 40% in 1964–65 and by a further 20% in 1965–66. The total number of units of furniture represented by this decline was so big that it was impossible for Jarrow to sustain its total production by making extra efforts to sell in other markets. It was because of these difficulties in the USA that Jarrow's total output fell by about 20% in 1964–65 and by a further 15% in 1965–66. Profits were reduced more than in proportion, and in 1965–66 reached their lowest level for more than a decade. Nevertheless, in 1967, Jarrow was supplying about a fifth of the furniture imported into the USA. Total imports, in turn, represented a fifth of the total US demand for furniture.

Total purchases of furniture in Canada had also been increasing rapidly and the Canadian market had similar characteristics to that in the USA. Jarrow Furniture accounted for about a third of Canadian furniture sales, although its market share had been under pressure for some time. In 1966–67, Jarrow had put a long-run marketing plan into effect in Canada and this was largely responsible for reversing the downward trend in Jarrow's market share.

In Europe, demand was more price-elastic and competition severe. Just under half the furniture Jarrow sold in Europe was assembled there. Since 1962, Jarrow's sales of finished products to Europe had fallen by about one-third. Those of units for assembly had almost trebled.

Competition in Jarrow's remaining export markets came from a large number of local producers, but its main international competitors were based in Japan and five European countries.

J.2 Objectives

Jarrow was operating on the basis of a strategy planned in 1967. The main elements in this strategy were: (a) to offset the inexorable contraction of sales to certain markets by increasing its penetration of the American market and (b) to diversify its production by moving away from its traditional product. The basic objective of this strategy was survival. Once the strategy had been agreed in principle, precise numerical targets for sales volume, market share, return on capital, etc., were set and written into Jarrow's corporate plans. They became the objectives of management.

Jarrow's basic pricing policy was to try to discriminate between its various national markets, with the price in each as high as was consistent with achieving other objectives, such as market share. In practice, Jarrow had found it both convenient and possible to arrange its national markets into groups, and was usually able to charge the same price for all countries within a given group, though it would adjust these prices on an *ad hoc* basis if necessary.

In the UK the prices charged had been limited by two inter-related factors. First, there was the contraction of the market already mentioned. Second, consumers appeared to have a view of what was an 'appropriate price' for the product and this seemed to be closely related to the level of prices charged many years earlier, when demand for Jarrow's furniture had been very high. The effect of these factors in keeping down Jarrow's prices was mentioned by the chairman in Jarrow's *Annual Report* for 1965. He said, 'The time has long since passed when we ... could pass onto our customers the cost increases which we suffered.'

In most export markets the situation was rather similar, but higher prices could be obtained in North America than elsewhere. This was another reason why Jarrow wanted to concentrate on the North American market.

The devaluation decisions were linked to these objectives in a general way, but also had the following specific objectives.

J.2.1 EXPORT OBJECTIVES

In export markets, the objective at the time of devaluation was to maximise the additional profit per unit of sales in the short run, provided that (a) long-term plans and objectives were not significantly affected by the action taken and (b) export sales were not reduced. In some markets, mainly in Europe, it was thought that demand was likely to be more than normally responsive to reductions in foreign-currency prices. In those markets, the long-term objective of the devaluation decisions was to maximise total extra profit through price reductions.

J.2.2   HOME-MARKET OBJECTIVES

Here, the aim was to maintain sales at as high a level as possible, and for as long as possible. This was to be done against the background of (a) a moderate boom in home-market demand of the sales and (b) the probable effect of this boom on the economic restrictions introduced by the British government at the time of devaluation.

J.3   Market Information

Jarrow Furniture believed that, in general, its market information was adequate. It had figures for the trend of sales and of market share in each overseas market, together with general information about trends in furniture design and in consumer attitudes towards those trends. Information was least detailed for the smaller markets, where Jarrow relied heavily on local assemblers to look after its interests. From Europe, Jarrow's agents sent in irregular, *ad hoc* reports but these were supplemented by frequent personal contact between the agents and those concerned with exports at Jarrow's UK headquarters. Statistical information for Europe was better than for most other markets.

However, Jarrow was best informed about the North-American market, where it saw its main growth prospects. Despite having good statistics for North America, it had a poor forecasting record there. The decision to switch Jarrow's main marketing effort in the USA to the higher-quality end of the market had been taken after Jarrow had commissioned a report from consultants in 1963. This tried to analyse thoroughly both market trends in the USA and Jarrow's competitiveness there. When the switch in the marketing strategy failed, a further report was commissioned and this was completed a few months before devaluation. While Jarrow Furniture believed that the new forecast was more accurate, it was well aware that another marketing mistake in the USA could prove disastrous.

Given this background, Jarrow made a special effort at the time of devaluation to obtain more information about its export markets both from its agents and from its internal information system. The aim was to decide on the best export marketing strategy. Each market was examined separately; markets were then grouped. This was done on the basis of rather rudimentary feelings about elasticity of demand in each market. Jarrow Furniture considered that, having taken this action, it had exhausted all useful sources of marketing information at the time of devaluation.

J.4 Internal Factors

The cost information available to Jarrow Furniture was excellent, but Jarrow did not recost individual products after devaluation. Its approach was rather to apply an estimated 'devaluation factor' to the goods it imported directly and to make separate estimates of the effects of devaluation on the prices it would have to pay for any other materials or components it bought and which contained imported raw materials. The upshot was a policy document which included the following paragraphs:

'Devaluation is having an immediate effect on our operating costs and this effect can be expected to increase over the next eighteen months, by which time it is likely that any benefits in terms of being more competitive in export markets (or more profitable through higher margins) will have been absorbed by cost increases.

'Imported materials will cost more immediately, although in many cases it is unlikely that prices will rise by the full one-sixth. Unless they are in monopoly situations, our suppliers must be competitive.

'The company's direct imports total some £x a year. In addition, we buy an almost similar amount of goods with an import content. Devaluation might put another $12\frac{1}{2}\%$ on this bill.

'There are numerous other effects to be expected, for more remote reasons, e.g. higher costs of transport; of freight; greater overseas demand pushing up home prices; the rise of other manufacturers' costs following the loss of the SET premium and the Export Rebate; and so on.

'The timing of the impact of these increases is difficult to assess. Some were instantaneous, while some may take eight or nine months before their effect is fully known. It seems likely, however, that our materials bill for the next financial year will be £y greater than at present.

'Wage rates will also increase, although by how much is a matter of opinion. A suggested working hypothesis is to assume an increase of 6% in hourly earnings by the end of 1968.

'At this moment, therefore, we have virtually the full benefit of our devaluation, i.e. one-seventh, which we could pass on to export customers. In perhaps eighteen months time, there will be no benefit left. One-fifth of our budgeted export sales for the current year are to markets which have devalued along with sterling, so that we are left with a theoretical maximum of about one-ninth of the remaining revenue to be obtained by maintaining local prices everywhere. One can envisage costs rising by this amount in the next eighteen to twenty-four months.'

These quotations show the kind of statement that Jarrow circulated about its assumptions at the time of devaluation. The assumptions underlay its decisions. For a time after devaluation, Jarrow kept a running record of all the price increases it suffered. The resulting figures were later used to check the overall estimates in the document.

J.5 The Decisions

The possibility of devaluation does not seem to have been considered seriously by Jarrow's management before it occurred. Certainly, no contingency plan was prepared. The final export-marketing decisions after devaluation followed a process of information-gathering and provisional decision taking, which was completed during the third week after devaluation.

We may conveniently distinguish three stages, consecutive in time and logic:

1 A 'basic principle' was defined which was 'to be followed in export pricing ... unless there is good reason for acting otherwise'. This principle was that foreign-currency prices should not be reduced.
2 Each market was considered individually in the light of the basic principle. 'Special situations' were identified where, in particular markets, price reductions or other action might be necessary.
3 Pricing decisions were then taken for the 'special situation' markets.

The basic principle was arrived at by consensus at a meeting of the chairman, the director of resources and planning and the export managers. This meeting was held on Monday 20 November. The 'basic principle' was set out in a document headed 'Pricing Policy after Devaluation' dated 2.12.1967. It is worth noting that

Jarrow's written documents, circulated to its staff after devaluation, referred to 'Pricing Policy' and not to 'Marketing Policy'.

The second stage ended with a meeting on Monday 27 November 1967, attended by the same people, plus other less-senior staff. While the decisions recorded in or implied by the minutes of this meeting were not all taken there, it was there that every national market was formally classified as either 'special' or standard.

The third-stage decisions were taken by the chairman and the financial and export managers a week later, on Monday 4 December. In the case of three 'special situations' (namely, Ireland, South Africa and Ceylon) responsibility for the decision was taken by the deputy managing director himself. The Board of the main group exercised no influence on these decisions, but was told what they were after they had been made and given a prediction of their effects.

J.5.1 EXPORT-MARKET DECISIONS

The final export-marketing decisions were:
1 To cancel a dollar-price increase of about 1.5% in the USA planned for January 1968. Instead, dollar prices were reduced by about 3%.
2 To raise sterling prices by 12.5% in Canada.
3 To raise sterling prices by 8% in European Markets.
4 To maintain sterling prices unchanged for all countries that had devalued, as well as Finland and Peru.
5 To raise sterling prices by 12.5% in a large number of markets (about 60) each of which was rather insignificant by itself.

J.5.2 HOME-MARKET DECISIONS

It was decided to postpone any price increases in the UK for at least six months.

J.6 Logic of the Decisions

Jarrow's approach was much affected by its rather traumatic experience in the period immediately before devaluation, with the substantial reductions in both sales and profit, mentioned above. The feeling that it was necessary to concentrate on short-term recovery explains why Jarrow set itself the objectives it did. Given its general strategy, every export market was considered separately, and the decision in each was related to the basic principle that, unless there were good reasons for doing otherwise, local-currency prices should be maintained.

J.6.1 THE USA

The original decision for the USA, announced immediately after devaluation, was to make no change at all in dollar prices. This was a tactical measure, aimed at countering 'almost a price-reduction hysteria' in that market, fed by the American press. The final decision (a dollar price reduction of $4 \cdot 5\%$ from the higher prices scheduled for January) was reached after face-to-face discussion with the management of Jarrow's distributing company in the USA. The latter saw that Jarrow needed to maintain prices and profits. At the same time, the US subsidiary felt hard pressed to obtain cheaper furniture in order to increase its local profits. Jarrow Furniture felt that, as it had been decided before the devaluation to treble the promotional budget for the USA, the smallest possible price reductions should be made.

In commenting on this decision, Jarrow insisted on its need for increased profits and emphasised that it foresaw the possibility of increasing its sales in the USA as a result of the dollar-price reduction of 3%. Indeed, it eventually increased its sales budget in the USA by 20%. However, the size of the price cut depended more on the bargaining power of Jarrow's American subsidiary than on any economic or commercial calculation by Jarrow.

J.6.2 CANADA

In Canada, the aim was to raise sterling prices by $12\frac{1}{2}\%$. Because it was customary to do so, Jarrow had been quoting firm prices to its Canadian agents, in October 1967, for the whole of 1968. These prices were quoted in sterling, and there was considerable reluctance by Canadian agents to see them increased after devaluation. Jarrow's main objective in Canada was therefore to persuade its agents to agree to pay higher sterling prices. If possible, they were to pay an extra $12\frac{1}{2}\%$; if not, they were at least to cover the cost increases caused by devaluation. After a trip to Canada by the export director and export manager, a sterling price increase of $12\frac{1}{2}\%$ was eventually agreed, which meant a reduction of 4% in the dollar price. Jarrow's position was strengthened by the Canadian press. Unlike the American press, it had conditioned the public to expect British costs, and so sterling prices, to increase.

J.6.3 EUROPE

Jarrow's European markets were roughly as important to it as Canada was. In particular, as we have seen, Europe was an extremely important market for units for local assembly. The decision to raise sterling prices in Europe by 8% resulted from two main factors. First, in Europe generally competition was relatively more severe, and price a more powerful determinant of demand, than elsewhere in the world. Second, Jarrow believed that the UK might well join the EEC at some future date. To prepare for this possibility, the firm felt that it should maintain, and if possible increase, its sales in the EEC. This was one of those markets mentioned in section J.2.1 where Jarrow felt that its long-run position could be improved.

Although Jarrow said that the long-run aim was to maximise extra profit, the choice of 8% as the rate of sterling price increase in every European market (except Denmark which had devalued by 7%) seems to have represented some notion of 'splitting the difference' over devaluation. It was not until much later that any estimate was made of the likely effect of the price changes on sales. However, it was vaguely felt that since price competition was particularly severe in Europe, a price reduction there might be more useful than in other markets. There was no study of the likelihood of competitive retaliation.

J.6.4 OTHER DEVALUING COUNTRIES

The decision to maintain sterling prices in all countries that had also devalued meant a fall in 'contribution' equal to the rise in costs caused by devaluation. It resulted from four arguments. First, in many cases, Jarrow already held such a large proportion of the total available market that any price reduction could have had only a minor effect on its sales volume. Second, prices in these markets had been increased in October 1967 when prices in about sixty-five minor markets were increased by a small percentage. Third, there was a vague feeling within Jarrow that its sterling prices in these markets were so far above those of its competitors that any further increase would endanger its competitive position, even though its share of most of these markets was very big. Fourth, Jarrow also felt that the task of explaining the need to increase sterling prices (whether caused by cost increases or otherwise) to customers in countries which had devalued by the same percentage as the UK would be a well-nigh impossible one.

J.6.5   THE REST OF THE WORLD

In most other markets, there had been the small percentage increase in prices in October 1967. It was felt that if there were no reduction in local-currency prices after devaluation, given that this increase had been made so recently, there would be customer resentment which might reduce sales. No attempt was made to estimate how big a reduction in sales could be expected. In the few markets where prices had not been increased in October, it did not seem that there was much to be gained from a price reduction, because Jarrow was so dominant in these markets.

J.6.6   THE UK

In the UK it was decided to postpone any increase in prices until May or June 1968. The reasons may be summarised as follows. First, the various economic measures which the government took at the same time as devaluation were thought bound to depress consumer spending, and so Jarrow's sales, because such spending was thought to be fairly sensitive to changes in government policy. Second, devaluation provided Jarrow with a degree of competitive advantage where it was selling its own furniture in competition with firms outside the UK. This advantage seemed worth preserving, at least until its value could be more accurately estimated. Moreover, a stronger case could be made to the Prices and Incomes Board for allowing Jarrow to increase prices once the effects of the loss of the SET premium and the Export Rebate could be calculated accurately, over a longish period.

J.7   The Results

In the year ended July 1968, Jarrow's profits were more than three times as big as in the previous year. However, about 30% of the increase represented a once-and-for-all profit from the conversion into sterling of large sums of money owed to Jarrow Furniture by foreign agents and customers at the time of devaluation, for goods they had received but not yet paid for.

In general, the devaluation decisions seem to have successfully increased Jarrow's export volume. Jarrow's total exports rose by $2\frac{1}{2}\%$ in 1968, thereby reversing the declining trend. However, little of the increase could be clearly attributed to the price cuts made at the time of devaluation.

As Table J.3 shows, Jarrow's export sales (in units) recovered satisfactorily in 1968 and, more especially, in 1969.

While Jarrow found it difficult to attribute any increase in sales to the devaluation decisions, the sales manager gave us his 'personal opinion' of what had happened in the USA and Canada. As Table J.3 shows, the increase in sales there in 1968 and 1969 was considerable.

TABLE J.3 *Jarrow's export sales: 1966–69* (index numbers of units sold: 1966 = 100)

Year	USA	Canada	Europe	Total
1966	100	100	100	100
1967	104	114	96	102
1968	124	155	97	105
1969	145	191	129	113

In the USA the sales manager believed that the small reduction in dollar prices had 'no effect at all'. He thought that the increase in exports was a result of several factors. First, 'promotional activity' was three times as big in 1968 as in 1967, as had been planned before devaluation. Second, advertising in the USA was increased by 30% in 1965. However, the sales manager admitted that here Jarrow Furniture 'might have been influenced by the greater availability of finance' after devaluation, because dollars earned from sales in the USA were now more valuable. Third, a new and broader range of products had been introduced. Fourth, two new warehouses had been opened, again in line with the development plan. Fifth, the sales force in the USA had been increased.

In Canada, Jarrow increased its sales volume by 38% in 1968. However, 1968 was the third year in which the new marketing plan had been operating and this in itself would almost certainly have had a significant effect on sales. However, the Sales Manager believed that devaluation 'unquestionably' assisted sales in Canada.

In Europe, performance did show improvement. The 7·5% reduction in foreign-currency prices was followed by an increase in sales volume of only about 1%, partly because competitors retaliated and cut their own prices. However, the downward trend in the sales of completed units (as distinct from parts to be assembled) was reversed, and in 1969 sales rose by about 30%.

In other export markets, experience was very diverse. Overall, however, Jarrow Furniture suffered a 10% fall in its sales volume, because of a continuing decline in its market, and the establishment of more local manufacturers overseas.

As for Jarrow's profits, in the year ended 31 July 1968 they were more than 400% those in 1966–67. About one-third of the increase was the result of a once-for-all profit on the conversion into sterling, at the new exchange rate, of foreign currency held by Jarrow, or owed to it, in November 1967. All export markets contributed to the increased profit in some degree. However, Jarrow Furniture was disappointed that its profit margins did not increase further. It attributed this to 'the higher than expected rise in costs, particularly of imports'.

The Export Director commented on the devaluation decisions taken by Jarrow as follows:

'I think that as far as markets which did not devalue are concerned, our policy in retrospect was a good one. However, in those markets which did devalue and where we did not increase our prices at the time of devaluation, we have been forced to push through price increases faster than we would normally expect to do, or wish to do, as a result of the cost increases we have faced since devaluation. However, having said this, I do not think we could have come to any different conclusion on this group of markets, as we would have found it virtually impossible to explain to customers who did devalue in line with us why we must increase our prices at that time.'

J.8 Import Substitution

The imported goods used by Jarrow may be divided into two categories.

First, some components were essential to Jarrow though they did not offer it the 'volume and other attractions' which would induce the firm to manufacture them itself. Nor were they available from other British firms. Devaluation made no difference to Jarrow's purchases of these goods. It did not lead to changes in relative prices big enough to lead Jarrow to produce the items itself.

Second, some components were similar to those produced by Jarrow itself, but of less-high quality and therefore cheaper. If the products incorporating these imported items were then exported, Jarrow could claim a refund of export duty paid. With these components, Jarrow was able to bring pressure on its suppliers to reduce their sterling prices. For specific items Jarrow mentioned reductions of 5, 9 and 11%. Apart from this, devaluation did not affect Jarrow's pattern of purchases. In particular, Jarrow did not attempt to seek out British sources of materials that were previously being imported, because there was no evidence that such a procedure would lead to net savings after taking account of the costs of putting it into effect.

Kendal Accessories

K.1 General Background

Kendal Accessories was a division of a large firm making a wide range of capital goods. Kendal itself specialised in producing a component sold mainly outside the parent group. There were few firms making the same product in the UK. However, exports were regulated by an export cartel, which fixed minimum prices for each major market.

K.1.1 THE INDUSTRY

Between 1959–60 and 1965–66 (years ending on 31 March) the home sales of the industry rose by 74%. In 1966–67 they fell by 6%, and remained unchanged in 1967–68. Most home-market demand was replacement demand and there were only about twenty customers. The high level of sales in 1965–66 reflected an increase in replacement demand, and the decline in the next two years was a reaction to this.

At the time of devaluation, Kendal Accessories had seven competitors in the home market. Kendal's market share was the biggest by a small margin and Kendal was the market leader. Competition had not been very keen for many years, largely, no doubt, because of a collective agreement to regulate UK prices. However, with the ending of this agreement, competition began to increase around 1966. At the same time, costs were continually rising. This left Kendal Accessories, as the price leader, in an unenviable position.

Between 1959–60 and 1962–63 the industry's exports fell by 29%. In the next three years they recovered somewhat, so that the 1959–60 level of export sales was regained in 1965–66. The decline was resumed in the following year, with the industry's exports falling by 23%, but there was a slight recovery (by 4%) in 1967–68. Table K.1 sets out the sales position for the industry and for Kendal Accessories.

The price of Kendal's product was often different in different export markets. For example, let us take the three most 'open' export markets. If the average home market price for the period

TABLE K.1 *Index of sales volume (1959–60 = 100)*

Year	Home sales		Export sales		Percentage of sales exported	
	Industry	Kendal Accessories	Industry	Kendal Accessories	Industry	Kendal Accessories
1964-65	154	258	86	73	27	28
1965-66	174	256	100	93	24	33
1966-67	164	193	77	87	20	38
1967-68	164	193	81	65	21	31
1968-69	126	169	55	33	19	21

1958 to 1959 is taken as 100, the f.o.b. price for exports to Market A, the largest of the three markets, dropped sharply from 103 in 1963 to 69 in 1964. It remained at that level until 1967, when it rose to 76. In Markets B and C the f.o.b. price remained at 103 from 1962 to 1966. In 1967 it rose to 109 in Market B, but remained at 103 in Market C.

Pricing in export markets was regulated by an export cartel, to which Kendal Accessories and all its UK competitors belonged. Some overseas business was allocated to individual firms on the basis of their exports to particular countries and there was a price notification scheme which, in times when business was good, meant that all UK firms tendered to the same country at the same price. However, while the price notification scheme was intended to keep prices up, trade was so depressed in 1967 that most export business was being tendered for at prices close to marginal cost.

K.1.2 THE FIRM

Kendal's sales in the home market usually rose and fell with those of the rest of the industry. Sales in the UK rose to a peak in 1964–65 and 1965–66, when they were more than $2\frac{1}{2}$ times the 1960 volume. They declined by 15 % in 1966–67 and, with those of the industry as a whole, remained static in 1967–68. Kendal's share of the industry's home sales rose to a peak in 1964–65, when it was 32 %. It fell sharply afterwards to 23 % in 1967–68, much the same as the 1961 percentage.

Kendal Accessories' exports had declined along with those of the rest of the industry after 1960, although there had been a sharp temporary rise in 1965–66 to a volume only 7 % below that of 1959–60. As Table K.1 shows, the fall was then resumed and the decline in sales was especially steep (25 %) in 1967–68. The main reason for the poor export record of both Kendal and its industry seems to have been an increasing amount of local manufacture in many overseas markets, usually under the protection of tariffs.

The number and geographical spread of Kendal's main export markets had been steadily reduced and its remaining export customers were all large and well-informed. The Eastern European countries had emerged as strong competitors for Kendal, mainly by charging low prices, at the time of devaluation. Japan was also beginning to compete keenly on price. In some cases, the prices quoted by firms from Eastern Europe and Japan were less than half those in the UK. Technical change also explained part of the decline in exports. For example, in one large market improved design had reduced the number of Kendal's components needed for a particular product by 50%.

K.2 Export Position

Kendal Accessories had been exporting for decades and, as Table K.1 shows, the percentage of its output exported was considerably greater than that of the industry as a whole. Indeed, in 1962–63, Kendal accounted for 58% of its industry's total exports from the UK; in 1966–67 it accounted for 54%. However, in the year of devaluation (1967–68), Kendal's share of total UK exports dropped sharply to 38%.

Exports generally yielded lower 'contribution' to profit than home sales. Priority in delivery had been given to the home market. However, the low level of sales in the home market in 1967–68, meant that Kendal was certainly not reluctant to export. The fall in its exports was mainly due to Kendal's inability to offer prices as low as those being offered by firms from Eastern Europe and Japan in some markets.

K.3 Objectives

Kendal Accessories set no precise objectives for either its home or export sales. For the UK, despite a worse performance in recent years, Kendal still hoped soon to have a 35% market share and to be making 50% of UK exports after a few years. Kendal had always attached great importance to keeping the goodwill of customers. It maintained contact with the senior managements of all customer firms and emphasised the need for its managers to attend trade fairs, etc.

K.4 Market Information

Kendal Accessories had only a few customers in any overseas market, and these tended to place their orders infrequently, sometimes only every few years. When pricing, Kendal Accessories was therefore in much the same position as firms which sold expensive capital equipment, bought very infrequently. Moreover, customers in overseas markets were becoming increasingly demanding, insisting on more rigid specifications at just the time when competitive pressure on prices was increasing sharply.

Kendal's sales manager felt that he was reasonably well-informed about the general competitive situation abroad. Kendal was given detailed export statistics by its trade association and could use the extensive foreign sales network of its parent group. Kendal had no separate export sales manager. Export sales were the responsibility of the sales manager, despite the fact that Kendal exported a substantial proportion of its output. In dealing with exports, the sales manager had to rely heavily on his personal experience. Sales reports from Kendal's overseas representatives were often vague and were not received regularly.

Kendal did not seek any extra market information before taking its decisions after devaluation.

K.5 Internal Factors

Kendal had only limited information about the effect of devaluation on its costs. There was considerable uncertainty in the firm about how far devaluation had increased the costs either of materials or of labour in the period up to March 1968, when all standard costs were reviewed, as was done annually. Meanwhile, Kendal had to decide how to value its stocks of raw materials and components after devaluation. As usual, these were equal to about three months' normal production. Because devaluation took place halfway through the financial year, it was agreed that only in the final three months of the financial year would raw materials and components used in production be valued at the prices ruling after devaluation.

Because the export market was depressed, with strong price competition, the prices being obtained in export markets before devaluation, for the component we studied, were usually less than its standard cost (including allocated overheads). The chief estimator had therefore been forced to work out the marginal cost for each tender separately. This practice was continued after devaluation. To that extent, the fact that Kendal's cost figures were not re-calculated until March 1968 was irrelevant. Uncertainty over the effects of devaluation on labour and raw material costs was more serious.

After devaluation, the chief estimator had discussions with members of the group purchasing and accounts departments, reporting the results informally to the sales manager before the latter attended the meeting of the export cartel. At this stage, no attempt was made to identify the specific effects of devaluation on the costs of exports. It was merely agreed that devaluation would result in an increase in the total cost of producing the existing level of output of $3\frac{1}{2}\%$. This was rounded up to 4%, to allow for the uncertainty over what would happen to labour and raw material costs.

K.6 The Decisions

The first reaction of Kendal's sales manager to devaluation was to feel that, since it was expected to increase Kendal's costs by only 4%, it would give him an opportunity to increase export margins significantly. He welcomed this because the divisional manager, and indeed the main Board of the parent group, had been complaining for some years that export margins were too low.

The first meeting of the export cartel after devaluation was held on 7 December, nearly three weeks later. At this meeting, the chairman and sales manager of Kendal Accessories argued that there was no need to make an immediate change in foreign-currency prices. The position in each market could be examined on its merits, and at leisure. Only as events made it necessary to change prices in particular markets, should this be done. However, some members of the cartel felt that it was essential to reduce foreign-currency prices immediately, at least in Hong Kong and New Zealand, where price competition from Japan and Eastern Europe was particularly severe. Kendal Accessories was one of two members of the cartel which had been allocated business in Hong Kong, but it was the smaller of the two and the cartel was not prepared to go against the wishes of the other member, who demanded an immediate reduction in foreign-currency prices in Hong Kong. In New Zealand, the situation was similar, though here Kendal Accessories had much bigger sales than the other member of the cartel which was allocated business in New Zealand. Despite its small market share in New Zealand, however, the other member belonged to a very large industrial group in the UK, and was confident of increasing its market share in New Zealand after devaluation. The firm therefore demanded an immediate reduction in prices in New Zealand. Because of the size of the parent group the cartel was reluctant to disagree. Although the sales manager of Kendal Accessories objected that competition in New Zealand was much less severe than in Hong Kong, the cartel agreed to reduce prices in New Zealand.

At this point, many of those at the meeting began to attack Kendal Accessories' idea of maintaining foreign-currency prices while the situation was studied at leisure. Instead, the meeting decided, there and then, to revise its whole export price schedule.

The meeting therefore went on at once to classify markets into two groups. The first contained those countries where the amount of business available was not significant, or where the cartel's prices were already competitive. The second included those countries where these conditions did not apply. The first group was made up of twenty-one countries. All countries but one in this group fulfilled the conditions laid down and, in all, foreign-currency prices were maintained at the same level. The exception was Malaysia, where Kendal did have a significant amount of business. Foreign-currency prices were also held at the same level as before devaluation, because prices in Malaysia were already extremely low. The second group contained seven countries (including New Zealand). Here, no change was made in sterling prices. This left three countries. The Sudan anb Cuba were both countries where competition from Eastern Europe was severe. After some discussion, foreign-currency prices there were reduced by 6%. In Hong Kong, the sterling price was raised by 6%.

The results of these decisions were complicated by the fact that some countries had devalued at the same time as the UK, though not necessarily by the same amount. Thus, the twenty-one countries in the first group included three that had also devalued by 14·3%, so that the sterling equivalent of the (unchanged) foreign-currency price remained the same. In the second group of seven countries, there were also three countries that devalued by the same amount as Britain, so that there was here no reduction in the foreign-currency price. Two other countries in this group had devalued by about 20%. For these countries, an unchanged sterling price meant an increase in local-currency prices, of about 3%. Again, Hong Kong had devalued by 6% so that a rise in the sterling price of 6% meant that local-currency prices were reduced only by about 3%. Naturally, the cartel realised that the local-currency prices of foreign competitors that had not devalued, exporting to these markets in countries that had devalued, would rise if they did not cut prices in terms of their own domestic currencies.

A notable feature of these discussions was that there was no attempt to recover the increase in production costs resulting from devaluation in the seven markets where no change was made in the sterling price. The same was true for the three countries among the first group of twenty-one, which had also devalued, and for whom the foreign-currency prices charged by Kendal's cartel were unchanged. Although each country was considered separately, only in three countries was the cartel able to agree on anything other than one of the two extreme pricing decisions. In all but three markets, either the whole gain from devaluation was taken as an increase in the sterling price; or the foreign-currency price was cut by the full amount of devaluation. Alternative policies for individual countries were not considered, and even in the three markets where special price reductions were made, the decisions reflected a rather uncritical response to strong pressures from individual members of the cartel. Wherever the foreign-currency price was reduced, the reason for the decision was the fear of competition from Japan and Eastern Europe. Yet no one seems to have considered the possibility that the competitors in Japan or Eastern Europe might retaliate by cutting their own prices.

The decisions taken by the meeting of the cartel meant that, in most markets where Kendal Accessories had built up a significant export business, foreign-currency prices were reduced by the full amount of devaluation. The main exception, as we have seen, was Malaysia, where foreign-currency prices were unchanged.

K.7   The Results

The results of the devaluation decisions were disappointing for the industry, but especially for Kendal Accessories. The industry's exports of the component we studied rose by 5% in 1967–68 (year ended March) but fell by 32% in the following year. In the same two years, Kendal's exports fell by 26 and 49%, respectively. Consequently, Kendal's share of UK exports of the component fell to 28%.

The fall in Kendal's exports was partly a result of technological change and partly a result of increased output (behind tariffs) by local manufacturers in some of its more important markets. However, it was also due to Kendal's inability to match its competitors' prices, even after passing on the whole benefit of the devaluation. This can be illustrated by Kendal's experience in Malaysia. It will be remembered that, in Malaysia, the foreign-currency price was left unchanged after devaluation because prices were already very low. Kendal Accessories therefore hoped to improve the profitability of its sales to Malaysia. A month before devaluation, Kendal had put in a tender at a price which we may denote as 100 in local currency. This contract had been lost to the Japanese, who quoted $77\frac{1}{2}$. When a new contract became available after devaluation, Kendal initially considered quoting 100 again, in line with the decision of the cartel to hold foreign-currency prices in Malaysia. However, having considered the situation, Kendal quoted 86, reducing its foreign-currency price by almost the full amount of devaluation. Even so, the contract again went to the Japanese, who undercut Kendal with a price of 72.

While agreeing in principle with the decision of the cartel to cut foreign-exchange prices in most export markets where his firm was actively engaged, Kendal's sales manager felt that in some markets, especially New Zealand, customers might have been persuaded to pay a little more. Unfortunately, as we have seen, Kendal's freedom of action in negotiating prices was severely restricted by the decisions of the cartel.

Although in general the decisions of the export cartel were adhered to, there were small adjustments to prices in some countries in succeeding months and several meetings of the pricing committee of the cartel to discuss the problem of falling export prices. Twelve months after devaluation, there was a wholesale reduction in export prices.

London Switches

L.1 General Background

At the time of devaluation, London Switches was a small independent company manufacturing consumable industrial products. There were only two producers in its industry and both home and export markets had been expanding rapidly.

L.1.1 THE INDUSTRY

It had always been difficult to obtain information about the trend of sales, whether home or export, in London Switches' industry. No reliable market survey had ever been made, so that London Switches had never been sure what its market share was. What was clear was that the UK market was expanding very rapidly, as were export markets. The industry at home was dominated by only two firms, which between them produced almost the whole UK output. London Switches believed that it accounted for just under half of this. Relationships with its slightly bigger competitor were cordial.

London Switches' total turnover had been growing fast. The largest element in this (some 40%) was sales of the products we studied, namely Products L and M. The value of total sales of these products had been rising rapidly in the years before devaluation. In 1969, total turnover from them was nearly 90% bigger than in 1965, with about three-quarters of sales made in the home market. Export sales had been rising even more quickly, and export turnover in 1969 was nearly three times the 1965 figure. Consequently, the proportion of turnover earned from exports of the two products had reached 26% by 1967. The proportion of output exported was even bigger if measured in physical terms, because export prices, especially for the Product L, were almost always considerably below prices in the UK. Indeed, exports were frequently sold at prices close to marginal cost, although higher prices were charged wherever conditions in overseas markets allowed this. In most export markets where London Switches had been successful in obtaining large market shares for the two products, it had done so in competition with its principal UK competitor, with foreign competition relatively unimportant. Table L.1 gives details of sales turnover for Produets L and M.

TABLE L.1 *Sales turnover (£) for products L and M (index numbers: 1965 = 100)*

Year ended September	Total	Home	Export	Percentage of output exported
1965	100	100	100	17
1966	117	113	156	22
1967	132	122	204	26
1968	169	151	289	28
1969	188	164	340	30

Prices had remained fairly stable since 1965, although cost increases, especially wage rises, had been passed on to customers.

L.2 Export Position

While London Switches exported only about a quarter of its output of Products L and M at the time of devaluation, it can be described as a strong exporter. As we have seen, the proportion of output of products L and M exported had been rising rapidly as part of a deliberate policy to ensure the firm's long-term growth, though there was no formal plan for growth. At the same time, Product M had only recently been introduced and it represented an important technological advance. London's export organisation was embryonic. Much of the firm's export business was conducted by the managing director, who spent a considerable proportion of his time travelling abroad.

Before devaluation, London Switches had decided to increase its export effort even further. As a result, its 1968 budget for expenditure on sales promotion abroad had been considerably increased from a rather low level. This increase in the export effort was undertaken partly because the new Product M had been accepted very rapidly abroad. It was recognised that London would have to take on more sales and administrative staff to handle the increased exports of the new product, but no decision about this had yet been taken.

L.3   Objectives

It was not London's practice to draw up annual sales budgets, so that no targets had been set for either home or export sales at the time of devaluation. The reason was that, for many years, demand had exceeded supply and there had therefore been little difficulty in increasing sales. In these circumstances, it seemed unnecessary to devote time to budgeting. One of London's most important objectives was to finance as much of its expansion as it could out of retained earnings. This helps to explain why capacity had not been increased some years earlier, when it was clear that the long-term sales trend for Products L and M was a rapidly increasing one.

L.4   Market Information

London Switches had little detailed information about export markets, which were mainly in Europe and the Commonwealth. However, it knew that export sales of Products L and M had more than trebled in four years and that its main competitor in overseas markets was the other UK producer. Since London Switches had no detailed sales budget, it made no serious attempt to forecast export sales. The market information it received from its agents came in irregularly and was extremely sketchy. However, since London's exports were growing so rapidly in 1967, the most important limitation on supply was capacity so that London saw no need to make detailed exports sales forecasts. The shortage of capacity could have been eliminated by increasing prices, but London was hesitant about doing this. It feared that raising prices to balance demand and supply could give some kind of marketing advantage to the other British producer, if only in increased customer goodwill.

When devaluation occurred, London Switches did not collect any extra market information. Its Managing Director judged that the response of the other UK producer to devaluation would be the most important determinant of London's level of sales in 1968.

L.5   Internal Factors

London Switches was unusual in our sample, having no standard costing system, despite the fact that it produced a standard range of products. Costing, including the allocation of overheads, was carried out 'on the basis of experience'. London Switches made a regular, monthly study of its cash flow, and of its raw material, overhead and labour costs, but did not look at the relative performance of its products in terms of 'contribution'.

Management was rather informal. Attendance at Board meetings was not confined to Directors; its managers were also invited when it was felt they could contribute or learn. The managing director claimed that this was an important reason why he was always well-informed about the current situation in London Switches.

As we have seen, London's policy of financing expansion only out of retained earnings had led the firm to take a conservative line on investment in extra capacity. As a result, there were times when London had too little plant. Indeed, this was the position at the time of devaluation. Existing capacity could not deal with the current volume of orders, and new capacity, due to be installed at the end of 1967, was bound to be occupied, for some time, simply in reducing the length of the order book.

Because London Switches' costing system lacked detail, its management could not quickly assess the effect of devaluation on total costs. Nor, as we have seen, did the firm know at all precisely what the 'contribution' from any individual product was. In taking the devaluation decisions, London's management simply assumed that the cost of imported raw materials would increase by the full amount of devaluation, and this turned out to be wrong. No attempt was made, then or later, to work out the effect of devaluation on the cost of individual products. However, the effect on overall costs was calculated correctly, before the decisions about devaluation were put into effect at the end of the year.

L.6   The Decisions

London Switches' immediate reaction to devaluation emerged at its regular management meeting on the following Monday 20 November. The consensus was that devaluation would provide a welcome windfall increase in profits, in a situation where much export business had been taken at prices close to marginal cost. Exports were rising rapidly at existing foreign-currency prices, and there was every reason to suppose that they would continue to do so. The only constraint was the amount of capacity that London Switches had available. Demand was rather insensitive to price changes and the small margin on exports seems to have been a result largely of a wish to ensure that London Switches' overseas agents, who also acted for other firms, devoted sufficient effort to selling London's products. The agents were also given the stimulus of good commissions. There were suggestions in the meeting that London's final customers would have been willing to pay rather more.

Three other factors seem to have been important. First, the existing plant was likely to be fully used for some time in meeting the outstanding orders. Second, the earlier increase in London's export-promotion budget was likely to increase its competitiveness, at least against non-British firms. Third, London Switches had already been planning to make an increase in selling prices at the beginning of 1968, in order to recover increased wages already agreed on for that date.

For all these reasons, London Switches' senior managers felt that the correct course would be to take as little action as possible, in the hope of keeping most of the benefit from holding foreign-currency prices constant in the form of increased sterling profits. It was recognised that some small price cuts might be necessary, in order to maintain the goodwill of London's overseas agents.

The problem was that London could not act alone because the other British producer was of much the same size. Any final decision had to take its reactions into account, because this firm was also London's main competitor abroad. The managing director of London Switches therefore telephoned the managing director of the rival company and suggested that the best reaction to devaluation would be to make only token reductions in foreign-currency prices, and then only where this seemed essential. London Switches assumed that its rival would want to pursue a similar policy, but this was not so. The rival firm felt that its own export effort would be best helped if both firms reduced their export prices substantially. After some discussion, the managing director of London Switches was persuaded to accept this view.

It was agreed that, from January 1968, both firms would increase their sterling export prices to all countries that had not devalued by 8%, thereby reducing foreign-currency prices by about 7%. For countries which had devalued, sterling export prices were to be increased by 5%. At the same time, a price increase of 10% was agreed for the home market, which took perhaps three-quarters of the sales of both firms.

L.7 The Results

In 1967–68 (year ended 30 September) London Switches' total sales of Products L and M rose by 28% as compared with their level in 1966–67. Home sales increased by 24% and export sales by 40%. This sharp rise in total sales was not the result of devaluation, which merely happened to coincide with the increase in capacity at the end of 1967. As intended, the extra capacity was used to reduce the large volume of outstanding orders. In 1968–69, the growth rate for both home sales and exports fell sharply, with the order book nearer to its normal size. The slower growth in home sales was also partly the result of the government's deflationary measures. In 1968–69, total sales rose by 11%, home sales by 8%, and exports by 18%. Again, part of the increase in exports was a result of reducing the size of the order book.

The managing director was unhappy with the decision taken at the time of devaluation, but we have seen that he had little room for manoeuvre. In an industry containing only two firms of relatively equal size, both making very similar products, he had always to charge the same prices as his competitor. In this case, their joint price was set by agreement with the competitor who, for his own reasons, wanted to set it at the lowest level acceptable to London Switches.

The problem in discovering whether devaluation was still affecting home and export sales in 1969–70 is that demand for Products L and M was then expanding very rapidly, because of technological changes. Of course, other influences had also begun to affect home and export demand for London's product. It is virtually impossible to separate the impact of devaluation on exports from these other factors.

Oxford Furnaces

O.1 General Background

Oxford Furnaces was a large, diversified engineering firm. It produced a variety of products, varying from complete machines to large engineering components, and exported a good deal of its output. We studied only one division, which was engaged on small-batch production. There were only four other firms in the same industry in the UK, and in export markets there were rarely more than two or three firms competing for any business.

O.1.1 THE INDUSTRY

Information about the performance of the industry was difficult to obtain. Oxford Furnaces could estimate how its market was changing only by discovering how many of the tenders it submitted were accepted. This gave only a rough indication of what was happening to its competitors, because Oxford Furnaces did not submit tenders for all contracts. Most of the contracts it did tender for were in the home market. The percentage of Oxford's output exported had fluctuated around 14% up to the time of devaluation.

Naturally, the number of tenders Oxford submitted was affected by cyclical changes in the demand for its products in the UK. The number of export tenders had also fluctuated in roughly the same way. Demand in the UK reached its lowest point for some time in the year 1966–67 (ending 31 March 1967), when the total number of tenders submitted was about 40% below the level in the year 1964–65. After a very small increase in 1965–66, the number of export tenders Oxford submitted had fallen in 1966–67, by about one-third. In 1967–68, tenders to the home market rose by about 20% but the level was still about 20% below that in 1964–65. Export tenders submitted by Oxford Furnaces jumped in 1967–68 by 75%.

The home industry was very concentrated, with only five producers, to whom Oxford sold components as well as competing with them. Oxford emphasised the importance it attached to maintaining good relations with these firms. Competition on

TABLE O.1 *Value indices of tenders submitted and allocated* (year ending March 1967 = 100)

Year ending in March	Total tenders	Total tedners allocated to Oxford Furnaces	Total home tenders	Home tenders allocated to Oxford Furnaces	Total export tenders	Export tenders allocated to Oxford Furnaces
1964	122	186	120	201	140	100
1965	144	145	143	139	154	179
1966	121	177	115	189	159	152
1967	100	100	100	100	100	100
1968	124	101	117	101	175	100
1969	173	264	139	232	419	450

prices and delivery dates was keen, but the firms co-operated a good deal over technical development and in dealing with general problems in the industry, though not on marketing. Since all competitors belonged to large industrial groups, they were better able than Oxford to afford a price war if competition ever broke out. This was a major reason for the emphasis Oxford put on maintaining good relations with its competitors.

O.1.2   THE FIRM

In the few years before devaluation, Oxford Furnaces had obtained between 7 and 13% (by value) of the UK contracts for which it had tendered. In 1966–67, the value of the contracts it won was less than half that for three years earlier. Although the total number of contracts available had also dropped, Oxford obtained only 7% of them. There was a rise in the total number of contracts available in 1967–68, but the volume of business Oxford obtained remained almost unchanged, and its success rate fell to 6%. Prices in the home market were depressed and competition increased.

Oxford's export sales had been erratic before devaluation and at a low level. They were practically the same in 1963–64, 1966–67 and 1967–68. However, they did rise sharply in 1964–65 and were still high, though about 20% lower, in 1965–66. Over the five years to March 1968, Oxford's export performance was disappointing, especially given the depressed state of the home market in 1966–67 and 1967–68. Like home prices, export prices were low.

In most overseas markets, Oxford Furnaces faced only one or two competitors. Apart from the four other British producers, only eight firms competed internationally for business. However, in many export markets there were also local producers. In the Far East, competition came mainly from the other British producers; in most other export markets, it came mainly from American firms, but there was sporadic competition from European producers in some markets, especially South Africa. Local firms were active competitors in South Africa, Australia, North America and Europe.

O.2   Export Position

Oxford Furnaces had been exporting for decades and had a number of manufacturing plants abroad. It claimed to be a keen exporter and, indeed, to have more experience of exporting than its UK competitors. Despite this, the role that exports played in

Oxford Furnaces' overall strategy was far from clear to us and its export effort did not seem to be well co-ordinated. There was no conscious attempt to charge different prices at home and abroad, though export prices were usually higher by the amount of extra shipping costs. Since the sharp increase in 1964–65, export sales had been falling and the proportion of output exported had declined to 14%.

Oxford Furnaces claimed to be better informed about export markets than any of its British competitors. Since it met few competitors in any overseas market, Oxford said that it could largely predict their reactions.

O.3 Objectives

While Oxford Furnaces had a sales budget, this was not regarded as a commitment to action, except of the most general kind. The operational objective before devaluation was simply to sell more than in the previous year, at profitable prices. Of course, sales were very low in the period immediately before devaluation.

In the division we studied, the purpose of devaluation was seen as being to increase exports. This was to be done whenever possible, provided only that they 'covered costs'. Indeed, there was a feeling that Oxford Furnaces should be prepared to absorb some of the increased costs resulting from devaluation.

Oxford Furnaces saw no reason to revise its budget after devaluation, and changes in export objectives, after devaluation, were not set out in detail.

O.4 Market Information

Statistical information about Oxford's overseas markets was very scanty. Even its own sales statistics were not set out as informatively as they could have been. For example, while there were figures for total sales in each overseas country, there were no similar figures for sales of individual products or groups of products. This was so despite the fact that there were also overall figures for sales in each product class. A further problem was that, while Oxford had made a tentative analysis of the reasons why individual contracts had not been obtained, the reasons were not known for the great majority of tenders submitted. Because earlier attempts to persuade its overseas representatives to provide more detailed market information of all kinds had been unsuccessful, Oxford relied heavily on the insights of the analysts in its headquarters.

As a result, the reliability of Oxford Furnaces' sales forecasts also varied between countries. Indeed, most of Oxford's managers regarded them all as unreliable and paid little attention to them. This left Oxford without a comprehensive sales plan. At the time of devaluation, Oxford's managers took marketing decisions on a piecemeal basis. For example, although Oxford Furnaces had forecasts for 1968 made as recently as September 1967, these were not explicitly considered when the firm took its decisions after devaluation.

O.5 Internal Factors

The cost figures used when pricing a tender gave estimates for labour and material costs, they also showed a standard mark-up separately for each of three types of overhead, namely: general, administrative and departmental (including process) overheads. On average, overheads amounted to about 50% of cost.

At the time of devaluation, Oxford's management regarded its budgetary control system as inadequate. The main cost information it provided was monthly job estimates (including the overhead allowances) for individual tenders. Cost information was presented in a consolidated form only every six months. While Oxford's managers *were* given monthly statements of expenditure, to compare with the figures in their budgets, these were summaries only. Detailed information was provided only every six months.

After devaluation, the deputy chief executive made most of the cost calculations required in order to take the devaluation decisions on the next day (Sunday). He confirmed these figures during the next few days in casual conversations with senior colleagues. He made no allowance in his figures for any rise in labour costs. In consultation with the purchasing officer, he estimated the cost increases for three imported raw materials that represented a significant proportion of Oxford's inputs. Taking the division's output as a whole., material costs were expected to rise by 3·4%. Separate cost increases were estimated for each of the three main types of overhead; together they represented 1·4% of the division's total costs. The increase in total costs resulting from devaluation was therefore put at 4·8%; this was rounded up to 5%. For exports, a further 'cost' increase of 2% was added to allow for the loss of the export rebate. The resulting increase in total export costs was further rounded up to 7½%. Oxford did not examine the costs of any outstanding tender individually before taking its devaluation decisions.

O.6   The Decisions

Devaluation caught the company unawares. The result of broadcast reactions to devaluation by leading politicians and industrialists over the weekend was a general consensus among senior managers that the right reaction to devaluation was to cut export prices as far as possible. Devaluation was seen as aimed at encouraging exports. Oxford's senior managers therefore concluded that exports should be increased by price cutting, wherever possible, provided only that the prices obtained covered the increases in cost caused by devaluation. The aim was not to increase export profitability, but export volume. Indeed, there was even a feeling that Oxford should be prepared to absorb some of the extra costs resulting from devaluation itself, out of a sense of public spirit. One of these 'costs' was the loss of the export rebate. To a degree which is hard to assess, Oxford felt that its response to devaluation should be 'patriotic' rather than 'commercial'.

All divisions of the parent company apparently shared this general attitude. At the next regular meeting of the main Board, the chairman strongly endorsed this view but, by then, the main decisions about devaluation had already been taken in the divisions.

Within Oxford Furnaces, proposals for the decisions about devaluation were worked out over the weekend by the deputy chief executive. He calculated the effect of devaluation on total costs on the Sunday, and drafted and circulated a memorandum setting out his proposals for responding to devaluation on the Monday morning. He discussed this informally with Oxford's chief executive on the same day. The marketing manager and divisional cost accountant were not consulted until later. The calculations and proposals were widely considered during the next few days, in discussions between the deputy chief executive and senior managers in Oxford Furnaces. There was no special meeting about devaluation. Rather, managers were approached informally, as and when they were available.

During the first two working days after devaluation, a number of managers looked at the big contracts Oxford was then negotiating. For each, they asked what would be the smallest reduction in foreign-currency price that Oxford would have to make if it were to be awarded the contract. After consideration of their conclusions, and of the deputy chief executive's memorandum, it was decided to follow two strategies. When Oxford was tendering for business against foreign competition, the aim would be to try to 'split the difference'; to reduce prices by half the net amount of devaluation after allowing for increased costs. However, where the competitors were mainly British, as in the Far East, it was felt necessary to reduce prices by the net amount of devaluation. This decision was taken despite the fact that, early in the week, the deputy chief executive had talked by telephone to Oxford's main British competitors, to discover their attitudes to devaluation. He discovered that they were very reluctant to cut foreign-currency prices on exports.

By the end of the week, however, this decision had been changed. Instead, the final decision was to increase the sterling prices of all products in all markets, including the UK, by 5%. This cut foreign-currency prices by 9%. The cost estimates made by the deputy chief executive, and generally accepted, had shown that devaluation would raise the total cost of producing the output sold in the export market by about 7·5%. Of this, 2% was the result of losing the export rebate. The final decision therefore implied that exports would bring in about 2·5% less sterling than before devaluation, though there was rounding up of about 0·7% in the 7·5%.

Oxford's reaction, and indeed that of its parent group, was described by Oxford's next managing director as a case of 'devaluation hysteria'. It resulted from the strong feeling, already mentioned, that Oxford Furnaces' patriotic duty was not to make extra profits out of devaluation but to reduce export prices by the full net amount of devaluation. This is why the initial decision to charge differential prices was altered. Oxford cut its foreign-currency prices, even though it freely admitted that price cuts of 9% were unlikely to induce Oxford's overseas customers to buy significantly more of its goods.

The need to reduce the amount of spare capacity that Oxford currently had was one factor leading to the decision, but making substantial price cuts was not necessarily the best way of doing this. Indeed, Oxford was already in a strong competitive position for obtaining export business. Since it had a good deal of spare capacity, it could quote short delivery dates and this gave it an edge over foreign competitors.

A few weeks later, Oxford's British competitors announced that they planned to raise their sterling prices by the full amount of devaluation. This led to an outcry from their customers, as a result of which much of the planned increase in sterling export prices was cancelled. Oxford saw this incident as confirming its own decision on export prices. However, it may be that the other British firms would not have been forced to cancel so much of their intended increases in sterling export prices had overseas customers not been able to quote Oxford's own decision. This was seen as implying that it was unnecessary to raise sterling export prices by more than 5%.

Oxford's decision is surprising because the firm claimed that both before and after devaluation it was opposed to reductions in sterling prices in the UK, and in foreign-currency prices overseas. Indeed, before devaluation, price cutting was seen as a last resort. Oxford even took work as a sub-contractor, in slack times, rather than cut prices. The speed, extent and uniformity of the price cuts after devaluation are perhaps best explained as the result of a temporary change in attitudes caused by the shock of devaluation.

O.7 The Results

While the total amount of business available to the industry both within the UK and in export markets increased after devaluation, the increase in export business was very much greater. Estimated in the rough way Oxford used, the amount of export business available more than doubled, while home business increased by less than 20%. The amount of business Oxford actually obtained in the UK more than doubled in 1968–69, but export business quadrupled. Having committed itself to a more positive approach to exports, Oxford actively sought business in markets which it had previously seen as offering too little profit. The rise in home orders was due mainly to an upswing in demand in the latter half of 1968, while most of the big increase in export orders came from Canada. Oxford was well placed to take orders here because it had finished establishing an export selling company just before devaluation. Sales to Canada accounted for about three-quarters of Oxford's total exports in 1968–69.

However, while the total amount of business that Oxford obtained increased substantially, it was not much more profitable. Some of the extra export business seems to have been taken at little more than marginal cost. The reduction in foreign-currency prices by 9% at the time of devaluation was probably too big because, as it had expected, Oxford's exports do not seem to have been sensitive to price changes. By announcing that it would reduce its prices by as much as possible, Oxford limited its bargaining power which, at the end of 1967, was considerable. Because it had a good deal of spare capacity, Oxford could quote early delivery dates. Indeed, throughout 1968, Oxford seemed to be offering earlier delivery than most of its foreign competitors.

In March 1968, Oxford Furnaces' managing director was replaced. His successor expressed dissatisfaction with the devaluation decisions. The attitude of the main Board to these decisions seems to have changed at about the same time. In discussions at the time of a scare over a possible further devaluation in 1969 the conclusion was that, if sterling was devalued again, Oxford Furnaces would make only marginal reductions in its foreign-currency prices. It would seek to maximise contribution to profit from exports.

Peterborough Tubes

P.1 General Background

Peterborough Tubes was part of a large, diversified group which dominated its industry. We examine the decisions taken after devaluation for two products, Product D and X-ply, both industrial raw materials. For both products, the company was virtually a monopolist in the UK.

P.1.1 PRODUCT D

The market for Product D, both at home and abroad, had been growing at about 15% per annum, in value, for some years. There was every reason to suppose that a similar growth rate would continue, although there had been a slight recession in UK demand in 1967. About 19% of output of Product D was exported to Europe, and a further 8% to other markets. The European market was growing more quickly than these others. While Product D was made to a fairly standard specification, adjustments were made to suit individual customers' particular needs, so that it was sold by a tender rather than at a list price. The amount sold was thought to be fairly unresponsive to price changes, but significantly influenced by delivery dates and technical reliability. However, competition from the small number of European producers was particularly keen and there had been some price cutting.

In 1967, margins in Europe were a little smaller than those in the UK. In overseas markets outside Europe, there was also some competition from a few American and Japanese producers. Peterborough Tubes was not worried by this, since it had a far more effective marketing and sales organisation outside Europe.

P.1.2 X-PLY

Peterborough Tubes made X-ply under licence from an American firm. It was a monopolist of X-ply in Europe, although it faced a great deal of indirect competition. X-ply was sold at list prices and, in 1967, total sales volume had been growing at about 30%

per annum for about eight years. The proportion of the output of X-ply exported was about two-thirds. As with Product D, the main markets were in Europe, where Peterborough Tubes also had a production plant. Outside Europe, Peterborough Tubes competed with its licenser.

P.2   Export Position

Peterborough Tubes' parent group was the most enthusiastic exporter in its industry, and this attitude was found in both the divisions of Peterborough Tubes that we studied. Both were able to use the parent group's extensive warehousing and distribution network overseas. For the whole group, prospects for sales within the UK were rather poor. Because Peterborough Tubes was a monopolist in the UK market, for both products we studied, it was feared that after a period of rapid growth the long-term future for sales in the UK might well be limited. This provided the justification for the group's increasing emphasis on exports.

P.3   Objectives

P.3.1   GENERAL

The group's general objectives in 1967 were summarised for us by the personnel assistant to the group financial controller, as follows:
'It was accepted at Board level that the target was to double the group's overall return on investment and that to this end a major reorganisation of the business was required. The operational structure of the group was changed, to reach the objectives the Board had set for achieving greater market shares in the more profitable sectors of the business. Objectives were translated into marketing plans and new measurement and control systems set up.
'All aspects of Peterborough's plans were discussed at various levels in the firm and marketing objectives were stated in writing.'

P.3.2   DEVALUATION OBJECTIVES

We were told that the objectives pursued in the devaluation decisions for Product D and X-ply were as follows:

Product D (export markets)
'To maximise long run profits by increasing volume wherever possible' (overseas marketing manager).

X-ply (export markets)
(i) *Europe*
To obtain the maximum additional revenue per unit of sales.
(ii) *Rest of the world*
As for Product D, 'the objective of growth is overriding, provided that a reasonable return is available' (overseas marketing manager).

Both products
(iii) *Home market*
To recover the increases in cost from devaluation as well as the other cost increases suffered in the period before devaluation. In this way, to restore profit margins to their levels at the time of the last price increases before devaluation.

P.4 Market Information

Peterborough Tubes had particularly good market information about the position of both products in Europe. For Product D, Peterborough had been able to negotiate information agreements, which gave it the prices charged by its European competitors. For export markets outside Europe, market information was less adequate. However, Peterborough's competitive position there was strong.

It was not thought worth asking Peterborough's overseas representatives for extra information at the time of devaluation, or seeking more market information in other ways.

P.5 Internal Factors

While profit margins were good, they had been under pressure for some time. Major changes had recently been made in Peterborough's organisation, as part of its plan for doubling the rate of return on capital. Although profit margins for Product D, and more especially X-ply, were above the average for the whole group, they had been squeezed in the three years before 1967 by increases in costs. There was therefore considerable pressure on divisional managers to increase their contribution to group profit.

After devaluation, the standard costs of the two products were completely recalculated, in an effort to work out the size of the cost increases that had accumulated since 1964, including the effects of devaluation. The marketing managers responsible for the devaluation decisions therefore had fairly detailed cost data. A selection of products, including Product D and X-ply, and representing about 50% of turnover, was completely recosted. For our two products, the calculations took account of all changes in costs since 1964, including the devaluation cost increases, and made an allowance for the improvement in productivity it was hoped to obtain from capital investment made before devaluation. These calculations produced the estimate that total costs were likely to increase by around 6%. These figures were used both to justify intended price increases to the Prices and Incomes Board and as a basis for export pricing decisions.

P.6 The Decisions

Devaluation took Peterborough Tubes by surprise, but was immediately recognised as an opportunity to increase export margins significantly.

The devaluation decisions for the UK and Europe were taken by the marketing managers responsible for sales of our two products in the UK and in Europe. For other overseas markets, the decisions were made jointly by these two men and the overseas marketing manager. The initiative lay with the marketing managers, who had authority from their divisional general manager to suggest changes. No instructions were issued by the divisional general manager or by anyone at a higher level of management.

The decisions taken on Product D and X-ply were as follows:

Product D
   (i) *Export markets*
   Local-currency prices were to be reduced within a range corresponding to sterling price increases between zero and about 10% depending on the competitive situation for the particular market and product. The average increase was about 9%.
   (ii) *Home market*
   Prices were to be raised to cover the estimated cost increases.

X-ply
   (i) *European markets*
   Local-currency prices were to be left unchanged in all markets except Spain and Denmark, where local-currency price reductions were to be made.
   (ii) *Other overseas markets*
   Local-currency prices were to be reduced by amounts differing

according to circumstances in each market, but always small enough to allow the increased sterling costs that had been incurred since 1964 to be recovered.

We now look at the decisions in detail. With Product D, the decision to make a reduction in foreign-currency prices of at least 5 or 6% for every product in each export market was based on the principle that 'if, in a particular situation, you can avoid quoting as high a price as you could in fact expect to get away with, then the dividend in terms of customers' good will will be considerable' (marketing manager, UK and Europe).

Each market was considered separately. For example, it was judged that, in South America, Product D was competing on equal terms with American products, so that a comparatively small price reduction would give a relatively big increase in sales. Each South American market was therefore considered separately and the size of the price reduction offered in each was determined by its particular circumstances. In Europe, price reductions were bigger, because German competition was keen.

Peterborough Tubes did not expect that these price reductions would always lead to an immediate increase in sales. As the marketing manager explained, 'a potential customer buys on technical grounds, so that the initial effect is to stimulate an interest in the product, which will take time before it is translated into extra sales'.

The decision to raise the price of Product D in the UK by the amount of the estimated cost increases since 1964 was virtually unchallenged within Peterborough. It was seen as only reasonable to offset the increases in cost that had already occurred before devaluation, and which had not been offset by higher prices, as well as the cost increases caused by devaluation itself. Peterborough's senior management strongly believed that all their British competitors were in roughly the same position and would want to raise prices as far as the national policy on prices would allow. It was not thought good tactics to raise prices by less than the maximum possible in the hope of gaining a competitive advantage over other producers, although this was apparently done by some competitors.

For sales of X-ply to Europe, the reasoning was this. 'If, at the limit, sterling prices had been held unchanged after devaluation, the prices paid for the output of the European plant would have been correspondingly reduced in terms of foreign currency. Such a loss of potential income was a risk inherent in any strategy based on the manipulation of prices as a tool to control demand, and a risk not justifiable in the particular circumstances'. The main factors were these. First, Peterborough Tubes was a monopoly supplier; the US company which licenced Peterborough did not sell X-ply in Europe. Second, the demand for X-ply was greater than supply, and growing rapidly. Third, in the early years of its operations, that is until 1966, the EEC plant had suffered substantial losses. In 1967, the plant was beginning to earn profits and Peterborough was keen to earn as much as possible in the short term in order to recoup as much as it could of the losses accumulated in the period before devaluation.

In other overseas markets, the American firm which licenced X-ply did compete, so that a cut in local-currency prices was thought desirable, in order to increase Peterborough's market share.

For the home market, the same argument for raising prices was used as with Product D. It was held necessary to raise prices by an amount equal to the total increase in costs that had taken place since 1964.

Apart from the cost information described earlier, no special data was collected in order to take the decisions. There was no contact with local representatives in any overseas markets, because the marketing manager took the view that this would not be worth the time, expense and effort it would require. The overseas marketing manager later said that, as it turned out, he and his colleagues felt that they had made unnecessarily big local-currency reductions in prices. The same results might have been obtained if smaller price reductions had been made, so that consultations with local representatives might have led to better decisions.

P.7 The Results

Peterborough Tubes' profits on its sales to Europe increased substantially in the year after devaluation, as did its sales volume. The volume of exports of Product D to Europe increased by about 23%, and sales of X-ply to Europe by about 14%. There was also an increase in sales to other overseas markets.

Peterborough had no doubt that devaluation had helped it in its overseas operations, especially outside Europe, where it was able to be more selective in choosing business. Devaluation had also made it easier to take a number of other decisions about, for example, export pricing, overseas representation, overseas investment, etc. For example, Peterborough Tubes had decided to expand its production plant for X-ply in the UK, primarily in order to sell X-ply in overseas markets outside the EEC. It also made investments to increase its capacity for producing other products, with the aim of increasing their sales in Europe. While these decisions were not decisively influenced by devaluation, they were made marginally easier by it.

Where devaluation had helped significantly was with some major marketing decisions. For example, after devaluation Peterborough had decided to send a team to South Africa, on a long term basis, to introduce certain products. Nevertheless, Peterborough's senior management argued that devaluation did not in itself make enough difference to induce Peterborough to develop markets which it would not otherwise have tried to develop.

In Europe, the devaluation decisions were thought to be very successful for X-ply, while with Product D they increased its competitiveness without provoking competitive retaliation. 'Contribution' increased on all exports.

Unfortunately, the potential benefits of devaluation for Peterborough Tubes were reduced by the pricing policy adopted by the producers of its main raw material. This material was unobtainable in the UK, and the overseas producers had formed themselves into an export cartel, charging uniform prices. After devaluation, the cartel made no change in its foreign-currency prices for the raw material; the sterling price of the material consequently rose by the full amount of devaluation. For finished products, however, the overseas producers reduced their domestic currency prices somewhat. So, while sterling prices of finished products rose, they did so by less than the full amount of devaluation. This swing in the competitive balance in favour of foreign producers led to an increase in imports into the UK. Even so, Peterborough was able to increase the volume of its sales of both Product D and X-ply in the UK by some 8% by 1968. Since it had also increased its domestic prices to allow for earlier cost increases, as well as the effect of devaluation on costs, profit margins in the UK improved.

Quantox Construction

Q.1 General Background

Quantox Construction was part of a group with an international reputation in the design and/or production of a wide range of expensive capital goods. These were supplied either as individual units or as complete factories, according to the customer's requirements. There were only two other producers in the UK, and both were smaller than Quantox Construction. Internationally, there was a handful of large firms in the industry, all of roughly the same size as Quantox Construction.

Q.1.1 THE INDUSTRY

The UK market for complete factories—the type of unit which Quantox Construction originally set out to produce—was very depressed in 1967, and had been throughout the 1960s. For various reasons, there was a tendency for demand for this kind of plant to be low simultaneously in all industrial countries. This was certainly the case in the mid-1960s. With business so depressed, the small number of producers found it difficult to obtain even small orders in their own countries, and the result was that business offered by 'third' countries was desperately sought after. There was very intensive competition over price, payment terms, service, product design, etc. More often than not, buyers took advantage of the world wide surplus of capacity to play off one producer against another to obtain better terms. Export margins were low and falling.

Q.1.2 THE FIRM

Quantox Construction dominated its own industry in the UK. It had recently taken over its principal British competitor, leaving only two small, independent producers who competed for the smaller contracts.

Q.2 Export Position

As with overseas competitors, the depressed state of the UK market had forced Quantox Construction to increase its export effort. In 1967, it was exporting about 80% of its output. Even so, its management was not fully committed to exporting. The policy was to keep sufficient capacity in hand to be able to give priority to the home market, even when demand there was at a peak. Quantox's hopes for long-term survival were still firmly fixed on the home market, which had always been more profitable than export business, and an upturn at home was hoped for in the near future.

There were potential buyers all over the world, but demand was very erratic because of the size of the plant being sold. The normal pattern was that several years of very slack business were followed by a rush of large orders, followed by a return to quiescence. Since 1945, Quantox Construction had exported plants to more than thirty countries, but at the time of devaluation less than twelve countries were thought to be potential buyers during the next few years.

Q.3 Objectives

Quantox Construction's objectives at the time of devaluation were very simple. The aim was to keep its plant and workers as fully occupied as it could, while losing as little money as possible. Quantox was prepared to treat many of its labour costs as fixed for some business, at any rate over relatively short periods of time. Even over fairly long periods, it was prepared to lose money rather than lay off all its skilled workers.

Given its depressed home market, Quantox saw devaluation as an opportunity to keep its plant occupied. It was prepared to take any business that offered what it regarded as an acceptable 'contribution' over variable costs. At the same time, Quantox was prepared to see contribution fall below even the level this implied, if it could thereby obtain contracts which enabled it to move into the production of a new type of plant which had been developed. Quantox thought that this new design would provide it with good business over a long period. In other words, it was prepared to 'buy' the experience needed to be able to offer the new plant to its customers, with confidence.

Q.4 Market Information

It was not difficult for Quantox Construction to be well-informed about the few orders likely to be available, from the small number of potential customers who wanted to buy plants at any time. Because of its international reputation, Quantox was invited to tender for all major contracts, and so did not need to seek new business actively. Its knowledge of its few competitors was also very good. Their behaviour was systematically studied and Quantox was confident that it was able at all times to give a detailed account of their order books, even showing the delivery dates they could offer and the credit terms they were able to give.

Q.5 Internal Factors

Because Quantox Construction had so much excess capacity at the time of devaluation, and was operating with such small profit margins, it had been forced to re-assess its cost structure completely. Its accounting system was now based on 'contribution', with fixed and variable elements in cost carefully separated. Indeed, we have seen that for some orders Quantox now carefully separated the fixed and variable elements even in labour costs, deciding which employees it would keep on, at any rate for a period of time, however unprofitable business became.

Q.6 The Decisions

Because it was so unprofitable, Quantox Construction welcomed devaluation as a means of restoring its margins. On the first working day after devaluation, there was a meeting of all senior managers concerned with exporting. They agreed to review all outstanding business, actual and potential. Where contracts had already been signed, it was not felt possible to increase sterling prices by the full amount of devaluation. Quantox thought that its customers would object to an attempt to increase prices by more than the amount which devaluation had added to Quantox's own costs. At the time, it was expected that this cost increase would be around 5%. With new contracts the aim was to look at each individually and suggest new terms, reducing foreign-currency prices by as little as possible. To put it the other way, the aim was to raise sterling prices by as much as possible, without actually driving away any business.

Since the whole world industry could expect orders in the near future from only about twelve customers, at most, this review was fairly straightforward. Final tender prices emerged only much later, after detailed costs had been worked out for each tender.

These final prices were arrived at by the managers directly concerned.

Q.7 The Results

It was not easy to find a direct connection between the general principles on which the decisions after devaluation were based and the tender prices finally submitted. We were allowed to study two tenders, submitted soon after devaluation. The reasoning behind the final decisions on the prices quoted for these contracts was as follows.

With the first contract, the immediate reaction of Quantox's European competitors to Britain's devaluation was to reduce the prices they were quoting by between 10 and 15% in the customer's local currency. The European producers feared that, with devaluation, Quantox would be able to reduce its own tender prices by this amount. Since they too were in difficulties in obtaining enough business, they wanted to make price cuts of their own first, in order to prevent Quantox from obtaining this contract. Since it had previously received an order with a similar specification from the same customer, Quantox believed that it would obtain this contract even if it quoted a somewhat higher price than the European competitors. Initially, therefore, Quantox made only a marginal reduction in its foreign-currency price. However, Quantox then discovered that its competitors had reduced their own prices by more than 10%, in anticipation of a major reduction by Quantox. It realised that there was now a wide gap between its own price and that of its leading competitor. Quantox therefore decided that it would reduce its foreign-currency price by 10%, but no more. The result was that a major European competitor, took the contract. In retrospect, Quantox saw this as something of a blessing in disguise. The competitor was now, if not fully committed, sufficiently busy to make it difficult for him to take further contracts. The result was that this European competitor became much less active in seeking business. As time went on, the market became firmer and Quantox was later able to obtain business at a much more attractive price.

The other contract we studied was one where Quantox was prepared to make a short-term sacrifice in order to obtain the business, because the contract was one for the 'new generation' of plants in whose construction it was anxious to gain experience. Quantox therefore carefully studied the marginal costs of producing this plant, distinguishing between 'key' and 'non-key' workers, in order to charge the minimum possible price for the contract. In this case, Quantox did obtain the contract and felt that its action was fully justified, especially because the same customer later placed another order at a much better price. Quantox did not doubt that the experience it gained in supplying the original plant gave it a decisive competitive advantage for taking the later business.

Rugby Processing

R.1 General Background

Rugby Processing was a large subsidiary of a very big diversified group, which produced both raw materials and finished products for consumer markets. Rugby Processing itself was mainly concerned with producing raw materials, and was divided into four divisions, A, B, C and D, of which A and B were housed in the same factory. All were process plants. Rugby's export effort had been increasing for some years, and in 1967 it exported over a quarter of its output. The product we studied was Product A, made in division A. It was sold in a large number of standard sizes and types. It was Rugby Processing's most important product, both in terms of turnover and profit, and also its original product. In recent years, Rugby Processing had been one of the largest contributors to the profits of its parent group.

R.1.1 THE INDUSTRY

The output of Product A almost doubled in the period 1960–68, rising sharply in 1968 after two years of relative stagnation. However, Product A was very similar to other products of the same type made by other firms. If the industry was defined to include these other products, then Product A's share of the total market had drifted downwards from 20% in 1964 to 16% in 1968. The price of Product A had been very stable throughout the period, rising by 2% in 1964 and a further 3% in October 1967. This second increase followed the introduction of the oil surcharge after the Six-day War. Imports of Product A were very small; in 1967, they amounted to less than 5% of UK production.

R.1.2 THE FIRM

There were only two producers of Product A in the UK. Rugby was by far the largest, holding about 90% of the market. The other firm was also part of a large group, but was not particularly concerned with producing A. For the whole range of products A, B, C and D, Rugby Processing and its parent group supplied about 40 % of the industry's total output. The rest of the UK output of B, C and D was produced by three large groups.

Rugby's parent group contained a number of firms using Product A, so that Rugby's sales had become increasingly important within the parent group. In 1967, for example, transfers of Product A within the group were equal to about half of Rugby's UK sales, and to about 30 % of total UK output. Until the mid 1960s, Rugby's rate of profit on capital employed, reckoned on a replacement-cost basis, had been very low. However, in the years 1964–65 and 1965–66 (ending 31 March) it was raised to over 13 %. It fell to 10 % in the year 1966–67.

Index numbers for production and sales of Product A by Rugby Processing are given in Table R.1, and this shows that until 1967 exports were around 25 % of output. However, exports fell in 1967 by 18 % in volume, and by slightly less in value, because of lower European demand. The main export markets for Product A were in Europe. Germany took about a quarter of Rugby's total exports and France a further fifth. Compared with the UK, per capita consumption of Product A was low in Europe, and Rugby had been concentrating its main export efforts there for some years before devaluation. Almost half Rugby Processing's total exports went to the EEC especially Germany and France. The EFTA countries took about a sixth, with a tenth going to each of the USA and the Communist Bloc. These proportions did not change significantly during the period we studied.

Export prices generally were slightly lower than those in the home market even before deducting extra transport and selling costs, export margins were therefore 15 to 20 % smaller than those in the home market. For a year or so before devaluation, Rugby's prices had also been slightly lower than those charged by its European competitors, the main ones being in Italy, France, Germany and Belgium. A small number of firms sold in the European market and the UK levied substantially higher import duties on Product A than did the main European countries.

R.2   Export Position

Because demand in the home market fluctuated considerably, Rugby was forced to export, at some times at least, if it were to keep its capacity fully employed. Originally, exporting had been conducted entirely on this contra-cyclical basis, but over the years sales to some European markets had become regular. For a decade before devaluation, Rugby had been exporting about a quarter of its output. In particular, it had sought to become

TABLE R.1 *Production and sales of product A* (index numbers for years ended March 1963–64 = 100)

	1963–64	1964–65	1965–66	1966–67	1967–68	1968–69	1969–70
Sales volume							
Home	100	128	132	115	117	140	137
Export	**100**	**136**	**136**	**111**	**152**	**171**	**160**
TOTAL	100	130	131	114	126	148	143
Percentage of output exported	25·5	27	26·5	25	31	30	29
Sales value							
Home	100	131	135	118	126	158	160
Export	**100**	**142**	**142**	**103**	**150**	**184**	**155**
TOTAL	100	133	136	114	138	184	159
Percentage of output exported	24·8	25·5	25	21·5	26	27	23

permanently established in the EEC where it believed the potential for growth in sales was greatest.

Accordingly, Rugby had built up a large distribution network based on the European offices of its parent group and had adopted a flexible pricing policy. It made no distinction between home sales and exports to Europe, so far as delivery dates or after-sales service were concerned; Europe was treated as an extension of the home market. This policy had proved successful and the minimum rates of penetration sought were being achieved during 1967.

R.3 Objectives

The main operational objectives at the time of devaluation were: to keep capacity fully employed; to break into the EEC, and to restore the rate of profit on capital (at replacement cost) from 10 to at least 13%. Rugby's policy had always been to keep capacity as fully employed as possible, in order to obtain economies from long production runs at stable prices. This reduced unit costs and enabled Rugby Processing to earn each level of profit with lower prices than those of its competitors. Rugby tried to avoid producing small quantities of special grades of its product, keeping down the number of small orders by levying special surcharges.

For several years before devaluation, Rugby had been making a sustained effort to establish itself in Europe, and especially in the EEC, by building up a comprehensive sales organisation and by cutting margins. This policy was about to pay off at the time of devaluation; exports to Europe had been rising sharply. Rugby's export prices in Europe had always been very competitive, and it was thought that the time had come to consolidate the position. It was hoped to push profit margins up to more acceptable levels, but without reducing market share.

R.4 Market Information

The company received regular reports from the overseas selling offices of its parent group, but these dealt with the whole of the very diversified product range produced by the group. While market reports were also produced for individual units in the group the time that the main overseas selling office devoted to preparing them, especially for Rugby Processing, was limited. As a result, they often had to be supplemented by special fact-finding visits to foreign countries, usually by junior executives in Rugby.

Nevertheless, each year the collection of information about overseas markets was co-ordinated as Rugby prepared its annual budget, when detailed studies were made of the prospects for sales, prices and competition generally in each of Rugby's major European markets. The smaller overseas markets were treated as residuals. There was no attempt to calculate elasticity of demand for Product A because its sales were rather volatile, whatever its price. The amount of Product A that Rugby Processing sold depended much more on shifts in demand by the consumer-goods industry that was the main customer for Product A. Such changes in fashion were not usually related in any obvious way to the prices of Rugby's products, or to those of its competitors. Hence, they could not be offset to any significant extent by price reductions by Rugby. Rugby was well-informed about the current levels of capacity and output of its few European competitors and believed that it could predict accurately what would be their reactions to any price changes it initiated. At the time of devaluation, it was not thought necessary to acquire any more market information.

R.5 Internal Factors

Rugby's main internal objective was to use its capacity to the full, in order to prevent a sharp rise in operating costs. Because of this, the rate of capacity utilisation was carefully monitored. Rugby's accounting system was based on 'contribution' and the cost information it provided was very detailed. Rugby's margins had been squeezed in 1966 and early 1967. Because of a slackening of demand within the UK, capacity was under-used and this had pushed up operating costs further than productivity improvements had been able to reduce them. At the time of devaluation, the situation had begun to improve markedly because of a recovery in sales during the summer of 1967.

Most of the raw materials which Rugby used were produced within the UK and their prices were little affected by devaluation. Indeed, Rugby's total production costs, both for the home market and for exports, were estimated to have risen by only $1\frac{1}{2}\%$ as a result of devaluation. This figure was calculated when Rugby asked the Prices and Incomes Board for permission to increase its UK prices shortly after devaluation. Much of the $1\frac{1}{2}\%$ increase in costs was due to the loss of the SET rebate.

R.6 The decisions

Because demand was recovering sharply in the summer of 1967, the Board of Rugby Processing had decided to take the biggest possible sterling profit if there was a devaluation. This decision was based on the view that since Rugby's capacity was being fully used at the time of devaluation, and since the export market was likely to grow in 1968 even without devaluation, there was little point in reducing foreign-currency prices for Rugby's exports. A major fear within Rugby Processing was that this would provoke immediate retaliation from its European competitors, which still had some spare capacity. While no explicit instruction was given to anyone, it was assumed by all senior managers in Rugby that the firm would take the maximum sterling profit, wherever possible, if there were a devaluation. Top management saw devaluation as a purely operational matter.

As a result, when devaluation took place, there was no special meeting to discuss it, and no detailed instructions were given to the export sales manager by the Board or the chief executive. The export sales manager simply continued to use Rugby's existing foreign-currency price list as the basis for all price negotiations. He did not seek any more market information than he already had and all his actions were later approved by the sales manager, in informal discussions.

Initially, then, sterling export prices were increased by the full amount of devaluation in all countries; foreign-currency prices were left unchanged. However, the result of detailed negotiations with its customers was that Rugby had to be satisfied with smaller increases in price for many of them. The final result was that, while Rugby felt that its export management had done as well as could be expected, Rugby was able to raise its sterling prices during the period immediately after devaluation by an average of about 12%, instead of the 16·7% it aimed at.

R.7 The Results

For the years ending March 1968 and 1969, the increases in Rugby's sales were as in Table R.2.

TABLE R.2   *Changes in home and export sales 1968 and 1969*

Year ended 31 March	Home sales		Exports		Percentage of turnover exported	
	Value	Volume	Value	Volume	Value	Volume
1968	+8%	+2%	+46%	+37%	26	31
1969	+26%	+20%	+23%	+13%	27	30

In the year ended 31 March 1968, there was an increase in the volume of exports by 37 %. However, most exports went to Europe, and the increase in demand from Europe in this period was mainly the result of fashion changes which led to an increase in the demand for Product A. This shift in demand continued in the year ending March 1969 and ensured a further increase in export sales volume of 13 %. Unlike the previous year, the year ending March 1969 was also good for the home market, with an increase in sales volume of 20 %.

With sales turnover rising more quickly than sales volume, there was an improvement in profit. This was restored to 13 %, on replacement value of capital, in the year ended March 1969, and rose sharply to 18 % in the next year. While the profit margins earned on exports were increased by devaluation, this increase came too late to have much effect on results in the year ended March 1968. Again the increase in sales value, sales volume and profit in the year ended March 1969 was seen as mainly the result of an increase in home market sales.

Stratford Equipment

S.1 General Background

Stratford Equipment was a fairly small company, a relatively autonomous subsidiary of a large, diversified group. It produced fairly cheap industrial products used by industry. It had only one competitor of any importance in the UK and few in the world. Sales in both home and export markets had been increasing rapidly.

S.1.1 THE INDUSTRY

Precise information about the size and rate of growth of Stratford Equipment's industry was difficult to obtain. However, since there were only the two British producers of any consequence, and since Stratford believed that its home sales were at least as large as those of its rival; it was confident that it produced at least half the UK output. Together, the two firms exported about a quarter of their turnover. The growth rate of turnover had been unsteady but rapid, with sales in the home market doubling between 1962 and 1967. Exports had also grown rapidly. Prices had been fairly stable, with little price cutting either in the UK or abroad. The product was cheap, so that its price represented only a small fraction of the price of the final product it helped to make. In selling, Stratford Equipment put the emphasis on technical reliability.

S.1.2 THE FIRM

Stratford Equipment believed that it exported a rather higher proportion of its output than the rival firm. This certainly seems to have been the case in 1967, when the proportion of Stratford's own output that was exported jumped to 34%. The rapid growth of Stratford's turnover can be seen from Table S.1.

Export prices were arrived at by making small reductions from home-market list prices. Local distributors abroad were expected

TABLE S.1 *Index of sales turnover* (1962 = 100)

Year	Home	Export	Percentage of turnover exported
1962	100	100	32
1963	164	102	22
1964	207	171	28
1965	242	186	26
1966	243	220	29
1967	252	272	34

to carry most selling costs out of their own margins, so that the return on exports was regarded as adequate, even though lower than on sales in the UK. There was no significant difference in the prices charged to different overseas markets.

Exports went to all parts of the world, and there was little concentration of sales in any individual market. In the USA (a market that Stratford Equipment did not enter until January 1968), the main competitors were an American company and a German-based firm with an American production plant. In Europe, the main competitors were the other UK producer and the German firm. The latter was especially active in Scandinavia, as well as in Germany. In other markets, the main competitor was the other UK producer.

S.2 Export Position

Stratford Equipment had exported a high percentage of its output since its establishment after World War II, partly because of the strong interest in selling—both at home and overseas—of the man who had become managing director by 1967. At the time of devaluation, Stratford had no specialists concerned with exports in its headquarters. The export effort was still directed by the Managing Director himself.

S.3 Objectives

The first detailed annual budget for Stratford Equipment was drawn up in September 1967 for the calendar year 1968; it was not altered significantly after devaluation. The main export objective was to increase sales in North America. Once a substantial increase in exports to the USA had been achieved, it was then intended to move into the South American and Japanese markets.

S.4   Market Information

Market information was not collected on a regular and systematic basis. It was felt that there was little need for this, since both home and export sales had been increasing rapidly for many years, and there was no reason to expect much slackening in them. Customers were conservative and preferred to deal only with long-established producers like Stratford, whose strength was seen as lying in their technical reliability. This represented a considerable barrier to new entrants. It was fairly easy to obtain adequate information about the pricing and selling policies of the few competitors, from discussions with customers and agents. Senior managers from Stratford, especially the managing director, made frequent fact-finding visits to the more important agents.

The large group to which Stratford Equipment belonged had a head office in the UK dealing with overseas business, which would provide market information on request. It had been consulted about the possibility that Stratford might enter the US market successfully with a new product, which was thought to represent a technological breakthrough, and which was to be launched in January 1968. Although the head office did not make a detailed report on this product, it took a pessimistic view of the possibilities, because the American market contained very few well-entrenched producers. The managing director decided to ignore this advice; to go to the USA and look at the subject for himself; and to rely on his own 'feel' for the market. This procedure had proved successful on previous occasions. Although his visit to the USA was not made until a few months after devaluation, this incident illustrates the difficulties Stratford Equipment had faced in obtaining sufficient information about overseas markets, and the reliance it put on the personal experience of its management.

Only a month before devaluation, Stratford Equipment had drawn up its first detailed sales plan, on the instruction of its parent group. The plan was rather nebulous about exports. It contained no precise export targets, and no other detailed market objectives for individual export markets. The discussion in this budget document about the marketing policies of Stratford Equipment's few competitors was scanty, general and rather complacent. Stratford's overseas agents had not been consulted while the plan was being drawn up.

S.5   Internal Factors

At the time of devaluation, Stratford was finding difficulty in meeting orders. It was already working three shifts so that the only way to increase output was by extending the existing factory in order to install automatic machinery. Stratford's restricted site made only a small extension possible, and even this was not expected to be completed before the middle of 1968.

Stratford had a standard costing system, based on variable costs. Though the standard cost figures were historical, the system did allow Stratford to calculate 'contribution' for each product group. Immediately after devaluation, the commercial manager made a rough estimate of the increase in total costs likely to result from devaluation, though it did not prove possible to work out detailed estimates for several weeks.

S.6 The Decisions

Stratford's initial reaction to devaluation was to emphasise the importance of the national interest. It was felt that the firm's duty was to give priority to the need of the UK economy for increased exports, so long as it was reasonably confident that this could be done without profit margins being reduced. This was certainly the view of the managing director who, we have seen, dealt with exports almost single handed. In practice, there was little that Stratford could do. Exports were already high and it felt that devaluation was unlikely to provide many new export opportunities, particularly since capacity was limited and demand was rather inelastic to changes in the price of Stratford's product.

Nevertheless, Stratford concluded that it would be improper to 'take advantage' of devaluation and that it should be satisfied with only a modest increase in export profits. This does seem to have been an element in some of Stratford's calculations. Although national considerations seem to have been important to the managing director at the time of devaluation, he knew that his German competitors wanted to break into a number of markets, even if that meant charging 'unprofitable' prices. In some countries, for example Norway and Austria, the German firm's prices were as much as 25% below those of Stratford. And while overall demand in any national market was relatively inelastic to price changes, one firm could obtain a big increase in sales if it made smallish price cuts that were not met by its competitors. The managing director of Stratford therefore considered that devaluation offered a timely opportunity 'to stand up to the foreigner', by reducing his prices in those markets where foreign competition was keenest. He also felt that unless Stratford made a reduction in foreign-currency prices of at least 6%, its overseas distributors would not make any price reductions to their customers.

There was a good deal of argument over the telephone with the other UK producer. Finally, it was agreed that sterling prices would be raised by 10% to all countries which had not devalued, effectively reducing foreign-currency prices there by 6%. For countries which *had* devalued, a price increase of 7½% was agreed, with a similar price increase in the home market. It was agreed to postpone all these price changes until January 1968. For the short intervening period, foreign-currency prices were reduced by the full amount of devaluation. However, we have seen that Stratford Equipment planned to introduce a new, technically improved product in January 1968. The price changes were linked to this.

One reason why the price increases were delayed until 1968 was that Stratford Equipment had big enough stocks of raw materials to last for three months. It therefore felt that there was no need to raise prices immediately to recover increased material costs. A further reason for delaying price increases was that, even before devaluation, it had been expected that raw material costs would increase at the end of 1967. It was also known that labour costs would go up early in 1968, by around 8%, because of a wage award. Including the wage increase, it was estimated that Stratford Equipment's total costs of production would increase by 7% after devaluation and the rise would have been bigger but for increased productivity expected once the factory was extended. By raising its sterling prices by 10%, Stratford therefore hoped to increase its profits while passing on some of the benefits of devaluation to overseas customers.

Since both Stratford and its British rival made the same price changes, their competitive situations relative to each other were unaltered. It is doubtful whether they obtained much advantage over foreign competitors. First, much their most important competition abroad came from each other. Second, a foreign-currency price reduction of about 6%, even if passed on in full by the agents, which was not certain, would do little to increase total sales of a product with an inelastic demand, even in the long run. In the short run, the problem was that capacity was already under pressure. As for competition with the overseas rival, even in the two markets where Stratford's position was being seriously eroded by its German competitor, the price disparity was so big that a 6% price cut would make little difference. Even if it seemed desirable to make price cuts in Norway and Austria, there was no obvious reason, except perhaps administrative convenience, for making exactly the same price reductions in all other markets. Prices there were not being undercut. Yet pressure was put on Stratford's overseas agents to cut prices to their customers, though they could have no obvious commercial reason for doing so.

However, there was another factor. Stratford Equipment was about to launch its new product, and was certain that this would be readily acceptable to the market and would give Stratford a significant competitive advantage over its rivals, including the other UK producer. Indeed, much of the extra capacity due to be installed in 1968 was designed exclusively for the manufacture of the new product.

S.7 The Results

In the two years after devaluation there was a dramatic rise in Stratford's export sales. The proportion of its output exported rose to over 60%, compared with 34% in 1967. This growth was entirely due to the company's success in America, which it had not dared to expect, following the launch there of the new product. There was, for example, the pessimistic report on prospects in the USA by Stratford's Head Office.

The introduction of the new product began in January 1968, and the Managing Director visited the USA in February. Until then, Stratford had not exported at all to the USA, so that it had to build up its marketing network from scratch. Despite the pessimistic head office sales forecast, three distributors were appointed and a resident technical-service team went out from the UK. At this stage, delivery and performance were much more important selling factors than price, and for several months Stratford carried the extra costs of using air freight in order to gain initial acceptance of the product. For a time, priority in delivery of the new product was given to American customers. This policy succeeded and, by September 1968, even with its extra capacity, Stratford Equipment was having difficulty in meeting large individual orders it had obtained from the USA. Accordingly, strict rationing was imposed on non-American customers, and it was not possible to relax these restrictions until 1969.

The decision to break into the American market had been taken before devaluation; it was contained in the budget plan of September 1967. The managing director claimed that his success in selling in the USA was not significantly influenced by devaluation. The sterling price for the new product in the USA had already been agreed, and it was not altered after devaluation though, of course, devaluation did reduce its dollar equivalent. As a result,

Stratford felt able to impose a price surcharge of 10% on sales to America in order to cover the cost of maintaining British technical staff permanently in the USA. The success of the new product was attributed to the technical advance which it represented and which rendered all competing products obsolete.

Tottenham Piping

T.1 General Background

Tottenham Piping was based in the UK but had substantial overseas interests. It manufactured industrial materials and components. There were few sellers in either home or export markets.
There were also few big customers. This study covers the basic
material sold by Tottenham Piping (Product M) and three
components (Products A, B and C).

T.1.1 PRODUCT M

About 70% of Tottenham's output of Product M was consumed
by the parent group in 1967. Of the 30% (roughly) sold to outside
customers, half was exported.

In the UK there were only four other producers, all smaller
than Tottenham Piping. One was independent, in the sense that
it was not associated with a firm making final products. The
remainder made Product M largely for their own use. Only six
firms used Product M. They chose to buy most, though not all,
their requirements from the independent supplier, because they
competed with Tottenham Piping and the other integrated
producers of Product M in selling final products. Tottenham
Piping and the other producers previously had a formal agreement
to set both home and export prices. The agreement covering home
prices had been abandoned because of the Restrictive Trade
Practices Act and Tottenham Piping was now the acknowledged
price leader.

Outside the UK, there were one or two local producers in each
of the smaller industrialised countries in Europe and six more in
each of the large EEC countries and in North America. As in the
UK, there were only a few buyers of Product M in each country.
There was also a limited amount of business available in countries
with no domestic production of M.

For some years, the world price of M had been drifting downwards and production capacity was much greater than demand.
Demand itself was growing only slowly, especially in Europe
where the local producers dominated their home markets. While

the pricing agreement had been abandoned within the UK, it was still nominally operating for exports. However, since the early part of 1966, the downward pressure on prices had been such that the system had broken down. At the time of devaluation, each producer was simply trying to get the best price he could, without consulting the others.

Prices for Product M were usually quoted in two parts. There was a charge for material and another for value added. This was necessary because world price for the principal raw material in Product M fluctuated rather widely. When quoting prices, Tottenham Piping merely gave an 'indicative' price for the raw material. When an order was received the raw material would be bought at the current world price, which would then be written into the order confirmation.

Sometimes, Tottenham used a substitute raw material. The decision on which to use depended on the customer's specification, the comparative prices of the two raw materials, and so on. The substitute raw material was also imported, but under long-term contracts at dollar prices. With the substitute, it was therefore unnecessary to make any allowance for a change in price before the raw material was actually bought.

Value added represented a very small part of the price for standard grades of Product M. With all producers in the world buying their raw material at the world price, it was virtually impossible for them to compete in each other's domestic markets in selling standard grades of M. Any possible advantage in production costs would be more than offset by transport and other incidental costs. All firms in all countries usually exported only non-standard items to markets where there were local producers, because for these items value added was bigger than for the standard product. There were, however, cases where the standard product could be sold in local markets. For example, Tottenham was able to sell its standard product in Switzerland because it was technically superior to the local equivalent.

T.1.2 COMPONENTS

Each of Tottenham Piping's three components was sold in a market with a different structure.

Product A
Tottenham Piping produced almost the whole world supply of this product. However, it was a monopolist only in a technical sense. There was no function which Product A performed that

could not also be performed by a wide range of substitutes. The reason why there was no direct competitor was that a large initial investment was required if one was to produce A. The smallness of the world market for A, although growing steadily, left room for only one producer. Tottenham Piping exported 20% of its production of A in 1967, as compared with 10% in 1962. The best markets outside the UK were the USA and Japan. The EEC was a difficult market because there was a tariff of 12% on Product A.

There was a price list for Product A, but prices were sometimes higher on exports than on home sales. However, the fact that there were many producers of close substitutes in all major markets put an upper limit on prices.

Product B

Product B was used in making components for a range of consumer durables. There were only two producers of Product B proper in the UK, and both belonged to Tottenham's parent group. In certain uses, there were no substitutes for B. With less-exacting uses, there was limited competition from alternative products. There were many more customers and users than for Product A and Tottenham Piping saw a big future for sales of B overseas. Total sales turnover for Product B was about £2M per annum and was growing rapidly. There were three or four producers in the USA, and others in Italy, France and Japan. Product B was normally manufactured to a buyer's own specification and the pricing procedures were similar to those for Product A.

Product C

Product C was a widely used component. There were substitutes, but they were the 'traditional' ones, and Tottenham Piping hoped to replace them by Product C because of its technical advantages. No other British firm produced Product C, but about thirty firms sold it in the USA, at least three in Europe and one in Japan. Tottenham Piping saw a market for Product C 'everywhere in the world' and expected both total demand and its own sales to continue to grow rapidly. In 1967, total world sales of C were worth about £15 million. Tottenham's turnover was approximately £1 million, about half of which was earned from exports, mainly to Japan and Europe.

Because the price of Product C was low relatively to that of the product in which it was used, the main need was for reliability. Price was a secondary consideration. Tottenham Piping therefore reckoned that within a price range of about 10%, demand was insensitive to price changes. Tottenham Piping offered a range of types of Product C at list prices.

T.2   Export Position

The parent group was a keen exporter and had been given the Queen's Award for Industry on more than one occasion. Its export performance owed much to the chairman's enthusiasm for exports. He personally approved the export targets each year, after discussing them with the managers immediately concerned and the latter had to answer directly to him on their export performance.

However, the underlying reason for this emphasis on exports was the difficulty of expanding home sales at a time when home markets for Tottenham's products were growing slowly and when Tottenham itself already had a dominant market position. Tottenham's growth depended directly on increasing its exports. It had therefore sought to obtain the bulk of export business taken by UK suppliers and had been successful.

T.3   Objectives

Tottenham Piping's fundamental policy objectives were set by the parent board. They were handed down to the boards of individual groups. Each group board translated them into operational objectives for each division in its own group in a joint exercise with these divisions. The objectives of any division's managers thus took the form of a set of precise targets for various aspects of performance; turnover, market share, profit, etc.

The objectives for Tottenham Piping after devaluation were as follows:

1 *Product M*   To avoid, or at least minimise the loss which would follow automatically if no action were taken.
2 *Product C*   To gain a marketing advantage which would help to expand sales volume and profit in both the short and long term.
3 *Products A and B*   To delay a decision until it was clear whether the price of Product M (which was a major element in the prices of A and B) would change, either because of devaluation or for some other reason.

T.4   Market Information

T.4.1   PRODUCT M

Information about conditions in the export markets for Product

M was very good, because most exports were sent to only twelve European customers, with whom Tottenham Piping had long-standing links. There was usually little competition from the other British producers because of non-competitive attitudes acquired when the export cartel was regulating prices still persisted. The members of the cartel still kept each other informed about the prices they charged on export business, although there was no longer any obligation to obtain each other's approval. Since the number both of customers and competitors was small, Tottenham Piping felt that it already had enough information about its markets at the time of devaluation.

T.4.2 THE COMPONENT PRODUCT

We have seen that Tottenham Piping (and its parent group) was the only producer of the components (Products A, B and C) in the UK, and that there were also few producers in overseas countries. Tottenham Piping was able to estimate the size of markets for all three components and trends in these markets. Tottenham Piping also claimed to know the marketing practices of the few competitors it met in each market. Here again no special market information was sought at the time of devaluation.

T.5 Internal Factors

With falling prices of Product M, which represented most of Tottenham Piping's business, profit margins had been squeezed. Margins on Product A, B and C were generally bigger, but Tottenham's cash flow position was unsatisfactory, though not critical. However, there had been an increase in overall demand just before devaluation so that there was little spare capacity.

Tottenham's accounting system worked on the basis of variable costs, and the amount of cost information available to management was considerable. It was therefore not thought necessary to recalculate costs after devaluation. Information for Product M was complete, in the sense that its price was known at the time it was bought. With Product C, the general manager drew on his experience of the market for this product and the information he had about its costs. He did not find it necessary to obtain any special information, for example from overseas representatives.

T.6 The Decisions

T.6.1 PRODUCT M

What happened was this:

1 A review meeting was held on Monday 20 November to

identify where 'we', i.e. the division 'were vulnerable as a result of devaluation.'

2 The conclusion was that the main problems would result from the cost changes on outstanding contracts caused by devaluation.

The only decision was to approach foreign suppliers of certain raw materials and ask for once-and-for-all price concessions, allowing Tottenham Piping to obtain the raw materials necessary to meet some existing contracts without loss. The possibility of increasing sterling profit margins on Product M after devaluation was not discussed. The existing margins were maintained.

T.6.2 PRODUCT C

To maintain sterling prices at their levels before devaluation.

T.6.3 PRODUCTS A AND B

No action was to be taken until it became clear that the world price of Product M had risen, whether because of devaluation or for some other reason.

T.7 Logic of the Decisions

T.7.1 PRODUCT M

As we have seen, export prices of Product M were automatically adjusted to take account of changes in the prices of certain imported raw materials, through changes in the variable element in price. To this extent, no special action was called for. Prices to customers in countries that had devalued automatically rose by the amount of devaluation. The other component in price was intended to cover Tottenham Piping's own costs. Its size was discovered by looking at Tottenham Piping's price list and making allowance for appropriate extras. If these price lists had actually been used in pricing, Tottenham would have had to decide whether they should be changed to take account of the effects of the devaluation.

As we have seen, export prices had been set on an *ad hoc* basis since early in 1966. Effectively, each price was set in discussions with the individual customer. The result of devaluation was therefore to make any given sterling price more competitive than it had previously been. Tottenham's price negotiators were given no specific set of rules about how big the permitted reductions in sterling prices after devaluation could be. Tottenham Piping also told us that no *general* decision had been taken on what to do about export prices. What appears to have happened is that those responsible for negotiating prices with overseas customers did their best to increase sterling prices. We are rather puzzled by this, since it appears to suggest that a general rule *was* being applied despite Tottenham Piping's denial that there was a general rule.

When devaluation took place, some orders for Product M had been taken at fixed sterling prices, despite the fact that M contained an imported raw material, bought on long-term contracts at fixed dollar prices. Here, the result of devaluation was to increase the sterling cost of the imported raw material, without any corresponding increase in the sterling price of M. This was why the Monday meeting decided that the suppliers of the raw material, with whom Tottenham had excellent relations, could perhaps be persuaded 'in their own long-term interest' to make concessions to 'help the company out'.

T.7.2 PRODUCT C

The view taken here was that with raw material costs little affected by devaluation, and with no reason to suppose that it would quickly have much effect on the price of labour, there was no obvious reason for increasing sterling prices. The decision after devaluation therefore centred on a judgement whether the marketing advantage that Tottenham Piping would obtain from keeping its sterling prices constant would lead to greater profit, in the longer run, than holding local-currency prices constant and earning an increased amount of sterling as a result of increased sales. This, in turn, depended on how far reduced foreign-currency prices would increase sales of Product C. After some discussion, it was decided that holding sterling prices would be more profitable. It was thought that the local-currency price reductions which this would allow would lead to a significant increase in sales. A further consideration was that at the time of devaluation significant productivity increases were being obtained in making Product C.

T.7.3 PRODUCTS A AND B

With Products A and B, there was no immediate decision on prices. The reason was that Product M made up a very large percentage of the cost of both products. Their prices therefore fluctuated in line with changes in the balance between the supply and demand for M in world markets. It was unnecessary, for Tottenham Piping's purposes, to separate the effects of devaluation on the price of Product M from any other changes. Indeed, it was probably impossible. It was therefore decided that the right time for price changes for Products A and B would be when the price of Product M increased, whether because of devaluation or some other reason.

T.8   The Results

The general manager responsible for Products A, B and C said that what was, in his opinion, the most important effect of devaluation had become apparent only after several months. It had not been sufficiently anticipated by him or his colleagues. This was the rise in the wages for various kinds of labour. The origin of this rise (which has been since fairly continuous) was seen by the general manager as partly due to the great publicity given to increases in the domestic prices of consumer goods in the UK after devaluation. He believed that this was largely responsible for big wage claims submitted after devaluation and for the subsequent increase in labour costs.

As for the specific decisions taken after devaluation, the general manager said that the company's requests to its suppliers to give once-for-all concessions had been successful; they had 'agreed to help'. Apart from this, he could see no clear effect of devaluation on the trading position. He added that the decision to keep sterling prices for Product C unchanged had undoubtedly been successful, with both sales volume and profit increasing significantly. Sterling prices for Products A and B had been increased on a number of occasions since devaluation, but the increases could not be definitely linked to devaluation. While export sales of these products had risen in both 1968 and 1969, it was not clear how far the increases were a result of devaluation.

T.8   Appendix

We now summarise comments by one of Tottenham's executive directors on the effects that devaluation had on the group:

'In theory, the effect of devaluation should have been to shift demand in our export markets to the part of our product-range with the biggest percentage of value added. Presumably, it was here that the competitive advantage in price given to us by devaluation was greatest. In fact, the shift did not materialise "perhaps because of psychology". Even more important was the expansion of demand in Europe as a result of the boom there. This tended to weaken competition in Europe and so submerged the effect that we could have expected devaluation to have on us, on purely theoretical grounds. The amount of potential business available to us in export markets was not much influenced by a devaluation of this size. Certain countries, for example Australia, Canada, Argentine and Hong Kong had domestic suppliers of "bread-and-butter" qualities of our products. Even after devaluation, it was hardly possible for us to offer buyers in these markets a worthwhile price incentive to "buy British". On the other hand, these markets did not have much demand for the qualities of product with higher value-added. With the latter products, the "price-competition" effect of devaluation would be proportionally smaller and the effect of non-price competition, for example on technical characteristics, would be greater.'

Index